about immigrants
into your

COMPLEX ALLEGIANCES

Constellations of Immigration, Citizenship

&

Belonging

WISING UP ANTHOLOGIES

SHIFTING BALANCE SHEETS
Women's Stories of Naturalized Citizenship and Cultural Attachment
2011

VIEW FROM THE BED: VIEW FROM THE BEDSIDE
2010

DOUBLE LIVES, REINVENTION & THOSE WE LEAVE BEHIND
2009

LOVE AFTER 70
2008

FAMILIES: THE FRONTLINE OF PLURALISM
2008

ILLNESS & GRACE, TERROR & TRANSFORMATION
2007

COMPLEX ALLEGIANCES

Constellations of Immigration, Citizenship
&
Belonging

Charles D. Brockett, Heather Tosteson & Anna Steegmann
Editors

Wising Up Press
Decatur, Georgia

Wising Up Press
P.O. Box 2122
Decatur, GA 30031-2122
www.universaltable.org

Catalogue-in-Publication data is on file with the Library of Congress.
LCCN: 2012936548

ISBN-13: 978-0-9827262-5-9

TABLE OF CONTENTS

IV. WHY DO WE GO?

V. WHY DO WE COMMIT?

VI. WHAT DOES *AMERICAN* HAVE TO DO WITH IT?

VII. WHERE DO WE BELONG?

. . . the task of democracy is forever that of creation of a freer and more humane experience in which all share and to which all contribute. . . .

INTRODUCTION

CONSTELLATIONS OF BELONGING
What You Will Find Here

We invite you to get to know, as we have, a wonderful group of people, talented, thoughtful, open, who are introducing themselves to you in their own words. We invite you to give them access to your own imagination because we believe you will find it enriched by their presence, whether their experiences echo your own or challenge them. Don't be afraid to step into their shoes or to imagine inviting them to step into yours. We especially urge you to listen for constellations of belonging—that sense that we fit, that we are accepted—to listen to where these experiences of belonging were in the past for this person; to where they may be now; to how these constellations have been challenged, recreated, or discovered; to what happens when someone feels the experience of belonging is lost to them permanently. We invite you to think about how identity, allegiance, and a sense of community relate to these experiences of belonging. We invite you to imagine the emotions you might feel, the decisions you might make if you faced similar circumstances—and why. Our aim is for all of us to feel our way more deeply into some of the questions that affect the immigration debate in our country today by basing our thinking as much on what we have in common as on what may distinguish us.

We have organized the collection by some of the major questions that we had and assume other people have about immigration in general—ones that are even more salient when people have active ties to several countries through citizenship, cultural attachment and/or residency. The questions we ask about why immigration matters, why people come to the U.S., why they stay, why they go, why they commit, why they develop cultural allegiance, or how they decide where they belong apply to people at all different stages in their own journey, here and in other countries. The answers are as varied as the individuals.

In *Why Does It Matter?* we begin by providing both an historical context for immigration debates in the U.S. today in Charles Brockett's "Allegiances Straightforward and Complex: The Social and Historical Context" and an experiential context in Heather Tosteson's "Listening for Belonging: I." We do so with the intention of relating these stories of complex allegiances to questions about the nature of national and local community today, questions that have direct relevance for many of us who live in increasingly diverse communities.

In *Why Do We Come?* we find people come to the U.S. to seek greater personal opportunity and also, like L.S. from the former Yugoslavia and Ara Sarkissian from Lebanon, because of powerful tides of history, the fragmentation of civil war, for example, sometimes several times over. Shan Yohan and Buddhi Masih both came to Atlanta from India as minority Christians, but each finds here a rather different constellation of belonging in the still segregated society of the South. Reasons for coming can differ significantly within a single family system. William Betancourt (part of the extended Losada family), although a birthright citizen by happenstance, experiences his own coming to the United States as an example of the classic immigration story, one he shares with millions currently, with all of us historically. Taye, who came to the U.S. through the diversity lottery, comes less for personal opportunity than for enlarged opportunity for his son.

Why Do We Stay? It isn't always self-evident why we stay in a new country. Except in the case of refugees and asylees, immigration always has a strong element of choice to it. But it also always has an undertow as well, as Marcelle Kasprowicz captures in her poem "Departure." We can feel, for extended periods of time, that we may have lost something precious that can't be replaced. We may have expectations or assumptions of welcome that are brutally shattered. In Emilio DeGrazia's memoir "Walking on Air in a Field of Green," he, like us, wonders at his father's persistence in the face of the callousness of his first employer, his dawning understanding of what could be involved in the American way. This question of what our first experiences here are like—and how they may come to define permanently where, how or even if we will ever feel we belong here—is one we suggest we all listen to closely because its various resolutions have many implications for us as a society. We find these questions still hotly burning in Natalia Treviño's meditation on what it means to be a legal Mexican immigrant. Jennifer Clark asks these questions from the perspective of a native-born citizen watching young people who have never been granted citizenship making the ultimate sacrifice for this country. Tom Sternberg began life in Romania with Hungarian as his first language, survived World War II there, then emigrated to Israel when it became a state, then came to the U.S. alone when he was fifteen. We can see in his story how the lives and choices of many immigrants are driven by large historical forces and the vagaries of chance and luck. But why Sternberg stays also says much about him, his unique constellation of commitments. Plamen Russev, forty years later, describes the similarly large seismic shifts that brought him to Harvard, a nineteen-year-old student from Bulgaria, after the fall of communism in Eastern Europe. He too discovers opportunities and freedoms here he did not know before, including the freedom of integrating more and more of his authentic self into his daily life.

Why Do We Go? We often assume that people who immigrate to the U.S. do so once and for all. This isn't always the case. Naturalized citizens often return to their country of origin. Their departure is not necessarily a rejection of their U.S. citizenship or cultural attachment. In the case of Yar Gonway-Gono, a woman born and raised in Liberia who learned to read at the age of eleven then went on to earn two master's degrees and a doctorate in the U.S. while raising five children, her decision to return to Liberia to help found a new community college speaks to her dedication to education, to the opportunities she experienced herself here in the U.S. and her desire to share them with young Liberians after decades of civil war.

Native-born citizens can also choose to leave the U.S. and spend the majority of their adult lives abroad, as is the case with both Alan Masters and Zoë Losada, both of whom have up until now chosen not to relinquish—or augment—their U.S. citizenship. Why does living in an expat community of Americans in a Costa Rican rainforest offer Masters and his family freedoms they can't find living in the U.S.? How does this intuitive and incremental decision shape the cultural allegiances of his sons? How does living in Venezuela shape Zoë Losada's understanding of her ties to the U.S., to her Baha'i faith?

Lauren Sergio (interviewed by her mother Alexandrina), who has sought and received Canadian citizenship, does not see this as a rejection of her U.S. citizenship, rather an amplification that permits her greater professional opportunity as a scientist and as a partner and parent in a same-sex marriage, a status which Canada as a nation recognizes. For Lydia, an American playwright living in Berlin, her decision to leave the U.S. and live in Berlin is reluctant, forced on her by the difficulty she and her same-sex partner experience because their relationship status is not acknowledged in the U.S. She has not transferred her cultural allegiances and lives in personal fulfillment but in a painful cultural and social limbo in Berlin.

In this section, we find as well the stories of young people, brought here as children, who are deeply identified with the U.S. as a country and as a culture. However, they have either been deported, like Saad Nabeel, or face deportation, like José Varible, to countries to which they have had little exposure and for which they feel little attachment, ones in which they experience no feeling of belonging. They deeply desire to become U.S. citizens. On the other hand, although the costs of her illegal status are clear to Mirjana, an illegal immigrant from the former Yugoslavia who has lived in the U.S. for over twenty years, she has no desire for citizenship, rather would prefer to live as a permanent resident alien, loyal to the urbanity of her New York City environment rather than a national culture or government. Her alternative is to return to a country, Serbia, that did not exist when she came to the States. Mariana Figuera and her husband Andy Martin (part of the extended Losada family), citizens of Venezuela and Canada respectively, have found wonderful educational and professional opportunities that result in a desire to continue to work here, but not necessarily a desire to change citizenship. The U.S. is where they met and married, so if they must leave, their different citizenship statuses mean that they will need to rethink again the role of cultural allegiance and citizenship in their marriage.

Why Do We Commit? Commitment, we realize from the stories in this section, is both legal and emotional and it often takes far more time than we imagine. Anna Steegmann's essay, "The New (Torn) American" vividly describes the emotions she feels at becoming a U.S. citizen after twenty-eight years residence here and how being a dual citizen allows her to embrace the full range of her attachments. Murali Kamma, a native of India, describes his attempts to try and explain to other Indians both here and in India what made him decide to become a U.S. citizen at one of the least propitious times in its economic history. The reasons they decide to make the choice for U.S. citizenship differ as much as they do from each other. But their legal commitment makes other choices of attachment and belonging available to them, ones they didn't necessarily imagine or assume. Nikolina Kulidžan, another of our talented writers from the former Yugoslavia, explores the experience of having a pluralist environment suddenly fragment, the loss of attachment that goes with it, and the complexity of the attachment she develops over time to the U.S., one that, finally, allows for social optimism again.

To get a better understanding of commitment, the stories of people who do not want to commit to citizenship but who wish to remain as permanent resident aliens are of interest. Barbara Toews, a Russian Mennonite from Canada has lived in the U.S. as a permanent resident since the age of seven, never relinquishing her cultural allegiances to her Mennonite faith and culture and also to her Canadian citizenship. Her attachment to the U.S., often disregarded in her conscious thought, takes on more meaning as she realizes what it would mean if she returned to Canada and was no longer assured of ready access to the country in which she has lived for the vast proportion of her life. Elwood Dunn, who came to the U.S. as an asylee from Liberia, has lived and worked in the U.S. for over thirty years but has never chosen U.S. citizenship although his wife and all his four children are citizens through birth or naturalization. He explains the powerful commitment he has to his own country of origin, Liberia, as an attachment so deep that transferring it feels like soul death. If we were to live in another country, how long would it take us to transfer our loyalty? Would we ever choose to? Why?

What Does Being 'American' Have to Do with It? What does it mean to *be* "American," to *feel* "American"? The authors in this section explore different dimensions of this experience. Jodi Hottel's poems painfully describe the experiences of her mother and other Japanese-Americans interned in World War II and the influence of that experience on how not only they but also their children understand what that word means. Julija Suput, while on a trip to Korea, explores what it meant to her to be a Yugoslavian, to experience the dissolution of that cherished identity as an individual and as part of a country, and what it might mean for her, now, to understand herself as "American." Both Debra Gingerich, a native-born citizen, and her husband Zvonko Smlatić, also from the former Yugoslavia, when on a trip to France to see his family, begin to understand that becoming American is something that can sneak up on you, surprise you. Joe Kim is a native-born American, who defines himself as Korean in body but not, like his parents, first generation immigrants, as Korean in culture. His wife, Janet, Korean-born and a permanent U.S. resident, teases him that he is a banana, yellow on the outside and white on the inside. On the other hand, they both observe that he is far more sensitive about being Asian than she is. How they explore, and expand, their allegiances to their partner's country of birth is one of the more fascinating dimensions of their marriage. Diana Anhalt's parents fled to Mexico from the Bronx in the 1950s during the McCarthy period without in any way renouncing U.S. citizenship or allegiance to the U.S. as a nation, rather to its policies. She explores the attachment she developed to the U.S. living in Mexico for over sixty years, and the attachments she discovers to Mexico, the country she always held at a little distance while living there, when she comes to live permanently in the States. In "A Feeling of Belonging" Heather Tosteson describes visiting a Somali strip mall in Stone Mountain, Georgia to explore some of the complex responses we can have as a native-born citizen when we engage with the reality of the waves of recent immigration, which in many places are so large they have substantially changed the nature of social cohesion in a community. Aurora Ferrer appeals to an understanding of American immigration broad enough to include all of our histories, all of our futures.

Where Do We Belong? In these memoirs and interviews, we have an interesting group of globalists by birth or by choice—and again we invite you to feel how those two conditions differently affect our feelings of belonging. Brian Jungwiwattanaporn talks about how, the son of a Thai father and American mother raised in both countries, he has always felt at a cultural disadvantage in both and how, over the years, he has learned to accept, with a struggle, his two inheritances as an amplification of identity, not a diminution. Paige Higbie describes the culture in which she does feel she belongs, that of the TCK (transcultural kid). We hear in her account, which is nostalgic, evocative, courageous and unsteady in its perspective (when do we use I, we, they, you?), the power and fragility of this fluctuating identification. Marcelle Kasprowicz describes how she juggles French, Italian, and U.S. identifications, some more successfully than others. In a joint interview, members of the Losada family (which includes a Venezuelan husband, a wife who is a U.S. citizen, their two children, who are dual citizens, and their infant grandson) explore the variations in their individual understandings of belonging and national and cultural identity. This meditation even extends to the next generation as they contemplate the five citizenships currently or potentially available to their newest member.

Emily Beeson shares her fascinating journey around the world soon after college on a traveling fellowship to visit Mennonite expat communities of U.S. or Canadian origin in the Dominican Republic and Paraguay and how she begins to understand how her own Mennonite heritage has affected her understanding of citizenship and cultural attachment. Thomas Spaccarelli, who has received dual citizenship from Italy on the basis of his ancestry and may apply for it in Spain on the basis of extended residency there, describes this accrual of citizenship as a natural development of his own experiential understanding of what it meant for him to grow up native-born and indisputably American in a multi-generational house with immigrant grandparents.

In the *Afterword* by Heather Tosteson, "Listening for Belonging: II" again we try to provide various holding contexts for these stories, ones that invite us to understand the questions we face now as a society that is *glocal,* where simple definitions of national identity may not apply, but local experiences of cohesive society need to. For our abiding question is very local and very personal. It is what Dewey would call making democracy a commonplace of living. How do we, with all this diversity, all this migration, all these constellations of belonging, create an experiential world in which we can create lasting bonds with our neighbors, bonds that acknowledge our differences and also, most importantly, acknowledge our mutual responsibility to create, through this acceptance, a new experience of belonging in the here and now. We emphasize this because there is a great cost not only to ourselves but also to those around us of living—often for years—in a place that we never acknowledge as bedrock real, especially in a democratic society whose major assumption is that we are all equally responsible for the structure and quality of the society in which we live. *Now.*

I

WHY DOES IT MATTER?

CHARLES BROCKETT

ALLEGIANCES STRAIGHTFORWARD & COMPLEX
Social and Historical Context

Complex Allegiances explores the various forms that allegiance to country can take, particularly for immigrants, whether naturalized or not, and also for the native born. For many people there is no complexity here. Allegiance is a very straightforward notion—Fourth of July, love of country, patriotism, the American Flag, willingness to serve, the Declaration of Independence and the Constitution, the Pledge of Allegiance itself.

War and Patriotism: This traditional understanding was vividly illustrated for me on Veteran's Day, November 11, 2011 when I attended the meeting of an American Legion Post in a Southern California community with my parents. My father served in the Navy during most of World War II. Many of those on the stage also protected their country during the same war. Many in the audience too had served their country and fellow citizens in the U.S. armed forces during a variety of conflicts.

In prior years my father had stood at the podium as the Post Commander. This year's leader gave an eloquent reading of the national American Legion statement for the occasion. "Regardless of which view of alternative history you take," he read, "we do know that without our veterans America would not be America." The statement quoted historian Stephen Ambrose, who once wrote, "America's wars have been like rungs on a ladder by which it rose to greatness. No other country has triumphed so long, so consistently or on such a vast scale through force of arms."(1)

Indeed, war often seems enmeshed with the concepts of nation, of patriotism, of citizenship for many of us. After all, "the rockets' red glare, the bombs bursting in air" is a central image in our national anthem. The possibility of war is at the heart of the oath taken by new citizens. Not only are they told to "renounce and abjure all allegiance and fidelity to any foreign prince, potentate, state or sovereignty" but they must also pledge "that I will bear arms on behalf of the United States when required by the law."

World War II had a long-lasting impact for many people on notions of patriotism and service. It was the true Great War, the one where the line between good and evil was clear, where the threat to the nation itself was a constant scary presence. People responded unequivocally. Completing high school for my father seemed irrelevant with the survival of the United States seemingly on the line. He tried to enlist a few months after Pearl Harbor but was told to wait until he had graduated from high school if he wished to train for aviation. He signed up the day after graduation but was assigned instead to a cruiser where he was trained as a radio operator because he was one of the few in his group who could type. The newly commissioned *U.S.S. Cleveland* sailed off to join the invasion of North Africa in the fall of 1942, 89% of its sailors never having been to sea. Then it was on to the South Pacific for the rest of the war, participating in many of the defining battles for that front.

My experience was very different. I was not going to leave college to fight in Vietnam, a war many of us regarded as the opposite of WWII's Good Cause but instead one that we saw as immoral, illegitimate, and counter-productive. When the draft notice came, I still did not respond to duty's call, becoming instead a war resister. This troubled my father though he tried only once to convince me that it was my obligation to respond to the duty call for my generation. My maternal grandfather, a veteran of both WWI and WWII, a man who never shied from voicing his strong convictions, felt obliged to call me outside from a family gathering and explicitly disown me (although in later years we both ignored this).

Allegiance Gets Complex: "My country, right or wrong." "America—Love It or Leave It." The question of allegiance has long fascinated me. What precisely are we pledging? Are there limits? Where? Probably for no generation have these questions been less problematic than for the WWII generation. It is not just for subsequent generations that the meaning of allegiance gets more complex. We forget that for the WWI generation the connection between war and allegiance was not so straightforward either. The issue of U.S. involvement in a European war was very controversial at the time. The war's relationship to the security of the United States was unclear to many, especially to many families who had hoped that they had left Europe's long history of senseless destructive wars behind when they left the old country and immigrated to the U.S. Once reliable public opinion surveys developed, they found in the late 1930s strong majorities that believed it had been "a mistake for the United States to enter" the war.(2)

When patriotism and allegiance are less about war and the willingness to fight, allegiance is free to become more complex. When possibilities of serious conflict and possibly even war threaten between nations then dual citizenship seems to many an untenable division of loyalties. Which side are you going to support? Even if the conflict is not with the country of your second allegiance, can we in the United States count on you giving as much support as the rest of your fellow citizens or might you slide your primary allegiance toward your second country? As one critic declares, "The chief concern about dual citizenship is that it encourages or results in shallower attachments to the American national community than would be the case if there were not stiff competition for immigrant loyalties."(3)

Several of the authors in this anthology disagree, finding no diminution of their U.S. allegiance because of their citizenship in a second country (or in at least two cases, the possibility of a third citizenship). The world does continue to shrink. Through economic relationships, travel, television, and the Internet we are more closely tied together across national boundaries. More of us now spend more time outside of the country of our citizenship, perhaps for years. War is inconceivable now between the United States and Germany or Italy and our core national interests only continue to converge. What then is the danger of dual citizenship involving such countries? Would not proliferating dual/multiple citizenships further bind countries together with common interests and fates, reducing the possibilities of serious conflicts?

Some thinkers see these trends accelerating with national identities and allegiances fading away in relevance, not just for a few people but for many. Perhaps some day . . . but I do not see this as more than a possibility for a distant future. For the present and foreseeable time to come issues concerning national allegiance will remain salient. One significant reason for this is the continuing importance of immigration to many countries, particularly the United States, bringing us to the focus of this anthology: the relationships between national allegiance and immigration.

Why Do We Come?

Immigrants come with their own stories and for their individual reasons. Often they leave behind loved ones and locations, carrying ambivalence and even grief with them to their new home. Their futures are uncertain. Underneath their individual stories, there is the shared assumption that through immigration their life will be improved—or at least that of their children. That improvement for many people throughout our national history has been largely material. Greater economic opportunity is expected in the U.S. whether one is an unskilled laborer or a highly trained professional. Others have been persecuted in their countries of origin and come expecting greater freedom. Some have seen their homelands ripped apart by war, in some cases even disappearing as countries. They come seeking greater security and hopefully peace. Others come for the most personal of reasons—they wish to be reunited with a loved one, perhaps a spouse or a child. All of these motivations are represented in this anthology, in some cases many of them within one person's story.

Positive Attitudes: U.S. residents also view immigration as a positive force for the country itself, even with the complicating impact of illegal immigration on attitudes. When asked at three different points across the last decade, "In general, do you think immigrants who come to the United States today help the country and make it a better place to live or hurt the country and make it a worse place to live?," pluralities consistently selected "better" over "hurt" with an average spread of nine points.(4)

Immigration Policy: U.S. policy on immigration has varied substantially through its history and accordingly so too have immigration levels and the size of the foreign-born population. Only mildly regulated until the 1920s, immigration to the U.S. boomed in the late nineteenth century and the first two decades of the twentieth. Major reforms in 1921 and especially 1924 greatly reduced this flow for the next four decades and institutionalized discrimination against non-Europeans. Landmark legislation in 1965 removed the country quota system established in the 1920s, instead creating separate ceilings for the two hemispheres; this division itself was removed in 1978. Priority under the law is given to family reunification, critical employee skills, and artistic excellence. Refugees were originally included as a priority category but were removed in 1980 and since treated separately.

Increasing Immigration Numbers: Although the precise number has varied, until 1990 the overall annual limit was less than 300,000 legal immigrants. In 1990 this ceiling was more than doubled. For the decade through 2010 the overall limit climbed again, averaging just over one million immigrants annually.(5) These changes are reflected in the percentage of foreign-born residents in the overall population. From the high of just under 15% in both 1890 and 1910 the rate dropped steadily down to 4.7% in 1970, its lowest point since data was collected (see Figure 1). Under the impact of

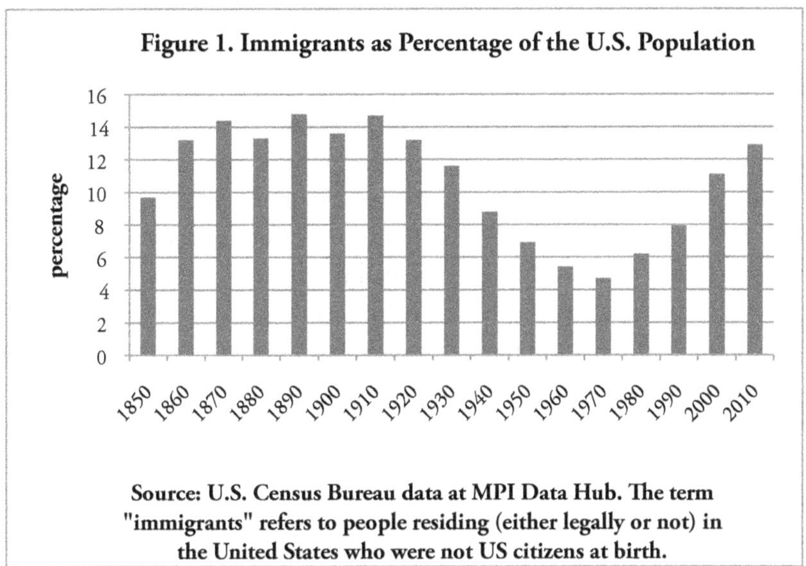

Source: U.S. Census Bureau data at MPI Data Hub. The term "immigrants" refers to people residing (either legally or not) in the United States who were not US citizens at birth.

the 1965 law, immigration (legal and illegal) then began growing faster than the overall population with the increase of the last four decades just as steady as the decline of the prior period. By 2010 immigrants, both legal and otherwise, had climbed back up to 12.9% of the total U.S. population. One reason why immigration is so controversial is because this increase was substantially at odds with the public's preferences (see Figure 2).

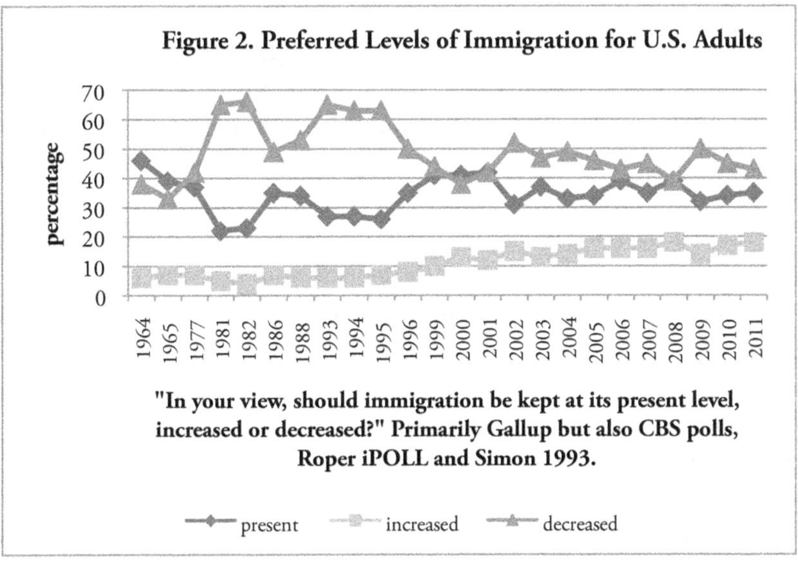

"In your view, should immigration be kept at its present level, increased or decreased?" Primarily Gallup but also CBS polls, Roper iPOLL and Simon 1993.

Why Do We Stay?

For many immigrants their expectations have been met sufficiently in the U.S.—and perhaps their reasons for leaving their homeland are strong enough—that there is no question that they are here to stay. Gladly. And often most gratefully. These are the heralded positive immigration stories that give many of us a warm reminder of those positive symbols of our nationhood: American Dream, Land of Opportunity, Home of the Free and Brave. These stories are real and they are included throughout this anthology.

Economic Challenges: But for a number of immigrants the reality they live is harder and staying is more complex. For some, assumptions that their hard work will gain them their comfort and perhaps eventual prosperity are not met. Particularly daunting are the circumstances of unskilled workers who went into debt to make the journey and who have committed to sending part of their earnings back home to support family members. Given their low wages, they find that they "must wring this surplus out of their own deprivation, forgoing everything but an ascetic existence."(6)

Social Challenges: For others the complexity might be more social. The dislocations of immigration can be difficult enough under any circumstances but often are more so for minorities. After all, much of their experience will be framed by the reception they receive from those already here. The first great wave of immigration in the decades before the Civil War brought many Irish and German Catholics to what had been a Protestant country. Stories of the discrimination they faced are legion. At the end of the nineteenth century and into the first decades of the twentieth, immigrants were still overwhelmingly Catholic but now even more different culturally from the early settlers, coming primarily from Eastern and Southern European countries such as Poland and Italy. This new wave of immigrants once again "inspired a virulent reaction from the native-born community."(7) This was also the period of substantial Jewish immigration—30% of all Eastern European Jews had moved to the United States before the doors shut in the early 1920s.(8)

The great wave of immigration following the 1965 reform has brought even greater difference, with most immigrants coming from Latin America, Asia, and Africa. Almost 30% of the foreign-born population in 2009 came from just one country: Mexico. Immigrants from the Philippines were next with 4.5% of the total, followed by India, China, El Salvador, Vietnam, Korea, and Cuba (at 2.6%).(9) Many immigrants have encountered welcome, interest, and assistance. Others, though, have had their experiences made difficult by responses ranging from explicit hostility to indifference.

Mexican Exceptionalism: Immigration and allegiance for those of Mexican heritage can be particularly complex subjects for just about everyone, be they native-born Mexican-Americans, non-Mexican-Americans, or immigrants from Mexico. This is not just because of the preponderance of people of Mexican background among the immigrant population but also because of a lengthy shared border, and very much because of a complex shared history.

Because so many people of Mexican descent who live in the southwest U.S. have live family roots on the other side of the border some observers see a transnational culture developing that draws perhaps more from its Mexican heritage than the mainstream U.S culture. This alarms some but delights others.(10) The elephant in the room for this controversy is the fact that the southwest came to be part of the U.S. primarily as a consequence of war. Very few people in the U.S. who I have talked with have known that the United States invaded the Mexican heartland in 1847, landing at Veracruz and marching on to take Mexico City. In contrast, any Mexican city of any size has an *Avenida Niños Heroes* and perhaps a monument in tribute to the six young cadets (one just thirteen years old) who, defending Chapultepec Castle, jumped to their deaths, taking their country's flag with them lest it be seized by the invaders.

The treaty ending the war formalized Mexico's loss of a little over half of its territory and the enlargement of the United States by California, Arizona, New Mexico, Texas, Nevada, Utah, a large part of Colorado, and small parts of Oklahoma, Kansas and Wyoming. Adding to the complexity of this relationship, until recent decades there was only intermittent effort on the part of the United States to police this border, in large part because U.S. businesses (especially farmers) welcomed Mexicans who were willing to work for low wages under harsh conditions without protest. Even today, with policies of much tighter border control enjoying widespread public support, possibilities of immigration policy reform often are complicated by U.S. agriculture's dependence on Mexican workers.

Even with this complexity, Mexican-Americans are proud to be U.S citizens. Surveys that compare levels of patriotism between different ethnic groups find Mexican-Americans generally do not differ from Anglo-Americans. However, when there are differences, it is the Mexican-American who is found by the surveys to be the more patriotic.(11)

Why Do We Go?

Repatriation: Not all immigrants will stay. Some never intended to—they came to earn money and take it back home. Some immigrants are disappointed economically or socially and eventually return home as well. Others have had fulfilling experiences here but unexpected opportunities or responsibilities call them back to the homeland. With increasing global interdependence, some observers anticipate contemporary immigration will feature far more of these returns than was the case in the past. In response, some scholars point out that there was far more return in the past than we remember. For example, a little over one-third of migrants entering the U.S. in the first two decades of the twentieth century ended up returning home. This was particularly the case for Italians—about one half of whom returned to Italy (although some of them then returned to the U.S., even repeating the journey multiple times).(12)

Illegal/Undocumented Immigrants: Others are here without permission—they are the undocumented or illegal aliens. Their individual stories are often heart-rending. But their numbers have grown so substantially that the issue itself dominates many people's views about immigration, complicating their reactions to individual immigrants who are actually here legally.

The best estimate is that 11.2 million illegal immigrants were living in the U.S. in March 2010 (3.7% of the total population), down from 2007 when the number peaked at 12 million.(13) The Immigration Reform and Control Act of 1986 was supposed to manage the illegal immigrant problem. Nonetheless, the number of unauthorized immigrants in the country tripled from 1990 to 2010. Most illegal immigrants come to the United States from Mexico—about 58% of the March 2010 total.

Not surprisingly California tops the list for the undocumented with 23% of the U.S. total, followed by Texas, Florida, New York, New Jersey, and Illinois. These are the traditional receiving states for unauthorized immigrants. Part of what has nationalized and intensified the immigration debate in recent years has been the growing presence of illegal immigrants in new areas, such as the southeast. The state that follows Illinois for total numbers is Georgia, now placing ahead of Arizona, which is then followed by North Carolina.

Recent public opinion surveys find U.S. residents deeply concerned about the size of the undocumented population. When asked in four different surveys in 2010, "How serious a problem do you think the issue of ILLEGAL immigration is for the country right now" the "very serious" response ranged from 56% to 66%. In another survey three-quarters agreed that the U.S. "is not doing enough to keep illegal immigrants from coming into this country." Finally, when asked in another survey whether illegal immigrants do more to strengthen or to weaken the U.S. economy, 74% selected "weaken."(14)

Why Do We Commit?

Our contributors are at different points in their commitment to the U.S. All are committed to some degree but not all have been prepared to take that significant step of becoming a citizen. Perhaps they never will, but their foreign-born children probably will and their U.S.-born children automatically are citizens. Some are almost ready for that level of commitment but then hold off, perhaps for years. Others when they do naturalize do not necessarily mean by it a switch in their identity and basic allegiance but instead an enlargement, choosing instead to retain their original citizenship as they also become a U.S. citizen.

Naturalization is not only an important step for the immigrant but it also is for the political community that they are joining.(15) Naturalization is not only "an important indicator of a person 's integration into a society,"(16) but studies also show that the new citizen is now "more likely to take up active roles in the civic life of the country, to vote, to join community action groups, and to be active in politics more generally."(17) Becoming a citizen is an indicator of commitment; upon doing so, that commitment to the nation often increases.

Accordingly, naturalization rates are important. In 2009, only 44% of the foreign born were naturalized citizens, down significantly from 64% in 1970 but higher than in 2000 (40%).(18) There is substantial variation in naturalized citizenship between the sending regions, probably related at least in part to composition of older and newer immigrant groups. Over 55% of the foreign born from Europe, Asia, and the Caribbean are now citizens. Naturalization for those from South America runs at about 46% whereas the comparable figure for Mexico is only about 24%. Of course, over half of the Mexicans are undocumented and therefore not eligible for citizenship.

What Does 'American' Have To Do With It?

With all of this diversity that immigration has brought, and so rapidly, the challenge for long-time residents is, as one author puts it to us, "How are we, in the United States, to embrace difference and maintain a common life?"(19) This challenge is especially great in those parts of the country that are now experiencing substantial immigration but had relatively little contact with immigrants in the past, such as the South. Few have written about this as well as the U.S. Commission on Immigration Reform in its 1997 Report to Congress. Known as the Jordan Commission for its chair, Rep. Barbara Jordan (D-TX), the report points out that legal immigration presents mutual obligations for citizens and newcomers.

Obligations of the Citizen: For citizens we have the obligation "to provide an environment in which newcomers can become fully participating members of our society." This means that immigrants are not to be excluded from our community nor kept from becoming citizens themselves.(20) Many citizens find this easy to do, welcoming immigrants into their neighborhoods, schools, and homes, some even volunteering to help with the often considerable challenges of adjustment to life in a new country. At other times, though, we fall short, as individuals and as a country, as several contributors in this anthology painfully portray.

Obligations of the Immigrant: Immigrants have their obligations as well, as summarized by the Jordan Commission: "to obey our laws, to pay taxes, to respect other cultures and ethnic groups."(21) But how much further does this obligation go, or does it? Given the ambivalence about immigration among the general public that surveys find again and again, it is safe to infer that many citizens do expect more. Figure 3 demonstrates one part of that ambivalence with a question that forces the respondent to identify immigration as something that either strengthens the country or is a burden on it. For the last decade the public has been essentially split on this issue. On both sides and by about the same amount, most respondents hold their position "strongly" (not shown in Figure 3).

I think what most citizens want from immigrants is a sense that the relationship is more than instrumental, that it is about more than working and taxes, although I cannot find surveys that would give me the evidence to support my hunch. In effect, the citizen is saying, "How can I welcome you into this community unless I know that you want to be part of our community?" This would be particularly true of the sizeable plurality that believes even with immigrants' hard work and taxes, overall they are a burden on the country. And, I would guess, it is most true in those parts of the country that do not have a long history of experience with substantial immigration.

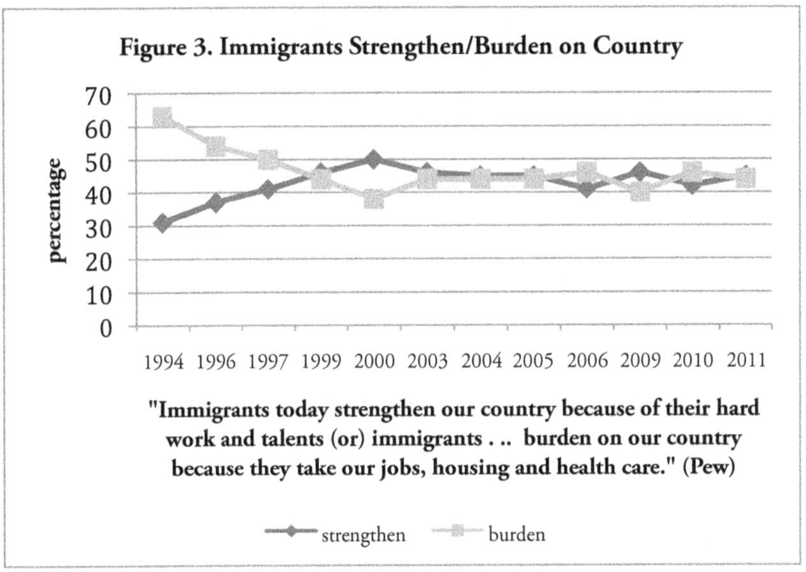

The Meaning of Being An American: We do have survey data on what Americans think "being American" means, as summarized by Figure 4. Two of the top four responses are political. "To respect America's political institutions and laws" is one of the basic obligations identified by the Jordan Commission to be met by everyone while "to have American citizenship" is the culmination of the identification process. "To be able to speak English" is the most frequent response, undoubtedly because it is necessary for the interactions that makes one part of a community and probably also as an indicator of the immigrant's desire for that interaction. And immigrants want to learn English. Unfortunately, their interest for classes far outruns the supply that we offer. The other leading response is "to feel American." What a welcoming response! We want you to feel like you are one of us. If you do, then you are. This anthology is replete with the stories of immigrants who have accepted this invitation, each finding their own way toward being American, as they understand it.

Since the United States has a long history of substantial immigration it is a well-studied subject, one we know much about. It is a process, one that is unique in its particulars for each individual but with many similarities in the challenges and the patterns. Immigrants learn about expectations in this new place and adjust . . . and adjust. Depending on one's age on arrival, the immigrant might have arrived already a rather fully formed person. Core values and customs might remain, but over time accommodations are made, demonstrated in new behaviors and views. One of the beauties of North America (including Canada too) is that one can become an American but retain much of one's original culture, indeed, making one's own contribution that will be valued by many in this "kaleidoscopic" nation.(22) It is also a multi-generational process, with elements of the homeland culture persisting into subsequent generations and associational preferences as well, but usually with diminishing strength, especially when marriage occurs outside of one's original national group.

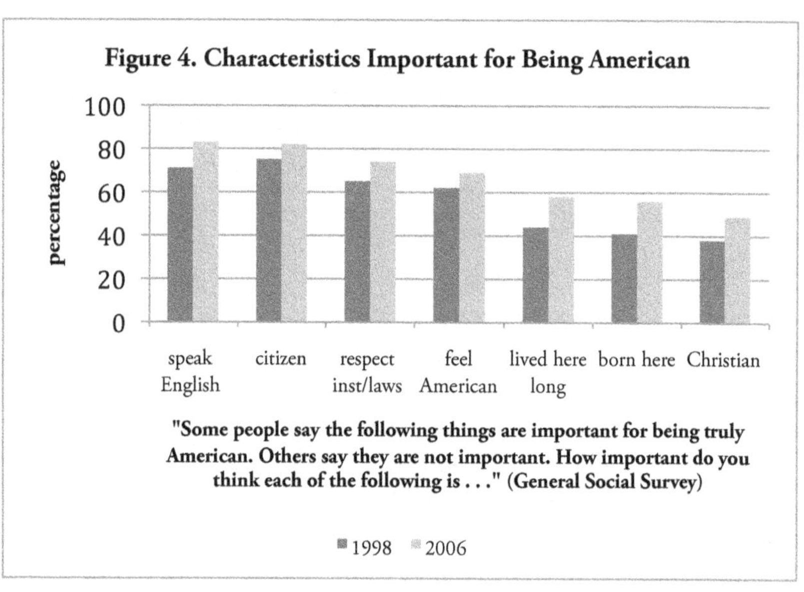

Where Do We Belong?

There may have been much more continuing contact between the Old World and the U.S. a century ago than often thought, as discussed earlier. However, contemporary transnationalism does present new features. Modern transportation and communication allows the immigrant to maintain much closer contact by phone and Internet with loved ones in their country of origin and to follow the course of current events. Visits are much easier in both directions. Indeed, for those who can afford the travel costs, economic affairs can be managed on the ground in both countries. Furthermore, U.S. society is much more accepting of cultural diversity today, reducing the conformity pressures immigrants faced in the past.

Multiple Allegiances: One of the most important differences is the growing acceptance of multiple allegiances, and even citizenships. Up until recently the naturalization pledge requiring the new U.S. citizen to "renounce and abjure all allegiance and fidelity" to any other nation was meant seriously. Since 1990 it has not, when the U.S. government "grudgingly recognized dual citizenship."(23) Other nations embrace it and large numbers now allow their citizens who leave and become citizens in another country to retain their citizenship—by recent count over 150 countries. The form that this takes varies widely. Some allow their dual citizens abroad to still vote at home, some even facilitate their voting from the U.S. Others even allow dual citizens abroad to still run for public office at home.

Today somewhere between twenty-five and forty million U.S. citizens hold passports from other countries.(24) This includes a good number of our contributors and in some cases, their family members—you will meet one young child who has the possibility of citizenship in *five* different countries. Others might not have dual citizenship but they do have dual allegiances. We have contributors who feel at home not just in one country but in two or even more. And then we have others who have lived outside the United States so much of their lives that even though they are U.S. citizens, it is not where they feel at home.

Allegiance to Principles: For many of us political allegiance is very straightforward. Having never left our birth country—or only for short trips—our loyalty is automatic. But for many people, the contemporary world presents new opportunities, including multiple allegiances. Because the United States asks you to affirm principles as the precondition for joining our political community rather than to embody any particular ethnic or religious characteristic, because to become *American* primarily requires that you feel you are *American*, the U.S. is particularly well suited for this world of multiple and complex allegiances.

Abraham Lincoln expressed so well the attractiveness of the core of American allegiance in his eulogy to Henry Clay, proclaiming that Clay "loved his country partly because it was his own country, but mostly because it was a free country, and he burned with a zeal for its advancement, prosperity and glory, of human liberty, human right and human nature."(25)

Endnotes

(1) American Legion, "Veterans Day Speech 2011." Web: 6.
(2) Rita J. Simon, *Public Opinion and the Immigrant: Print Media Coverage, 1880-1980.* Lexington, MA: Lexington Books, 1985: 32.
(3) Stanley A. Renshon, *The 50% American: Immigration and National Identity in an Age of Terror.* Washington, D.C.: Georgetown University Press, 2005: 26.
(4) www.pollingreport.com/immigration.htm.
(5) Office of Immigration Statistics, *2010 Yearbook of Immigration Statistics.* Washington, D.C.: Department of Homeland Security. Web: Table 1.
(6) Sarah J. Mahler, *American Dreaming: Immigrant Life on the Margins.* Princeton: Princeton University Press, 1995: 98.
(7) Jacob L. Vigdor, *From Immigrants to Americans: The Rise and Fall of Fitting In.* Lanham, MD: Rowman & Littlefield, 2009: 35.
(8) Vigdor: 36.
(9) Daniel Dockterman, *Statistical Portrait of the Foreign-Born Population in the United States, 2009.* Pew Hispanic Center, 2011. Web.
(10) Read side-by-side Samuel P. Huntington, *Who Are We? The Challenges to America's National Identity.* New York: Simon & Schuster, 2004; and Armando Navarro, *The Immigration Crisis: Nativism, Armed Vigilantism, and the Rise of a Countervailing Movement.* Latham, MD: AltaMira Press, 2009.
(11) Rodolfo O. de la Garza, Angelo Falcon, and F. Chris Garcia, "Will the Real Americans Please Stand Up: Anglo and Mexican-American Support of Core American Political Values." *American Journal of Political Science,* 40.2 (1996): 344-45.
(12) Nancy Foner, "What's New About Transnationalism? New York Immigrants Today and at the Turn of the Century." *Diaspora* 6.3 (1997): 358-59. Also see Ewa Morawska, "Immigrants, Transnationalism, and Ethnicization: A Comparison of This Great Wave and the Last." *E Pluribus Unum? Contemporary and Historical Perspectives on Immigrant Political Incorporation.* Eds. Gary Gerstle and John Mollenkopf. New York: Russell Sage Foundation, 2001.
(13) Jeffrey S. Passel and D'Vera Cohn, "Unauthorized Immigrant Population: National and State Trends, 2010." Pew Hispanic Center, 2011. Web.
(14) The source for all survey responses reported here is www.pollingreport.com/immigration.htm.
(15) Information on the requirements and process of naturalization can be found at: U.S. Citizenship and Immigration Services, "A Guide to Naturalization." Web.
(16) Task Force on New Americans. *Building an Americanization Movement for the*

Twenty-First Century. U.S. Department of Homeland Security, 2008. Web: ix.

(17) William A.V. Clark, *Immigrants and the American Dream: Remaking the Middle Class*. New York: Guilford Press, 2003: 164.

(18) Thomas A. Gryn and Luke J. Larsen, *Nativity Status and Citizenship in the United States: 2009*. U.S. Census Bureau, 2010. Web.

(19) Michael Walzer, *What It Means to Be an American*. New York: Marsilio, 1992: 17.

(20) U. S. Commission on Immigration Reform. *Becoming an American: Immigrant and Immigration Policy*, 1997. Web: 28.

(21) U.S. Commission: 28.

(22) This is the preferred term of Lawrence Fuchs, a preeminent scholar of U.S. diversity. See *The American Kaleidoscope: Race, Ethnicity, and the Civic Culture*. Hanover, NH: University Press of New England, 1990.

(23) Michele Wucker, "Changing Concepts of Citizenship and Nationality across Time and Space." *Getting Immigration Right: What Every American Needs to Know*. Eds. David Coates and Peter Siavelis. Potomac Books, 2009: 41. For a particularly good account of the subject see Foner, "What's New About Transnationalism?"

(24) Wucker: 41.

(25) Quoted by Walter Berns, "Patriotism and Multiculturalism." *The Many Faces of Patriotism*. Ed. Philip Abbott. Lanham, MD: Rowman & Littlefield, 2007: 3.

of the American

with

made,

upon

HEATHER TOSTESON

LISTENING FOR BELONGING
I

For to get rid of the habit of thinking of democracy as something institutional and external and to acquire the habit of treating it as a way of personal life is to realize that democracy is a moral ideal and so far as it becomes a fact is a moral fact. It is to realize that democracy is a reality only as it is indeed a commonplace of living. John Dewey

Citizenship is hard. It takes a commitment to listen, watch, read, and think in ways that allow the imagination to put one person in the shoes of another. James Leach

Narrative, I believe, is designed to contain uncanniness rather than to resolve it. It does not have to come out on the 'right side.' . . . the 'consolation of narrative' is not the comfort of a happy ending, but the comprehension of plight that, by being made understandable, becomes bearable. Jerome Bruner

Our nervous systems are constructed to be captured by the nervous systems of others, so that we can experience others as if from within their skin, as well as from within our own. A sort of direct feeling route into another person is potentially open and we resonate with and participate in their experience, and they in ours. Daniel Stern

This collection was inspired by several questions that grew in importance to us as we listened to the stories and meditations on the immigration experience included in our first citizenship anthology, *Shifting Balance Sheets: Women's Stories of Naturalized Citizenship & Cultural Attachment*. The word *We* is central to all of them. The phrase *Finding the We in Them, the Us in You*, is one we use to describe our approach to pluralism. *We* means to us both a pronoun and a posture of communal, consciously shared direct experience. We, in general, use *We* to refer to a group that we feel part of. Here are some of the questions that concern us:

Where do we, wherever we were born, whatever our citizenship status is, now place our 'We'?

What are we giving back to the place—and society—in which we now live?

What effect does being welcomed, or denigrated, in a new country have on where we place our 'We'?

What is the rate of change that is possible for a community, local or national, to sustain and still experience itself as a community, a group that feels ties of social reciprocity, of affection, respect, obligation, and unity of purpose and feels those not as a promise for the distant future, but as a reality now? Here.

These are all, finally, questions about belonging. The question of immigration, however complexly organized it is, remains for me a doorway into that even more powerful and pervasive question of belonging.

When I ask myself why I am so intensely interested in this question of belonging, what comes to mind is a morning on the beach in Chiapas, Mexico in the fall of 2004. We were spending several months in San Cristóbal and had decided to exchange the mountains for the sea for a weekend so had taken a bus down to a rather deserted beach town. We found a hotel some distance from town. The second morning there I decided to go for a walk alone on the beach, something I love to do. However, there are many stray dogs in Mexico and, especially in the morning, they can band in packs. One large pack was milling on the beach, so instead of walking away from town I decided to walk toward it thinking the dogs would be less likely to follow me. If they did it might be better to be near other people. The dogs eagerly trailed me. As long as they kept their distance, I decided, I was relatively secure. I did pick up my pace. However, just as I began to pass a few houses and restaurants, still closed at this fairly early hour, another pack of dogs appeared from the other direction. The two packs eyed each other warily, tails alert, a few growls rumbling, then they all turned toward me. Their interest was daunting. I decided it might be wise for me to step into the water.

The surf was stronger than I expected, sucking the sand loudly out from under my feet. I swiveled around to check where the dogs were. Suddenly a large wave washed up and slammed against my leg at knee height. Without warning, my leg gave and I found myself flat on my back in the waves. I tried to get up, but my leg collapsed again. Down the beach I could see an old man and a younger woman. I yelled in Spanish for help. *¡Socorro!* They did not respond, indeed turned away. I yelled again, louder. I varied my cry, *¡Ayudame!* I tried to get up again, fell again. I saw someone else coming along the beach and yelled louder. The dogs were all edging closer, fascinated. I had this moment of amazing clarity and realized that I was going to yell until someone helped me. All social inhibition disappeared. I was both desperate and eerily objective. Curious. How long would it take? Finally, many yells, falls, and several passers-by later, a young man paused beside me. His girlfriend walked determinedly on. I explained to him in Spanish that I needed help to get back to my hotel. I had hurt my leg.

"Just walk very slowly," he said.

I explained that I couldn't, that my leg wouldn't hold. He looked interested now.

"I had something like that playing soccer. It is probably a muscle. Are you sure you can't walk on it?"

I crawled to standing, then tumbled back down again when I tried to walk. "If you can help me get to the street, I will take a taxi."

So, to his girlfriend's obvious disapproval, he gave me his arm and helped me hobble, my leg erratically collapsing on us, the block to the main road. But the three taxi drivers he hailed looked at me and shook their heads. They would not take me back to my hotel. I was too wet. Sandy. Unkempt.

"I think I will have to take you myself," the young man said at last. He told his girlfriend, who responded angrily, but went into their hotel and brought out a towel to save the front seat of their truck. She stood, arms crossed, scowling, as we drove off. As we drove, the young man asked me, "Do you like Chiapas?" "Oh yes," I said immediately. This was a well-practiced interchange that I had had numerous times in our months there. So, we had a surreally normal chat about the beauties of Mexico and Chiapas, the kindness of the Mexican people. I had this vocabulary down pat. "*Una gente muy amable, muy inteligente, muy trabajadora, muy simpática,*" I said. As we approached my hotel, he suddenly lit up and said, "Oh, is that where you are staying?" And then he looked at me more closely. "You were at the restaurant last night having dinner with your husband. I saw you there." With this new context, some switch was flipped and, at that moment, I could see that I had suddenly, mysteriously, become fully human to him. So the smile and thanks I gave him when he left me precariously standing in the hotel courtyard were genuine from several different levels.

But I had exhausted my objectivity, so when the maids in the courtyard looked at me with the same blankness as the people on the beach and turned their backs and started to chat with each other, and through the window I saw my husband standing on the other side of the guardhouse chatting with someone, oblivious to my presence, I just began to howl, in English, "HELP ME!!!!"

This experience has had a profound impact on me—and it is the basis of much of my own thinking on community. My definition, obviously, is very basic. When I scream for help, especially if I scream in the language of that country, I want to be able to assume that I will be answered. Honestly, when I scream I want that universal language answered anywhere in the world. I expect every immigrant and émigré wants the same. It is hard to imagine the basis for any continuing relationship that doesn't have this assumption at its core. I had, up until then, always assumed it was a given, instinctual. (When I have shared this story, people have asked me if I thought the reluctance to get involved was because I was American. It honestly hadn't occurred to me, and I still don't think it was the reason. Living in Mexico at different times, observing how Mexicans respond to other Mexicans in distress who are strangers to them, I think I was being treated as they would any stranger, even *una compatriota*. It is my uncomfortable assumption that immigrants living here in the U.S. could have had a similar experience. I think it has more to do with where we draw the line between us and strangers.)

I now think these are very appropriate questions to ask of anyone who asks loyalty of me: If you find me bleeding on the street, would you stop and help me? Would you call an ambulance? Would you stay until it came? I think these are questions that people in our country these days may be asking themselves *about* each other—but not *to* each other—more than we imagine, especially in highly diverse areas. What would happen, I wonder, if we began to ask them openly, with all that vulnerability exposed, claimed as our common good?

For this anthology, I was clear that my interest was in emotional complexity, stories that didn't fit conventional assumptions about citizenship and cultural attachment, but did reflect the lives of people we knew. I wanted to push my own thinking and feeling about citizenship and about community and about belonging. I wanted to do it by encouraging us to listen to stories of real people each in his or her unique situation as an immigrant or émigré facing choices in the thick of their lives, to see what choices they made, and to wonder what, in their situations, we ourselves would do. I wanted our collection to have what I call novelistic complexity, by which I mean a layering of individual stories that intersect, echo, contradict, amplify each other. I wanted that other wonderful quality of a novel, that sense that with all that multiplicity of story, a coherent affective world is forming, created by something more than mere proximity, something that has to do with our own listening, with the meaning-in-the-making that is essential to all stories. I wanted that affective world to intrigue and surprise, to validate our own experience and introduce us to experiences that are radically different, to make a safe place for troubling complexities that at other times we try to deny or suppress. A world that can't be reduced to a single character's point of view, or summed up in a lesson. I wanted us to be changed by participating in that world in the way that we are by art, not by journalism or scholarship, from the inside out, starting with the heart.

I knew I wanted my own contributions to this collection to be about listening—because I had done a lot of it in the process of developing this anthology. To begin, I am going to be sharing experiences of listening that have strongly influenced or been influenced by this book but are not directly included in it.

I was drawn into all this listening because this anthology was more difficult to create than some of our others. Fewer people submitted. Perhaps people found the issue of complexity more aversive than alluring—difficult to put into words, intimate and precious, but also dangerous to share with people who were unfamiliar or intolerant of it, people who could possibly use it to challenge one's right to belong. So we actively solicited writing from people we knew, here and elsewhere, whose stories we thought might help us understand better some of those questions we felt rising about citizenship, attachment, and belonging. We wanted to hear from people who did not want to become citizens but wanted to live here, people who were citizens but preferred to live their whole lives abroad, people who had several allegiances, people who felt rebuffed in their allegiances. They wrote, then, assured of an open, attentive listener who wanted to know the messy stuff. We also made a joint extended effort (see the interviews by Charles Brockett, Anna Steegmann, Debra Gingerich, and Alexandrina Sergio) to interview people who were not writers but who had interesting stories that would not find their way to print without a listener interested enough to record them.

The stories gathered here are intriguing and take us far beyond the long-standing assumptions about immigration that Marcelo Suárez-Orozco identifies in "Everything You Ever Wanted to Know About Assimilation But Were Afraid to Ask." These assumptions include making a clean break with the past, struggling to assimilate, and creating a new life for yourself better than the one you had before. I am very fond of that immigration myth, addicted to it really. I never tire of learning about the challenges we face leaving everything we know; the courage and tenacity required to live, work and love in a rawly new and not necessarily welcoming environment that challenges many, sometimes all, of our most cherished assumptions; or about how that difficult journey can, unbelievably, lead to that most precious of conclusions, integrity and belonging. *Again.* After setting up life for myself on those terms in twenty-two different places in sixty-one years, I could well call it my personal meta-narrative—one that only immigrants and expats seem to *get* in the same way I do. Not as an oddity but an essential human condition. This *condition* I share with pioneer ancestors as well as immigrant ones, and with many mobile Americans (like my own family) who move more than once in their lives for jobs, education, family. It has affected how I understand community, what it is, where it is located, whom it consists of, and how I recreate it for myself time after time. I am always listening, in all these different places, with all these different people, all these different social structures and cultural mores, to what it is we *really* share—where and to what extent it is safe to rest in the gifts of our common existence.

But however much I like that myth, the reality is always more difficult, nuanced, changing. What we felt was a choice can quickly come to feel like something uncontrollable and unwanted. What we left can feel as if it deserted us. The community, national or local, we once belonged to was often far more divisive and our sense of belonging far more provisional than we care to remember. There are doubts about what part, if any, we played in that uncomfortably remembered conflict or alienation. If our allegiances remain strong in several directions, these complexities of both situation and response increase. This complexity is very difficult to share, especially with people who haven't had similar experiences, but also with ourselves. It provokes all kinds of feelings, half-thoughts, doubts, but it is essential to the experience and when someone *gets* it, they *get* us in a profound way.

It is exactly these difficult to describe experiences we have selected for and heard into speech for this anthology—ones that resist language because they cut across language and familiar categories, are steeped with intense but inchoate feeling, ones that make the listener and the hearer see themselves in new, not always flattering, lights. In the polarized atmosphere in the U.S. today, it is a brave and generous thing to be willing to do so.

THE SILENCED CENTER

To cooperate by giving differences a chance to show themselves because of the belief that the expression of difference is not only a right of the other persons but is a means of enriching one's own life-experience is inherent in the democratic personal way of life.

John Dewey

Words matter. They reflect emotion as well as meaning. They clarify—or cloud—thought and energize action, sometimes bringing out the better angels of our nature, sometimes baser instincts. Stirring anger and playing on the irrational fears of citizens inflames hate. When coupled with character assassination, polarizing rhetoric can exacerbate intolerance and perhaps impel violence.

James Leach

Both these anthologies have been inspired in part by a strong concern about the increasing polarization in our country that is amplified by the media, both mass and social, and its impact on our sense of national community and on democratic process: in particular, a concern about the silenced center. I often think that our public conversations now are like a family dinner where two highly opinionated people, perhaps Uncle Bert, a Republican banker, and his sister's son, John Jr., a rising star in MoveOn or Occupy Wall Street (or both) have appropriated the head and tail of the table and, within ten minutes of serving the roast, are holding the whole table hostage to their vociferous debate. This year it happens to be about presidential candidates. But it doesn't really matter what it is. Religion. Taxes. Same-sex marriage. Abortion. Charter schools. Terrorism. Wars. Legal or illegal immigration. They always stake out positions as far as possible from each other. They are not listening to each other. The argument rapidly becomes personal. John Jr. questions his uncle's honesty, intelligence and compassion. His uncle questions his patriotism. Occasionally, one or the other looks around the table for affirmation when he feels he has scored a particularly good point, but no one else is encouraged to join in. Nor do they show any inclination. Quietly, with a glance here, a smile there, the rest of the people get up, clear the table, take their own conversation elsewhere. Their departure, if it doesn't go unnoticed, is written off by Uncle Bert and John Jr. as complacence or shallow-mindedness.

As Ara Sarkissian says in his interview, there is a *We* in daily life, but with the extremes now so loud and relentless, it is almost impossible to hear. But that centrist voice is very important to hear—for one thing, it is a *listening* voice. It has a sense of the multiplicity of viewpoints involved. It sees something good—and something questionable—in everyone. And it usually speaks as we saw just now through action or silence. If someone asks a centrist what they think about a candidate, a policy, they may say they have not decided yet. If they are still thinking about it, they may well use stories to get a feel for the real life complexities involved. They know someone who . . . and, on the other hand, they know someone else who. . . . They take things with a grain of salt, or a whole saltcellar these days. They also take them personally. On many issues their evaluations are highly contextual, contingent. This can be misconstrued as indecision, but they really mean it when they say: *it depends on the circumstances*. It is my assumption that we would make wiser real life decisions, policy decisions, listening more closely to their thoughts even if they are difficult to elicit. Listening as well to the manner in which those thoughts are often shared: story.

In the case of the current immigration debate, we need to move beyond these polarized positions where immigration is *only* right *or* wrong, patriotism is *only* rigid, xenophobic, and authoritarian *or* an unquestionable virtue. Most people with direct experience with immigrants—or patriots—already have. They just haven't been heard yet, not necessarily because they aren't clear about what they think but because they may feel they will be attacked. The more complex and nuanced their thoughts, the more they may feel that. It is easier to speak with a vote, an act of volunteering, or random kindness. What those choices to speak through actions rather than words, however understandable, fail to do is to allow us to know how numerous we are. They reduce our common good. They do not change the tenor of our daily environment where Uncle Bert and John Jr. (and their media amplifiers) loudly go on giving as good as they get. The volume is deafening and distorting. They give people—for example legal immigrants and naturalized citizens who wonder why they are being treated as intruders, or people with some reservations about the rate of change in their communities—the idea that these hyper-articulated extremes have such broad tacit social support that the rest of us have no choice but to speak in their terms. We can fight back or succumb. Either. Or. Either. Or. This feels like a real loss to all of us at every level—intellectual, social, personal, political and moral.

It is important when we ask people to share their experiences with immigration to recognize the level of discomfort and social anxiety that request can cause, especially in our current environment, and the courage it takes to overcome it even if people want to share their stories and thoughts. I want to share some of the things that happened during this interviewing that bear most directly on this issue of silencing in the way any good centrist would—through story.

One thing I want to draw our attention to is who is missing from this collection: Muslims. Although we strove for breadth in this collection and spent a considerable amount of time working through both public networks (like local Muslim speakers bureaus) and private networks, we were not successful in finding Muslim immigrants willing to write or be interviewed on this subject. I want us to hear this absence although I am hesitant to guess the reasons for it. I'm fairly sure there isn't personal animosity toward us, or even to the project. It may just be the difficulty of exploring such complex subjects, especially if one fears the ultimate audience might be hostile, even more so if these meditations were to be included in something as permanent as a book. Certainly one Turkish physician I spoke with, someone who works for the government and has been a citizen for decades, made it clear she found the current attitude toward immigrants, specifically Muslim immigrants, so hostile that she would never even put her thoughts down in a private journal, much less share them, even anonymously, with the world. The level of that self-silencing makes me ache.

There are other reasons for hesitating that may have nothing to do with U.S. attitudes toward immigration at all. For several months, I have been in a fascinating dance of yearning and withdrawal with a thoughtful Middle Eastern man in his thirties whom I will call Rôhat. He works at a popular restaurant we often frequent. It is very successful, a family business. We have always been struck with how well the restaurant combines dimensions of the owners' two cultures. It has belly dancers and hookahs, is a local hangout for college students, for African-Americans dressed to the nines for a fancy night out, and also for families, especially Indian and Pakistani ones from the surrounding neighborhood. The belly dancers (all Caucasian) are as often teaching their shimmies to two year olds as they are dancing in place so that adults can slip a folded bill under their waistbands. The young men who work there seven nights a week are constantly attending to customers, except when, on belly-dancing nights, they take to the floor with a group of their male friends to dance their own dances in a vigorous ring.

Rôhat's brother had generously offered to help me locate possible contributors for the previous anthology because through the restaurant he knew many women who were immigrants from different countries. When we decided to do a second one, I went back to the restaurant to see if I could enlist his help again. This time, it was his own story, this successful accommodation of cultures, that interested me, as well as the question of whether minority status in your country of origin (a Kurd in Iraq or Turkey, an Armenian in Lebanon) made it easier for you to assimilate in a new culture but more difficult to commit, and whether you brought the ethnic tensions that were so defining in your country of origin with you to your chosen country. Instead of finding the brother, I ended up in conversation with Rôhat, who had taken charge of this restaurant while his brother went on to manage a new one they were opening. Rôhat was obviously fascinated with the project. He had studied political science at university before he came to the U.S. He wanted to go back to graduate school, probably in global studies, he confided. He thought about these issues often. "The young people who come here, they drink and they party. They have no idea how it is in the rest of the world." He spoke as much in wonderment as criticism.

"Would *you* like to participate?" I asked him.

He hesitated, then said sadly, "My English is not good enough."

It was, and I said so. But obviously his facility in his other two languages was greater and these issues were close to his heart so the frustration he felt was high. I suggested that we use the process to improve his English, so the experience would be helpful to him if he decided to go back to school. He could write and we could edit, or if he thought it would be less frustrating to be interviewed, we could do that.

Rôhat still seemed to hesitate so I told him to think it over and offered to bring him a copy of the first anthology to look at and also to make up a list of questions that he could review. We met at the restaurant one afternoon and talked some more. As I was driving away, I saw him settling at a table outside the restaurant with a cigarette and the book.

When I called Rôhat a week later, he apologized and said he didn't know enough, that we should talk with his uncle who was a leader in the local cultural society. We dutifully did, but nothing came of it.

I worried a little that with this request I had created an uncomfortable situation for him, so we purposefully didn't make contact with him when we went back to the restaurant. However, he personally came up to greet us every time we were there and said how sorry he was that his English wasn't adequate. Responding to something in his intensity and tone, I would say each time, "If you change your mind, there is still time."

It became a fascinating dance. We didn't want him to feel uncomfortable, but there was something in his obvious interest that kept me asking him about his plans for school, for further study. He brushed them away. "There is no time," he said. "We work every day." I told him he would be invited to our publication party because he had been involved in the project and I thought he would like to meet the other people there. He was excited at the prospect.

A month ago, when we visited, again he came and sat with us and asked us how we were. He asked about the publication party. We joked that we didn't know if we would ever be finished, whether there would be a party. He then looked at me and pressing his hands together and drawing them to his chest said, "I so much want to be part of this book—but it is not possible." He gestured to the teapot. "My friends would say I am like this. A good surface. But you open it up, it is only air. Nothing. Who am I to talk? They have no chance. It is not fair."

"Your friends here?" I asked. No, he told me. His friends back home.

"I feel so stuck," he said. "I cannot move. I feel this might help me—" He gestured as if tearing through something. "But I cannot. My friends, they do not have this chance. And my mother, I would not want to upset her."

"Perhaps you would like to talk to your friends through the book, show them what your life is like now?"

"They do not speak to me. I just left. I did not tell them I was leaving. It is not like here. We must respect our mothers, so I left. But my friends have mothers too. They are still there. They did not go. I left without saying anything to them."

Suddenly he scrambled to his feet and ran across the room, knocking his head on a hanging lamp as he lunged to stop the song beginning to play from his ipod through the sound system. "That is not a nice song," he said laughing as he sat down with us again. It was rap of some kind, and from the speed of response, I assume probably obscene. Ruefully, he rubbed his forehead.

"In my culture," he continued, "you do not say what you think. You cannot."

"Not even with your family?" Only, I began to surmise, with your friends.

"If I were to do this, put this in a book it would be there forever." He shook his head.

My husband, responding to his obvious distress, gave him our order. A waitress who had been impatiently reminding him that there were drinks to mix, orders to ring up, sighed with relief.

As we were leaving, he came up to us again, obviously torn.

"You feel you betrayed your friends by coming to this country?" I asked.

"I did betray them. They do not speak to me. What could I do?"

A look passed between us as we bowed to each other. Guilt on both sides. I had wanted him to have a safe place to explore his thoughts, to speak back gently (he is a gentle man) to the callow students who come to puff hookahs and, if of age, to slug beer or sip martinis oblivious to countries with famine, civil war, rebel movements, Arab Springs. I wanted him to feel that he had a voice. Instead, I felt I had left him more isolated than before.

I couldn't shake my concern for him, for these desires, intense, painful, and so necessary for his own development that I had unintentionally activated. So I wrote him a letter in which I suggested that he write out the story he so desired to tell for himself alone, that he was its most crucial audience. Once he had heard it himself, he was free to choose to share it or not, but everyone should have the freedom to listen to their own story without fear or coercion. This was, I told him when I handed him the sealed letter, exactly what I would tell my own son, for whom also my deepest desire is inner freedom.

This sense of the danger of self-revelation was also echoed by Taye, whose interview is included, but his moment of doubt came after the interview not before. Taye is a tall, handsome, endearingly warm and open man. Years ago when I moved here, we connected at the local branch of the county library (where he is a librarian and I am a very frequent visitor) when I asked him what his name meant in English. He blushed as he told me. It was wonderfully heroic, something that pleased and embarrassed him in equal measure. He was comfortable agreeing to be interviewed as a diversity lottery winner, but it took a couple of missed e-mails and appointments for the interview to take place. Some months later, when I sent him the transcript for factual corrections, he took several weeks to respond. It took face-to-face contact at the library to get him to do so. At that time I asked if he wanted to donate an image of himself to art, a light-hearted request I was making generally of contributors but only if they felt comfortable. "Is that necessary?" he asked. His discomfort was so obvious, I told him of course it wasn't and asked again if he wanted to use a pseudonym for his interview. "I think anonymous is better," he said with a sigh of relief. (He ultimately chose to use the name Taye, "He has been seen," a common name in his country.)

Before Taye sent back the transcript he wrote me a letter in which he said that his wife had come in while he was editing the transcript and began to ask him questions about it and that got him thinking as well. He knew he should have asked these questions before but thought it was not too late to ask. What was the purpose of the book? Who was its audience? Was his story going to be the only one included? How did it benefit his community? He hoped we could talk about these things so he could get peace of mind.

I felt stricken at his obvious discomfort—and exasperated because we had gone through all this before the interview or I assumed we had. I'd given him our website link. He'd seen the first anthology, indeed had shared flyers about our call for interviews with members of his church. Copies were in the library system. But I also realized that he had done this interview for me because he liked and trusted me personally—that his wife, who did not know me, whose judgment he also honored, now expressed doubt and anxiety and made him feel that he had possibly made a mistake, one that he could not remedy without insulting me.

I methodically went through each of his questions, responding to his question about the benefit to community in this way: *Our sense is that it benefits the community we are all creating here where we live by helping us understand each other's experience, by focusing on what we share and what we can learn from each other.*

I went on to add, *It would also help me to understand what it is you are most concerned about. Do you think that your story can be used against you or your Ethiopian community in any way? I can't possibly imagine that is the case. Your story is one of someone who is very thoughtful, responsible, accomplished—exactly the kind of person that the diversity lottery is designed to encourage. I think many people will be very impressed with what you and your wife and son have managed to do—the courage and persistence it has taken to come to a different country and the benefits you bring to this country.*

It troubles me more than I can say, as his friend, his neighbor, and an American, and expect it will trouble other people who read his interview, that he might even wonder about that.

These questions about silencing, about the felt dangers of speaking one's truth, and my own responsibility as a listener came up for me as well when Natalia Treviño and I went back and forth over her manuscript, which we had asked her to write based on some wonderful conversations and e-mails we had shared about all the different forms of cultural attachment and citizenship in her immediate family. Natalia's memoir speaks for itself, but as a friend and colleague, I was also aware that several times she used the word "dangerous" to define her participation here, a word she hadn't used for her submission to the prior citizenship anthology. And she had a point. We had invited her to revisit the powerful emotions she experienced as a child asked to distance herself from her beloved Mexican identity without a clear or comparably valuable American identity to take its place. The anger and shame she felt at the tension between her need to belong and the seemingly impossible choices she was asked to make to get there in both the Anglo and Mexican communities are still alive today—as are those choices in some form or another. But she has a voice of her own, warm, pained, persuasive, to speak with now, one that everyone, even she, can hear. One that will, I am sure, free others to hear their own.

In his interview Ara Sarkissian, whom I have known since he first came here from Lebanon over twenty years ago, discussed this issue of the silenced center in immigration debate. But we also shared another interesting reminiscence about a silence that wasn't about suppression, rather spoke louder than words, and was heard. When Ara first came to Watertown, Massachusetts, my son was his first friend, his only friend he corrected me, in high school. "I was so traumatized when I first got there I couldn't speak," he said. For the first two weeks he and my son (who is no stranger to silence himself) played chess without exchanging a word. I can actually remember my son telling me he had finally made a friend. "What is he like?" I asked him. "I don't know," my son said. "I haven't asked. We just play chess." Somehow, in that silence a bond was formed that still lasts today.

I reminded Ara of how he had also, without a word, left on a side table in our dining room a packet of photos of his school in Beirut. I had opened it up with his assent and spread them out on the table. They were of rubble. They said more clearly than words that there was no going back. We never talked about them. They remained spread out on the table and each time he came over to visit with my son I would ask in passing if he wanted to take them back home and he would say no. I'd say fine, and they would stay there.

"I don't remember that," Ara said twenty years later, amused. "I wonder why I did that? I guess I needed to feel at least one person here in this country knew what my world was like. I guess I decided it was going to be you."

"That's what I thought too. I felt it was my job to hold them for you until you were ready to take them back."

Ara, on our Skype interview, had been for him astonishingly open, had probably spoken to me more than he has to my son in their twenty-year friendship. Silently, he lifted his young daughter up for me to see on the computer screen. He beamed. When I used photos of the two of them he sent me as the basis of some of the images for this book, I felt we had completed some charmed circle. Without a word.

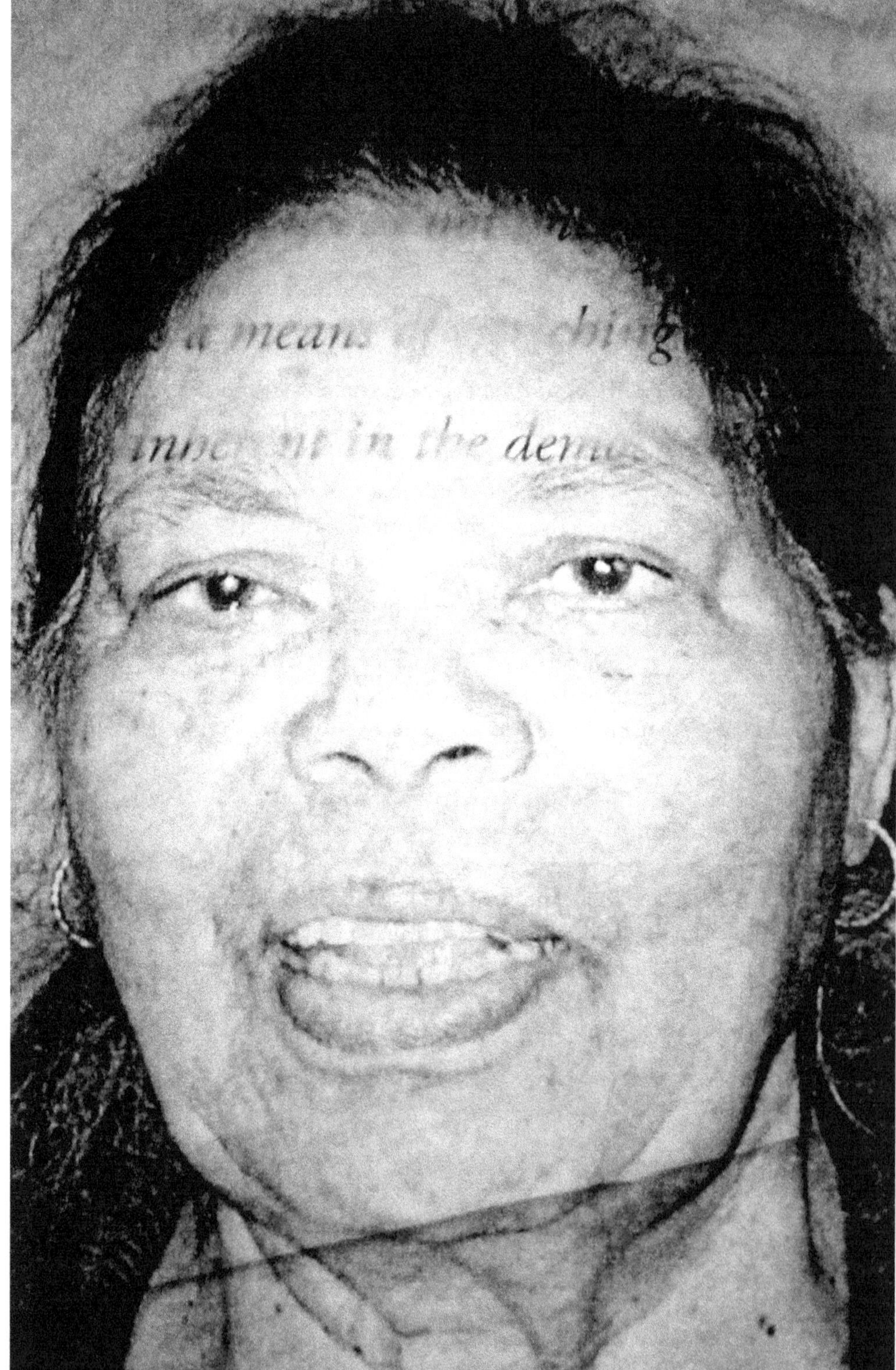

II

WHY DO WE COME?

MARCELLE KASPROWICZ

NATIVE LAND

I walk with you

I am your ship
your crew
your trade winds
your sail
I am your anchor

Terra firma
I remain
and you take me with you

You take me with you
alter-ego folded
and well-behaved
in your trunk

I am the wheat still green
of your flesh
the ripe wheat
in your hold

I am the wine
which does not turn
the livestock which renews itself

I am the burning
the dull pain of exile
I am your voice
the one I have baptized

I am your sealed references
I am the footbridge
which delivers you
to the new land
and there
I am your firewood
and your spark

Have no fear
I walk with you

DEPARTURE

Tomorrow
when I climb aboard
when they pull up the boarding bridge
space will tear between us
along an incurable wound

The crew endlessly
will shovel in
time
The three majestic stacks
will belch their thick black smoke
and in its wake
the hull will squirt
a slow star-spangled snail trail
along the sea

Like paws
we will press our fur-lined mittens
against our ears
and deny
the horn's lament
wrenching our hearts

L.S.

THE VISA RITUAL

The plane from Charlotte landed in Madrid at sunrise. The flight seemed longer than usual because my thoughts about the upcoming visa appointment kept me awake most of the night. This time, there is no particular reason to worry about a possible denial. I have already assembled all the necessary documents and the process should be merely a routine. After nineteen years of being on different types of temporary visas, I, of all people, should be accustomed to this process.

Yet I could not shake off my apprehension that something might go wrong this time; something like the fact my actual residence is in the U.S., the country where I have lived most of my adult life and where I have a stable employment, rather than in Spain, the country where I became a citizen six years ago and where I have no prospects of residing in a foreseeable future. How did I end up in the situation that inevitably raises eyebrows of new acquaintances when they realize that I am still legally a temporary resident in the U.S. after all these years? The short answer to this question is that I did not plan any of it. The long answer is that a combination of my curiosity about new cultures, the outbreak of the war, as well as my career ambitions had something to do with it.

Most of my childhood I spent in my room, the sanctuary where I was surrounded by my piano, favorite childhood toys, books, photographs, notebooks and journals. To my parents' dismay, I grew increasingly withdrawn from other children in the neighborhood and preferred to spend time in the world of my own imagination. On the positive side, the more I read and the more I learned, the greater my curiosity became about the world beyond my own. When I was fourteen, on a summer vacation, I met my future pen pals, who told me about high school student exchange programs. Several of them planned to spend a senior year abroad. Upon returning home and checking with my parents, to my surprise, they were fully on board from the onset. As hard as it was for them to let me go, they saw it as the only opportunity compelling me to leave my safe hermitage and become more prepared for life.

In less than twelve months from then, we would become refugees of war. We left behind not only everything we possessed, but also the life we knew before the war. We left in a hurry on the night when the first tanks appeared on the streets and bridges of my city. We became uprooted, humiliated, and scared about what would happen next. The plan to spend a year abroad would have been a distant dream had it not been for another unexpected turn of events. My parents' savings, which had previously been appropriated by the government, could be released to cover educational expenses. I left for the U.S. soon after the school year ended. The bus to the nearest functioning airport, which departed from a highway rest area near the border, was full of young people embarking on a similar journey.

I did not know back then that nine years would pass before I returned again. During the first five years of living in the U.S., I was a stateless person because my passport corresponded to Yugoslavia—a country that had in the meantime ceased to exist. As I waited to be granted either the Croatian citizenship based on my birthplace or the Serbian citizenship based on my mother's birthplace, I reapplied each year or two for a renewal of the status of a foreign student or a temporary worker. I applied for my first student visa to attend a community college. The outcome of the application was uncertain because ideally I would have had to leave the country in order to switch from an exchange visitor status to a student status. But given my unique situation of statelessness and the war that was heating up in my home region, an exception was made in my case.

What ensued in the following six years was a chain of student visa applications, as I switched first to another community college as a result of relocation, then a four-year college, and afterwards a master's program. When it became apparent to me that my country continued to remain politically unstable, I decided to apply for a political asylum as a refugee of war. I turned to a lawyer recommended by friends who handled many other cases from my country. The lawyer required half of the amount to cover the fees ahead of time. My parents sent me their last savings. The first application was denied in several months. The letter indicated that I should appear in court for a deportation hearing.

If I had to leave the U.S., returning to my birthplace would not have been a possibility. It was the city that my family, ethnic minorities who were the target of violence at the onset of the war, had abandoned eight years ago.

The only other possibility would have been to join my parents in their new city. But that possibility was even less probable, as their city was under air strikes at the time. They had already spent every night the previous month hiding in a bomb shelter. My contact with them was reduced to sporadic telephone calls when I was lucky to reach them past the busy signal or when someone answered on the other end. My other concern, in case I left, was that I would lose everything I had accomplished thus far if I was unable to return. I had just completed my master's degree in business administration and was starting my first job.

I applied for an appeal explaining my case in more depth, as advised by my lawyer whose main interest, in retrospect, was to receive the second portion of the payment. In the meantime, my company filed the papers for a temporary work visa. Several months later, while still waiting for the results of the temporary work visa, I received a negative response to the appeal informing me that I should appear before the deportation judge in one month. My former host mother volunteered to join me on the date of the hearing as a moral support. My lawyer did not come in person. While we sat in the waiting room discussing what I should say to the judge, a woman sitting in front of us overheard our conversation. She was surprised to find out that my lawyer had not shown up and told me that I should not have been there in the first place since my application for a temporary work visa was still pending.

Inside the hearing room, surprisingly even more crowded than the waiting room, my name was called first and my lawyer answered the conference call already knowing the court's decision. The judge informed us that this was the final denial without a further option to appeal. I was to pack my bags and leave the country in one week. At that moment, the lawyer from the waiting room stood up in the back of the room informing the judge that my work visa application was pending. The judge was caught off guard, surprised that my own lawyer had not mentioned such vital piece of information that would result in the termination of the proceedings and a positive outcome for me. The case was closed. Thanks to the accidental acquaintance with a person who was genuinely humane, or to my host mother's loud protest, or to my mother's prayers, or all of the above, I was lucky that day.

The work visa arrived in less than a month. Burying everything under a layer of dust of unwanted memories, I turned once again to my other, more hackneyed, yet happier spheres of life. The work hours were long but I enjoyed learning new things. I was in love even though the distance was difficult to bear. With my own immigration status resolved and the political situation in my country stable, I was beginning to make plans to visit my family for the first time since I left.

My plan was intercepted, once again, by events I could not have foreseen. I was asked to set up a new position that would serve as a liaison between Europe and America in the company's European headquarters. In order to accomplish this, I had to move to the Netherlands and apply for a temporary work permit in the European immigration system. I accepted the offer even though it was a difficult decision that required me to put all personal factors aside for the time being. I had to wait four-to-six months for the approval of the temporary work permit. I also had to postpone visiting my family once again.

After the first month in the Netherlands, I received the news that my last living grandmother was diagnosed with cancer, which was already at an advanced stage. I contacted the immigration authorities regarding a possible exception in this case of emergency that would allow me to travel outside the Schengen zone to visit my family. I could leave but could not return back to the E.U. or to my job, I was informed, because the temporary work visa for the E.U. had not been approved yet. The geographic proximity was just an illusion. What mattered in reality was the distance determined by my travel limitations across political borders.

I was trapped by the immigration system once again. This time, however, I was not alone. My husband at the time, a Spanish citizen, had his own share of immigration troubles. When he completed his master's degree in the U.S., I was already six months into my residency in the Netherlands. He was required to return to his home country for two years due to the type of student visa he had as a recipient of the Fulbright scholarship. Having already spent six months on two different continents, I was not prepared to continue living apart indefinitely and decided to leave my job and join him in Spain. Unlike my experience in the U.S., from the first moment I stepped onto the Spanish soil, I became a permanent resident, and shortly thereafter a citizen. The first thing I did when I received my residency papers in Spain was to visit my family.

I was eighteen when I left my family for the first time and twenty-seven when I returned. My twin brother was as unrecognizable to me as I must have been to him. My parents held me in their arms for a long time when they saw me at the airport. The first week, we did not need to sleep and eat. We could not stop talking and crying. Their lives were entirely different from the time when my brother and I were children. Now, they lived in a city I had visited only a few times in my life. Their new apartment was small and overcrowded with books and old furniture from my father's childhood home. Even though I was back with my family, I was clearly an outsider for this was no longer my home or my country. My family did not know whether to laugh or cry when they heard me speak my mother tongue for the first time after so many years. I preferred to see them laugh, and so they did, particularly during mealtime conversations.

I remember writing to my parents while I was still studying in college that I had decided to pursue a career in business. My mother remarked that she was very surprised by my choice since the type of work I appeared to do the best was related to education or learning. But whatever you choose to do for a living, she wrote, your father and I support your decision fully. I wrote back that I had no choice if I wanted to become independent economically. That was the most practical thing to do for the time being. Later on, if an opportunity appeared, I wrote, I would make a career switch. That opportunity came with my arrival to Spain. I was sure this time that I wanted to dedicate the rest of my life to an academic career. I found a temporary job as a language teacher while preparing to apply for doctoral programs in the U.S..

Having completed my doctorate about a year ago under the student visa and started to work as a college professor, my status changed to that of a temporary worker. This meant that the first time I leave the United States territory since the change of the status from a student to a temporary worker, I would need to obtain a visa in the United States Embassy in Spain, my new home country. I lost one country—the country of my childhood. But I lived in, and became attached to, several other countries over the past nineteen years. While some limits to my ability to cross borders remain, there are no limits in how many countries I can feel at home.

WILLIAM BETANCOURT

Interviewed by Heather Tosteson

I SEE MYSELF AS ANOTHER IMMIGRANT WHO CAME HERE TO SUCCEED & TO HELP THIS COUNTRY

I now live in Fredericksburg, Virginia, but I'm moving this month to Waldorf, Maryland. I work for the U.S. Navy as a mechanical engineer. I do designs for ships. The reason we're moving to Maryland is that my wife just got her dietician's license and found a good job in D.C. I work in Dahlgren, Virginia. Waldorf is halfway for both of us. Before, the commute was killing her. I don't like Virginia or Maryland very much. I like Washington, D.C., but it's very expensive to live there. I'm looking for a beach (I'm a big surfer). I just spent three months working in California and I loved it. I'm trying to see if I can move us to California. We're not buying a house here because we know we'll go to California when we have a chance.

Birthright Citizenship

My parents are Venezuelan, but I was born in the U.S. The way this happened was my Uncle Freddy was studying here for his PhD, in North Carolina at Duke University, and my mom came to visit him and decided to stay and study English. She ended up in Washington, D.C.—I think my uncle told her there was a good language school there. There she met my dad, who is also Venezuelan. He was studying engineering here. They got married, so she stayed in the U.S., finding a job at the Venezuelan Embassy. But after I was born, things changed. My father was very young, my mom was about ten years older, and he didn't want the responsibility. He was busy "studying" (I think it was more studying some other women). So they got divorced. My mom went back to Venezuela. She said she wasn't going to stay here alone with a baby and no family to help her. We returned to Venezuela when I was one, so I never really knew the United States then.

First Exposure to U.S.

I didn't feel like an American growing up. Everything was Venezuelan-related in my growing up and schooling in Venezuela. But when I was twelve, I came to Florida with my Aunt Zoë and Uncle Freddy and their family. I had fun with them, but I had a hard time at school, especially in Naples, where we first lived. I was in fights every day with Mexican students. I got broken ribs. My aunt was horrified when I told her about it this year. I didn't tell her at the time. Even now, I don't like the Gulf Coast of Florida, so I avoid it. I stay on the East Coast. I didn't tell my aunt that the reason I was in fights was because I was wearing glasses all the time. She kept telling me, "You can't see very well. You have to wear these, it's for your own good." They were very nerdy looking glasses with big frames. Everyone was messing with me. I didn't think of the Mexican kids who bothered me as being more American. They were very uneducated and they did not care much about school. I was making very good grades. I was in the seventh grade, but I had had the material in the fourth or fifth grade in Venezuela, so it was very easy. I began to understand I had advantages over the other kids. But it was weird. It was very different from my experience in Venezuela. I had many friends in school there. But in this school I was fighting from the very first day. There was a guy who was sixteen and in sixth grade. He was the one who broke my ribs. He had lots of hair and he was shaving already—and I was this little guy with big glasses.

But overall the experience in Florida was good. We had fun at home. But my cousin Vanessa was a teenager and I was fighting with her and also her brother Davin. So after six months, they sent me back. It was not only the fighting with my cousins, but also my aunt was going to start her master's degree at the University of Florida and they were going to need more money to sustain their family. I was away from my mom for the first time, which was hard too, so I was okay with going back home.

Emigrating to U.S.

The best thing for me has been returning to the U.S. when I was twenty-three and what we've accomplished since then. My wife is a warrior too.

I didn't have living in the U.S. in mind when I was growing up. I had to come to the U.S. because things were getting bad in Venezuela. I didn't like the direction the country was taking. I didn't like Chávez and

I didn't like the opposition. And some stupid things happened. I earned a mechanical engineering technology degree from the technical college that is part of Simón Bolívar University. It takes three years and then you can go to work right away. But I finished right after Chávez took over and companies were hesitant to hire people due to the uncertainty of the country's future. But when I wanted to go for a bachelor's degree and wanted to transfer credits for some of my classes, they wouldn't let me transfer them. It was the same school, but they wouldn't honor their own classes. So, after a six-month job search, I decided to go to the U.S. to get a degree there. I went by myself and brought my wife to join me four months later.

I had a friend who had gone to Miami who said he'd help me. I had just married and we took our $1800 in savings and I came to Miami. I tried to find a job. For three to four weeks, I was here with no job. I had to apply for a Social Security card and it took some time to get it, so for three to four months I was working illegally. I was working sixty to seventy hours a week, including weekends. Then I got my Social Security card and I could go to temp agencies. I was sleeping on the sofa in the apartment of my friend and his wife. But they were getting divorced (my friend had another girl). It was a mess. I was sleeping on their sofa and the wife came to me one night saying she couldn't sleep, and I told her she could sit up as late as she wanted watching television. I turned around and went to sleep. I was waiting for my wife and I did not want more problems in my life.

When my wife came to join me my friend's wife didn't like my wife, so she kicked us out. And there we were—just married, no job and no place to live. But there's always someone to help us. A cousin took us in. A week or two later, I found a job in a company. There was a job opening, and they helped us find an efficiency for $480 a month with utilities. I was working there until 9/11. Then I was laid off. I couldn't apply for unemployment, so I kept switching jobs until I got some experience. I worked fixing coffee machines. I worked maintaining carwash machines. I did both mechanical and electrical work.

I took a one-year air-conditioning course that had a lot of electrical and mechanical engineering in it and I liked it. So, in 2003, I went back to college to study engineering. I got financial aid and had good grades and won four scholarships. I've been treated well here. I got the scholarships and they gave me transfer credits for my schooling in Venezuela, which in Venezuela they wouldn't give me. In three years, I got my BS in Mechanical

Engineering. I did two summer co-ops in upstate New York before finishing my bachelor's and after graduating I got three job offers. I took one of them and I went for my master's degree while working fulltime.

Financial Troubles in Florida—The American Way

I got greedy. I thought, I'm in America, I have to be a millionaire. So I decided to buy properties. I bought two apartments in Florida. But then the depression came and I lost my job. I couldn't find a job in Florida so I came to Virginia. My wife stayed in Florida finishing her degree. I got rid of the two properties through bankruptcy. I bought one for $220,000, which now is worth only $50,000. I made the bank an $85,000 cash offer but they wouldn't take it. They were suing me for $180,000, so I had to declare bankruptcy.

Now my wife has her license as a dietician and has a very decent job. So do I. We are doing well. We're saving money now. We're saving almost $4,000 a month. Within a year, we'll have enough for a good down payment on a house. We'll make better decisions now. I sometimes think my aunt influenced me to buy the properties by her example. My Uncle Freddy tends to believe in Murphy's Law and on the contrary my aunt is the one who is always pushing and willing to take some risk. I thought, I need to make an investment. I don't want to be a loser. Do you know Hershey filed for bankruptcy three times before he made his fortune in chocolate? So, no, I don't think I'm going to stop investing. I think I'm going to be more cautious. I'm watching documentaries constantly now about *everything.* All the politics and business behind the crash. It was just terrible luck I bought in 2006. But I want to know why those things happened.

Deconstructing Attitudes

While growing up in Venezuela, I remember that my family thought everything was great in Russia. During the Olympics, for example, my family would be rooting for the Russians and Cubans. They had these crazy ideas about how good socialism is. But I've been watching documentaries and reading and have been checking out what was really happening in Russia. I am also looking at the other side, learning about what the CIA was doing—as well as the KGB. So I can know more and have a more educated opinion. I want to know all sides.

When I was working in upstate New York, I worked for Lockheed

Martin taking care of the facility. I remember my family telling me, "You have to find another job. You're making weapons of mass destruction." I said, "OK, I have to find another job *that is better.*" I wasn't making weapons of mass destruction. I was taking care of the facility.

But I didn't apply to any military companies. I thought I'd never be able to explain it to my family. However, when I got my master's degree I couldn't find a job in the private sector. My only offers were from the Air Force, Navy and Army. When I was thinking about taking the jobs, I was feeling awkward about my family, what they would think if I took them. And then I decided no one was going to take care of me. I had to take care of myself and my wife. Some of them thought that I would never amount to anything—because my mom didn't get a college education and I was lazy in high school. Not that they thought I wouldn't do anything at all, but that I'd probably end up being a handyman or sweeping floors.

At first, I was very ambivalent about working for the Navy. I didn't want anything to do with the military. But before that I worked as a project manager at a cement company in Florida. Then there was the crash in Florida and I was looking for a good job and this job is a very good one with good pay and vacations. As a project manager, I was supervising and working on logistics, so I had no time to design. But my master's degree is in design and manufacturing and here I am able to design, and I really like that.

I have nothing to do with designing weapons. I'm designing boats. I like the work. It's complicated and satisfying. They care about me and I'm getting many raises. The more I'm in the military, I realize it has saved a lot of people. Kids who were getting in trouble join the military, and now they have a job, a career. There's a bad side to it, of course. You can go to war and get killed. I'm working for the Navy and Marines as a civilian government employee. It's the best of both worlds. The last three months I was working on a ship. I like in this job that you can move around if you get bored. There's always something interesting to do.

Renouncing Dual Citizenship

When I went to work for the Navy in 2009, I had to renounce dual citizenship. I had to do this to get security clearance. Not top security. I don't think I could get top security because I come from Venezuela, which isn't so popular with the U.S. right now.

They gave me a two-hour interview for my security clearance and they said, "Don't renew your passport. Are you willing to surrender your passport?"

When I was living in Venezuela, I got a letter from the U.S. Embassy that said, "You're now twenty-one. You have to decide if you want to be a U.S. citizen." I signed the letter and sent it back. That was my back-up at this interview. I told them, "Go to the U.S. Embassy in Caracas and check it out. I did this independently when I was twenty-one."

So, I won't renew my Venezuelan passport. Right now, I don't even go to Venezuela much. It's cheaper to go to Europe than to Venezuela, and all my family will come and visit us here.

My Wife Is a Warrior Too

My wife's name is Diurka. We've been married for eleven years. We're having so much fun. People can see that. We were at the housing office in Waldorf to sign the leasing agreement, and when I was out getting the registration from the car, someone asked her if we were newlyweds. That's what we project.

She's staying down in the new apartment now and when I left this afternoon, she was crying, and I said, "Come on, baby. I'm coming back." You don't find that closeness very much. She has helped me so much to become the person I have become. I do the same for her.

When I was young, I had very low self-esteem. My wife was my first real girlfriend. My wife comes from the same background. She also was an only child with a single mom. We never saw our fathers. We each had an uncle who was like a father figure. She is a warrior too. She has always believed in me.

I thought no one would want me for a boyfriend. In Venezuela, women measure you by your career, by the car you drive, and by the amount of money you have. I didn't have those things. I told my wife when I met her, "You don't want to go out with me. I don't have a car." And she said, "That's all right. I don't have a car either. We'll just walk. I want to be with you." After six months, we got married. And now it's eleven years.

My wife is thirty-three. We're coming out of bankruptcy. We don't need children yet. Every time I tell my mom that, she gets pissed. I don't think our mothers will come and live here. They're single moms. They have their lives there. They're retired. They have many friends. My mom gets bored after a week. The first week is perfect and the second week we start fighting.

My mom has low self-esteem, I think it is just the way she was raised. Every time she sees herself in the mirror or a photograph, she says she's too ugly. When I was a kid, she was always complaining about how we were going to pay the rent, the groceries. I heard this all the time. When I was nine years old, we went to a convenience store down the street and I saw a can of tuna and it was the biggest can there. I took that can and put it in my knapsack and I took it home. When we got there, I took it out of the knapsack and put it on the table. "Now you don't have to worry about food," I told her. I didn't know what else to do. I just didn't want her so worried. After this she told me that I was not supposed to steal and that it was bad what I did, but even after that, we ended up eating tuna for lunch. I guess she was too embarrassed to return it to the store.

I didn't want to have a kid and do that kind of stuff to him. I thought, "If I don't go to school and get an education, I'll be broke. I will end up doing that to my kid." I knew I had to get an education. That's what I saw from my uncle. He had an education (a PhD) and also from my other aunt, Marcela. She had an education and she raised two kids by herself. Both of them could get things for their children.

Differences Within Families

My Uncle Freddy was always there for me. So is my Aunt Zoë. She's not blood, but she's always been there for me. I love her very much. They've been supporting me all along in my life. I don't think that my Aunt Zoë being an American made it easier for me to think about coming to live in the U.S. A lot of the time, she feels more Venezuelan than American. Sometimes we have conversations where she really sounds that way. Now that she has bought that apartment in Jupiter, Florida, she's more relaxed about the U.S. It's easier visiting with her here.

My attitudes are different from my family members. Some of them have radical ideas about events that happened throughout history, for example, conspiracy theories about 9/11. Stories about people launching missiles at the Pentagon in daylight without anybody noticing, and things of that nature. Once you understand the engineering behind how the towers failed, how lightweight steel behaves under high temperature and how the design of the towers contributed to its collapse, you can understand that the disaster wasn't created with bombs.

Some others think that there are too many rules to follow in the U.S.

and that the government wants to have full control of your life. "This is a dictatorship!" I heard things like, "How come we can't drive over the speed limit?" "Why do we have to cleanup after our dogs?" "Why can't we drink and drive?" I even heard once, "Why are there so many U.S. flags displayed in this country?" I thought to myself, is it a bad thing to feel proud of your country and what its flag represents? How is that affecting you? Why are you making an argument about it?

Like in every country there are good people and bad people, I don't think you can judge a country only by if you agree or disagree with its government. I like life here. What is it they say, "If you get used to eating sirloin, you can't go back to hamburger?" I've been trying to explain that many times to my family, but I think that the only way that they would understand is if they were in my shoes. There's always more than one side and not everything can be black or white, there are also shades of gray.

Assimilation

Both my wife and I are U.S. citizens now. Sure, we are also Venezuelan. The way I see it, it's like the Italians. Even after several generations, they still feel Italian and American. I've been treated very well here. I don't plan to go back. (It will take at least forty years for Venezuela to get straightened out.) This doesn't mean I'm ever going to start hating *arepas*. I'm never going to say I don't love Venezuela. I love where I come from and where I am. I have the best of both worlds.

My kids are going to live here. I see myself as another immigrant who has come here to succeed and help this country. After ten years, we're succeeding, paying taxes. We can take a vacation, buy a car. I like it. I don't like it when people say they hate the U.S.

I didn't agree with the Iraq war. I agreed with the Afghanistan war to begin, but it's going on too long. But I can't say the U.S. and all Americans are bad. It's like saying if you don't like Chávez that all Venezuelans are bad.

I'm not all Venezuelan, I'm not all American. I'm a little of both. I have friends from all over the place. I have Indian friends who worked with me in Miami. I visit with them when I go back because they're my friends. I have many Latin friends. I have a rock band (I've always had one). We are called Empty Trends. We're playing now in pubs in D.C., Alexandria. We were recording today. We have guitar, bass, and drums. The drummer is a close friend. He's American and his parents are from Holland. The female singer's family is Irish. The guy who plays bass and guitar is Puerto Rican. As you may see the U.S. is a big melting pot!

It's the same with food. I eat all kinds of food—Thai, Indian, everything. If I don't like it, I don't try it again. I do the same with people. If they're nice, they're my friends.

Now I don't want to go back to Venezuela. I get too stressed when I go back. I was robbed at gunpoint at nine, had a knife at my throat at eleven. I'm tired of it. Even after all these events I will always love my Venezuelan people and culture.

One of the things that made me take advantage of all the opportunities here, was because I *didn't* have those opportunities in Venezuela. It's like giving opportunities to a pampered child—they won't use them. But you give them to someone like me, who wasn't pampered, and they'll take every one.

something
the habit
realize
is a moral fact. It
a reality only as it
commonplace of living.

TAYE

Interviewed by Heather Tosteson

I CAME MAINLY FOR MY SON

I would strongly like to stress that this is just my own information based on personal background and opinion and doesn't represent any group or area of Ethiopia at all.

Growing Up in Ethiopia

I was born and grew up in a small town, Gimjabet, about 450 kilometers southwest of Addis Ababa. It was a good small town. It had a high school, a bank, telecommunication and other service-providing sectors. There were about 1,000-2,000 residents.

My parents are farmers. I have three brothers and four sisters. I'm the youngest. Sometimes it's good to be the youngest. You get a lot of support from your brothers and sisters, although your parents are older.

My father can read and write but he had no formal education. He learned how to write and read from a religious education. We belong to the Ethiopian Orthodox Christian church. In the area where I grew up, there was one priest teaching lots of students how to write and how to read religious books, nothing else was close by. My mother couldn't read or write. She did not have the opportunity.

Now things are changing. There are schools even in remote areas. Most people can read and write. But many parents couldn't. Some of my older brothers and sisters can't. They are farmers in the area. My sisters didn't go to school. When they were young, the school was very far away. When it was my time to go to school, schools had been built, but they were too old by then to go back to school. But now most of my nephews and nieces are in school and very successful. I'm helping my nephew right now. He is in medical college in his second year, studying for an MD I have two nieces in college too, and I am helping them as well.

I have no immediate family here in the U.S. I came with my wife and my son, my own little family. It is very hard for people who come by themselves. Many people are homesick here. The Ethiopian Orthodox Church here is where I go and feel at home. There is a very nice social life there. We pray, eat, and chat together.

Education

After I finished high school, I came to Addis Ababa. My wife and I met there. She was born there. I finished high school in 1990. In 1991 when I was supposed to go to college, the socialist government was overthrown and it was a big mess. All the schools were closed. I had to live with my uncle, a businessman in Addis Ababa. Finally, I went to college in Addis Ababa. I studied library science. My wife had a diploma in accounting. In her family, her two sisters also went to school and finished high school.

I liked going to college. Why did I choose library science? When I first moved to Addis Ababa, I worked at the British Council Library and loved it and wanted to work there. It was the best library in Ethiopia and fully automated. I worked there from 1994-2005. It was a model library. What you have now here in the DeKalb library is what they had there fifteen years ago.

While I was working at the British Council I learned about the lottery and I began filling out applications. I tried three or four times before I succeeded.

National and Cultural Identity

I am very proud of Ethiopia back then and now. We have a wonderful culture. We are a very welcoming culture. People are very polite. Ethiopia has never been colonized. I had a chance to notice that when I was working at the British Council. There were many people from other countries coming to use the library. Everyone had to stay in line, but a friend of mine, who had a chance to visit other British Council libraries in other African countries, told me that for people from some other African countries it was harder for them to do so. We Ethiopians don't have an inferiority complex. So our response is, here I am Ethiopian. I am free. I don't have to worry about my standing.

In Ethiopia there are more than eighty languages and tribes. People are predominantly followers of the Christian and Muslim religions. We have a great compromise. We celebrate Muslim holidays and Christian ones. The government closes for both. People know how to live together. In 1991 when the government lost control, nothing happened like in Somalia. People didn't harm each other.

Each tribe has a little bit different culture, but when you come to the country level, everyone believes they are Ethiopian, especially whenever there are foreign invaders. However the dress and food between groups are very different and we enjoy that difference.

Most Ethiopians speaks three or four languages. Everyone has a mother tongue, which they learn inside their family. My language was Agew. At school, every subject used to be taught in Amharic, but now most major tribes create their own curriculum with their own language. However, in third grade you start learning English and through grade six, it is taught as a subject. After that, from seventh grade to college, every subject is taught in English. Amharic is the national language, but everyone who goes to school can understand English, even if they can't read or write it so well.

Preparation for Coming to the United States

For me, the preparation to come to the U.S. wasn't difficult. I think that is true for people coming through the DV (Diversity Visa) lottery. They must all be high school graduates. Refugees are different. A certain education level is not a requirement for them.

While I was preparing to come to the United States, I had a chance to work for seven or eight months at the U.S. Embassy. I wanted to know more about Americans before I came, to be at least familiar with American culture. At that time, I already had my lottery letter and I was in process. Security at both the British Council and the U.S. Embassy was very high because of terrorist activities in the area, especially after the attack at the U.S. Embassy in Nairobi, Kenya took place.

My impression of the Americans I met there was positive. I like Americans. Ethiopians in general are pro-American and pro-Israel (maybe because of religious associations). Working there, I thought I had a good chance to get one step closer to getting to know them, but I didn't really have much chance because then our visa came through.

Winning the Lottery

Each year, you can have one application per person in the lottery, so I applied in both my name and my wife's name. After I tried for four years, my wife's name came up. She had mixed feelings about winning the lottery.

She used to work at the British Council too. We had a good life in Ethiopia, so she had mixed feelings about leaving that life to face the unknown. She was so close to her mother. I asked her to try it because I thought it would be better for our son. I thought he would have more opportunity.

We made the decision mostly for our son. We had a good life in Addis Ababa. We were trying to build a house. It is very expensive to build a house in Ethiopia, but we were contributing to an association to build a house, but we left that to come here.

We said to ourselves, well we can at least make there what we do here, so let's try it.

Was it surprising to win the lottery? I was surprised. Thousands are applying every year, maybe millions, so it is surprising.

Lottery Interview

When you win the lottery, then you have to go in for an interview. I worked at the U.S. Embassy, so daily I saw people coming in to interview for different things. What I could see was many people were happy to get a recommendation. Expectations were very high. Lots of people thought of America and imagined everything would be different and life would be much easier there.

What questions did they ask in the interview? Mainly questions from the application. Some people see this as an opportunity and make a false marriage, but we were listed together in all our applications. So they asked how long had we been married and we told them. For some people, they need to get proof they are husband and wife. I know people with real marriages who have been denied. In our case, they asked us where we were working, how long we had been married, how old our son was, and where we were going in the U.S.

Early Adjustment to the U.S.

I was a little closer to American culture and to what the reality might be. Thank to my friends here, they informed me not to expect too much and I had internet access to check some reality and even some states' history, geography and culture. Lots of people come here with high expectations and little knowledge, and when they face reality, they become unhappy because they haven't been able to match expectations. For people coming through the DV lottery, there is no help here. You don't necessarily have any family here. You don't have an employer. If you have a sponsor, usually you get them through a third person and have never met them.

Atlanta wasn't my choice. For me, the U.S. was just the U.S. There wasn't a particular city or state. My good friend in Minnesota and his brother-in-law in Atlanta, they knew about the weather and explained it to me. And the weather and the living cost were better in Atlanta.

My sponsor was the brother-in-law of my close friend who now lives in Minnesota. I had never met him before. Luckily we got along. We stayed at his house for three months before I found a job and had earned enough money to rent an apartment.

Sometimes, sponsors would say they were family members, but they really weren't. Now, a sponsor isn't required. They only ask for an address in the U.S. where you would stay. When we came, in 2006, a sponsor was a requirement. We gave my friend's address and we were very lucky that he was willing to act as a sponsor.

Why did he do it? Some people like supporting people. Even after this, he has helped three or four more people. I think he is that type of person. He and his wife are very friendly. People from Ethiopia are very welcoming, so when I came to my friend, he helped us because that is just what his nature is.

The same thing happened to us. A few weeks ago I received a call from a friend who lives in Washington, D.C. He is here as a political asylee. He told me that a friend of ours from the British Council had also won the lottery. This friend was going to come with his wife and daughter here to us in Atlanta. I told him he could come and stay with us, but to wait until he found a job. We have a guest room and can afford the food. But I was worried about his having a job before he came because the job market is very bad now and people come with very high expectations. He has this opportunity and I don't want him to lose it. But it needs to be balanced with reality. He finally found family to stay with, on his wife's side, in Denver and they decided to go there. But he could have come here.

First Impressions

My first impressions of the U.S.? Oh, when I was thinking about the U.S. back in Ethiopia, even with all my preparation, I don't think I was prepared for what I saw. It was March when we arrived. All the trees looked as if they had died. I wondered, "Is this a desert?" I was expecting tall buildings.

I looked around and saw a rural area. And all the streets and stores were the same. For instance there was a Subway store near my sponsor's house that we used as a landmark. After a week or so, when driving with my friend, I saw another Subway store that looked exactly like the one near to our house and said, "What is that?!" I was very confused. They were just alike. I couldn't tell the difference. I felt lost.

We were all afraid of getting lost then. One day we went out to walk and saw a parked Coca Cola truck and decided it was our landmark, our sign. But when we came back, it wasn't there and we were lost. And also the houses looked the same.

I didn't have a job. And I couldn't get a job until I had my paperwork. Within fifteen days I had my Social Security card, and within a month, my green card.

I had my first job near my friend's house, which was in Lithonia. It was a woodwork company producing materials for roofing. I had some woodworking experience; I applied as a walk-in at many companies including this one. My friend took me to them. After another week, I had a job at the Hilton Hotel. The pay was higher. It was a night job. I chose it for my son. That meant in the daytime I could take care of my son. My wife also found a job fairly soon.

We waited some months before getting an apartment of our own. My son was going to school and we wanted him to finish the year. We made the decision to live near Clarkston, because there is a little center of Ethiopian stores there and access to public transportation.

Race and Cultural Assumptions

Lots of people here don't even know that the country of Ethiopia exists. I had one shocking experience at the Hilton. I was working as a bellman and my friend was working security. Two white men, in their mid-thirties, came up to us and they asked if we were brothers. We said yes, that we came from the same country.

"What country?" they asked.

"Ethiopia," we answered.

"Ethiopia! People there are poor and small. You can't be from Ethiopia," they said.

But Ethiopia has many millionaires as well as poverty. There is a misunderstanding here. I know we had a famine from 1983-1985 in some part of the country. To get support and attention from the international community, journalists and humanitarian agencies took many pictures of starving people. For some people, that is all they know about Ethiopia.

With other people, especially at the library, I try to ask them about their culture—not to make assumptions. The person could be very educated in their own country's language. Most people coming from Ethiopia have their first degrees, some of them even have master's degrees and PhDs. There is a man I know who was a college professor but now has no job. People don't see their past lives but think everybody is the same.

What Constitutes Home Now

For me the institution that makes me feel most at home is the Ethiopian Orthodox Church. Some of my friends go to an evangelical church. Other Ethiopians have a mosque. What I like about the Orthodox Church is it is exactly the same service anywhere in the world, it is the orthodox liturgy.

When it comes to making friends, I don't have an American friend. Most of my best friends are Ethiopian. I have colleagues, yes, but I don't have a close American friend. It is hard to make friends because of differences in our culture, even our eating habits. At my work place, when I have lunch, people look oddly at what I eat and they keep asking what it is and test it to see how it tastes. I had an American neighbor and I invited her to my house when we were having a party. She had never seen food like ours. In our culture, you must have something for people to eat and drink when somebody comes to your house. Perhaps my son will have more American friends.

After two years here, I think most Ethiopians feel at home. I can say it is a great country. People are very welcoming. To narrow the gap, our children are now more American. They speak like Americans. Most of them don't know how to speak and write and read Amharic. They watch only American television. It is hard for someone who came in middle age to feel completely at home in another country. But that is not true of our children.

With your children, you have to help them with their school work. To do this, you have to learn more about America. It helps you feel more American yourself to know you are helping raise your own child to feel American.

The name Taye is used here as a pseudonym. It is a common name in Ethiopia and means "He has been seen."

SHAN YOHAN
BUDDHI MASIH

Interviewed by Heather Tosteson

EVERYONE HAS THE OPPORTUNITY HERE

Shan (Shantilata) Yohan, in her eighties, and her friend Buddhi (Buddhwanti) Masih, in her seventies, both immigrated from India. Christians, they first came to Atlanta on scholarship to study religion. Subsequently, Shan earned a doctorate in counseling and taught until retirement at Georgia Perimeter College. Buddhi earned a Master of Library Science from Atlanta University and worked there until retirement as an academic librarian. Both are now widowed.

Growing Up in India and Thoughts of Coming to the States

Buddhi: I never thought of coming to the U.S. We didn't have any connection and financially it did not seem possible. I never thought of it. But a friend of mine was a social worker and she came to the U.S. She was a missionary, and I took over her job when she left India. When she came over to the U.S., she thought it would be nice for me to come over here as well. Her husband was already over here. So she made the connection with a friend who was in school here at the Interdenominational Theological Center (ITC), and made it possible for me to get a scholarship. Shan was teaching there. It was easy to get a scholarship at that time. I came here as a student studying religion. When I finished, I looked for a job and decided to do other studies as a librarian. I got a job at Atlanta University, and then I thought, why not stay here? The job supported me financially and sponsored me for a labor certificate. Those were good days. They helped me get a green card. Since then, I'm still on the green card.

Shan: Yes, I did think about coming to the U.S. I grew up in an area of India, central India, where there were missionaries, American missionaries, and I played with their children and felt part of their family.

When I got married, my husband was teaching in a seminary. He was elected as a fellow to go to Union Theological Seminary for one year. I said I wanted to go too. I had gone to college.

So, he went to Union and I went to Vanderbilt and got a Master in Higher Education.

Then we heard about ITC. We called and they said, "We want international students, and we will take you both with scholarships."

After one year, he went into the PhD program at Emory in Sociology of Religion. After he completed his degree, I said, "Now it's my turn." So I got my PhD from Georgia State in Counseling and Psychological Services.

My husband went to work at Georgia Perimeter College, and they were so happy with him, they hired me when I finished my degree. We both taught at different campuses, and that is our life.

When I got the job at ITC, they said, "We need some kind of international recognition." So they helped us and our two sons get green cards. At Georgia Perimeter, because it is a public institution, they said we had to become citizens, so we got our citizenship in six months. It was a big deal in the sense that we wanted to live here and work here and we needed to be citizens to do that, so we agreed.

Buddhi: In 1976, I received my green card. It is not mandatory to become a citizen. I checked the date for my card recently. I was apprehensive about the card. I wanted to go back to India, but I was afraid about coming back. I went to the immigration office and they told me that many people are permanent residents and they don't have to become citizens. Since my son is over here and the grandkids are over here, I'm thinking now it might be better to apply.

Shan: India also allows dual citizenship.

Buddhi: I'm considering that too.

Childhood

Buddhi: I was born in the mountains, in Uttar Pradesh. My family wasn't Christian then. There were missionaries there from the U.S. They were evangelical Methodists. My parents were the converts.

Shan: I was Disciples of Christ. My husband was Anglican. When I got married, I became Anglican. But he was working in a Methodist seminary, so we changed. We wanted to be effective workers.

There is a distinct Christian identity in India. It was developed by American, English, or German missionaries. Our parents were the converts. We grew up Christian. We felt different, but we didn't segregate. We were taught that you integrate and try to convert.

Christians rejected the caste system. Christians when they converted became outcasts. They were considered lower than the untouchables. But personally, I never felt like an outcast. We never lost our confidence. We went to Indian schools. I never minded the challenges Christianity posed.

Children, Citizenship, and Racial Identity

Shan: My sons were born in India. My husband and I became citizens in the 1970s, but my older son became a citizen on his own. My younger son took a *very* long time to become one.

Buddhi: My husband came after I got my permanent residency. When I applied for him, he also got it. My son was born here. He has beautiful twin children, now three and a half. He is married to a black woman from here.

Shan: Here in the South, I felt a strong sense of identity but I also felt discriminated against because I was neither black nor white. The discrimination was subtle.

Buddhi: I worked in a black institution until I retired. I always felt it.

Shan: At ITC, it was very African-American oriented. The faculty were okay. They wanted it to be international. But I always felt excluded by the students in the program.

Buddhi: My son went mostly to black institutions. He went to high school in south DeKalb and then went to North Carolina Central, which is a black state college. We were trying to tell him to go to more mixed schools, but his identity is combined with black identity. In Atlanta, at Georgia State, where the population is mixed—black, white, Indian— he associated with the black community. He's happily married. They care for me too. My son went to Georgia State and is a physical therapist and he helps me with my knee. We still have our cultural differences. He is mostly with her family and he identifies with them more than with white people. And they care for him too.

Shan: My sons went to DeKalb schools too, but the ones in the north of the county. Then they went to Georgia State. They both married white girls from Georgia and we have two grandchildren, a boy and girl.

Buddhi: South DeKalb, where we lived, is mostly black. The basis of the prejudice is that the African-American community does not perceive us as African-American. They think we are closer to the white community.

In India, we come from a caste system. Here they discriminate against color.

Shan: We had experience with both black and white. Saint Timothy United Methodist Church, where I worship, has thirty nationalities.

Cultural Identity

Shan: I feel we have become part of this country. I feel I'm an American.

In India, I feel integrated. People are fascinated when I talk in Hindi, especially small children. One of my nieces said, "I have never seen an American before, Aunt Shan."

We're *all* part of the human race. When I started the Interfaith Dialogue Group, I had this revelation. I saw how the rejection and exclusion *got* to me. I decided we need a group especially for women. The first meeting was in 1995 at ITC and there were about a hundred women from twelve different faiths. There was a hunger there and a hunger in me. I have received a lot of fulfillment from this group over the years.

Indian History

Shan: I identify with Gandhi, but he didn't become a Christian although he was friends with a lot of American missionaries. The missionaries' ultimate motive was to convert. Stanley Jones was a good friend with Gandhi. They prayed together, read the Bible together. Jones asked Gandhi, "Are you thinking of converting?"

Gandhi said, "I want to tell you something. I almost became a Christian, but I decided against it. I was thrown out of a train in South Africa because I was not white. How can you do that as a Christian? The life of Christ is the most beautiful life—but I can't be a Christian."

But to me, Gandhi was the *best* Christian.

Buddhi: He was the *father* of India. I still think I'm Indian. To me that means people like Gandhi who fought for freedom. But when I see why they're having conflicts now, I wonder.

Shan: I consider myself *Indian*-American. I don't want to get rid of the Indian.

My sons see themselves as *Indian* Americans, and my younger son *looks* American. He has very light skin. He talks very American. My older son looks like his father. His skin is brown.

Buddhi: I talked to my son in Hindi. He understands and talks in

Hindi. When we call back home, my relatives adore that he speaks Hindi with them. The grandkids also understand Hindi.

Values of Citizenship

Shan: You can be a voting member of the society. I am proud to be accepted as a leader in church, community, and in education.

Buddhi: I think it is freedom in the history. Freedom to grow, to be who you are. As a permanent resident, I can do anything you do. In India we don't have that freedom of choice, religion, culture. I think that citizenship gives you the opportunity to participate.

Shan: In America, you can become anything you want—and I believe in that.

Buddhi: I think citizenship gives you all the privileges and conveniences. I'm not greedy, but I like the conveniences.

Shan: I do feel that in the U.S., people gave us scholarships. They gave us respect. All you have to do here is make use of the opportunities.

Buddhi: Everyone has the right here.

ARA SARKISSIAN

Interviewed by Heather Tosteson

WHERE IS THE 'WE'?

Fatherhood is wonderful. It makes you think about many things. It doesn't necessarily offer answers, but it puts out questions. I do wish I had had my daughter fifteen years ago because I can't live with the lack of sleep—and back then I felt I had the answers. But hopefully I am a bit wiser now.

What is America?

If you think about America as an ideal—it's a very unique nation-state that is not based on any ethnic allegiance, as opposed to most other places. In Germany, most people are German, and in Poland, Polish, etc. Perhaps in South America it might be a little different because people came from elsewhere, but in most other places there is a ruling ethos tied to the character of the nation-state. There is the mass culture idea of America with people obsessed with how white their teeth are, the extra large Diet Coke bottles and Disneyland. But when you think about what the heart of the country is, for me it's the South. It's true that the South has a past filled with things that are so obviously problematic, yet it seems to me the place where one can find the roots of the non-mass American culture—Appalachian music, banjo playing, cooking, hospitality, a sense of independence from *center*. Maybe it will take another generation or two for this culture to disappear into the *mass*. People often describe the U.S. as a place where people will give you a coffee, and then point to the time, whereas in most other places people would stay for hours and hours. But it feels like in the South, you could visit with someone for six hours, quite unlike in Boston.

I think, having been here for twenty years now, that this idea of America as a homeland is starting to take hold here. The notion of "I was here before you," prevalent in many other places, is starting to take hold here as well. Perhaps it just happens when a country gets to a certain age. People are developing the same sense of attachment and protectionism that you find other places. I don't know if it is controllable. Is it just something that is natural? I can't figure out if it is something you can control. Perhaps it is just a result of thinking in a box. I think about this a lot. People assume they share a lot and a lot gets brushed under the rug for them to think this way. But every twenty or thirty years here there are riots. What is interesting is that people have very selective memories. Each time it is as if it never happened before. Everything is in the past and "the past" is always untouchably far away.

This is strange for me being Armenian, because we remember what happened 1300 years ago, where battles took place, who won and who lost, and how it affected the future. Why can't people here remember what happened in L.A. in the 1990s? Maybe there's something I can learn from them here. Maybe it is good to forget. And then I think, maybe there's something they can learn from me, maybe they should learn what they shouldn't forget. When you get your citizenship, no one tells you what is the right answer.

Growing Up in Lebanon

I just visited Lebanon last January for the first time in ten years. My last visit was twelve years before. It seems I go about every decade. For me, it felt like a normal place to live growing up. War was something we just grew up with. I was four years old when war began. This was a civil war, so in addition to invading armies, there were invading sub-armies invading neighborhoods. In a way it was bizarre, to be honest—like a very bad movie we just stopped watching.

There were many of us Armenians in Lebanon then. There aren't now. Maybe there were about 150,000 Armenians out of about three million people living in Lebanon. Armenians congregated mostly in the capital. We had our own neighborhoods where maybe half the people spoke Armenian. It didn't feel like a transitory environment. The only choice other than making it a home was to emigrate again, which after a while becomes tiring. Even if you yourself did not emigrate originally, after the immigration of the previous generation, you felt as if you needed to stay a while.

The Lebanese system was set up to distribute rights along sectarian lines, and Armenians, like other groups, had representation based on their population. We knew we were not Arabs, the dominant population in Lebanon, yet we were Lebanese, which is a multi-layered concept.

We were citizens of a nation-state, there wasn't necessarily allegiance to a tribe. It wasn't that different, at least legally, from being a citizen of the

U.S. in terms of pluralism. Obviously, there are many differences, culturally and otherwise, but as far as feeling yourself a citizen of a state, you did. It was different from here where in the process of becoming a citizen there are resentments and some people treat you like an outsider. But there we felt comfortable more or less.

But during the civil war, it became less so. People had to declare allegiance. Armenians felt caught. They were between the factions. Should allegiance be based on religion (other Christians) or political ideology? This is what made the sense of belonging disappear. It was religious differences versus ethnic differences versus political differences that in the end made Armenians uncomfortable. Our interest was always to have everyone get along because we were the least powerful group. It was for us an historic continuation of the tensions we endured before.

Armenian Diaspora

The intensity of one's experience of the diaspora had to do with time and also location. My grandmother came from western Armenia, a region outside of the current Republic of Armenia. She was born in 1901 and during the massacres and deportations of 1915 she was a teenager. She lived until she was almost one hundred. I had access to her and I could learn where her village was on a map. In Lebanon, everyone has grandmothers like mine. She actually waited her entire life to return to her village in western Armenia. Having direct intense contact with someone like that causes you to stop and think. These people had inherited land, inherited memories, culture. For political reasons that had nothing to do with them but with larger powers carving up the surface of the earth, these people happened to be on the wrong side of the map. So I really understood from these people what that period of history meant.

My parents' generation was the first to go to school. They went because they were living in Lebanon and they were expected to have the same literacy as everyone else. They were always grateful to Lebanon because it made it possible for them to move from illiterate to college graduates.

My father's sense of being Armenian was emotionally no different from my grandmother's, but practically it was. For example, my grandmother never understood modern furniture. Her house in Lebanon looked like a house in eastern Turkey. What she understood was a piece of wood, which she covered with a carpet. She couldn't understand why we would buy a wooden chair from a store.

Attitudes Toward the U.S. Growing Up

My father was principal of a school that had American benefactors and used American textbooks along with French ones. They had some sponsors from America, but the curriculum was not based on the American system. Like all Lebanese schools, it was based on the French baccalaureate system. I guess it meant something to us at the time as children that it was called an American school.

Before 1982, when Americans bombed Beirut, we had a different view of the U.S. Many people felt the Americans would help end the conflict. It was a new country. It didn't hate anyone. It wasn't like Europe where the nations fought among themselves. They invited everyone over. They had a Statue of Liberty, anyone could go there, and money grew on trees. We had this notion—and our books were American, so we wanted to learn *American* math, square roots in English not in Arabic or even French.

But by the 1980s, with Ronald Reagan and the Americans bombing Beirut, and the increasing tensions with the Arabs, people's hope in America changed, and so did ours. To see a U.S. warship bombing the hills from the coastline was an image one could not easily forget. We really weren't sure what it meant. Everyone understood it was politics, that normal everyday Americans would never condone such actions. We thought it was a renegade army, a renegade president. But we lost the hope we had, and I think many people in the world did, that there was one nation with enough of a stance of neutrality that it could help bring peace.

Why Family Left Lebanon

We talked about it for a long time. My father's siblings were all here in the U.S. since the 1960s. Ever since the war started, they were trying to convince us to leave and we kept thinking no, this will end at some point, this will not go on forever.

I have another uncle in Germany who was trying to convince us to go there, but it would not be as simple to get legal papers. We didn't want to go to Germany or show up anywhere in Europe and sell sandwiches on the street. We wanted to go somewhere where we could be legally accepted. The easiest thing was to go to America.

We were reluctant to leave because Beirut was a good place for

Armenians. There were many Armenian schools and multiple Armenian daily newspapers. It was almost like being "home." We all understood that if we went anywhere, it would be different, there would be a serious shift in who we were. It was a struggle deciding whether to go or not. But the war seemed to never end. I'm sure my parents considered the future of their children when making this decision. Not only to "build a better future," but also to avoid the ugly truth of civil war, such as militias who could just drive around and pick up fifteen-year-old boys and say, "You're coming with us." We lived in an area where that wasn't such a drastic reality but it was seeming more imminent. We were close to the green line dividing the city, and it was not a comfortable place to be any longer.

I turned eighteen a few weeks after I arrived. My mother, younger brother, and I came first. It took another year for my father to join us, and three years after that my second oldest brother joined us. Because he was over eighteen when he came, he had to apply independently.

By the time the initial shock of being transplanted began to wear off, the civil war in Lebanon had ended, but no one was really sure if it would start again. In retrospect, we could have gone back—but we could not have known that. Part of us longed for it. You miss the little things—the smell of the sandwich shops or the way you can have a coffee for four hours. There was always a desire to go back to that so-called leisurely life.

First Impressions of the U.S.

I experienced the U.S. public school system for about five months. It was bizarre. The sense of discipline here was completely opposite to what I was used to. It seemed to me at the time, and it still does at some level, that there was such gross disrespect toward authority from students. There was chaos between classes. Everyone was always going to their locker and combing their hair, it seemed like I wasn't in a school, but in the green room of a Broadway production. Imagine coming from Lebanon and two days later hearing some girls chewing gum and talking about their cheerleading practice. I'd never heard of cheerleaders. I had no idea how to respond. The boys were always smoking in the toilet. They seemed like eighteen-year-old children. No one over twelve years old would have acted that way in Lebanon.

They kept moving me from class to class, because it seemed like the math and the chemistry were things we had done when I was eleven. They kept phasing me out of classes, not because I was bright but because I had had a different level of education. I couldn't quite understand how these people were going on to college—but later I learned that people in college would learn what we had in high school. Sometimes I thought, maybe I'm at the wrong school or that maybe it was a school for the ungifted! I realized I could not buy a bottle of beer since I was under twenty-one, and yet eighteen year olds were at the time fighting in the first Iraq war. It all seemed surreal.

Armenians in Watertown

The Armenians in Watertown not only come from different places like Turkey, Syria, Lebanon, and Russia, but they have come at different points in time, not only absolute time but also how early in their life they came. There are people here who think of themselves as Armenian, but it is because their grandparents came a hundred years ago from Turkey. They speak maybe five words of Armenian, but they somehow feel they are Armenian too. Many of them are very nice people but for me they seem like Americans. Then there are people who came young, but they are now in their sixties. They speak a little more Armenian, they know a little more about Armenian food, but again they seem more or less completely American. Then there are the more recent immigrants. So there is a whole spectrum of assimilation in Watertown. It is interesting to watch—and now I feel I am part of it. I have been here twenty years. I made a promise to myself that at the point when I had lived here half my life I would go someplace else—but then I had a baby! So I have gone to a different place, just not physically.

I had a difficult time finding a sense of home in Watertown because of the breadth of attitudes. I think it is the different levels of assimilation that causes problems; it raises the issue of what is healthy assimilation. What parts do you keep? What parts do you change? That was a constant struggle for me. I think it still is.

Feelings When Armenia Became a Country

We came to the U.S. at the end of 1989. When Armenia became a country in 1991, we did some rethinking, but it was a similar issue to Lebanon. My oldest brother went there from Canada soon after the Soviet Union collapsed. But Armenia was the smallest of the sixteen republics and it wasn't a place with many resources. There were questions about what would happen tomorrow. It was a place with brutal winters. And 1991 was the first time since the fourteenth century, except for a very brief period between the end of World War I and 1921, that Armenia was a sovereign entity. Can you imagine the disorganization! So many of us decided to wait. A few years later there was the war with Azerbaijan, and we never wanted to be in a war zone again, so the idea of moving there was shattered, at least temporarily.

I did think about it again much later on—after it was clear war wasn't going to start up again. At one period I was visiting Armenia a couple of times per year. I was seriously considering moving there but there were several problems: family considerations, financial considerations, and fears of beginning the entire cycle of emigration inherited from my grandparents. It seemed each generation since then felt obligated to move again and I just wanted to have a chance to sit still for a few years.

My oldest brother is still in Armenia. He has similar problems there to what I have here, simply in different shading. He's still an immigrant in Armenia.

Becoming a Naturalized Citizen

I became a citizen in 2005. It was much later than I was first eligible. When I was first eligible, I decided I didn't care. I didn't even think about it. Then later I thought about it and I filled in all the forms, then I never sent them in. I don't know why. Then I decided it was the oath. It was now around 2000. There was this oath saying that I'd fight for the United States Army. "We" were bombing this and that place, and likely planning to bomb some others soon. For some reason, I decided to make a big deal about this in my head. If the oath had required me to help decide whether to go to war, it would have made sense. Eventually, though, I realized things were not so black and white.

I don't necessarily feel different now that I'm a citizen. It didn't change very much for me. Voting, of course, is different. I voted for the first time. I thought electing the current president was a beautiful thing. I care if we have another guy talking about wars or another guy who ideally, conceivably is different. (How different remains to be seen). But the notion it was not a typically upper-class white person was important to me. It was important to me that he had spent time somewhere outside the U.S.

Even though at times I don't feel I belong here, I care. I want *us* to have this change of direction. If I were not a citizen, I don't think I would have thought so much about it. So it did become a positive thing. So maybe I was crazy to delay. I would say, "I can't vote, so what does it matter to me?"

But maybe it wasn't because of them, but because I wasn't voting. It may have been that I was keeping myself from voting, I was shirking my responsibility. So I think citizenship helps me clarify whether I'm here or not. I felt I was physically here, but I always felt before that I should be going somewhere else. (Maybe that is a very Armenian attitude.)

My friends in Europe (when I was going there a lot on my way to Armenia or Lebanon, or to do a music project) were living in Germany and France. They would tell me, whether you like it or not, you are becoming more American. I would ask them, "Specifically, can you tell me specifically what it is that is American?"

What they pointed out were things I felt were *good* things. Simpler things. Letting things go. Being practical. Risk-taking. Saying, "Let's just go and find out."

Working Full-Time, Going to Harvard at Night, Pursuing Music Studies, Composing and Performing

I never thought that I was doing so much. I think most people would do the same thing. It's about the cards you are given. If the cards say you have to work, you have to work. You can't just run away. I always felt I didn't have the time or luxury to think about what I was doing. I could easily have given up the school, the music, the work. But I felt I wanted to do all of them. Actually, I am surprised now that I did all those things!

But it's nothing compared to a villager in the winter, where they have no running water in the house, no gas to heat their house. They have to go out and chop wood for six months until they can go out and plant crops again. I didn't feel like it was that much of a burden. It wasn't what I saw my grandparents had to live with. They just did it. They never complained, they just did it. I felt I had a job inside where it was warm. I had school between work hours, then after work hours, sure, but I didn't have to walk in the snow, there was always a bus. When you can sit on a bus, you don't need to discuss that it is winter. Everything's heated. But for many people in the world, there is no bus coming. And if there is, it certainly isn't heated. Why can't we do a number of things? Besides, we only sleep eight hours a night. What was I going to be doing instead? Watch television? Eat potato chips? Whiten my teeth?

Marriage

I was married in 2009, two years and two months ago. My wife's name is Arminè and she is from Armenia. She came here to go to graduate school, then her advisor recommended that she work for a year. And then we met. We were married within eight months or so. It was very quick and somewhat surprising. She is an economist by training. She had a degree as an economist in Armenia but here she was enrolled in the School of Law and Diplomacy at Tufts, but as it pertains to economics. Now she works for the Commonwealth of Massachusetts as an economist.

I don't know that we really discuss differences in what we think it is to be an Armenian or an American. The significant difference is perhaps in our attitudes toward "organized" Armenian activity, which is rooted in the fact that she grew up in a place where she belonged—an Armenian in Armenia, whereas I am a diaspora-born Armenian. For example, I have a set of Armenian friends who are a support network for each other for cultural activities within the community. We try to have a concert or to do something for the children because we want to emphasize cultural aspects of being Armenian. But my wife would ask me, "Why do you care?"

She makes a valid point. But I think it really brings out the differences between someone who grew up in a place where she belonged—an Armenian in Armenia. She never had to find other Armenians or make a plan to do something with them. In Lebanon, where we were a minority, Armenians would get together in their neighborhoods and do things for their community. My wife would likely prefer that I work on my own craft, but my instinct is that since we are not in Armenia, we need to seek out other Armenians and work with them.

For her, contributing means having a professional life, doing the best you can in the place you are. To her this means doing well in school and in your professions—and the rest of it will take care of itself. The truth is probably somewhere between our two instincts.

Where Is the 'We'?

The difficulty about the *We*, about including others in that *We*, is that question: *Why should I include you in my We when you live in your own community and marry your own?* I think people ascribe reasons to why immigrants congregate together that may not be completely true. They may be the same reasons that people born here get together and watch movies about cars crashing or baseball games.

We for the immigrant is different from that of the native born. That is something difficult to cut through and understand. How can you say, "We should kick them out?" Who is the *We* who is speaking. Are *We* the people who are here? The people who have a piece of paper? Those with a passport? Those with a green card? Those who eat cheeseburgers? Or is it again those with whiter teeth than the rest of the world?

I do think of myself as Armenian first. Armenians have such an attachment to the past, you always end up returning to it. There is such a sense of injustice and loss, we can't just let it go. The *We* for my daughter may be different. (My daughter is not a dual citizen. At least not yet.) Obviously by the choice of having an Armenian wife, that affects that *We*. There are many things that are different about having a Russian Armenian wife—and it makes it refreshing. I never envisioned marrying an Armenian from Lebanon, it would be like marrying my sister or someone I grew up with. Here there is enough difference to make it interesting, but the very fundamental things we never need to explain to each other.

If I had decided to marry someone across race or culture, that would have been seen as decision to integrate. But I wouldn't be able to be myself. I would always be *explaining* myself. I'm not sure it is about being exclusive, but about not having to explain yourself every morning.

The image of the *We* in America is so interesting—because the country is so big and the conversation takes place on such a mass level, but somehow it is only the most extreme and pointless views that get echoed. I think that the *We* does exist, but no one hears it. I live in an area that is very Italian, with some Irish, and no one asks us where we're from. I have a feeling if I went to Virginia, people would ask us *Where are you from?*, but they would only ask it once. In other words, I think the vast majority of people assume we are *We*.

All these political pronouncements of "send them back" are ridiculous and I don't understand why they warrant radio or newspaper time. It is scary to think who decides that they do. There is a sense that *We the immigrants* cannot get equal air time under any circumstance. Have you noticed how few people there are on the radio who speak with a foreign-born English accent? The conversation on a mass level is skewed tremendously. But the conversation on the "people" level I think makes much more progress than we hear about.

III

WHY DO WE STAY?

IAIN MACDONALD

OUTSIDE, LOOKING IN

Raised to talk "properly,"
with speech devoid
of those broken glass-and-gravel gutturals
that mark the true Glaswegian,
one may, removed to California,
adopt the well-modulated Scotsvoice
so much admired by Americans,
but, once back amongst one's own,
will find one's accent wavering
under each muscular influence,
lost and exposed
as an orphan seeking home.

ROUND TRIP

For years, after summer visits home,
I'd unpack in California, and the scent
of my mother's laundry detergent
(because you can't pack dirty clothes!)
transported me 6,000 miles.

Back in Scotland, I encounter it again
during those final weeks
while washing the stained items
brought home daily from the hospice,
breathe it in once more
while folding four clean nightdresses;
a greater number, I already know
than will be required.

REDISCOVERED COUNTRY

My eyes, accustomed
for a quarter-century
to northern California's
conifer-green fall,
startle to the gold profusion
flaring throughout
this Scottish autumn
of my mother's slow dying.

Scarlet berries
cluster the rowan tree
in the hospice garden;
later, on the drive home
through the tear-swept rain,
every hedgerow is on fire.

GLOBAL VILLAGE

The Chinese man next door
is shouting yet again
in (to me) incomprehensible Chinese;
and I wonder, yet again,
what series of events
brought him so far from his homeland
to find himself stuck here
with an uncomprehending neighbor
so far away from his.

RESIDENT ALIEN

Each burning day
that first Virginia summer,
as climbers
spiderwebbed overhead
trimming shade trees planted
unwisely close
to million-dollar homes,
I high-stepped through debris,
a battered Husqvarna
growling at my side,
disentangling limbs
to feed into
the chipper's hungry maw.

Each evening,
the apartment's a/c
chill on my shower-humid skin,
I'd suck down cold beer,
switch on the portable tv,
and try to decipher
the strange game
flickering across the screen.

A home run
spoke for itself;
likewise, a catch
equaling an out.
But how long
could one guy
keep "fouling off" a pitch,
and what, precisely,
was the pitcher
aiming for?

Finally, it was Peter,
one of the climbers,
who set me straight.
Sticky with bar oil and resin
at the end of yet another
ten-hour day,
we were annihilating a six-pack
of blindingly cold Bud
when I confessed my ignorance.

Profanely impatient
with any screw-up on the job,
he now quietly outlined
the simple arithmetic
of balls and strikes,
patiently explained
the glorious absurdity
of an invisible target
subjectively defined.

Then, as though to share a secret,
he leaned over and told me
that the true beauty of baseball
lies in a well-turned double-play.

Of course,
he had to use a pencil
and sandwich wrapper
to diagram the moves,
but that night
with Yankees vs. Orioles
on the tiny screen,
I began to understand.

Thirty years later,
three thousand miles west,
and in the chill
of a northern California fall,
with Giants vs. Dodgers
on video stream,
the sharply hit grounder
is still snagged cleanly,
the feed to second
is still smoothly perfect,
and the hard-fired throw
to first
still beats the runner
by half a step
as it has always done,
must always do,
in that frozen, perfect moment
where America makes sense.

EMILIO DEGRAZIA

WALKING ON AIR IN A FIELD OF GREENS

A trip back home to my birthplace, Dearborn, Michigan. Autumn, 2004. How do they remember, those who do not have our words?

The traffic thickened as the city sprawled. The farm fields that once lay on both sides of the highway leading from Detroit to Ann Arbor had all been planted with houses, factories, strip malls and parking lots. I had grown up in these parts, knew the streets, names of suburbs and city limits. But the city limits, like my absences, knew few limits now. All was Growth, incessant urban swelling and swirl, a vast anonymous cityscape stretching toward the Minnesota small town six hundred miles away that was my escape from it. I remember certain boyhood episodes too well: The way I forced one more half-breath into an overblown balloon, the little laugh when it suddenly burst, leaving behind shreds of rubber, limp as pieces of flesh torn apart by a bomb.

What hometown was there to go back to? Dearborn, Michigan, my place of birth in the upper bedroom of a rental on Calhoun Street. The landmarks still there—the Montgomery Wards at Michigan and Schaefer, Fordson High, gothic and majestic Hemlock Park, with its worn hill and basketball court, and, of course, the Ford Rouge Plant, the world's largest automobile factory. Even miles away on Gregory Street where my sister's small Cape Cod house stood with its chestnut tree and hanging flower baskets swaying with the breeze, the Ford Rouge was seldom out of sight or mind.

And there, inside that house, my Papa, now ninety-eight, was willing to speak only when looking at a past staring at him.

So I asked him before he slipped into one of those silences just this side of sleep: "Papa, what was the worst moment you ever had here—in America?"

The question deepened the calm stare that became habitual after my mother died two years ago. Since then, after seventy-two years of marriage, the present held little interest for him. He was here and not here, his face unmoved by any movement in the room, his eyes owl-like as they took in a wide expanse from a distance he was fading into. The steadiness of his gaze, and the precise words he attached to memories convinced me that he had achieved an impartiality synonymous with the ubiquity of the events unequally present in his ninety-eight years. Words, even when taken to story length, seemed small next to the silence his wisdom required of him.

"That's a hard question," he began. "You know, your Mamma and me we came here in 1936."

During the Great Depression. From San Pietro, a small town in the mountains of southern Italy where people scraped a living from rocky soil hardened by centuries of wind and sun. He was hearty and young then, doing better than most as a stone mason in the village where things remained unchanged except for the names of those who left to try a new life in the U.S., Australia, South America, or cities of northern Italy. Leaving San Pietro had never really been seriously discussed, until Mamma discovered that her father's U.S. citizenship gave her the right to emigrate. The time seemed wrong to leave. They had just moved into the new home my father had built, a big stone house with balconies overlooking the Via del Popolo, and my sister Francesca was only two.

"So I went to Franco Sesti," Papa said, "to see if I should go or stay. He was the doctor in our town, a big shot. He told me, 'Carmine, laborers in America have more than the dons in Italy. Go! But I hate to see you go.'"

Papa left unsatisfied, in part because he had to abandon a masonry job midstream. He worked until nightfall on the last day, until Mamma showed up, hands-on-hips, to tell him she'd go to America without him if he didn't come home right now.

The next morning they abandoned their house, its handmade furniture, the tear-filled stoic faces of Papa's parents, and then the small crowd that gathered on the Via del Popolo to wave farewell hankies as the young couple and their daughter Francesca made their way by mule cart down the mountain road to the Amantea train that sped them to Naples and the small cabin of a ship that took eleven days to complete the journey to New York. They had enough bread, cheese, and *sopressata* for the first six days of the trip, and they made a bed for little Francesca from the clothes packed into the big suitcase they lugged all the way to Detroit, thinking everything they owned was in there—not only the suit Papa was married in but a half-dozen beautiful dishes given them as a wedding gift, and a cast-iron frying pan and silverware and underwear and linen with flowers embroidered by hand, and a hot-water bottle for Mamma's painful side, and a sprig of fig tree taken from the ancient big-leafed grandmother of all trees hanging over the road just outside of town.

"And there we were in New York, the big suitcase, Francesca crying she wanted something to eat, nobody taking our Italian money in exchange for a banana or piece of bread, your Mamma unhappy with me, saying hurry up with that suitcase, let's go back, where will we stay tonight, and me lost with no words in my mouth."

They found their way. First they spent two days with a cousin in the Bronx, who abandoned them in Union Station as the train took off for Pennsylvania towns and the cramped houses of relatives where they tiptoed through their days trying to be helpful and invisible to hosts who wanted them to move on, especially nights when Francesca woke up crying and wouldn't stop. The long-awaited letters came—first from Pittsburgh, where Papa sold fruit on the street for fifty cents a day, then finally from Detroit, where Maria Sesti, the doctor's daughter, had a small apartment waiting for them, and maybe, God-willing, just maybe some day, a job in the Ford factory. It was February, 1937.

"And when the train stopped in Detroit, Maria Sesti wasn't there. So there we were in the cold. Without words."

"Was that it, then," I asked, "the worst moment you had here, in America? Waiting there in the cold?"

"No, we waited seven hours, but she came. No, she said, no job in the Ford factory. I have to find other work."

They lived in the upstairs room of Maria Sesti's Dearborn house in those days, huddled behind a small rounded window in the gable looking out at the branches of an old elm that hid from view the sidewalk below. Papa paced away many minutes and months in that room, maddened by Francesca's crying, looking for any small task to perform around the house to make himself not only useful but worthy. Finally, in the middle of a hot July afternoon, Maria Sesti brought him good news. A job.

"In the Ford factory?"

No. On a road construction crew in Lincoln Park. They needed someone to mix cement.

"Me?" Papa said. "What do I know about Lincoln Park, where it is? How do I get to Lincoln Park?"

About ten miles from the Dearborn house. "Maria Sesti says to me, I'll drive you there."

"And how do I get back?"

"She says, 'I'll tell the boss to drive you home after work.'"

He slept little that night, his heart pounding with excitement and fear that maybe they would not like him enough. He would show them how hard he worked. He was up before six, and Mamma too, who fixed him a lunch big enough for six—half a loaf of bread to eat with a frittata made of spinach, onions, and cheese, a banana and orange, and a special treat, a Hershey's chocolate bar she had hidden from Francesca's hungry grasp when she bought it at the corner store. This would go down just right with the bread.

Maria Sesti pulled the Model A in front and off they went, Papa fingering the one dollar bill in his pocket until Maria Sesti stopped for gas and he showed it to her and said, "Here, I will pay for the gas." And when they arrived at the Lincoln Park site, ditches alongside a roadbed being plowed through two flat fields, he marveled at how quickly they had arrived at such a faraway place. For a moment he stood and stared at the fields that went on and on beyond the weeds and tall grasses to perfectly straight lines of corn that converged like railroad tracks to an infinity out of sight. America. All these wonderful fields going on and on! Who had such land over there, in Italy? Who could imagine such wealth?

But he was immediately afraid of the boss, a thick-necked man who stood hands-on-hips nodding as Maria Sesti spoke to him, and whose first words to him were commands Papa understood only because the man's gestures were as big as his voice. So Papa smiled, took up the shovel and began mixing sand and cement, happy when the boss walked away to a crew on the other side of the ditch, happy too when the sweat began to flow in the hot sun, drenching the shirt that Mamma had ironed for him the night before. The hours on that first day of work flew, even as the sun glared down from a cloudless sky. Work was good. If you want to eat you have to work. So he was nervous when the other men laid down their tools. Work was a refuge, its routine a ritual he could understand in silence. He would rather work all day than eat, rather than interrupt the routine that would require him to use words he did not have. But if you want to work, you have to eat. Warily he found a place to sit nearby the others, smiling when they laughed and nodding when they looked his way. Carefully he opened the lunch bag Mamma had packed for him. Then—thoughtlessly, habitually, naturally—he did the necessary thing: He held the bag open in front of them so they could see what he had. He took the bread out and offered it all around, then the orange. Here, please, take something. Please, would somebody tear off a piece of bread?

They laughed and all said no. He understood the no, and smiled at them. But why did they laugh when he finished off the bread with the chocolate, choking both down past words trying to get out?

He left the banana in the bag and happily returned to his work, cheerful even when weariness began to weigh on him as the sun began to lower itself into the western sky. All the men slowed their work as the lights of early evening made shadows of them against the sky, the boss small in the distance as he sat with his head in his hands on the stump of a freshly cut tree. Papa also paused to gaze at the lovely colors gradually descending on the fields. Italy was out there, far away in those colors.

He felt a lightness in his chest. In two weeks he would be paid for ten hours of lovely work accomplished today. His hands hurt when he wiped away sweat from his nose, but cement always smelled good to him.

He knew it was time to stop when he saw the others throw their shirts over their backs and put their tools in the truck. He also walked to the truck, laid his shovel in carefully, and stood. In his lunch bag he had the banana he had planned to give to little Francesca when he got home, but a better idea came to him. He had only forty cents in change for the gasoline he had bought and didn't know how many more times Maria Sesti would expect him to pay for gas, so he would offer the banana to the boss.

He smiled and waited for the boss to finish talking to the last worker, a boy still in his teens who was about to get in a car with three others from the crew. As the car rumbled off across the half-finished road and the boss made a final round over the work site, Papa waited next to the truck.

And when the boss finally came to the truck, he smiled, thinking no, not yet, I will offer him the banana when we're on our way, no, not now, it wouldn't be right. It would seem like a bribe.

"How you getting home?" the boss asked as he stood by the truck door, laying his arm against him to hold him away, make a way for himself.

Papa was paralyzed. He pointed—first at the boss, then at the truck. "Me? No?" With two fingers the boss made a walking motion in the air. "No. You walk."

Papa hunched his shoulders into a question mark. "*Io* . . . you . . . ?"

"No. You walk." Again his two fingers walked in air.

"*Io*, no . . . ?"

"Dearborn. That way."

He pointed west, where the sky was already fading toward gray. Then he got into his truck and drove away.

Papa's worst moment must have happened right then, when he stood there alone with that banana in his brown paper bag.

"What did you do?"

"I started to walk. Me and the banana in my bag."

He walked until he came to a main road, then followed it a long way, thinking yes, maybe this will take me back. Could he ask a car to stop for him, wave his arms? What would he say? How could he make himself understood? He turned and waited when cars came up on him from behind, tried smiling and waving at a few as they passed. Two cars slowed but nobody stopped.

He walked on until he came to another wide road. Should he turn here? He looked down the road as far as he could see, then searched the sky. The sun was slipping down beneath treetops. Home, the upstairs room with the small window looking down, was somewhere out there where the sun was going down. He would have to hurry. How would he see in the dark?

He crossed the road and cut across an open field. If he kept a straight line maybe he would arrive. He hurried, broke into a run thinking no one would see him here in the field, anger rising in his chest as the sweat again began to flow. Why did you come here, his heart said as he ran. Run before the sun goes away—run all the way to the Old Country. You left your new house there. What is here for you? Waiting for someone to offer a ride to the same place tomorrow morning, the same boss driving away at the end of another day's work in the same truck, laughing this time as his fingers walk away on air.

Exhausted, he slowed to a walk in the middle of the field. Nothing planted in this field, all grass and weeds. Such waste. What a man could do with such land over there.

He stopped and took a deep breath. He saw it then: The chimney stacks above distant treetops, the plume of black smoke rising, then spreading itself into a thin layer in the windless sky. The Ford factory. There, somewhere straight ahead beyond this field. If he could keep the smokestacks in sight he would not be lost. He would get home tonight, and maybe someday he would get a job in the factory.

He walked on, wading into a patch of mustard greens, moisture beginning to appear under the thick young leaves of the plants, and their little yellow blossoms just beginning to unfurl. So many of them, reaching all the way to the trees. Another day in the hot sun would turn this field into a yellow plain. It would be beautiful, but the plants would go to seed, no longer tender and too bitter to be sweet. What a terrible waste.

I should stop, he said to himself, and fill my bag before it's too late. What a terrible waste. In Maria Sesti's kitchen Mamma would boil the greens, then fry them with garlic and olive oil. That would be something when he got home, more than the banana already turned brown in the bag.

But he had to hurry home from work, somehow find his way. What if the night came on and he no longer could see the smokestack or smoke? Maybe some other time he would come back for the mustard greens. On a Sunday after church, when he and Mamma would have time to fill twenty bags.

But no, the city was so big and he was lost. No, how would he ever find it again, this field so green?

NATALIA TREVIÑO

AND CROWN OUR GOOD

I grew up in San Antonio, Texas with a mother who spoke Spanish to me and Sesame Street, which spoke Bert and Ernie to me. My first words, my dad says, were in English, in the snow-covered state of Minnesota, but with two parents from Mexico, and my mother being a stay-at-home mom who only knew Spanish, it is very likely that my first words were a blend of Spanish and English.

I was born in Mexico City. My parents were from Monterrey, Mexico. We came to live permanently in the U.S. when I had just turned four years old. The flight from Monterrey to San Antonio is one of my earliest childhood memories.

While we waited in the airport for the plane, I sang what must have been a favorite song, the ABC's in English. I think we must have been waiting a long time in line, because my parents tell me I was singing it over and over, dancing around the merciful people waiting with us. I probably felt that the people in the airport enjoyed my song. I probably sensed approving eyes on me, and laughter. More than likely, they were humoring me and my poor parents who were tolerating their child, proud of her voice, unafraid to sing this extraordinary song.

Once on the plane, a lady set a tray with dreadful looking food in front of me, but at the corner of the tray sparkled a piece of candy in its gold wrapper. I knew I was not allowed to eat candy. I had to earn it. I wanted it, and so I decided to eat all the food first. This was going to be a big task because I didn't like food, especially strange food. It was a big decision I remember vividly. I knew this plane trip made it a special day, like a birthday and that my mom would probably give in. Somehow, during the meal, in the excitement of the descent, my plate disappeared and so did the candy. I had sacrificed and received nothing, and I knew it would be ages before another piece of candy came my way. I remember getting off of the plane, without my candy, feeling angry and cheated.

Many immigrant children arrive to the United States feeling this way, but for much better reasons than a lost chance at a sweet.

One friend of mine, Jen, who came from Korea when she was nine, tried to get her four brothers and sisters to run away to the mountains when their parents came for them from America. Her parents had saved enough money, moved to America, created a life here, saved more money, and went home for their children. Jen had a hiding place in the mountains all figured out. Her siblings said no. She wept. How could they leave their playground? Or their grandmother, all they ever knew?

Another friend of mine, Sonya, came from Poland when she was fourteen. Her father left Poland when she was twelve during its Solidarity movement when their home city, occupied by Russia at the time, had become intolerable. Lines of people in front of stores where there were rumors that bread or shoes or eggs had arrived, when all that was available was a shelf of vinegar. He traveled as part of his job, so on what seemed like one of his normal business trips, he left Poland and did not return. He never said a word to his daughters about what he was about to do that would change their lives forever. Her mother also said nothing to them. They did not know when they would see him again, and they did not know why he left. He would carve out a new life for them in another country. Sonya did not see her father again for two years. After starting a life in Austria and then settling in America, it was time for them to be together as a family again. Finally, Sonya, her sister and mother went to the American Embassy and were each tested to see if they were "fit" to come to America.

Sonya makes quotation marks with her fingers when she says the word "fit." The embassy gave them a test because they wanted able-bodied immigrant workers, people who could contribute. The lady who worked at the embassy was abrupt, cold, and bent on making Sonya feel inadequate, but Sonya passed the test. Her mother passed too. Her sister did not. Sonya says her sister was actually deemed "unfit" to come. Her fingers punctuate the word, and her face folds in pain as she remembers this. Her sister, slightly mentally disabled, and desperately excited to come to America, would not be able to join them.

This brought an unimaginable horror to Sonya's family. Would they leave her sister behind? Would they send Sonya on her own and split the family? Would they ever be a whole family again?

In the darkness before dawn, after months of begging for a second chance at the test, Sonya, her mother, and sister left their home and belongings and took a taxi to the embassy on the chance that her sister might be accepted the second time. Having given up their publicly owned house to a neighbor on the chance they would be leaving, they did not know if they would return to nothing. Her sister somehow passed the test, and their journey across the ocean began.

The intimidating lady at the embassy who didn't want to let her family in, who would be willing to cut her family in half was Sonya's introduction to America.

The conversation about immigration is about all of us. Whether we are Asian, European, Latin American, Middle Eastern, Pacific Islander, or indigenous to our respective land, most of us come from a legacy of attachment, detachment, migration and settlement. What I keep hearing in the conversation is that immigrants, both legal and illegal, are punished for coming. Both Jen and Sonya, and so many others I have talked to begin to tear up when we talk about it.

Maybe the issue is that government agencies do not accurately represent what life will be like for the immigrant family. Once they arrive, life is very confusing. Images of American freedom seem attractive. The U.S. government proclaims, "Welcome." But the neighbor down the street might proclaim, "There goes the neighborhood." Immigrants hear: *We are welcome. We are not welcome. We are desirable. We are not desirable. We are cheap labor. We are cheap? We are in the greatest nation in the world. It asks for the meek! But do not ask for help. Do not take our social services. Do take this job. We need fresh vegetables. Do not take that job. Or that job. Take care of our children. Stay away from our children. Stay on your side of town. Why do you not learn English and blend in? Why do you not go back to your own country? What do you do for this country?*

What is so confusing about this conversation on immigration, especially for Mexicans, is that we who immigrate legally are often treated like we immigrated illegally. We are all lumped together, and it does not feel good. We never broke a law.

But in a way we should be lumped together. We emigrated from the same country. We have accents. We smell of different foods. Some of us had the means to come on an airplane with papers, and some of us jumped on a train in the middle of the night. We sat on its roof for the trip north. Some of us died. What scares me is that most of what I hear about "those people," the people I have been lumped in with, is that WE are expendable.

There is a project happening out of the University of Michigan. It is called The Undocumented Migration Project directed by anthropologist Jason DeLeon. Researchers are collecting artifacts left behind by thousands of undocumented immigrants, such as shoes, letters, and photos in the desert between Mexico and Arizona. DeLeon wants to exhibit them and tell this story, perhaps to build compassion or to accurately document this migration. Some people think these artifacts are just trash. The Smithsonian has contacted DeLeon about being a venue for the exhibit.

I worry about what this confusing conversation may mean for my son. I was driving him and his best friend home one summer day. I adore his friend, but the boys are in full middle school swing. We saw some construction workers digging up a part of the road at the entrance to my neighborhood. The men were clearly brown. It was 110 degrees outside. They were hunched over with heavy tools in their hands, concentrating. His friend muttered jokingly, "Dude, there are your people."

I wonder what my son felt in that moment. I heard him take a breath and say, "Yea, those are my people, man," in a Mexican accent. They both laughed.

I wonder if I should I have lectured these kids about indigenous people or honest, hard work? About privilege? Or have I done that enough with my son already? I think my son was made to feel inferior in that moment, and he had to defend himself by aligning himself with the joke. It is a joke that the dirty brown men working outside are his people.

Thankfully, my son owns his Mexican heritage, and he loves the deepest reaches of Mexico he knows. He has relationships with his family there. He and this not-so-adorable-anymore-friend actually look like brothers, fair-skinned and blonde, which adds a complexity, making it more comfortable for them both to mock the same people. But what were they mocking? Hard work? Brownness? Knowing how to lay a pipe under the asphalt?

No. They were mocking Mexicans. What kids mock each other for is random. The wrong jeans. The wrong shirt. The wrong side of town. Or is it really random? Are they not mirroring adult prejudice?

If you wear blue shoes, and people mock them, you might become ashamed of your blue shoes. If you feel a loyalty to your shoes, you may keep them and hide them, you may want to throw them away, or you may wear them defiantly. My son does not hide his Mexican heritage, and yet there are moments like this he must navigate on his own.

And what if one of those men were his uncle? It would have been perfectly possible. Loyalty and pride do not always go hand in hand. We can be loyal to our family but not proud of the people in it, and when that happens, there is pain and shame.

What happens when we finally get our papers? When I became an American citizen, I was no longer comfortable saying, "I am Mexican." It was complicated now. I wasn't sure if I was hyphenated, Chicana, Hispanic, Latina or still just Mexican. I wanted to know what to say. I was also not comfortable saying, "I am American," because no matter what the paper said, my friends knew it was not true.

There were so many times when I was told, "You don't even look Mexican!" or "You don't even have an accent! How is that possible?" and "At least you don't look Mexican!"— in the most flattering tones. This happened with almost every new person I met when I was growing up. I know it was always intended as a compliment. But it became eerie that so many different people said the same thing. Of course I looked Mexican. I looked like my relatives, all of whom look Mexican. In Mexico, I blend in. The comment has never been true. But I was lucky because I passed unwritten tests; I was accepted into Anglo homes and friendships. They were telling me I was lucky.

I did not know it was a bad thing to look Mexican until they told me what a GOOD thing it was that I did not. It did not make sense, and while it made me feel shame, I also enjoyed, on some level, the message of approval. It is unsettling when I think of it now. I shudder when I recall how this compliment made me feel special. Saved.

This tricky "compliment" cheated my friends who did look more like "typical Mexicans." They always sounded angry when they explained to me that they were not Mexican. Their parents spoke Spanish to each other and to their own parents. To me this meant they were like me; only they were born here. The being born in a location part seemed arbitrary to me, not your language or your family traits. Because they were born HERE, they said, that made them NOT MEXICAN. They told me they were white. But I could see with my eyes that they were brown. Now when I think about their angry tones, I realize that while those tones were being said to me, they were directed at the people who made them feel inferior. No one told them, "Well, at least you don't look Mexican!" No one smiled at them like they had won the lottery.

The kids in my neighborhood felt they had the right to call me wetback. For the longest time, I wondered why only my back stayed wet after my shower and no one else's did. Maybe because of what they said: the greasiness of it. I did not know what was so funny about it, but I did not like the laughter. My mom would call me down the street to come "take a chower." The kids laughed. I laughed. Eventually, I started trying harder to reach my back with soap and water and to dry it as best I could with the towel.

After my toweling off plan did not work, I decided to ask my dad to check my back. I asked him if it was wet. He looked at me like I was crazy. He checked it. It was dry. I asked, "Then why are the kids calling me wetback?" His face became ash for a moment. He told me about the river, Mexico, our papers, our plane trip, which I still remembered vividly because of that candy. He told me I could tell them I have papers. We did not swim. That made me feel better. I had armor—papers, papers I could not read, but that said my back was dry.

Did this mean I could join in and mock those who did swim across the river? Was I now on the right side of the line with my dry back?

Today I get emotional when I hear patriotic songs about America. It's a bit embarrassing because these songs evoke a gag reflex in some of my native-born American friends. I think this is because I loved these songs when I learned them in school. The lyrics "Oh beautiful, for spacious skies and amber waves of grain" told me what a beautiful place this country was. It had purple mountains and fruited plains. It was worth the lives of soldiers who loved mercy more than life. And brotherhood was what crowns were made of.

I sang these songs fully when I was a child, and I believed in the words I sang. America was beautiful. And free. I was five and six learning these words and ideals. These songs, taught by the same teacher who taught me how math and letters worked, had to be just as true as one plus one equals two. I believed in America just as much as I believed in God, but just like God, the America in that song was something I could not see with my own eyes.

I worry for kids who will grow up like some of my friends who were teased for their dark skin by their own lighter-skinned siblings, afraid of being in the sun, scrubbing their skin, picking make-up colors that lighten their face, picking hair color and contact lenses that will lighten their look, angry that their elbows look "black." These are the very kids who fiercely say skin color does not matter. And they are born here, legal. Then there are the kids who were not born here, who have no papers that defend them, and their dark skin betrays them. Not saved.

And they are learning "America the Beautiful" at school like I did, maybe believing those words too, wondering, *when can I see the beautiful part?*

I worry that all they will know about being of color is the shame and anger part. How the shame mounts with the wall going up along the Rio Grande River, with Mexican-American authored books and historical photos being banned from public schools. How the shame mounts when people assume all of us are illegal, and therefore criminals.

My father encouraged safety and assimilation. He was practical, only talking to me and my brother in English in the house to make sure we knew how to speak correctly. My brother and I only spoke English to each other. My father did speak to my mother in Spanish, and she spoke to us in Spanish, but we were not allowed to blend the languages, so I spoke to her in English. She understood me, but always spoke to me in Spanish. *No problema.* Now that I know more Spanish, I switch to full not-so-great Spanish for some topics, and since she knows more English now, and some topics are just more accessible in English, she switches to English for certain sentences, but it has taken about forty years for us to get this right. She is reading Jane Austen. I am reading the original letters of Frida Kahlo.

I craved going to Mexico as a child, and I still do. My aunts, cousins and grandmothers kept me in the loop though my Spanish was terrible. I craved to see my mother so happy and alive with her family in Mexico, some dark-skinned, some olive-toned. Her best friend from childhood, from a very humble neighborhood, was a blonde-haired, blue-eyed woman. She was my "aunt," my *tia*. To me she looked and sounded as Mexican as the rest of my family, so it was hard to understand what it was I did not look like.

When I was about eight or nine, I made it a point to look closely to see what exactly changed when we crossed the border. What made America the beautiful look so different? I knew I could tell I was in one country or the other, but I wanted to know why. This is when I first noticed each piece of trash left on the side of the road in the area around Nuevo Laredo. It was just not a clean road. America, just a few short miles that way—clean. Littering laws. I imagined when I grew up, that it would cost me nothing to pick up each piece of trash, one by one for as many days as it would take. It would be worth it. In my mind, as we drove, I picked up each piece of trash I saw. It made sense to me that since I was not a citizen, I belonged to Mexico and needed to help it "get better." After I was done, people would like it, and of course, I could talk to them about making littering laws that would help them be more like Texas.

But I was at a disadvantage with this dream of "helping" Mexico because I was not a true Mexican over there; I spoke a poor version of Spanish, which made me an embarrassment to some of my relatives, a joke to some of the kids in the neighborhood there, and, at best, a novelty to the people who were kind. If only I could hurry and grow up so I could do something about this, in silence though because I knew people have their minds already made up before you talk to them. The last thing they would do in Mexico is listen to a girl. They were just fine. Well, the trash on the road told me they were not fine, and over there in America, no one thought Mexico was fine.

Today, with the violence rampant in my family's city of Monterrey, the reminders that Mexico is not fine abound. I have cut myself off from traveling there in the last three years. I am heart broken every day because of this. I can barely speak about it. My family over there is pretty mad at me. But if my father stressed any idea above others when he was raising me, it was to stay safe.

He did not allow me to walk with my hands in my pockets. He did not allow me to drink any water, unless it had been boiled for thirty minutes first when we were in Mexico. We travelled with jugs of San Antonio tap water to drink and brush our teeth. Sometimes we ran out and had to boil what came out of the Mexican tap. My cousins were disgusted and offended by this. In our home in San Antonio, my brother was allowed to go fishing at "the pond" behind our house. I was not. My brother was allowed to ride his bike at "the trail." Not me. Death and murder were literally around every corner. Illness was an even larger worry. I had a serious illness when I was four and by the time I was eight I had had five operations—for urinary tract malformation, ear infections, and a "tied" tongue. More operations came when I was a teen. Dad took great pains to keep me alive. He constantly reminded me that since I was a girl, I was "prey" to male passersby. I was never to have my window open. I was not allowed to have any part of my bedroom furniture in front of my window because it would block me from getting out in the fire we were sure to have.

Today, if I do something that puts me in danger, I feel I am slapping my father in the face. I feel I have no right to do that after all he has done to keep me healthy and alive. So I do not travel to Mexico now to further my research, my writing, or my relationships with elders and my beautiful nieces and nephews. I am not sure whether I am risking danger here—by writing about immigration, by even wanting to find the "we" in "We the People," but Dad thinks I like danger. He thinks I want to go to Iraq and help them reconstruct.

Marriage would be tricky for me. I knew I wanted to marry a man who would help me continue my relationship with Mexico. I knew he would have to know Spanish to be a part of my family. That seriously limited my hopes for dating any guy I met. When I met my first husband, I thought, "perfect match." He was half Mexican, and he loved Mexico as much as I did. Our son is the result of that marriage. Some things are more important than trips to Mexico, though, and I got out of that marriage. Later, I met an Australian who emigrated here so we could be married.

Family trips are now over multiple borders including ocean borders. My husband wants to become an American citizen so he can participate in civic voting like he did in Australia, where he was required by law to vote. He has very mixed feelings about being an American citizen because he saw so many celebrity Aussies give up their citizenship when they became famous in Hollywood. He always saw that as a kind of betrayal. Now, after moving here, he understands how complex that decision may have also been for those famous Aussies who became Americans.

Politics have always been a large part of his family life, and here he feels left out of the process. He wants to be a part of "We the people" since he has to live by the rules of these people. He works here, pays taxes, owns property. He belongs to the "we" in all but citizenship.

When he becomes an American citizen, it may be easier for him to think "We Americans" than it was for me. He is a tall, pink-skinned, Anglo man who looks like he carries authority in his pocket. While his accent sets him apart as a foreigner, he passes that unwritten test of being accepted into the white culture wherever he goes. And who does not like Australians? They are known as warm, as loving life, as being down to earth. He will have an easier time than my friend with an equally distinctive accent—from Dubai.

My brother's immigrant experience is so different from mine. He was forced to start first grade without knowing English. Soon, he was failing. My parents went to a parent-teacher conference after six weeks had gone by. The teacher met them and indignantly said, "Well, your son does not listen to me. He does nothing that I tell him to do!" My dad said to her very slowly, "He does not speak English." He says she turned gray with shame in that moment. She had no idea. This is before bilingual education existed, and we did not live on that side of town, the side of town where the kids spoke Spanish.

It was no surprise that my brother was never into getting teacher approval or high grades. He did learn the language. He was into fishing, hunting, and he was silent most of the time, fishing, aiming, shooting, honing the skills that would make him the physicist and engineer he would later become.

He graduated from high school, but was not hoping for more than to work at a hunting and fishing store. He had no desire to go to college. My dad and I begged him to try it. I distinctly remember telling him he could become an engineer who could design faster, more accurate weapons of his choice. He liked that idea. He gave it a go. He found out he had a talent in physics, and he went to a nationally recognized physics program.

From what I read about statistics about Hispanic males, my brother is a rare bird. There are not many physicists with a name like Treviño. The national trend for Hispanic males who graduate from high school and college is decreasing. But my brother, who did not know English, did not like school, was Mexican and should have been getting a girl pregnant and becoming a mechanic, has his own consulting company now as an engineer, and he goes fishing whenever he wants.

This is the experience so many immigrants want for their children, a chance for a better life. My friend Jen is a dentist. All of her siblings are professionals too. My friend Sonya is a public relations officer. That is so interesting considering her first disastrous experience with American public relations. But like these two women, and others I interview about their immigration experience, a common thread in their stories is their feeling of grief and powerlessness. With many children and women, it is the men who bring them. With my friend from Dubai, it is his father who "forced" him to come. It is the men who often decide to "vote" with their feet and come to America.

The women I have met come for love and family. Some men, like my husband, also have come for love, and I have a young friend just finishing high school named Mariana who came for love too—when she was ten.

She remembers feeling terrified of leaving Mexico because she would leave the only world she knew. She had never traveled here. But she was desperate to come because her mother lived here. Her mother married an American when Mariana was five. They filed for papers for Mariana to come. The marriage was both real and legal. They submitted the papers immediately. Months went by. Her mother came to visit. They both cried when she left. She did not understand what was happening. More months. More visits. She tears up when she recalls the partings. Her mother could have gone back to Mexico, but that would have slowed the process even more, and she had promises from lawyers and the immigration officers. Finally, after five years of separation, her mother broke the law and brought her child here illegally. Somehow, Mariana excelled in school. She has lived here for eight years illegally. Her papers came through a few months ago.

I asked her now that she is on the path to citizenship, was there a time or place when she could imagine herself saying, "we" and mean "We Americans." At first, she could not think of how. She told me, as if I were a native to this country, "Foreigners are not welcome here."

She thought for days about this, and she finally answered when we spoke at a panel on immigration I organized. She said she feels she can say, "we" and mean "We Americans" when she thinks of her classmates at school. She is an honors student graduating twelfth in her class. She tutors students. She does community service. She is a school athlete. Her academic and sports teams travel and compete together. She shares in the joy of improving the world around her, this American world where public opinion and policy have been both hostile and generous to her. She is on track to attend a major university on scholarships. Now that she is a legal resident, she has privilege and choices.

Residency during the naturalization process is a huge transition period, often colored by mixed allegiances, anger, shame and confusion for most youths. When my mother became a citizen, I remember being horrified by the pledge she gave, that she vowed to take up arms against Mexico if needed. I was frightened and furious, but I was fifteen. I wonder how my husband will feel when he takes his oath, to possibly take up arms against Australia. It is unthinkable.

Some people ask, and with good reason, "What are you doing for America since America opened her arms to you?" When powerless children and teenagers come against their will or for love and family alone, civic responsibility is not an issue. Survival comes first for all species, including immigrants. When we are teens, no matter our legal status, we are only thinking, "What is in this for me?" The question of, "What are you willing to do for America when America opened up her arms to you?" hurts.

If the immigrants are here illegally, then they follow unwritten policies that govern them: there is shame in their presence here. They accept it. They know what jobs they can and cannot try for. They know what income they can expect. They know where they can and cannot live or get medical help. They know where their kids can go on the weekend. They know they have to live in secret. They know they cannot afford that restaurant or that one, even though they clean its floors from midnight to 3 a.m. They know that they will do a job for a fraction of what it is worth. They know it will be hard labor, labor the Americans will not do for that amount of money. Those are their policies. They give up their rights and their lives.

For my husband who never wanted to come to America in the first place, residency has been a period of happiness over our new life together, but it is tinged by loss and mourning his home country and missing immediate family and friends who live across the planet. It is not easy. He works, pays taxes, and follows the law. He loves this country for its example and ideals. Do most Americans do more than this?

What I see in so many of these immigration stories, including my own, is that there is a personal attachment an immigrant is often seeking, an attachment to a family member who needs them to be here, or who is already here, a future wife, a mother, a father, someone they love. That attachment has power. That is the power that will bring someone across a river, bridge, or shining sea.

For many immigrants, immigration is more about seeing the new country as a new house, a new, temporary shelter. We go in because of WHO is in the house, not really because of WHAT is in the house. We may not be attached to the ideals of the house when we arrive. We may not know what they are. We will have to learn the stated and unstated rules of the house. We may not like all the people in that house, but there are people in there we would die for.

What I have discovered is that these are love stories. That is where there is the greatest "We," a we that would cause someone to risk the lethal trip over, or to spend a life savings. There is the unlimited human need to be with those we love and to take care of them as best we can, even if we have to depart from them, risk our lives, or break a law to save them.

I think the larger "We" has the potential to hold and save all of us. It appeared when we hear that an Italian cruise ship hit rocks and seventeen died. It appeared when my neighbor's house down the street burned down. We all came out of our houses to breathe in the same pungent smoke. We all spoke the same nonverbal language of fear, horror, loss, hope and grief. Accents and differences disappeared. Everyone wanted a reason. Some wanted to place blame and secretly wondered what did that man do to cause this fire? Eventually, we stopped and realized, *oh yea, this could have been my house burning down, with my family in it.* On September 11th, we all knew it could have been any of us in any of those planes or buildings. In that humbling moment when we feel a tinge of shame, when we know that it could have been me, the "We" has the potential to become infinite.

JENNIFER CLARK

EXPORTING THE DEAD

"Every year, the corpses of hundreds of immigrants are flown from San Francisco to their home countries."
San Francisco Weekly, Lauren Smiley, January 20, 2009

When an elephant dies
bones rest and relatives remember;
wrinkled trunks inhale the scent of skull,
then silently caress ivory tusks.
Massive feet rise, and soft
as a whisper, stroke that which remains.

When a human—deemed illegal—dies
the good death begins; it is in
the business of "international transfers"
that a life no longer is legitimized.
Documents once withheld
made up for now, an offering
of papers—presented to the corpse—
certified and sealed, pinned to
that which remains, like a
note from a guilty parent:
we withhold love no longer.

It costs more to fly dead
than alive, even though the dead
don't ask for pillows.
In this sport of exporting
we pretend they're alive.

So when a human dies illegal
bones fly home
or glide on the backs of waves
to Mexico, Nicaragua, El Salvador
for singing relatives to bury.
A mother folds her arms and hugs herself.
A sea of feet stand above blanketed bones
and remember that their dead once lived.

TOM STERNBERG

Interviewed by Heather Tosteson

I DON'T THINK LOYALTIES CAN BE JUDGED IN A VACUUM

Until the age of twelve, I lived in Romania; from twelve until fifteen, I continued my childhood in Israel. Then upon arrival to America at the age of fifteen, life events forced me into adulthood.

Childhood and Early Cultural Attachments in Romania

I grew up in the town of Arad, which was the westernmost city in Romania very close to the Hungarian border. It had between sixty to eighty thousand people. My mother tongue is Hungarian. Politically, we belonged to Romania because after the Paris Peace Treaty following World War I, Hungary ceded this territory to Romania. But culturally, there was a much stronger Hungarian rather than Romanian influence in the inter-war years even though all the new citizens were expected to change their loyalty due to a paper document drawn up by the victorious nations. Once I went to school, the education was in Romanian.

No one could fail to notice the hatred between the Hungarians and the Romanians but it was not unique. Practically all the Balkans were made up of small national groups who hated each other throughout the centuries. By and large we are loath to admit that our patriotism and other prejudices are not personal choices but results of millennial historical forces. However, in my case, we as Jews feared and hated both the Romanians and the Hungarians, as both didn't need a reason to butcher us. My uncle would never refer to Romanians without adding the adjective "fucking Romanians."

World War II was the most seminal event in my life due to the war's impact on everything I came to understand—family disruptions, Holocaust and personal tragedies of Jews and it's terrible damage to my natural optimism; it was not until I came to America that I regained my inborn instincts for believing that the world has islands of happiness punctuated by mountains of misery. During the war, from eight-year-old eyes, the world was not so nice. There was no food and to this day I tend to hoard it. The world looked bleak and angry. There were more times of anguish than happiness, though I don't consciously think I have suffered psychologically; but it did underline for the rest of my life a need to assess all misfortunes in a relative and realistic way.

After my father was shipped off to labor camp my uncle took care of me. We fled in a train together with thousands of other scared people, out of the city and into the mountains as the German armies were approaching. There my uncle had to bargain with the local peasants to hide us from the Germans for sky-high prices. The importance of available cash money to save one's skin made a mark on my psyche. While we were fleeing in that train, I remember that an airplane shot up our train car. In desperation my uncle placed me on the floor under the bench he was sitting on. There on the floor under the bench was a man who was shot moments before and he stared at me with open eyes. I remember that; I was eight. It didn't mean anything to me. I don't think I understood that he was dead; anyway I didn't quite understand at that age what it meant to be dead—it was just something that was to be avoided.

During this war period, my older brother Mordechai and I lived with my uncle and then with various families, strange families that we did not know, as my parents were separated, by the war or by choice I don't know. My guess is they didn't have a good marriage. I didn't miss my mother. I got separated from her at an early age, in 1942 when I was five years old. Truly the one and only incident I remember of my mother is when I was going to sleep and she played my favorite tune on the piano: "How Much Is That Doggy in the Window?" My older brother was always more attached to my mother as he had more time to bond.

She went to get a job in Bucharest. Since she spoke English fluently, she got a job in the British Embassy, where she met someone, an Englishman. My mother went back to England with him but the man was married. So later, my mother also immigrated to Israel where her two sons were soon headed as well. When the war was over she came back to Arad in 1946 for a very short visit. That's when she brought me a Kodak box camera and the magic of a box permanently saving a moment in time impressed me greatly and probably pointed me into a life in the sciences and engineering.

In 1944, when the Russians came through Arad on their way to

Berlin and on to final victory, my dad came back from labor camp—alive, but just. My brother and I lived with others until 1946 when my father remarried. My stepmother had been in Auschwitz. Then they had a boy, Haim, who came years later to the U.S. to join my newly created business.

My father and uncle were the only two who survived the war out of nine brothers and sisters in that family, or that was the story then. But only two years ago and eight thousand miles away, I accidentally learned from a professor of French at Emory University that she was a great-granddaughter of one of my father's sisters who also perished during the war. My brother and I wonder why our parents didn't tell us who survived so we could gather in the survivors. There were four years between the end of the war and when we went to Israel in 1950, so they should have known and reconnected. Knowing how family oriented my father was I'll never know why he did not tell us.

Moving to Israel

Escaping to Israel after the war was primarily a question of who among the Romanian officials you could bribe. You couldn't take anything of value with you. Emigrating forced my parents to be impoverished as it did all escapees from Europe. The Romanians loved that they could grab all the goods the Jews were forced to abandon in their country—apartments, furniture and personal effects. My uncle couldn't raise the money to bribe for his emigration papers. He served jail time after the war for some so-called economic crime. The newly arrived regime of the communists had a long litany of capitalist crimes they could again persecute the Jews with.

My older brother left Romania in 1946 when he was thirteen or fourteen. On the way to Palestine, he was captured by the British and interned in Cyprus. When the State of Israel was declared, he was allowed into Israel. My mother headed to Israel at that point too. Everyone ended up in Israel. But it was not a nice place where people had individual freedoms, unfettered rights or economic opportunities—they just survived. By the time we arrived, she'd already hooked up with a British colonial official. He was also Jewish, so after the Mandate when Israel became a state, he decided to stay. He lost his eldest son in the oncoming War of Independence 1948-1950, the first Arab-Israeli war. He was fifty and didn't want children around, so I could only come for visit from my father's house but couldn't live there with my mother.

However, my mother was the one who met a military man at the U.S. consulate in Jerusalem, the one who eventually financed my coming to

America. It was her plan to have me come to America. I think, now, that she did love me—but I didn't reciprocate. I think she thought this would help me. At the age of fourteen, ping-pong was my passion. There was a YMCA building in Jerusalem with a ping-pong table and I hustled some games with strangers. One of them was Chief Petty Officer Wallace Hudson, who spent his free time between shifts playing many ping-pong games with me. I was very good at that age, and he was quite good. We started a friendship. His life was constricted. He was a radio operator at the U.S. consulate and the only place he was allowed to come between shifts was to the YMCA. At that time Wally was thirty-five years old and had two children and a wife in Tennessee.

He got to talking to my mother about me as I didn't speak any English except counting to twenty-one—the usual end of a ping-pong game. Somehow, my mother or Wally got to talking about the fact that there wasn't much of an educational future for me in Israel given my scientific interests. We were poor, for us there were just basic existential issues of life and death—and the army. They decided it would be useful for me to go to the U.S. and live with Wally's family in Tennessee. I wasn't that happy with Israel at that time. In Haifa where I lived with my father, we lived in tents. There was no ping-pong. I didn't like working in the fields of the kibbutz. I also didn't have a great attachment to my mother. There wasn't a lot holding me there; even at fifteen I somehow had an understanding of the U.S. potential. I liked that Wally had the money to buy chocolates and oranges. I liked that he had a car. I felt that coming to America was going to be chocolates, oranges and cars. In Israel, everything was rationed. You could have rationed milk at fifteen, but no chocolates. Only my two-year-old brother could have chocolate. But Wally was able to buy it in the American canteen and offered me all I could eat.

I was very interested in science, in chemistry and math. I had a chemistry set, all made up by hand, even when I lived in Romania. I think my mom must have thought I was Nobel Prize material. She was wrong in that though I did have some very purpose-driven dreams, among them a university education.

Coming to the U.S.

When I first came to the U.S., Wally was there already having been reassigned to the D.C. area. He took me to Jefferson City, Tennessee to live with his family, but this small-town school was not approved by the

State Department for foreign students. The same was true of Greenville, South Carolina where Wally's extended family lived. So I went right back to Washington, D.C. where Wally was stationed. He had a brother living in Alexandria, and that school was approved. So I was deposited with his brother at the age of fifteen and a half. Four months later, Wally was shipped off to Korea for two years and I was stranded among very nice strangers.

I arrived in July 1952, and by September I could speak well enough to go to school at George Washington High School's ninth grade. It was easy to learn everyday English among kids my age. When I arrived, I spoke Hungarian, Romanian, French, which we studied in pre-war Europe, Russian, which we studied after their occupation of Romania, and both local official Israeli languages—Hebrew and Arabic. University-bound students needed a foreign language to be academically rounded so I had to learn yet another language; I chose Latin because its grammar is in many ways similar to Romanian and thus did not take much homework time as I worked every day after school. Then in college there was to be another two years of foreign language requirement. But they agreed to excuse me from this requirement and I substituted another useful life-skill instead: fencing. Languages aren't hard for me to learn. My poor father took many years to learn Hebrew. But my wife, Jette, now she is something unbelievable with languages.

My formal education in Romania ended at eleven. In Israel, I was living on a kibbutz and went to kibbutz school. I pursued my interest in science. Now, in high school, I took to learning in a big way. They put me in ninth grade, maybe on the basis of my English or small size but within a month they upped me into the tenth grade, possibly because my math skills trumped my English skills. Very soon, Wally, on his way to Korea, began to circulate me among local Jewish families who wanted to help a semi-abandoned fifteen-year-old Jewish kid. So I began living with different local Jewish families where my experiences were not pleasant, so I chose to live with his brother's family, still attending GWHS. His brother and his family were nice, simple country people. I liked them but I was not comfortable in their house due to the poor living conditions they themselves had to endure with no space to do homework or read and the black-and-white 9" TV constantly blaring

I took a job at a shoe store on Saturdays, and I learned that I could rent a room for $1 a day. So, I took a second job after school and worked in a pharmacy from four every afternoon to seven in the evening. I took a bus to this lady's house who had a room for rent. She worked for AT&T. It was a nice big room with a bed and a table. I lived there as well as other rooming houses for three years. There were very many kind people who took to me and helped me. For instance, there was this very old Jewish lady from Poland, Mrs. Klein, the grandmother of one of my high school classmates who served me daily bowls of chicken soup and bread as I was running from school to work.

Two and a half years after learning English, I won a statewide prize in public speaking and some thirty years later my trophy was still encased among the school's more highly regarded football achievements. But my interest was in chemistry. In my junior year in high school I was chosen to attend Virginia's Boy's State in the summer. It was held at VPI, Virginia Polytechnic Institute, in Blacksburg, Virginia. I went there as it was the only engineering college with in-state, reduced tuition for Virginia high-school graduates and thus something I could afford by saving during my summer jobs. However, after admission and well into my first year at college in the fall of 1955, I was declared a foreign student having to pay twice the tuition charges of my fellow Virginia high school graduates because I did not have parents in Virginia. I did get even the following year as I decided not to buy the semester meal tickets but to get a job serving food in the cafeteria where as a dishwasher I could eat freely a hundred times more than my tuition increase. This lesson of trying to outsmart the rules has fortunately stayed with me all my life.

College

When I went to VPI, I was eighteen years old. The Israeli government called me back to fight between my sophomore and junior years. I spent three and a half years in the Air Force. But by the time I returned to Israel, I had been away for five and a half years, speaking and living totally in an English world and I had completely forgotten my Hungarian and my Hebrew. In the service I quickly relearned Hebrew and this reinforcement has now buried the language deep in my brain so that now I speak it fluently even if seldom.

(Many years later living in Denmark, I got a job with a London-based computer company on the strength of my Hungarian, which was none at that time, but I knew I could relearn fast. They never thought that somebody would claim to speak a language that he did not, but my experience with re-learning Hebrew in the Air Force gave me the gall to apply. The big surprise came soon when this international company had a Hungarian delegation attend a meeting. Their regular translator had not arrived so the English marketing manager remembered me and called on me suddenly because I was the only other person in the company to speak the language. There was no way out. My English boss opened the session by welcoming the visitors with warm English business *schmaltz,* then paused and looked at me for the instant translation. Without skipping a beat, without remembering a single word of my mother tongue, I began speaking some awful gibberish that to my boss must have sounded like good Hungarian but completely dumfounded the Hungarians. I didn't know how to escape but at that very moment the doors flung open and the real translator entered, apologizing profusely for his late arrival due to traffic. I evaporated from that room. Years later I met up with some members of that Hungarian delegation in Budapest, where I was later stationed due to my great language skills that by that time, as expected, I had relearned. We all had a hilarious time remembering, especially the miraculously happy ending to what for me had been a frightful event.)

When I was decommissioned from the Israeli Air Force, I knew I wanted to work in chemical engineering and thought I would eventually do so in Israel. I was an Israeli citizen because any Jew arriving in Israel automatically receives Israeli citizenship, if he elects, based on religion and ethnicity. But it would have been an extremely difficult, if not impossible, burden for my family to finance my further schooling there. Also in Israel contrary to the U.S. in the late fifties, one could not work in summer jobs and earn enough to finance a whole year of schooling. I also noticed that the Middle East was noisy, conflicted, intolerant and not respectful of individuals or personal boundaries. Very different from Anglo-Saxon Americans.

On return to my undergraduate school in the U.S., my roommate was studying for a PhD in statistics, a subject I had never heard about. I got interested in it. Later I realized that statistics was a useless field with only a BS I knew I needed to learn much more statistics before I could use it effectively. I decided to go to graduate school. There was an extremely good applied PhD program at VPI and I received a scholarship. It would have been easy to stay only paying for food and board. But I decided to go to Stanford in California for both scholarship and adventure.

Marriage

I met my future wife Jette in September 1963, the first day she arrived at Stanford. It was a year after I had started my master's program and I had three months to go. I had decided I wasn't going for the PhD.

I met her because she came down to the student center. She was barely twenty years old, Danish, and had come to work as an au pair. I was twenty-six. She was smoking heavily. She had just escaped from a restrictive family. As an ice-breaker, I asked to borrow a cigarette which to a European girl was natural; in fact good manners requires that when taking a cigarette from a pack, you pass the packet to all present.

I already had a girlfriend who was leaving in two weeks for a semester in Spain. She was leaving her car with me for safekeeping. I took her to the airport and came right back to Jette but this time not just for a cigarette but for a date; I have never left her since. Jette was living in Menlo Park. We had a good time. I forgot about the other girl.

Our first connection was sexual, she came from a liberated country from a sexual standpoint. But then we saw each other more and more. She was living a very monastic life as an au pair. They locked her up with the child she was attending. The parents didn't occupy themselves with the baby so the only love the child received was from Jette. Jette was into the baby in a big way.

I finished my degree in December 1963. Two months later in February we went to get a marriage license and Jette took the baby with her to the county marriage registry. After obtaining the license, I said jokingly to the registrar, "Now we no longer have to call him 'little bastard.'" Jette has been asking about that baby for years. I finally made some inquiries and found out that he had died a year before at the age of forty-four. He was manic-depressive. "He never smiled," Jette always said. "I always remember him never smiling."

I left Stanford after obtaining my MS degree because I was interested in getting married, getting a job and leading the American dream life. It was the height of the Cold War. I couldn't work in the space or defense areas because I was not a U.S. citizen and these were the innovative growth industries of the Cold War era. So my first professional work was with General Mills in Minnesota, specifically, in quality control. The day we married, we left for the new job in my tiny little red Fiat 500. We drove to Philadelphia and to the New York World Fair—an overwhelming, grandiose affair. We saw Wally and his brother and his family in Washington. I introduced Jette to all of them as they were a big part of my past life. We saw the Jewish drugstore owner whose personality I had eagerly captured, especially his belief that everything had a solution and who attacked all troubles with smiles, verve and optimism. Then we moved to Minneapolis and found an apartment. Maya, our daughter, was born there.

Citizenship, Adversity, and the Social Net

When I began working for General Mills, I wanted to become a citizen, but I could only do that if the employer applied for me. General Mills did, but the condition was that I had to leave the U.S. to pick up a work visa and immigration papers in another country. I was supposed to go to Canada, but it turned out I didn't have to. I became a newly minted green-card carrying immigrant in Minneapolis.

Six months after we married, Jette got ill and was diagnosed with Multiple Sclerosis. She was twenty-two years old. She applied for a green card but she chose not to become a U.S. citizen. When I read up on this disease, I saw it could be a terrible disease. I decided she should not give up her Danish citizenship, because when things got bad she might need to be cared for in Denmark since care is offered to all handicapped people there. We have relied on this scenario during all our forty-eight years of married life, but a few years ago when things got unrelentingly bad, we couldn't execute this master plan. It wasn't a happy solution because our family would be separated. All three of us are together now. I do not know to this day how the chronically ill can lead decent lives without outside financial support. I have a good financial situation, but two-thirds of my retirement income goes to nursing care. The house and car are paid for. We are comfortable. But I am worried that we may outlive our money. I am seventy-six now and Jette is sixty-eight but with the same youthful and innocent smile as when we first met. I often feel strangled by the disease. Not because I regret the limitations of the past, which we overcame as best as we could but because of the hopelessness of it all. It is a difficult issue. I can't get myself to put her in a nursing home either here or in Denmark.

I've done fairly well financially and for about three thousand dollars a month we were able to bring over here Danish au pairs who came mainly for the foreign travel and adventure but maintained themselves by being caregivers. Now Jette needs more intensive care. She has three different machines attached or inserted under her skin and for almost ten years a morphine pump attempts to reduce pain caused by more than forty-four years of sitting in a wheelchair.

We tried to shield our daughter, Maya, throughout her growing up years from much of this shit. For the twenty years after she left home, she felt she needed therapy. We didn't see why she needed therapy but she definitely has benefited in understanding her feelings toward life and her own fate as part of her mother's tragedy. Now in her adulthood she is able to be both engaged with us as well as to carve out her own individual mark in life. She is a research scientist and a frequently published author in highly regarded scientific journals within her fields of interest. From her additional income from her private statistical consulting business she often helps us with major expenditures.

Amazingly, despite what fate dished out to her Jette has not rebelled against her lot in life. She has been able to mentally adjust due to her inner strengths and my hopeful encouragement that they will eventually find a cure. That fantasy is no longer working so she now relies on her memories and stoicism.

From an early age I have felt that chance encounters and outcomes are a major determinant in one's fate. Lots of people have varying degrees of misfortunes, all relative, and it is important to put them into perspective and not to feel sorry for oneself. With me, I've never expected much of life, not nirvana nor eternal happiness. If you're constantly fed this imaginary idea about a perfectly happy life, then I think it is more difficult to live in adversity.

The pressure of this disease is such that we don't always reflect on the best in ourselves. I am short tempered but we both recognize our deep commitment, even in the days when we may not like how we behave to each other. We have talked about joint suicide many times. It is no joy to handle these issues. She talks about it more than I do, perhaps four times to one of mine, and often asks me to help her end her life. At those times, she says it's not worth living this way, but her depressions, which have a credible base but no rational solutions, tend to be short lived.

Our Daughter

Maya and I bonded very early in her life. Within the first week of Maya's life, Jette was using crutches. As she could not keep her balance when moving and transporting Maya in our apartment, she sat down in the wheelchair and put our daughter into her lap. Jette never left the wheelchair; that was forty-four years ago. Thus, from Maya's first month, I bathed her, fed her at night and would take her for the first strolls of her life. She was a skinny baby with a very well-formed little round head and red hair. On these strolls I would compare her to all the fat babies and conclude that she was the most beautifully formed baby.

My daughter sees herself as very American and is deeply concerned with the world around her. She has a very close relationship with Denmark and with the Danish side of her family. She speaks fluent Danish. I didn't pick it up in all these years where my household buzzed with Danish. They don't enunciate the words; just half grunts. Maya is also very loyal to her Jewish roots. She is not a Zionist, though. We have different views on this. I very much admire her character and values as well as her achievements and am proud that she chose a career in public health rather than purely pecuniary pursuits.

Bankruptcy

I created a computer business in the travel industry employing seventeen people including four sales offices. It was growing fast and doing well, but then the airlines, competing with each other, entered the field. It was a fierce fight between unequals, and as I had a lot of debt I was unsuccessful trying to play in the big leagues. I had to abrogate part of the debt. I had a small business loan of three-quarters of a million dollars. I divorced Jette and left everything in her name so it would be protected from creditors.

From day one after our divorce we continued to live together. She had no relation to the business so banks couldn't take the house away as it was in her name. I hid behind this legal facade and settled with the bankers and the government, which had guaranteed the loan, through a long-term repayment arrangement. Subsequently, I got a job in my original field, statistics, taught at university level at Emory and Morehouse, worked for the federal government in the health and disability area and paid taxes for another fifteen years.

Dual Citizenship

I think Americans have difficulty understanding experiences in lives of others because in the context of the last half century, Americans have enjoyed an unprecedented historical period of world-wide progress, in no small part due to America having charted a more humane life system than any other of the many past and powerful empires. To this day the U.S.'s vision is the one most wished for, craved for and copied.

I don't think my loyalties can be judged in a vacuum. My inner self is at home only in the United States or in Israel. If I had to choose at random an American or Israeli to admire more, I don't think I could choose based on nationality but on the person's achievements and humanity.

If my dual citizenship is questioned or tested, it's helpful to be logical and factual to exclude unreliable emotions. Are you going to support Israel? The U.S.? I can clearly divide these seeming contradictory issues in any particular situation by whether in that instance I logically side with the American or Israeli positions. There is no conflict because nothing is in a vacuum but in some sort of relationship and common sense is a better guide than prickly feelings. If you asked me, "If Israel and the U.S. went to war against each other, who would you support?" My answer would be simple—I always hope to be able to choose the winning side.

every concept by the question "What
to anybody will its truth

PLAMEN RUSSEV

Interviewed by Heather Tosteson

I FEEL MY ROLE IS TO BE A NEVER-ENDING LABORATORY

Childhood in Bulgaria

I was born in Stara Zagora, which is in the middle of the country, halfway between Sofia and the Black Sea. It's near the Rose Valley and is one of the larger cities in Bulgaria, fifth in size. It has a pretty good cultural life and a rich history. The city has had eight names throughout history, including Old Bulgarian, Slavic, Thracian, Greek, Turkish, so it is very much aware of its history. There was a building with all eight names of the city in a mural painted on its side, and as a kid I loved looking at that as I was into geography and enjoyed saying the foreign sounding names. Stara Zagora was razed a few times, so it is a modern city now built on a grid and visually there are no clues to its history. But it's all there, right under the surface. For example, when they were expanding the old post office building, they discovered Roman frescoes and built an atrium around them.

I grew up during very closed-off times in Bulgaria. There was a thirst in people for knowledge outside what was allowed. There was a strong urge and drive to get more information, to get to the *truth*. All official information was censored. The same stories ran in all the newspapers and on the radio and TV. It didn't matter where you saw or heard them, they were all the same, endless redundancy.

It was endlessly frustrating. People felt they were being treated like idiots. In the 1970s and 1980s people were becoming very aware of how much the regime was suppressing any contact with the wider world, especially the West, and many intellectuals engaged in a form of *mental emigration*. In their minds, they started imagining living abroad, usually in the "free West." There is an old Bulgarian saying that "a book is a window to the world" because it shows us things we may never be able to see with our own eyes. Learning languages, I realized that every language is a *door* into the world. Intellectuals learned languages to tap into every idea they couldn't find at home. Everyone was reading between the lines. Writers *wrote* between the lines. Key characters in our films at that time were speaking between the lines.

I was definitely acting along Bulgarian operational lines when I came to the U.S. Even now I am very tuned into the unspoken. But in Bulgaria it is a survival skill. Here, where it is a more open form of communication, seemingly having no oppressive forces, we end up substituting other oppressive stories. Here it could be your religious beliefs. So I am very tuned into the unsaid. I also prize speaking openly and clearly, which seems to be an American value.

In high school, I began my own mental emigration at the end of my first year there. I had been studying English forty hours a week and by the end of the year I was fluent. One day, as I was riding on the train back from Sofia, I found myself thinking in English. We started learning Russian in kindergarten, and the study became more intensive from third grade through the end of junior high. Then, I went to a foreign language high school—a Western languages (rather than a Russian language) high school. It was very elite, very selective and provided outstanding academic and language instruction in English, French and German. You had tough entrance exams and had to have the highest scores to get into the English department because everyone wanted to study English as their primary Western language. In addition, we continued studying Russian and had to choose one more Western language. So by the time I graduated from high school, I was fluent in English and Russian and had three solid years of first-year German because I ended up being the only one in my class who consistently wanted to learn German year after year.

Throughout that time, overall there was a sense of repression, suppression. People couldn't breathe. There was only a very tiny box in which they had to fit. It was a very fractured experience for everyone. Publicly you had to be one way. Only with your closest friends could you speak your mind more openly. None of that was allowed or tolerated elsewhere. We learned very early on what we had to say publicly and what we could say at home.

Sense of National Identity

There was a lot of shame about being Bulgarian at that time. Bulgaria has a rich and long history, but the focus tends to be on the Ottoman domination (which lasted five centuries). We were ashamed of large chunks of our history, especially when we were parts of various other empires, and we felt great pride in the times when Bulgaria itself seemed like an empire, such as in the thirteenth century when its borders were washed by three seas. There was a sense of deep shame but also of grandeur.

The sense of shame continues until today. Shame comes from where we are, on the *edge* of Europe. Even a very recent Bulgarian film refers to Bulgaria as the place "where Europe ends but never begins." There is a strong desire to be part of Europe, but it coexists with the belief that we're not exactly as *they* are. There is a value judgment there, an assumption that the West is better. And there is shame in our petty ways of being that are common—in the small tricks and petty theft of ordinary people and the grand theft of the (now elected) politicians, shame that we're not living a life of integrity. The shame is a cauldron that holds all those things.

There is also genuine pride in being both European and non-European. It is a split identity. Listening to a mix of Bulgarian music I just made, I hear how intense it is to be Bulgarian. You can feel it in the music, which can be very classical and then wildly, exotically Eastern.

How do we forge an identity that allows all this to coexist? Shame makes us feel and act very small. Can we use that to fuel our growth somehow?

Childhood and Family

I am an only child. My mother is a professional musician. My father is a civil engineer, but he also used to sing in one of the amateur choirs in Stara Zagora. My father's father was one of the founders of the city opera, where my mom worked. My mom started me playing the piano at four and a half. It was too early. I totally did not feel the music. I played like a robot, without any emotion. It was total torture—both for me and for my mom. I played the piano for ten years. Mom was very persistent because she saw it as a discipline, and music was also her passion. But she stayed open to changing her ideas of what I could become. When it was obvious that I would not be a virtuoso pianist, she began to say that I still needed to learn the piano because I was going to be a great conductor.

But when she noticed later on how I was responding to languages, she could let go of my becoming a famous musician. It gave her peace that I would be really good at something. I do have a good musical ear, which is probably why she persisted. But in general my mother was more of a driver when it came to my intellectual development. My dad was more observant, a provider. He would take on additional work to provide us with as much material comfort as he could.

Materially, I grew up very comfortably, or as comfortably as was possible in Bulgaria at that time. You can tolerate many inconveniences.

My parents still live there. They had different relationships with the regime. My dad looked at it as a huge inconvenience. He did the best he could to navigate the system without getting too involved with it. My mother had a more complex relationship. For the sake of her child, she was willing to work with the system. She became a member of the Communist Party so I would be able to go to the Western languages school and then a good university. She was ready to sacrifice her beliefs for her child. My dad would say, "I just can't sell my soul to the devil," referring to the Communist Party. And my mom would answer, "For my child, yes!"

But then it became immaterial because, by the time I finished high school, it had all collapsed. By the time I graduated high school in 1991, the world had been reshaping itself for about two years.

Decision to Study Abroad

I grew up with the idea I was going to study abroad. Both my mom and my dad almost expected it and talked about it since I was very young. My paternal grandfather had studied in Germany. In the larger scheme of what it meant to be Bulgarian, toward the end of the Ottoman Empire and after its collapse, many Bulgarians started going to Western Europe for their higher education. At that time, our national identity centered on the notion that getting a good education wherever available, including abroad, was an indication of being a good Bulgarian. That idea was deeply ingrained into intellectuals. My grandfather couldn't complete his studies in 1930s Germany because of Hitler's rise to power. So perhaps in my family's perspective, I was going to complete something that he was not able to do.

Originally, during communism, my options were to study in Moscow or Berlin. I was going to study foreign relations to become a diplomat, which is why it was important for me to study abroad. But it wasn't just that. This interest in foreign lands felt like it was mine from very early on.

When I was a child, I spent hours with my head buried in a small political atlas "traveling" around the world. I loved all the different colors designating different countries and the sounds of the names of foreign countries and cities. I loved discovering that not every country had the same language.

At seven, I remember listing every country I could name and declaring I would learn its language, perhaps starting with the countries surrounding Bulgaria—Greek, Turkish, Macedonian, Serbian, Romanian.

By the time I was finishing high school, the Berlin Wall had fallen and my foreign options were no longer limited to Russia and Germany. So I wrote to many schools in the U.K. and in the U.S. I applied to many and I was admitted to many. But only Harvard had a need-blind admission process that ensured that, once you received an offer of admission, the school would do everything possible to help you with financial aid so you could attend. And that is what made it possible for me to start my studies there.

In high school, I frequently went to Sofia to spend at least a part of my school vacations with my aunt and uncle. I would visit the press center of the U.S. Embassy. It had a library with glossy magazines, one of which, *Spectre,* was a digest of various articles from U.S. magazines translated into Bulgarian that they gave away. I remember reading an article about Harvard on my train ride back to Stara Zagora at the end of one winter break, and I felt a very strong but deeply buried desire in my heart. I secretly hoped that one day I would be able to visit this amazing university, just to walk through it.

So, a few years later, when I received a telegram that said "Congratulations on admission to Harvard," I was incredulous. It was the first U.S. college application I had ever filled and sent out. I had received the application from Harvard just a week before it was due, so I felt that I might not even be considered and had turned all my hopes to attending the University of Chicago.

Coming to the U.S.

When I came to Boston, I thought, *The grass is greener and the sky is bluer here, how do they do it?* I was so excited and thrilled. My parents were excited for me too. Only later did I realize what deep pain it had been for them to see me leave home so young, especially for my mom. But we were all very aware that it would take years to clean up the post-communist mess in Bulgaria so I was better off coming to the U.S.

About two weeks into classes, I found myself completely exhausted at the end of each class. I wasn't used to American accents (only British accents) and American students seemed to mumble and use endless strings of unfamiliar colloquialisms. I had to reach another level of fluency. I was fluent, but in a rather bookish English.

The thing that really made the experience good was that I had a structure and a reason why I was here in the U.S. But I used it to limit my experience as well. I thought, I'm here to study. I can't disappoint my parents and others by wasting my time on things that have nothing to do with studying. I perfected being terribly harsh on myself. Before, Mom and Dad had mirrored that for me, but I reached an entirely new level at Harvard. It was up to me to stay focused, and I didn't allow myself many deviations from my purpose.

I found it all very rewarding, but I intensified the pressure. I didn't really know how to take unplanned breaks. However, Saturday was my sacred no-study day. I would explore a different part of Boston or Cambridge. Parties made me uncomfortable—everyone was drinking cheap smelly beer. Eventually, my life became a more nuanced experience as I realized that this was my real life now, it wasn't just a transitional stage. Early on, I made pretty good friends with two of my roommates, but not the one with whom I was sharing a bedroom. He was a mechanistic science whiz but difficult to relate to. He was from California, and he liked walking in the snow in flip-flops. It triggered my harsh judgmentalism.

I never liked bumping up against the limits of my knowledge, but Harvard does that. So, I had to intensify my efforts and dig deeper into my studies. Some of my friends were living in the same way. But I didn't share my inner experience with anyone. It was very rewarding and very lonely. I was continuing that split that was so important in Bulgaria where the public appearance is safe and perfect and the inner experience is hidden and not expressed.

I ended up creating an intellectual cocoon, familiar but not necessarily comfortable. It did allow deep and expansive growth intellectually. I majored in social studies, which is an honors-only major (i.e. you have to write a senior thesis to graduate from it). You had to apply to get into it because of its intense academic requirements. Of course, I had to choose one of the most intense concentrations. It kept other aspects of my life at bay.

But they all came rushing in after I left college.

Remaining in the U.S. after College

After graduating, I spent my summer working in Cambridge and then I got a job in Atlanta with an Anglo-French company. All its clients were in Latin America. I'd learned Spanish in college. (I took one language class every semester, so I could relax, play and have fun while still studying and learning new things. It was a form of self-care. My senior year, as a special treat, I took two language courses.)

In Atlanta, there wasn't this focus on academic performance. It was a new city, a new setting, a new job. I had a couple of friends from college. I began to meet people, to stay in relationship.

At first I tried to do what I had done in college—study and focus. This was an IT job and I had not had a single computer class in college, so I felt I had to prove my intellectual agility, and in this way it was allowing me to replicate my college experience. But the move was also requiring me to face another big part of my life.

There was no way I could have been out as a gay person growing up in Bulgaria in those days. There wasn't a single positive reference to gay people in Bulgaria. As soon as I got the message, *This isn't right*, I knew I could never let anyone know. But here I was in the U.S. now. Many people were out in college, but I was scared of them. I thought they would know about me, sniff me out somehow. Any relationship to me felt very scary. To be in relationships with women felt fraudulent and I couldn't do that. I kept imagining, but I was terrified in real life.

In Atlanta, I was lonely without companionship. Confronting this loneliness, I thought a relationship might be a way through it. It took me a few years, even after dating, to finally come out to myself. I was just experimenting, I told myself.

In Bulgaria there may have been something in the criminal code about homosexuality, but more important was that early on I noticed that it wasn't OK. I buried this part of myself so deeply my parents had no clue until I came out to them in 2005. I kept hoping they would have figured it out by then, but they hadn't. When I did come out, they were able to respond with great love and affection. When I saw that, I felt sad about what I had deprived myself of in my relationship with them during all those years.

Living in Atlanta allowed me to come out in ways I couldn't in Bulgaria. Jacob Needleman says that the essence of the U.S. is a space that allows you to find an authentic expression of the completeness of being human: the U.S. allows the exploring of spiritual paths.

It was certainly easier to accept myself and come out when I had spiritual awareness. In communist Bulgaria we were all atheists. Being Christian was dangerous.

The Atlanta gay scene was more open and I had space to explore and come out. But it was also a rather conventional gay scene that turned its back on our spiritual side. I became quite alienated from the gay scene. I got tired of being seen as a piece of meat—desired or discarded, it was the same dynamic. It was such a narrow way of relating, stiflingly narrow. I am interested in being in a conscious relationship and this year I feel that I found my tribe through a group called Gay Spirit Visions (GSV). It was a transformational contact for me. After the first gathering I realized that, for the first time I had been surrounded by gay men in a social setting who related to me as a human being, not as a piece of meat. They have seasonal conferences, the last of which was in the North Carolina mountains, with about a hundred people. It was clear to me that every man who was there was consciously attending to his own development as a whole person. It is a community of truly kindred spirits. And that experience allowed me to start melting away the shame that came from my prior experience of being gay. I realized that I had a very narrow experience of being gay that had been limited to the very predictable and monotonous interactions and conversations that took place in bars, clubs and houseparties. Thanks to GSV and the meaningful human contact I can have there, I am finally experiencing life as a gay person in much richer, fuller and integrated context.

And that is one of the deep appeals for me of being in the U.S.—it allows me to find and give honest expression to my full being in all of its dimensions.

Cultural Allegiances and U.S. Citizenship

Bulgaria is part of the European Union, but it is still very backwards in some respects. All of Eastern Europe is very backwards with LGBT issues. And there are all these other European Union countries where gay marriage is legal and has equal standing with heterosexual marriage. It is an interesting situation because, as a European Union citizen, you are not confined to the situation in only one state or country.

But this question doesn't influence my applying for U.S. citizenship. There is a practical dimension to my interest in doing this. I haven't applied before because of technicalities that had to do with changing my visa status at different points. Once I have U.S. citizenship I will not need to maintain a certain number of days being physically present in the U.S. If I am away for a long period of time, there won't be consequences that U.S. residents (i.e. not citizens) face. So, I guess the immediate effect of having U.S. citizenship is that it would allow me *not* to be here. Because I wouldn't *have* to be here, it would allow me to make a more conscious choice to be here. I will have dual citizenship. Bulgaria allows dual citizenship and I am not interested in throwing away my E.U. citizenship.

To be a dual citizen would be appealing. It gives me the flexibility and freedom to be in either country or continent.

Given my interest in life coaching now, I am interested in being in the place where I can be of greatest service. If I were in Bulgaria, it would be interesting to see how my being a U.S. citizen might help support that work, whether it might open up a door for professional development and contact, perhaps it might even allow me to be a cultural ambassador between the LGBT community there and the U.S.

Emigration from Bulgaria

A good number of my high school classmates have left Bulgaria, perhaps twenty to thirty percent. We had good access to other countries because of our language skills. There are very few people who have gone back to Bulgaria. Of my two best friends from high school, one is in New York and the other is in Malta. After that first immigration wave, not so many Bulgarians are going to the U.S. now. Most are going to other countries in Europe instead.

Immigrants and Friendship

About a third of my friends are immigrants, but being an immigrant from Bulgaria can be radically different from being an immigrant from Switzerland, for example. I think people who have never immigrated can understand the immigration experience but with difficulty, as a mental construct, not through sharing an actual experience. Having said that, I'm quite aware that the majority of people have had the experience of otherness, of being an *other*. It looks like privilege in some cases, but it is mostly a liability these days. And some people don't even acknowledge that experience of otherness.

Languages

In college I added Spanish, French, and Portuguese to my languages, and I can fake Italian as a result. I've always liked foreign languages. The more I can learn the language of a country, the more it enriches my experience there. For example, I've noticed that in France, if you can pull off the accent, people are quite forgiving of your grammar and will pull you into all sorts of interesting conversations. But when I tried to learn and speak Mandarin, I had a hard time getting the different tones right and frequently got blank stares when I mixed them. It felt a bit like a psychological slap, like a very direct statement: "I have no idea what you're saying regardless of how hard you're trying." And so I constantly felt like an outsider.

When I am learning a new language, early on my thinking is very systematic, so that I can learn the patterns. Once I've become comfortable with the patterns, then I get into the more organic experience and flow of the language, then I can go with the overall sense of things. I have fun with languages, especially in mixing different registers of speaking, but only in English and Bulgarian have I reached that level of fluency.

In my work at one law firm, many of my colleagues were threatened when a colleague and I began to speak Spanish together. I just didn't want to forget my Spanish. But they would usually ask, "What are you saying about us?" It was an intense experience of discomfort for them not to understand what we were saying and, most of the time, it had nothing to do with them anyway.

Civic and Political Participation in U.S.

For a good period of time I was rather indifferent to civic participation. I think my attitude as a long-term resident was, you don't allow me to vote so I don't care. But then I learned that I could vote in some local elections, and I had to reconsider my attitude. Now that I know that, and it is also getting close to my becoming a citizen, I think about it more. This happens at a time when I'm dissatisfied with what I'm seeing happening politically here, so it becomes more important to be able to vote.

I have always been more involved in contributing to social causes than participating in political campaigns. I've also served as an election protection volunteer, as a poll monitor. And I've always felt very proud of this, especially because I can't vote, but I can ensure that U.S. citizens' right to vote is properly observed and exercised.

What I have really been interested in recently is contributing to creating community. I have an awareness of the need to rebuild community, especially conscious gay community, not just locally but globally. Recently I've had a strong need to communicate what I've learned here to LGBT groups or activists in Bulgaria, to write and offer to help. I don't feel it as a requirement, but as a personal need. It is important to me that I can contribute something positive from my own experience.

But going back to Bulgaria requires almost going back into the closet. I'm out to my parents, but not the rest of my family. That would be affecting my parents' lives more than mine, and I don't think I have a right to do that. I am gradually coming out to other very close friends there. My friends and I have found a way of navigating the questions around this so the relationships aren't affected. But if I had a partner, then it would be different.

Studying Law

Getting a law degree was purely an expression of intellectual interest. In my first job, my brain felt like it was turning into mush. I felt I needed to re-engage my mind.

My educational experiences in the U.S. have been at both extremes. I went to Harvard for my undergraduate studies, and then to Georgia State for my law degree. They were such different schools, one a very old and established private university and the other one of the youngest public law schools in the U.S.—thirty years old compared to four hundred years. At both, I got some benefits for being "exotic"—I think one of the reasons I got into Harvard was because I was one of the very few Bulgarian applicants in the early 1990s and I received one of the few scholarships in law school because I was one of the very few Harvard graduates that ever applied there. I felt I got an excellent education at Georgia State College of Law. I was fascinated with what people can create intentionally, and with people studying law as a second or third career. There was a depth and complexity to the students and the experience that wouldn't be there with younger students who go to law school right after college. I didn't even for a moment doubt that it was a good choice for me. I had outstanding and mediocre teachers.

I practiced transactional law—at first commercial lending, then corporate law. The work I do now as a lawyer is on a contract basis. I work with large law firms on specific projects. If it is litigation, I am helping behind the scenes to run the case. It is less intensive of time and energy than other ways of practicing and a good source of income. Law started out as a purely intellectual interest for me, and I found the practice of it difficult because it doesn't always allow you to maintain that intellectual integrity. And, in the meantime, I grew into the need to develop and express more aspects of myself than just my intellect.

I have become very interested in life coaching and breathwork in the last couple of years. I enjoy relating to people in ways that support their development. Life coaching makes sense to me in those terms. I got into it in 2008 after I left my second law firm with the idea of doing cross-cultural consulting. As I was looking at intercultural communication, I ended up discovering some inconsistencies between what people say and do. I was so aware of the same fracturing in me—of the values that I could not embody in my work as a lawyer in a big law firm. I saw it also in cross-cultural practitioners and I didn't want to go there again.

So what I did was make a list of all the ideas I had had about what I wanted to do, the paths I had considered taking—NGOs, social development, European Union institutions, European NGOs, contract lawyer for European firms, translator, interpreter, legal recruiter. I decided to take one step along each path and see what I would discover. In some cases, there was no real path and I had to scratch that option. But because I had so many activities to explore, I would feel a sense of relief. Oh, now I can let that possibility go. Some paths were blocked. Coaching ended up being the path that kept taking me further on and on.

I completed my studies and obtained certification as an Integral Coach with New Ventures West, which has a very holistic approach. Some of the other schools I researched were more transactional, more narrowly interested in achieving specific outcomes. That didn't appeal to me as much. It felt shallow. My interest is in how we support human development in the largest way possible. So far, what speaks to me is coaching, breathwork, and exploring how our narratives shape our experience of life. I like helping people develop new or deeper competencies.

Perhaps for me the U.S. is the place where the definitive answer to any question is not going to be given, but where it is going to be worked out over time. There is a dynamic bonding between perception and belief, between the conscious and the unconscious decision to be a certain way. It is really interesting when conscious commitment comes right in contact with the automatic habit. And in that contact the opportunity for growth, change and expansion arises as we engage in one conscious experiment after another. In some ways, I feel my role is to be this never-ending laboratory.

MARY O'CONNOR

IMMIGRANT

I'm making a home for a seven-and-a-half-foot olive
whose aunt was a eucalyptus: it's dripping with slivers
of sage-y dusty green, and its trunk is straight
and leafless for most of its height. It was a bargain.

I drag it to the bath and give it a shower that wets the whole
room. Still dusty. But I'm going to make a home for it
here in these pale white northern flats, so different
from my wet, temperate and its hot, oily real

home. Nothing I can do about that: I set it beside
the forced heat and give it light and water; I spread
a Chinese mat with roses under it. When I look up
from the mat I can see it shelters me in a spiky distant mood.

Yes, it will do as a tree to sit under, uncomfortable, awkward
in my tastefully furnished living room where nothing clashes.
Now you're here, tree, let us be uncomfortable together,
and see what it is like to just be a me and a tree

cut off from our natural environments, each out of place
in this place. A tree to sit under and refuse to know
anything wise. A tree to sit under, gazing out
over the furniture I've massed on the living room floor

against the wilderness.

DRIVING WEST ON HIGHWAY 212 TO EAGLE BUTTE, THANKSGIVING DAY

I pitch with the highway's light pitch at 65 miles an hour
tuning to weird stations, slowing for little towns,

passing through expanses of harvested grass and hay
—a house every few miles, with a frightened tree

wrapped round it like a mother. That terrible wind!
"My poor battered house." "My poor guardian tree."

But here is a village of sorts: a field of wooden chalets
Tin-roofed holiday houses that get smaller as I approach—

ah! hog huts for farrowing sows, prosperous in private quarters,
their piglets shielded by the slope of the roof to thrive in their turn.

This is where the deer and the antelope play, and dash themselves
into cars; my eyes are peeled at the gullies on either side, and beyond them

the slopes where the cattle are all black cutouts against the stubbled hillock,
moving stick-legged, ruminant, bending to graze. I hope they're getting

what they need from the prairie. Under the zing of wind in the powerlines,
under the massed clouds keeping their distance, past a field of wrecks proudly

arranged by model and year, past memories unmarked of plunder and
massacre,
past a bare church, St. Basil's, that locks its sacred space close on a yellow
hill.

It is colder. When I get to Eagle Butte, I will answer the door to a woman
needing
gas money to drive her son back to prison after his turkey dinner.

I am clutching the wheel and thrown out on the bank of what happens,
caught up and lost in the movement of the big world.

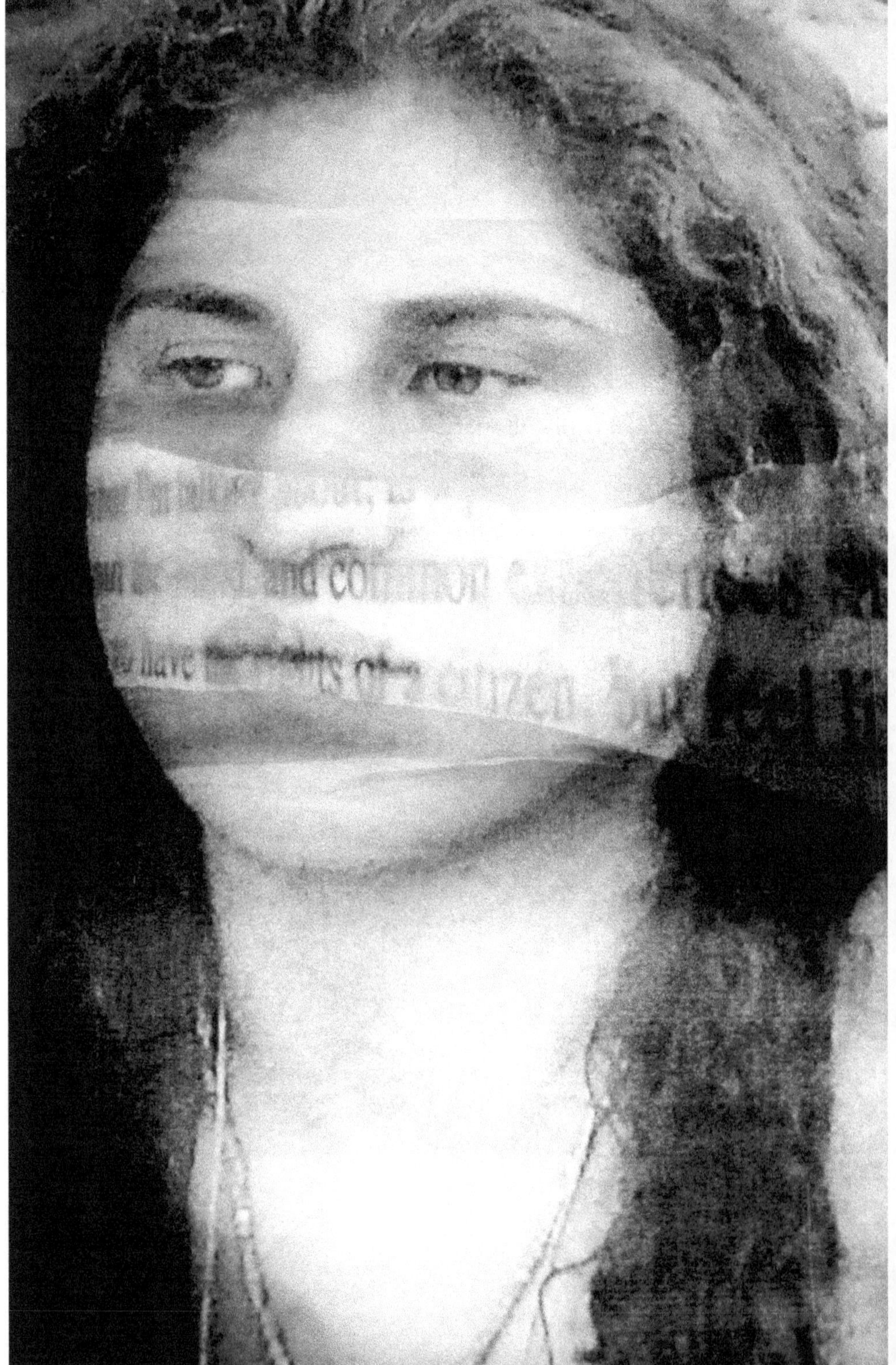
and common
citizen

IV

WHY DO WE GO?

YAR DONLAH GONWAY-GONO

Interviewed by Heather Tosteson

TO ME, EDUCATION IS SACRED

Yar Donlah Gonway-Gono is a naturalized American citizen from Liberia. She has a PhD in Women's Studies. Her dissertation examined acculturation in Liberian women living in Atlanta. In the last year, she has returned to Liberia at the request of its president, Ellen Johnson Sirleaf, to become president of a new community college in Nimba County, one of the areas most affected by the Liberian Civil War. She was first interviewed by phone as she was preparing to leave for Liberia to assume her new position and again, more fully, a few months later when she had returned to celebrate holidays with her family in Minnesota.

When I was talking with the women in my study, they said that coming to America was also an opportunity to see themselves in the culture in which they were raised. This was true of me as well.

Growing Up in Liberia

I grew up in a small town, Flumpa, in Nimba County, the second largest county in Liberia. The emphasis was on the farm, not on education. The first process of growing up was to work with your mother if you were a girl, learning to cook, or with your father if you were a boy. The community of women taught girls how to dress, eat, how to behave.

Later on, my father took us to Lamco, Yekepa, where we settled in Sawmill Camp, a small town of low-income families. He worked at Lamco Vocational Training Center as a security guard. It was a different life. People came from very different walks of life. They were very poor and some worked as housekeepers in rich people's homes. My mother was a housewife and subsistence farmer. Young girls who went to school got pregnant and left very early.

My father was part of the indigenous community, not the

Americo-Liberians. My mother birthed eight children, seven of whom lived. I was very close to my mother and helped take care of my younger brothers and sisters. My father kept me at home to help my mother. My younger brother (Peter) and sister (Yei) both went to school first.

One time, my siblings and I were sick with a cold. The custom was that the company provided some type of document for the worker's children to be treated at a nearby clinic. We went with my father to his place of work for the document. A colleague of my father's asked my father, referring to me in these words: "Is this smart looking little girl going to school?" My father's reply was: "This one will stay at home to help her mother." But the colleague's job was to enroll the workers' children for school and he enrolled me. So in 1968 at the age of eleven, I went to school for the first time. I was in a classroom with children five years old. The names of the children were written on the desks, but I couldn't read so I didn't know where to sit. I understood that if I could not read I would not be able to do anything, so I got my younger brother to teach me the alphabet and the numbers. Once I learned to read and write, school was everything to me. My mother thought my going to school was going to take her help from her. And the neighborhood girls became jealous and they would steal my uniform and books. But when I entered the door of the school, that was all that mattered to me. I did so well that at the end of the year they gave me the sixth grade exam and promoted me to seventh grade.

I developed a passion for learning and took it as opportunity. I was not meant to go to school in my culture and in my family, but I told myself I was going to go on and get as much education as I could.

In eleventh grade, I got pregnant. But I told my family I was going to have the baby and continue with school. I took my baby and found someone to help the baby and continued to go to school. For me, nothing was ever going to stop me from learning. There was something mysterious in it. I was not going to give it up. This help didn't come from my village. No one in my family could read and write, except my younger siblings who went to school before I did. There was something in my being that kept me going. Life was very challenging; I was encouraged to move forward regardless.

At first, because I was really good in science, I wanted to be a medical doctor. My father kept me at home because I was the most caring child. So, I was going to continue my love for caring by being a doctor. After graduating from high school, I wanted go to college. I took several college entrance exams and passed, but did not have a scholarship. I was really desperate and did not want to delay going to college. It was during this time that I found a seminary that was enrolling students. I decided to go and give it a try. When I went to the seminary, I went for the education. I didn't grow up in a Christian family. My family didn't do organized prayer. There were missionaries who came and worked with families like mine, but not my parents. But in high school, my friends were going to the Methodist church. I went to the church and that is how I came across the seminary.

I took the entrance exam for the seminary and passed, but I did not have the money to enroll. The dean said I came in at the top: "We can receive you." But I didn't have a background in Christianity. I thought I would go and do nursing. They kept saying that they would send me to study library science. But in seminary, I began to study and learned to preach. I went into the nearby villages to conduct worship services and preached to the parents in many of the congregations about the importance of education for all their children: "Send your girls and boys to school," I told them.

At this time when I was asked to write about my call to ministry, I got confused and did not know why I was in the seminary. In 1980 it was uncommon for women to attend seminary. The feeling of being out of place kept me confused and I did not know if I was in the right career path. The situation reversed when I went to Monrovia to intern. I worked with Rev. David Tweh Toe who made a difference in my life. He began to teach me about counseling. He encouraged and empowered me to be a good leader. From his mentoring and nurturing me, I realized I didn't only have to do medicine. I could be there and be a healer in the church as well. I then began to mentor adolescent girls and boys as well as troubled teens. Most of my messages have always been about education.

At seminary, one striking thing for me was the question of call. At the end of my internship, I still couldn't answer. I just wanted to keep learning. When I was going back to Gbarnga where the seminary is located, three questions came to me: Do you know *how* you started school? Do you know who helped you? Why? The answer was a Christian family helped me go to school, and I understood that my call to ministry was for me to help other people access something sacred, and that for me, education was sacred.

Coming to the United States

The way I came to the United States was that there was a conference in Monrovia and the main speaker, Major Jones, was from Atlanta, from ITC, the Interdenominational Theological Center. He said that for young Methodists there were scholarships available to study there. I researched and sent in my documents and was accepted to study there. I came in 1986 and studied there for three years and graduated in 1990. Then I spent a year at Candler School of Theology at Emory University and in 1992 entered the doctoral program in women's studies at Emory. I was part of the first group.

I left Liberia with the intention to return to help train pastors. My focus was always education, connecting students with the church and with education. But when I finished at ITC, the war was still going on, so I thought I would return later. When the war ended, I was raising five kids and finishing my doctorate. When I finished, I wanted to serve and to help my family. But I needed to help my own children get an education, at least college degrees, first.

My first real job was at Georgia State, then I went to Wesleyan College for one year. After that I went to Oklahoma to serve an all-white congregation. I love to make history. This congregation had never had a woman pastor, let alone an *African* woman. I told them we are all one in Christ Jesus.

Then my husband took a job in Minnesota. My kids didn't want to live in a small town, so we left Oklahoma and moved to Minneapolis, where I served at Park Avenue Methodist from 2004 to 2008. Then I began to study for a degree in marriage and family therapy. I needed to refresh. Counseling—marriage, divorce, recovery—came easily for me. It was natural for me because I had been there. When I came from Liberia, my first marriage didn't work. I had raised my kids myself. I was nine credits short of my degree when the President of Liberia, Ellen Johnson Sirleaf, asked me to come back and become president of the Nimba County Community College.

When I came to the United States I had three children. I got pregnant in the eleventh grade, as I mentioned, and dropped out and went back to the village to do everything the illiterate people did. The father was a poor school kid. When I finished high school, I had my second child with the same father. When I was in seminary, a pastor in training, I married, and my third daughter was eight months old when I left Liberia to come to study. My other daughters were five and six at that time. When I went to the airport to take off, a woman from the Bishop's office came out and asked me, "Which do you value most, family or education?"

I told her, "Both."

She wanted to discourage me from coming.

I worked hard to bring my daughters here. The first to come were my husband and our daughter, who was then seventeen months. Then I sent for my other two daughters in 1987. I had to pay to have someone fly with them. It cost a lot but it was the only way to bring them safely.

My oldest daughter now works for Georgia Power. She is married and has her own life. My second daughter is a registered nurse. She is married with two daughters. My third daughter is a registered nurse and has a daughter. My older son, who is twenty-two, just graduated from the University of Wisconsin-River Falls. My youngest son, who is nineteen, was enrolled at Fort Valley State University, but did not like it there. He is now planning to train for the Air Force. He was doing marketing and communication in college, but got depressed when we went to Liberia and dropped out.

I had my youngest son when I was in my doctoral program. He is the child of my second marriage. I have been married to my second husband for twenty years. He is a Liberian also.

My second husband became a naturalized citizen in 1979. We went to the same high school in Liberia, but I didn't know him until later. I met him in Atlanta. He was around when my children were young. When he met me, I had done my master's degree and was now accepted in the PhD program. I had four children then. He was fascinated by what I was doing. We came from a similar background. His father died when he was young and his mother raised him. He went to Kennesaw State and earned a degree in business administration. He also studied at the University of Wisconsin-Stout and then worked in Minnesota.

Acculturation in the U.S.

The U.S. was a transforming factor for me as it is for many immigrant women. The U.S. offered opportunity. "What do you African women want with two masters and a PhD?" a female professor at Emory University asked me. "There will be a need for credentials," was my answer. "And there are questions I'm asking in that PhD program that I wouldn't have asked without it. It's my liberation. I don't have to be from a family that has everything to have an education."

When I asked young women in my study, they said they are of both cultures, Liberian and American. They said they take the best from each. From the Liberian, respect for adults and thinking about others. From the

American culture, independence—avenues to develop the self that you are. For me, when looking at parenting of African culture compared to the United States, in indigenous culture, parents expect children to provide for them and have trouble with independence.

Now Liberian culture is a strange culture for me. My way of thinking has changed. I'm more of a servant in my own thinking. All the Liberians are asking me, "Are you going to give this to me?" There is no talk of service.

Naturalized citizenship was important for me because it helped me have security and stability in securing a job and helping my children. If my children were in Liberia, I don't know if they would have finished school. They might have gotten pregnant and stopped. There is a girl who grew up with me, went to school with me, who now has ten children. In the U.S., there is still discrimination. People will always look at me as African. There are advantages and disadvantages to citizenship. It means that you have access to jobs and people can't deprive you of them because of discrimination, and you can't be deported.

But becoming a U.S. citizen doesn't mean that I haven't passed on all that my mother gave me. There has been an important reproduction of parenting. My mother, when I was pregnant, tried to find all the best foods for me. My father raised me to be responsible. I sometimes thought he was very hard on me. He would come home and if there was anything out of order, he would say, "Why are you sitting here? Why can't you sweep?" I thought he was mean. But now I realize that without that I couldn't raise five children and work three jobs.

I have passed much of this on to my own children. My older son (who graduated from college with a degree in finance and economics) was having difficulty in school when I was going through my divorce. His teacher told him, "Tell your mother you can't do a seventh grade job." I told him to tell her, "I can do a seventh grade job." He told the teacher that and we left. I put my study on hold and helped him through summer school, and he had straight A's that year.

Liberian society made me very sensitive to women's issues, especially sexual exploitation. A young man can take another woman, even if he has a family. There are no mentors for women. I was very sad when I was pregnant in the eleventh grade, and my mother told me, "You are so beautiful. You will make it." When my mother told me that it went straight into my brain. I walked in the street and I thought, "I am the most beautiful person on earth."

And I passed this on to my children. And I think I can now pass it on to the students at the Nimba County Community College (NCCC) in Liberia, where I am appointed President. There are thirty-nine high schools in Nimba County. I tell the students, "You sit in life taking this class for granted. But you shouldn't. You should take it for an opportunity."

In seminary, they said, "You are not from a Christian home. You don't belong here." But I told them, "Christ was not for the righteous, but for sinners like me, women with two children." We too could study.

Americo-Liberian and Indigenous

My last name is indigenous. People laughed at me before and said, "You are not a Johnson or a Cooper." In America, we Liberians are all equal. We are all immigrants. We all have an accent. The U.S. was a leveler. Here what matters is how hard you work. In Liberia, people look at you as inferior if you are village born. My ex-husband was an Americo-Liberian. In classes, he would talk about the villages, the village girls. He meant me. But the professor would say, "This village girl is *so* smart."

Recently in Liberia, I was at a group meeting of Americo-Liberian women. A white woman introduced me as the President of Nimba Community College. At the end of the meeting the president of the group passed by me without saying anything. (It was almost like working with some white people here at the Minnesota and Oklahoma Conferences.) I ran to the leader, introduced myself and gave her my card and said, "I'm sure we will work together." When people are lost, they act like they are so important.

But the indigenous community itself is very divisive. There are ethnic cleavages and conflict as well as many other issues of disunity. It's not just tensions between Americo-Liberians and the indigenous. Liberians in general are divided based on many factors.

Now people consider me Americo-Liberian because of my education. In Liberia, and even in the United States, I am isolated by my education. They run away because of my PhD. Even women.

My husband now works as an environmental health and safety manager at a mining company in Yekepa, Nimba. He was willing to go back to Liberia. He went back before me in 2009. Even though I wanted to go back, I had three granddaughters. I said I wouldn't go until I was called.

Even as a naturalized citizen, I still wanted to return to Liberia to help. I have siblings and nieces and nephews there. I feel I can have a home in both places. Minnesota is my home too. I fell in love with snow when I came here. I look at what is good in America and what is not. Generally, there is a giving spirit in America that I really embrace. At the same time there is a selfish spirit too. There are some people who define living only through themselves.

Africa is meant to be a communal society. There is communal parenting and sharing, but we have lost it all. Many of the elites who were mission trained and colonized still think and act as though they are better than others. I think people who behave and think like that are lost. That is part of what I don't like. I like leadership, but I think it is wrong to worship leaders. The lack of autonomous thinking in Liberia—I don't like it. Everything is group. At least if you have a point of view, then it can be respected. But it is a long socialization process for people to think that an individual point of view is available. There is a real fear of being isolated.

Returning to Liberia

My place is to go there not just to run the community college but also to improve the community for women and girls so that they can see themselves differently. People think I am dismantling things, just by being who I am. It is possible to become labeled, isolated. I feel lost in the culture in which I was born and raised. My whole professional life doesn't fit there. I have to let go of some parts of that.

My current experience is teaching me that this experience I have had in the United States, the education I have been able to have, means so much. When I go to schools, they call the girls to come and see. Wow! I didn't know the PhD meant something. Women want to call men "Doctor." When I go places, no one cares about me until people call me "Dr. Gono." Then they look at me differently. (And charge me more in the market!)

When I went back in October of last year, President Sirleaf had a press conference. I didn't know that some of the biggest political figures in Nimba County had applied for the job. Two men began to write about how my appointment is political, even though I have never met President Ellen Johnson Sirleaf. "She has not written any book," they said. "The first college in Nimba, and the president is a woman," they said. They thought I didn't have the experience. They don't know anything about me. They don't know what it is to pastor 2,000-3,000 people, many of them doctors and professors. They don't know anything about me. I'm occupying positions that only

Nimba men and Nimba politicians have held. These are the guys who have destabilized Liberia.

I see my job as expanding and integrating. I come as an indigenous, but not really: I've learned that you have to be prepared, systematic. That is a value from here (the U.S.). Even though the leadership team is all from Liberia originally, it is different for me. They will tell you something that isn't true but which, just by saying it they're getting to feel sure it is true—for example, that a particular building is a bank, when it isn't. Or they will say we're doing well—when we're not. We are all learning. I am learning too.

In interviews, often people don't look at me. One young man, he kept looking out the window. I told him, "Why are you talking to me and looking somewhere else? Who are you talking to? I am the only one here." I told him four times. He asked, "Are you saying that my culture is being used against me?" It is true that we don't look at our elders, but I told him four times. He needed to learn something new.

Part of the value I maintain here is the value of human rights. People can't beat their wives or steal and get away with it.

After twenty-five years away, I look like an outsider. Even at the market, people inflate their prices. While walking in Sanniquellie, I met this guy who did that and asked me, "Where are you from?"

"I'm from Flumpa. I'm Mano," I told him.

He said, "You're not!"

Just in time my older sister arrived and introduced me to the man. "Meet my sister who came from America."

The man replied, "I knew it."

They look at you and know you are not from Liberia.

Aftermath of War

Nimba County suffered a lot in the war. But people are also using the war as an excuse for failure. Just like black people in the U.S. use slavery as an excuse. I say, "There is no war. Sirleaf has brought repatriation." There are also people in Nimba who are thriving. Lots of adults and younger people are leading businesses.

My daughters ask me about my siblings, "Mama, why do they beg so much?"

I see my siblings in the same houses they had with my father. I think of my father, how he wouldn't be recruited for slave labor, how he moved away instead. But his brothers and sisters were different. Many of my cousins never went to school. I see they are so old now. If my father hadn't moved away and sent for us, maybe we would never have had our opportunity.

ALAN MASTERS
Interviewed by Heather Tosteson

TWENTY-EIGHT YEARS AND COUNTING
The Decision Was, and Still Is, Incremental

Alan Masters is an ecologist who has lived and worked in Monteverde, Costa Rica for most of his adult life. For the past fifteen years he and his wife have directed an international studies abroad program there. Alan originally came to Monteverde as a graduate student in 1983. In his years in Monteverde he helped found the Cloud Forest School to provide environmentally focused, bilingual education for members of both the U.S. expat and Costa Rican community living there.

Growing Up in Chicago: The Limits of Experience

I grew up in a suburb of Chicago. It was a pretty affluent suburb. Quiet. I lived there through high school. I didn't travel much as a child. This was in the 1960s and 1970s. No one I knew had even been on an airplane except my grandmother. We went on car trips. My dad had been in the army in Germany but didn't talk about it. It wasn't in our vocabulary.

Where I came from, there was a very local view of the world. When you grew up, you were probably going to live in a suburb very close by. It was a *very* local view. My family went to places like Missouri. That was very far away. Or Wisconsin. I had this grandmother who was a globetrotter to us. She went to Florida sometimes and even to Europe. But that was unusual. And none of my friends had been traveling like that. It was something other people did.

I didn't even think of going to college until my junior year in high school. My father was a high school drop out. My mom barely finished high school. My father didn't think college was necessary. He was not encouraging. On the other hand, he wouldn't stop us. In our world, at eighteen you were on your own, so you could do what you wanted. And my dad did have a point. There were five of us. Three went to college and two didn't, and the ones that didn't make more money than those of us who went. My mother wasn't discouraging. She was more of an "Oh, whatever you want to do, darling" mother. The assumption was that you were following your calling.

The brother just ahead of me was always in Spanish club and taking Spanish lessons in high school. My younger brother and I tore him apart about it. We tore him apart for having dreams. I don't know why we did that. He hung out with the international students at our high school. They'd all get together at our house sometimes.

He applied and was accepted to study for a summer somewhere in South America—maybe Ecuador? He even received a scholarship. But my dad was unwilling to cover his living expenses. My brother was heartbroken. I remember feeling bad for him. I didn't think my father was right to be so tight.

In college, my brother was a linguistics major. He was hell-bent on going abroad. It was his dream. He was an inspiration, yes, but he also was thwarted. I saw both.

He finally did go abroad. When he was studying linguistics, he went in with Spanish as his first language. He had to choose a second, non-Romance language. The people at that time who could pay most for tutoring, which is how he helped support himself, were Arab speakers. He became friends with them, converted to Islam, and they arranged a Kuwaiti marriage for him. Now he lives in Kuwait, has five sons, and teaches English at the University of Kuwait. He never made it to a Spanish-speaking country.

All his children are U.S. citizens.

Funny. I really did pick on him for speaking Spanish and eating weird food. Now, I'm speaking Spanish and living in Costa Rica. But in high school I chose to take Latin—for medical school. I remember my guidance counselor saying Spanish and Italian were close to Latin but *living* languages—and I told her I was never going to live outside the country and stuck to my guns and studied Latin.

Choosing Ecology: Broadening Horizons

I went into undergrad as a premed major. I considered biology a route to medical school. I liked it, learned it easily. But it was through those classes that I first thought of going abroad. In my third year, I took general ecology. I thought it was a pollution club, that kind of stuff—air contamination, river pollution. But it wasn't. It was about non-human species in a natural community context. Trees. Butterflies.

I went to Illinois Southern University in Normal, Illinois. It was a Mayberry-like town. But there I was, in the middle of the winter, looking at slides of butterflies in Ecuador. I saw those slides and I knew I wanted to be there. It wasn't for culture, history or language—I wanted to see a tropical rain forest. I talked to a professor about grad school and I ended up going to the University of Florida, where he had gone. I submitted many applications and got accepted everywhere, but I decided to go to Florida because it was halfway to the tropics; so if I didn't get to Ecuador, I'd at least get to see some tropical forest.

When I went to Florida to graduate school was the first time I saw the ocean. I drove. I still had never been on an airplane. The first semester one of my professors had a grant and had funds for fieldwork. He told me, "But you'll have to be in the field in December." That sounded all right. They were looking at Monarch butterflies, where they spent the winter. So it was high altitude, not tropical, but that was ok with me. We went for a month and a half. We drove from Florida through the Panhandle, Alabama, Louisiana, Texas. There's a little strip of tropical rainforest on the Gulf Coast of Mexico, so I did see some. We went through the desert and then into a high mountain system *covered* with butterflies. It was exotic. We were camping all the time. I loved doing the research, but socially, well, it was a group of biologists, and, you know, they're rather odd ducks.

But I liked the camping and being in nature. Where I grew up there were nature preserves, but they were places of drugs and crime. We were discouraged from going there. So, I really enjoyed my contact with nature. But it was only a month. Then I was back in school.

Monteverde, Costa Rica

I applied for a two-month summer course in Costa Rica. Eight weeks of study. I flew down. My first plane, and my first experience doing research with people my own age. This was great. We were moving from place to place. Working fourteen-hour days. Exposed to many things. One place we visited was Monteverde, and I just knew that was where I was meant to study—and there was money for participating in the program there.

So of the twenty students in that program, two were given fellowships to return. I received one of them. You had to submit a proposal to gather preliminary data for your thesis project. So the next summer I returned to gather preliminary data and then I submitted a bigger proposal. When I was there, I met my future wife, who was also working there. She was from Michigan and had just finished her undergraduate degree and was working as a field assistant to two biologists. We fell in love.

She stayed and I went back to Florida, then came back the following year, 1985.

She applied to Florida for graduate school and took courses there in 1985-1986. I was a little worried when she applied to the same school, just in case the relationship might not work out, but it did. We returned together in 1986. I had funding for two years of straight fieldwork, and we have been here since then pretty much constantly.

How We Came To Stay

We never figured we'd live here permanently. We were just thinking of the next stages of our studies. By then, we had friends, knew people. It was like renting a house and *living* there, nesting and playing house, not like camping in a field station. We could pretend to be adults. We had a dog. We wanted to be biologists but we still wanted to be people too.

We each did our own research and also helped each other out. There were about ten biologists here and we'd get together weekly to discuss our work. It was good for us. Monteverde is a Quaker community. It is English speaking, and I didn't speak Spanish at that time, so it worked for me.

Our decision to live in Monteverde was incremental. When we left in 1988, my wife Karen was pregnant with twins. The pregnancy was unplanned, but we weren't bothered. We were committed to each other. We married in Monteverde in March, so when we returned to the U.S., we were married with two on the way. The babies were born in August. Karen dropped out of graduate school for a year but completed her degree a year to the day after the twins were born.

She didn't want to do her doctorate in Florida, so we went to Princeton. I had finished my doctorate and could go where we needed. In 1990 when she needed to do her fieldwork, our decision was influenced by the fact that we *knew* Monteverde. We could get childcare. I could get a job there. The twins were three years old by that time.

The work I did is what I do now, teaching undergraduates through CIEE, the Council on International Educational Exchange. At that time, it was just a summer program, not a full-year program, but it was enough money. I also taught in the University of California program. So we spent two years here for Karen to get her fieldwork done. At the end of those two years, CIEE asked me if I wanted to direct their full-time semester program. I told CIEE that I would do it for two years. I thought, after Karen's finished, we'll see what we do next.

But by then, the twins were eight years old. We asked ourselves, do we want to go back to the States, put them in after-school? One or the other of us would have to do a postdoc. It is hard for couples with degrees in the same area to find work in geographical proximity. You need to find different universities in the same place. That's not easy. And it would mean a divided family, everybody struggling. Or we could stay here in Monteverde with a job we could share, with help with the kids.

The kids were now in school, speaking Spanish. We didn't want them to lose that, so we decided we would direct this program. We built a house in 1997. I think that was the point where we committed consciously to living here, but only until the boys finished high school. But they've finished, in fact they've finished college, and we're still here. So I guess we must have made another decision somewhere. Now we just have to deal with mid-life crises! *Is this the right career?* The answer is, it is. If we got fired, we feel we could get another job. If that happened, we might go back to the States. We talk about going somewhere else—the Amazon, Ecuador. We live in a remote place, but it has lots of artists, PhDs, English and Spanish speakers. It was rural when we came, but to go back to not having a phone—honestly, now that would be hard.

Monteverde

If there was no Monteverde, I don't know that I could live in Costa Rica. I think Monteverde is what I fell in love with. But a small liberal town in a conservative area might have a similar feel—Austin, where one of my sons lives now, or Gainesville in Florida.

I know making Costa Rican friends was very difficult at first. There were so many things—language, culture, have and have-nots, education and economics—that kept us apart.

The Quakers didn't know the language and the culture. They were poor when they came. But we share many values. Without the Quakers it would be hard to spend so much time here. The same with the biologists. So many elements that worked for me converged in this little town.

Monteverde used to work well for jacks-of-all-trades. If you were interested in pioneering, and we were then, it was great. Your sink breaks, you fix it. Your roof leaks, your car breaks, you fix it. It speaks to a pioneering spirit and that was what I was into then. Remember those *Foxfire* books that taught you how to make everything? I read all of them. And we lived it. We had a wood-burning stove and a hot plate. We had sugar, flour, and a Fannie Farmer cookbook from the late 1800s because that is the one that worked for us. I guess it was like the early 1970s for some people. I'm a little too young for that, but we were living that hippy ideal of living off the land. I *wanted* to do that.

And, at the same time, Monteverde always had artists, writers, coffee houses, skits, charades, Scrabble on Friday and bridge on Wednesday. It was a retirement community for all ages. Granted, one with mock cheesecake made with leftover curd from the dairy.

It's a quirky place with quirky people. I've known people for so long now, they've seen our children grow up. There is a depth in all these relationships that I like. All these surrogate parents and grandparents. This more than compensated for its limits. The town is so small you *can't* burn bridges and I like that. If people make you angry in the States, even in a small town, you can write them off. Someone here may be angry with you, but you're teaching their children violin in the afternoon or you have a winch to pull them out of a ditch. You have to be more forgiving.

Residency and Citizenship

My sons are U.S. citizens. Until 1997, we were not committed to living here. It is difficult to get residency, but in those years you could have ninety days on a tourist visa before you had to leave the country and come back in. There was only a small fine if you over-stayed your visa. Now I wish we'd gotten residency earlier because our sons *feel* Costa Rican but they don't have the status.

Residency has many steps to it and only after you've received it and lived here for seven more years do you have the option of soliciting citizenship. Costa Rica doesn't ask you to relinquish any citizenship.

Sons' Citizenship and Cultural Attachment

One of my sons graduated from the Rhode Island School of Design and is setting up a studio in Philadelphia. He wants to go on for an MFA. His twin brother is in graduate school in Austin, Texas studying Latin American history. He would love to set up a program similar to the one my wife and I do here in Costa Rica somewhere in Latin America—but with more of a language and cultural focus rather than our scientific one.

Both my sons spent a year in Germany studying abroad. So our artist is also thinking of going to Berlin to pursue artistic opportunities there before he goes back to school.

The two of them graduated from high school when they were fifteen, so we sent them to Germany to study for a year, and they graduated from there at sixteen. Then they went to Simon's Rock in New York, which is for young students. They graduated from there at eighteen. After that, they took a gap year and the one who went to RISD went to Munich and the one who is now studying in Austin went to Italy, where he fell in love with an Albanian girl he is still serious about. He goes back to Italy regularly to see her. We're trying to get a visa for her to come and visit us here in Costa Rica, but Albania doesn't have reciprocity with Costa Rica yet.

My wife and I are now Costa Rican residents. The boys are residents of their respective states, Pennsylvania and Texas. But the boys will say they are Costa Rican if you ask them. They would say they grew up in a North American household in Costa Rica. In this way, it's very similar to when I was growing up in Illinois and many of the kids' parents came from European countries. The kids were American but they identified as Albanian or Italian at home.

I wanted our sons to be bilingual and bicultural. That's why we decided to stay here. At the Cloud Forest School, which we helped start, they were the only gringos in their grade. At first they were outcasts, outsiders. But from kindergarten on they quickly became insiders. They weren't ambassadors for other gringos. They didn't see that as their role.

The way we dealt with language was we spoke English at home. At school, the instruction was in English, but everything else took place in Spanish. Even now, my sons' friends will speak English to me and Spanish to them. There are definitely rules to the use of the two languages. If someone is monolingual, everyone uses that language. When my sons are here now, they will only speak Spanish unless they are speaking to us. In the Spanish-speaking community, they only use Spanish. Our only rule has been no Spanglish. They are pretty good about that now.

If they knew you spoke only one language and have never tried to learn the other one, like some of the Quakers here who have lived here for fifty years and still don't speak Spanish, they wouldn't say anything, but they might feel some value judgment. They now speak four languages—German, Italian, English and Spanish—fluently. They're polyglots. They think the kids who went to Friends School here are oddities, that they live in a bubble; even when they speak Spanish, they aren't comfortable with the Costa Ricans. My sons are.

They are very idealistic. When they went to Simon's Rock, they tried to join the Latin American association on campus. They are blonde, they look Anglo, and they have no accent, but they don't see themselves as Anglo. But in that group they weren't seen as Latin—by kids who couldn't even speak Spanish!

My sons don't get the U.S. This need for people to say, I'm this or that. They say that when people get together, the first thing they have to say is, "I'm Italian. I'm Mexican." My boys say, "You're *none* of these things. Maybe your grandmother was Italian, but *you're* not." They feel like outsiders in the U.S. They don't feel it's theirs.

My parents now have a kid who lives in Kuwait and a kid who lives in Costa Rica. They have bilingual children and grandchildren. I think now they are envious and proud. My parents live on the border of Mexico, in El Paso. They have Mexican-American friends. When my kids visit them, my kids will speak to my parents' friends in Spanish. My parents are in their eighties and can't learn the language, but they respect it.

My five nephews in Kuwait are more proud to be American than my sons. The cachet of being U.S. citizens is higher there than in Latin America. They are more conservative culturally and *proud* of the States. My boys are more critical of the U.S. They aren't ashamed, but they aren't proud. They are not going to yell, "U.S.A! U.S.A!" when Bin Laden is killed. My oldest nephew in Kuwait is the same age as my sons. On his Facebook page, he lists his hometown as Chicago, Illinois. My sons list theirs as Monteverde, Costa Rica.

Civic Engagement

My national interests are still with the U.S. I still vote in elections. We keep residency in Washington and vote for the governor. I follow news, write my congressman, vote.

In Costa Rica, my engagement is more limited. It is merely local.

I divert a lot of resources into schools and the Monteverde Conservation League. About national issues here, I feel that I'm not Costa Rican enough to deal with them. A few years ago, with the free trade decisions here, although I feel strongly on the issue I didn't speak out here. I speak out in the U.S. and with a U.S. audience, but when the issue came up here in Costa Rica, I felt this was *their* decision and I shouldn't weigh in. As a U.S. citizen, I may be against it, but I will talk about it there, not here. I still feel as if I am a visitor here.

If I became a citizen here, I think I would feel *less* like a visitor, but really culturally I'm a gringo. I don't think I'd ever walk into a room of *Ticos* [Costa Rican slang for Costa Ricans] and say, "I'm *Tico*." Many *Ticos* tell me they *feel* I'm *Tico*. I'm definitely seen as a resident. I may have an equal vote with citizenship, but not an equal say. My *sons* would feel equal.

ving dif ce a chance to sh

of the belief that the expressio

a right of the other person

experie

ZOË TOSTESON LOSADA

YES, I GUESS I AM AN AMERICAN…

As I write this, I am looking at the mountain, called the *Avila* that is due north of Caracas, through the huge windows that dominate my small apartment, bought with great sacrifice, in cash, eight years ago. Before moving here, we lived in a small town southeast of the city. I drove to work each day, for at least nine years, on the winding back road to the city, past another town, forests, slippery roads, hills and valleys, through fog and smog, past a convent and poor slums or *barrios*, which I watched grow, sometimes overnight. This road was an obstacle course, where I encountered wrecks and mudslides, beauty and absolute squalor, children waiting in the darkness before dawn, and, above all, the early morning and late evening bustle of people struggling to earn their keep in a precarious world. For the most part, I drove a series of used cars—the most memorable being a venerable 1971 Mustang that went through a long period with a damaged starter. Dressed up in my work clothes (Venezuelan work places require a certain level of elegance!), I would start this car in the early morning by opening the trunk and spilling a bit of gasoline into the starter. (I also remember a huge Malibu, which would suddenly and startlingly lose its right front wheel from time to time in inconvenient places like major highways, despite endless repairs.)

My arrival time, both to work and schools in the morning and to home in the evening, was entirely unpredictable: sometimes heavy rain or heavy traffic would impede the way, for hours, and sometimes I would damage the car in one of the numerous, and very large, holes that impeded my progress. If I left Caracas too late, I would often have to drive through an impenetrable fog, and I learned to fear the darkness and the rain—the lack of visibility, the possibility of sliding off the slippery roads, and the very real possibility of being the victim of a crime.

Once, years ago when the children were quite small, a huge hole wiped out the road. We parked, for an astronomical sum, one dilapidated car in the parking lot of a restaurant on one side of the crater and another car on the road on the other side, and then slipped and slid along the mud with the two children in the morning when we went to Caracas and in the evening when we went home. This lasted a couple of weeks. (I thought this was a uniquely non-U.S. experience, but of course that is not true. I just read today about a community of Vermonters, who, isolated by the flood-destroyed roads, have developed their own super footpath through the woods.)

Strangely, despite the relative ease and comfort of my childhood in a middle-class home, spent mostly in North Carolina, we did go through a similar period when I was a child. I remember living in a lovely house in the woods, miles from the nearest town, but within walking distance of a lonely forest. We walked (in my mind anyway) an endless road to get to the bus stop, shivering in the cold morning air, like the Venezuelan children I would see at dawn during my long drive from San Diego de los Altos to Caracas, neat in their school uniforms, waiting for the schools to open.

Before moving to the apartment in San Diego de los Altos, we rented a large house in a forest, full of orange and banana trees. This house had some drawbacks—bats would fly in sometimes, and, if I were alone, I would take refuge in one of the rooms with the children until my husband came home. There were rats in the forest as well that sometimes ate the clothes on top of the washing machine, which we kept on the porch. I remember my feeling of shame when my daughter blithely explained the origin of the holes in her T-shirt to my stepmother. Nevertheless, it was a beautiful house with a view of endless hills and forests. I spent my son's pregnancy there, growing huge. We prepared *hallacas* (a laborious Venezuelan Christmas dish) with rabbit that year—the rabbits raised in back of the house by my husband.

Looking back, I remember that the U.S., where I had lived until I was almost twenty, seemed like an unattainable dream during those years. I found life in Venezuela to be hard, and the comparison with the very comfortable lives of most of the members of my family was striking. I would travel to my father's huge house in Chestnut Hill in Boston during the summers and compare. Yet, although we did spend some time in the U.S. in the early 1990s, I was not, at that time, tempted in any real way to permanently return to the U.S. I had made my life since early adulthood in Venezuela, and it seemed part of my identity, like speaking Spanish and drinking *café con leche*.

On the other hand, I was never tempted to give up my U.S. citizenship or even acquire Venezuelan citizenship. Despite what I think is a quite deep understanding of the country and a certain sense of belonging, I have never felt Venezuelan, and I know that I will always be considered a foreigner in this country. I am not sure what keeps me apart. Perhaps it is language—I speak Spanish, yes, but with an accent that does not exactly seem like that of a *gringa*, but is certainly not that of a Venezuelan. I have spoken with immigrants to the U.S., however, and despite real difficulties with English, they do feel a real sense of belonging to the U.S. in a way that I do not feel to Venezuela. I do not explain this, but wonder if it could be the difference between the two countries. The U.S. is, finally, a country of immigrants whereas Venezuela, despite a large influx of European immigrants right after both World Wars, is smaller and much more insular. I also wonder if the feeling of difference comes more from myself than from any outside source. It is possible that I simply do not want to become Venezuelan, because being in this country but not of it is as much a part of my identity as being an American and not living there.

Strangely, contradictorily, even though I have spent thirty-six of my fifty-six years living outside the United States, being American is part of me. I know this in part because of the sadness I feel when the U.S. government, again and again, behaves in the world in a way that I, childishly and naively, believe they should not. I am never surprised now when I discover some nefarious activity that can be attributed to some branch of the U.S. government, and I am always deeply disappointed, and I always feel a sense of personal responsibility.

My first thought of myself as an American came during a conversation with my father when I was four or five years old. He was telling me about the role of the United States of America as a peace-promoting influence in the world. This was the end of the 50s, remember, before the corroding effect of the Cold War and the Vietnam War on the patriotism of some fellow citizens, including, finally, my father. "If we believe in peace, Daddy," I asked, "why do we go to war?" And he answered, as I have answered, later, many times to my children or my students when I don't know the answer, "that is a very good question."

My father later developed a skeptical attitude regarding our country's role in the world, often echoing my question. He was the one who first expressed concerns to me about the ill-fated Plan Columbia, which deposited billions of U.S. dollars into the pockets of Colombian generals in a supposed effort to control the cocaine trade through that country (a policy that was implemented in 2000, suspiciously close to the election of the rabidly anti-American Venezuelan president, Hugo Chávez). "If I lived in Venezuela," he said (which I had, for years, as had his Venezuelan grandchildren), "I would be concerned." The day that the U.S. invaded Iraq in

2003, he told me, barely audible due to the disease that finally robbed him of his cherished ability to speak, that he was ashamed to be an American.

A sad commentary, which makes me sad to write, because my father loved his country and would never have contemplated living permanently anywhere else. And when I, who have chosen to live most of my life outside my country of birth, think of being an American, I first think of him. I also think of the other members of my family, my three sisters, two brothers, nephews and nieces (several of whom are Venezuelan), my uncle and cousins. I believe that my older sister and I, because we have spent most of our adult lives outside the United States, have a profoundly different perspective of the United States and being a U.S. citizen than the others, despite their extensive travels and generally wide and deep knowledge of global affairs. I know other expats, many of whom, like me, have married foreign citizens and had children in foreign countries who, like me, return to the United States like visiting foreigners, marveling at the strange habits of the inhabitants of this huge country and wondering where they fit in, if anywhere. My real life is elsewhere even if, like my journeys to work on the endless road, it is not always comfortable or safe. I think as well of my daughter and son, who now, well into their adulthood, have not opted to live in the United States, despite my efforts to ensure their U.S. nationality years ago during their childhood. And I think of my brand-new grandson, who is a Spanish citizen born in Australia, and for whom his parents, particularly his father, who is not a U.S. citizen, are working hard to obtain U.S. citizenship.

So . . . what does it mean for me to be an American? First, having lived the majority of my life outside of my country of birth, but in the Americas, I am careful about calling myself an American given, as I have been told many times, we are all Americans in a strictly geographical sense. True, the U.S. is the only country that uses the word "America" in its name, so perhaps the term "American" is justified in that sense, and in deference to brevity, U.S. citizen is quite a mouthful, and it is longer in Spanish. The objection people have to the term American seems to have less to do with geography, however, and more to do with power. In Venezuela, many people think of the U.S. as an unattainable dream, or, on the other hand, an uncontrollable and essentially malicious power. When my Venezuelan husband watches the government T.V. channels, the word *emperio* (empire) to refer to the U.S. and its abuse of power in numerous parts of the globe, is used continuously. The anti-government channel, in contrast, seems to imply frequently that the U.S. is a fount of rationality and good governance, as well as a possible deliverance from the frightening leftist chaos that the present Venezuela and Venezuelan government are perceived to be and the abuses of the U.S., while acknowledged, are considered necessary.

In truth, at least in regards to foreign policy, I coincide more with the anti-U.S. opinions of the government. And yet, like the Venezuelan government, which depends upon the steady stream of income it receives from oil sales to the U.S., my feelings regarding the U.S., and my belonging to the U.S., remain ambiguous. I criticize the interventions of the United States in other countries, and I find my fellow Americans to be impossibly insular at times, often unaware of even the existence of other cultures and even countries, as if nothing exists outside the borders of our country. I have never voted in a U.S. election, not feeling my citizenship enough to go through the hassle and paperwork that registering to vote from Venezuela would require. My citizenship does, however, somehow mean more to me than the ease with which I travel with a U.S. passport. I have never returned to the U.S., for example, without feeling some sense of returning home, without wondering what my life would have been like if I had stayed, and without, lately, a feeling of loss for the United States that I had imagined existed as a child.

When I was eleven, some years after that conversation with my father, I met a young girl, a classmate in the sixth grade, who was sitting across from me in the library, a natural red streak in her dark, long, glossy hair and a kind look in her intelligent eyes. This turned out to be a pivotal meeting in my life, because she gave me the opportunity to make a lasting change in my perception of and role in the world. This meeting took place a few years after the Cuban crisis and the assassination of President Kennedy, events that affected me and are now inescapably entwined in the complex tapestry that is my memory of my childhood, (although they affected me much less than, say, the devaluation of the Venezuelan Bolivar in 1980 or the election of Hugo Chávez as President of Venezuela in 1998). It was also after the summer I spent with my family in Annecy in France, the last summer that my family was intact. I spent hours sailing on the lake that summer, alone with my mother, as she grieved and raged, knowing, I realize now, that her troubled marriage was over. I came back with a new clarity that fall, somehow over the depression that had dogged me for years, and entered a sixth grade that was formed to jump-start the integration of public schools in Chapel Hill, North Carolina. For that year, all sixth grade students were bused into one building and so, for the first time in my life, I interacted with fellow students who were black and/or poor, like my new friend.

Her parents had come to Chapel Hill from farther up north, and she had gone through periods of real hunger and abuse. Her mother worked in a secretarial position and her father, a brilliant, troubled man, was mostly unemployed. She lived in a tiny house with her two brothers and two sisters, very different than the custom-made house I inhabited with my mother, sister, brother, and numerous dogs (my father was in the process of moving out that year). Yet I spent hours in her house, in part because I was fascinated by her religion, the Baha'i faith. Eventually, later that year, I became a Baha'i and, now, forty-five years later, I remain a Baha'i. One of the tenets of this faith is belief in the unity of all people and the necessity of a world government. Although nationality and citizenship are respected by Baha'is, we consider cultural and national differences to be immeasurably less important than our shared humanity.

Starting in seventh grade, I often traveled to large Baha'i meetings, without my family, interacting with Baha'is of all backgrounds, nationalities, and races. I remember eating watermelon on the porch of impoverished Native Americans, feeling like a foreigner no more than a two-hour drive from my house. In fact, I might have felt less a foreigner a few years later, when I traveled to Venezuela and little by little, made the series of choices that ended with me living the majority of my adult life outside of the United States. Until now, I have never thought that those choices had anything to do with the world citizenship that is such a central part of being a Baha'i, but perhaps the belief that nationality matters little has made it easier for me to live in another country and accept the inevitable differences of culture simply as natural variations of the human state.

In my professional choices, as well, I have reinforced my feeling of myself as a citizen of the world rather than a member of any particular nation. I work as counselor in a small international school, and have, as part of my work, worked with children, adolescents, families, and colleagues from all over the world. At times, the differences between cultures and languages have felt as if I have been placed in an Escher diagram, where nothing feels right or rational, where up becomes down without a discernible reason. I have learned to listen, to observe, and not to judge. I have often been reminded of my sister hissing at me once, exasperated, in an amateur art show, "can't you just take it in without JUDGING so much?!" I was continually, and apparently annoyingly, expressing my opinion, "I like this, I dislike that," when she wanted to just experience. As a counselor, I have learned to enter and experience the world of the people I work with and, ironically perhaps, in my role as a college counselor, to interpret and explain the unique and strange world of U.S. colleges and universities and the convoluted process of admission into them.

As I sit here, the sun has now set over Caracas and the spectacular sunset has spread out across the mountain and the city. Every evening is different, with a range of colors from deep orange, like tonight, to light pink. Sometimes the colors tinge the entire sky, and sometimes, like tonight, the color concentrates in one corner of the horizon. And each day, the mountain awakes with a different face. Sometimes, when wild storms convulse the city, it disappears behind the clouds and wisps of the fog slide in through our windows. Whatever is the mood of the mountain, I feel privileged to be here and to witness its beauty. It is part of me, as is being an American, and being a Baha'i, and being a member of the human race, in all its beauty and its tragedy.

ALEXANDRINA SERGIO

CAN YOU TAKE THE COUNTRY OUT OF THE GIRL?

Me: *OK now, tell me this: Do you get teary-eyed when you're watching the Olympics and they play "The Star Spangled Banner"? Does your heart go pitter-patter?*

She: *Well, I get choked up over "O Canada" when the Canadians win, even if they have competed with the U.S.*

Me: *I didn't ask about context. This is a gut check. When you hear "The Star Spangled Banner" at the Olympics, do you get an involuntary emotional surge?*

She: *Yeah. I do.*

Me? I'm Sandy, The Mother.

She? She's Lauren, The Daughter.

She was raised in a Connecticut suburb, born into a politically involved family that planted campaign signs on the lawn at election time, wrote many letters to the editor and spoke at town meetings and legislative hearings. Tall flagpole in the front yard. She had a high-school boyfriend. She scarfed down roast beef and ham with the best of them. Storybook American childhood.

Today she is a city-dwelling vegetarian married Canadian lesbian.(!)

As I rejoiced in the child she was, I revel in the adult she has become. Her evolution has been marked by the blessed awakening to her sexual orientation and the happiness of her legal-from-the-start marriage to her beloved Meg. I easily grasp how she has become an avowed city person, her basic metro-life training having taken place in Montreal and Toronto. I understand how she became a vegetarian: hard not to be when Meg had espoused the practice long before they met. The being Canadian thing, though, has prompted questions. She holds dual citizenship—feels privileged to be able to be Canadian without renouncing the place of her birth; but if she were forced to make a choice? How deeply rooted is allegiance to one's native land? How broadly can we define citizenship? We talked about it.

Me: What do you think makes one feel a *citizen* of a particular country?

She: For me, citizenship is defined on two levels: the pragmatic and the emotional. The legal considerations, i.e., where you can vote, who issues your passport, where you can be employed, along with where you have your long-term life, where your family is—your geographical location: these are pragmatic considerations. Then there is the emotional level, involving cultural identity and a sharing of the country's ideals and social values. I have been a Canadian citizen for twelve years, and became one happily and comfortably, since my admiration for and agreement with Canada's more socialistic and tolerant society had grown since I first arrived in Canada as a student in 1984. But I certainly can't deny my strong ties to the United States. My family is there: my parents and siblings, aunts, uncles and cousins!

Me: What was your understanding of citizenship when you were a citizen of just one country? What is it now that you are a citizen of two?

She: My earlier concept of citizenship was limited because I had had no exposure to any culture other than that of my geographical location: the eastern U.S. It wasn't until the 1990s that multi-culturism became part of the U.S. educational process, and so I defined my citizenship only in pragmatic terms—didn't really consider other aspects of it. Too, I was in school then, with homework and the beach and soccer games crowding out more philosophical contemplations. Living in Canada awakened me to the emotional aspect of aligning oneself with a particular nation as a citizen. I found I rapidly adapted to a new cultural ethos: one somewhat less frantic than many, with a social contract that assumes an obligation to help the less fortunate and social policies that attempt to nurture a more healthy, balanced society. The hallmark of this national attitude is the Canadian healthcare system, a huge point of pride in Canada. And of course, the altruism is, as well, enlightened self-interest. I want to know that the child sitting next to mine in school has access to the same excellent health care that my child receives. Too, I am now seeing what I consider to be the advantages of a different political system. I now live in a country with a multi-party, parliamentary system that exerts tight controls over political donations so that it is harder politically to give social advantages to a select few entities. I like that.

Me: How did differences in U.S. and Canadian acceptance and legalization of same-sex unions affect your decision to become a dual citizen?

She: Not at all; but it has had a profound influence on the probability that I will stay in Canada. When I became a citizen of Canada it was for practical reasons. I attended McGill University in Montreal for both undergraduate and graduate degrees, then followed the opportunities that opened up for post-doctoral study at the University of Montreal. By that time I was settling in to Canada and had discovered that I loved city life. Perhaps if I had spent my childhood and youthful years in New York City rather than in a somewhat staid suburb, the impact wouldn't have been so dramatic and the change wouldn't have been so seductive. But I hadn't and it was; and besides it was getting tedious to have to renew my visa every year. (Confession: about that time I took up hockey and to this day regularly take to the ice as part of a women's team. That's pretty Canadian.) I gained permanent resident status in 1996 and full citizenship in 1999. The following year I was appointed to a position at York University in Toronto and my fate as a Canadian was sealed.

In 1999 marriage was not on my radar, but I knew that as a lesbian I already faced considerably less discrimination in Canada than I would back home. While there always seem to be individuals who harbor prejudice against homosexual people, Canada's Charter of Rights and Freedoms specifically disallows discrimination and this strongly influenced/influences a more accepting environment.

Me: Meg has both U.S. and Canadian citizenship. Tell the details of her dual situation.

She: Meg was born in Canada, but because her mom was born in the U.S., she has been a U.S. citizen since early childhood. She was able without problems to attend an American university for her undergraduate degree and to work in California for a number of years. She returned to Canada to attend graduate school, we met, and the rest is ourstory.

Me: They were married in 2003 on the shore of Lake Ontario in a legal ceremony presided over by an elegant judge of the Ontario Court of Justice. I wore a truly kick-ass big hat. It was wondrous.

Me: Would you consider coming to live in the U.S. again? What might persuade you to do so? To not do so?

She: We have talked about it, mostly fantasizing about hypothetical dream jobs in the States. I have been building credentials in my field and Meg will soon have a PhD and be looking for a position. With dual citizenship we both should have a broader array of possibilities open to us; but in reality, that isn't the case. At present there are a limited number of places in the U.S. where our marriage is considered legal and where our family would have available the respect and benefits accorded to families with heterosexual parents. [Lauren and Meg have two children, ages five and seven.] Even if we found dream jobs in a state which does recognize same-sex marriage, the federal government does not recognize marriage between same-sex partners, and until the federal Defense of Marriage Act, which defines marriage as a union between a man and a woman, is repealed, our marriage and family are second class as far as numerous federally-based family benefits are concerned.

Me: Do the kids have any concept of citizenship? Do they have dual citizenship?

She: Both of them were born in Canada and feel quite Canadian. They loved watching the Olympics, rooted for Canada and sang "O Canada" at the top of their lungs. Still, they are keenly aware of their U.S. family and know I am their "American Mom." They know Grandma and Grandpa and their aunties and uncles and cousins and a great-grandmother live in the U.S. We fly the U.S. flag on July Fourth and sing the National Anthem to them. So they do feel a connection to the U.S. We will seek citizenship for them as soon as some questionable tax laws regarding U.S. citizens living out of country are clarified. The children are eligible for citizenship by virtue of their mothers' citizenship and having it will allow easier border crossings and opportunities in education and employment when they are older. Too, and as important, their American heritage is part of their identity and being a U.S. citizen underscores and honors that.

Me: Where do you vote?

She: Meg and I both vote in Canadian elections and we vote in U.S. presidential elections. We could vote for other U.S. federal nominees, but on principle do not. We feel we are not sufficiently knowledgeable about candidates other than those running for the presidency. Being able to vote in the country where I live is very important to me. I would find it hard not to be involved in political life, not to take part in the electoral system and have a say in who is making decisions that affect my family. And indeed, we display campaign signs in our front yard—just like when I was a kid!

Me: Do you feel you have particular civic responsibilities to each country? What are they?

She: I believe I am obliged to keep myself informed about public/

political issues in Canada and let my opinions be heard through raising my voice (or pen . . . or yard sign) and by voting: the usual civic responsibilities. As well, I feel that my work accrues to the benefit of my country. It is not only as a scientist but as a citizen that I can contribute to Canada's international reputation in neuroscience. My concept of my responsibilities to the U.S. takes another form. I find I am often viewed as the apologist/expert in the room when discussion of U.S. politics and policies gets heated and I do stand up for America and, should the talk get disparaging, let people know that I'm American.

Me: Evidently you're still proud to be an American. Now I'm confused. Do you feel your attachment to one country is predominant? Which one?

She: I'd have to say Canada is the primary attachment. I have lived in Canada for twenty-seven years. I have a job that has put me in touch with others in my field throughout the country—scientists with whom I work collaboratively, and I received an outstanding education in Canada, with a good part of my graduate work funded by government grants. I am grateful for this. Perhaps the strongest tie lies in the circumstance of my children having been born in Canada. They are Canadians and their country accepts them and their two-mommy family.

Me: Does having dual citizenship diminish your attachment to one or both countries?

She: No. I was born in America; was nurtured in America; am the granddaughter of a man and a woman who came to America from other countries. Nothing can change these things. They are part of who I am. My attachment to Canada is in the foreground now because I live there. It is my community. United States: my past and present; Canada: my present and future. Both are honored.

Me: Would you feel comfortable renouncing either citizenship?

She. No. In fact, I would be quite angry if I were forced to renounce one or the other—angry at a circumstance that might require this. While my civic and social values align more closely with those of Canada, my children are Canadian and my adult life thus far has been a Canadian life, still I was born in the United States and there is ultimately an indefinable strong connection that remains no matter what the paperwork indicates. I am grateful that when someone asks what my nationality is I can answer Dual.

ANNA STEEGMANN

AN AMERICAN PLAYWRIGHT IN BERLIN (Lydia)

Lydia has invited me to her peaceful oasis, an enchanted garden patch, one of hundreds in a colony of allotment gardens in Berlin-Charlottenburg. She proudly points out her fruit trees, all thirteen of them. The plums and various apples are ripe and fragrant and she offers me a taste. Too late in the season, I have missed out on roses "as big as trees" and "lilac bushes of every hue." She had not been a gardener until she came to the Rosstrappe Laubenkolonie but her passion for her "perfect witch's garden" is evident. Lydia originally conceived of the garden as a place to write, but ends up spending most of her time gardening—tending to her trees and flowers, her herbs and vegetables. A cabin provides shelter from the rain and cold, but that won't be necessary today. Berlin has been blessed with a succession of glorious summer days. *The garden has done wonders for Lydia*, I think, for she looks like a Zen-practitioner untouched by the stress of urban living. She serves tea made with lemongrass from the garden. We settle into the rickety lounge chairs under the plum tree and chase away the bees. I place the tape recorder on the small table between us and press the record button; she suddenly looks as if she is uncomfortable to be the center of attention.

"I was raised in DeKalb, Illinois, sixty miles west of Chicago. My mother is a Londoner. My father is American. He's a poet and taught poetry and Buddhist literature at Northern Illinois University and translated poetry from the Japanese. I was conceived in Japan. My mother was pregnant with me on the boat coming back to America. The back-and-forth life has been the only constant in my life. As a little girl I lived for a while in Japan and also in Iran. We often spent six months to a year in London. I loved London most of all. I fell in love with the theater there."

A smile lights up her face as she remembers the plays she saw in London.

"And your decision to move to Berlin?" I ask.

Lydia answers with a question of her own: "Did I make the decision to move to Berlin?"

She takes a deep breath before she continues. "I met Halina in March 1991 in New York. We fell in love. Within one year I gave up my New York apartment to live with her in Berlin." She tried to return to the U.S. in 1993 and accepted an offer to teach at the Virginia Commonwealth University. She had a PhD in theater from the CUNY Graduate Center and this was a great career opportunity, a tenure-track position in the English department. But it did not work out. "After six months I knew I could not live in Virginia," she says. "There was nothing there for Halina. The university was kind enough to give me time to think about it. They urged me to take a leave of absence but I knew it wasn't going to work. The academic year of 1993/94 was the last time I had any semblance of stability or a well-paid job."

Her voice sounds graver than seconds before. *As if she's contemplating the weight of her decision, what could have been instead,* I think. "Berlin is a good town for dancers and painters from abroad but not for me as a playwright," she says. "Living here has been very hard on my career. The theater is a collaborative art form; you develop relationships over time. I had just started writing plays when I met Halina. My first play was produced at the Denver Center Theater in 1993. I was naïve. I thought I could leave my plays with my agent in New York and take off. I thought I could live in Berlin and come back to New York, renting a place for a month or two every so often and pick up where I left off. I would make connections with people in the theater when I was back in New York but then I would leave again and the connections would dissipate. As soon as you're gone you're gone. I had the same experience in other American cities. I had a production in Chicago. I met people from this theater and that theater; they'd be interested and then I was gone. Once a famous actress told me, 'Who do you think you are? If you work in theater you have to be either in New York or London.' Eventually I understood that playwriting is not about writing a play and sending it off. It is about doing a play by someone who's in town, someone you have a relationship with. I am ambitious for my work but was never ambitious enough to leave Halina behind in Berlin."

Lydia entered my life through Halina. Halina and I were both undergraduates in the early 1970s at the Westphälische Wilhelms Universität in Münster. Lydia's longtime companion is a famous feminist activist. Halina was elected to the Berlin House of Representatives where she fought, among other things, for equal rights for homosexuals. They were married in Berlin on August 9, 2001.

"Halina and I are part of a civil rights struggle. This affected both of us. Halina fought for gay marriage rights for five years in Germany. We won the fight."

Their *registrierte Lebenspartnerschaft,* their registered civil union, entitles Lydia to live and work in Germany. She is eligible for health insurance and all other benefits open to spouses of German citizens. Although New York State has recently permitted gay marriages, Halina is not allowed to work and reside in the United States. I ask Lydia to clarify. "We are a binational gay couple and we have no right to live together in America. Clinton signed the Defense of Marriage Act in the dead of night. He sold gay people out. The act states that no federal rights will accrue to gay couples; no state has to recognize the marriage of another state. There are no immigration privileges for gay couples. Unless DOMA is repealed, unless the Supreme Court upholds the right of every American to marry, there is no chance for Halina to legally reside and work in the U.S."

I do not have to ask how Lydia feels about that. I can hear the anger in her voice.

"I guess you could say I sacrificed for love," she says. "Halina sacrificed too. She gave up her job in Parliament because she couldn't go back and forth. She has had to be the main supporter for us for most of our years together."

I ask Lydia if she ever feels homesick for America. "I have a deep nostalgia for the Midwest," she says. "I'm back in touch with old friends from grade school and high school. I envy those who are rooted to one place. I have a fantasy about small-town America, about living there again, but I know it won't happen."

I ask her what she misses about America. "I miss my New York friends, I miss speaking my language," she says. "Don't get me wrong; Berlin is a super place to live. And there's so much I dislike about America—the debasement of politics, the non-existent social system, how difficult it is to live in New York. Nevertheless, I feel at home in America; I have my references in America. I write for an English-speaking audience. My themes are American. The German references are so intense, so deep; they go back so many centuries. It is such a literary world."

I ask her about her career, the roadblocks.

"Germans are not interested in intimate personal plays and psychological portraits. They like plays with stories and themes a director can go to town on. They are not concerned with what is human. For them, theater is the theatrical expression of ideas. America, on the other hand, is a playwright's theater. The theater is focused on human psychology. The process is centered on the play itself, with directors playing a much less prominent role. In terms of my aesthetic, I fall somewhere in between—utilizing both human psychology and the expression of ideas in a way that makes my work unfamiliar territory for either culture. In terms of my academic career, I spent ten years in various graduate programs but here, because of my poor language skills, I can't teach what I'm qualified to teach."

I ask her about her poor language skills.

"I did make an effort to learn German. I tried a few times. Still, my German is terrible. I use the excuse that I go back and forth all the time. But it is an excuse. Everyone speaks English in Berlin. I have a big list of reasons why I never learned German. I can understand a great deal but I cannot speak. Some of my American friends speak perfect German. Some people are good at languages. I am not. I had resistance to coming here, psychologically—part of my family was murdered by the Nazis."

No wonder, I think and remember that Halina has Jewish roots also.

"Living abroad has affected my English. I sound odd now. When I get back to the States people comment on how I speak. I tend to say *Ja* at the end of a sentence. I never wanted to be one of those people who have a funny untraceable accent but now I have become one of them. I consider myself an unwilling exile. I think this is what separates me from many other Americans in Berlin. They want to be here. They have connections. They think Berlin is hip."

"Would you become a German citizen?" I ask.

"I might if there was some particular benefit to it," she says, "but I don't think there would be one. And I would never give up my American citizenship."

"What do you call yourself?" I ask.

"An American playwright based in Berlin." She chuckles. "Funny that word 'based'; it sounds as if I'm in the Army."

"Where is home?" I ask.

A long pause.

"I guess Berlin is home now," she says.

Another long pause.

"It took me a long time, twenty years, to say that."

Another pause.

I ask her about the American expatriate life in Berlin.

"I listen to NPR religiously, I read *The New York Times* online, I am getting total American coverage. I'm a big fan of *Democracy Now* and NPR's *This American Life.* This morning they had a funny piece about New York supers."

She thinks for a while. "I've somehow become a big defender of Americans since I live abroad. I joined *American Voices Abroad.* The group started in Berlin and was formed around opposition to the Iraq war. Now they are all over Europe and the world. The German press loves our group because they like to see the other perspective, the other Americans. But Berliners in general are friendly toward Americans. You know they like their *Amis* because of their history. People see me as a friendly American. I am happier here now than I used to be. But I do have a sense of relief when I'm back in America. America is my world."

"Can you imagine returning to the U.S. to live?" I ask.

"Psychologically, emotionally, yes," she says. "But not when I think about the social system. I don't know if I can survive the political direction the country has taken. For the first time in my life I am proud of Germany. Chancellor Angela Merkel is stepping out of nuclear energy. This is a huge progressive step for the planet."

I ask her if she has any advice for American newcomers.

"Really learn the language, immerse yourself in the culture, get to know different people even if you think you won't be staying long. Because you never know."

ate, arrest, impr

mising young people

tax paying cit ns; and

deported to co ntries

JOSÉ VARIBLE

Interviewed by Charles Brockett

JOSÉ DREAMS OF BECOMING A U.S. CITIZEN

José Varible is one of six siblings. All of his brothers and sisters are U.S. citizens. Much to his dismay, José is not. Nineteen years old when I talked with him, José was in jeopardy of being deported from the country that has been his home for the last ten years.

"You know you could do a lot better," José tells me over the phone from Wisconsin, "but you can't when you are undocumented. It keeps you from doing so much of what you want to do. I get depressed. Lately I have been feeling really bad . . . alone. I am seeing a doctor."

"I grew up here," he emphasizes throughout the conversation, "it is not my fault that I lack papers." José was born in Toluca, Mexico, which is not too far outside of the capital city. "My mother had a small neighborhood grocery store. One day it was held up for 50,000 pesos, and they told her not to report it or they would kill her. That is when she decided that they would leave for the U.S." At the time, his parents had two children.

José was nine. "I learned English quickly and by the seventh grade I was doing well." Indeed, he speaks an almost-accentless English. His illegal/undocumented status was not an issue in high school. The U.S. Supreme Court ruled in 1982 that public education through high school must be offered free to all children, regardless of their immigration status. But that does not apply at the college level. And the same philosophy certainly does not apply to employment. Since 1986 it has been against the law to knowingly employ workers who are in the country illegally.

"Friends in high school would tell me about job possibilities, good jobs, but I couldn't take advantage of them because of my lack of documents. I didn't want to tell my friends I was undocumented so I would make excuses." Talking with José, it is clear that making these excuses cost him psychologically. His friends wondered about the excuses too. Knowing this added to his distress.

Without documents, he could not apply for financial aid for college, so he took classes at the local community college. But since he could not work regularly he was hard-pressed to make his tuition. Neither could he get a driver's license. He tried his best to get by with odd jobs using skills he developed at repairing computers.

Adding to José's sense of the unfairness of his position is the situation of his family. The sister who migrated with him later married a U.S. citizen and is now a citizen herself. His parents had four more children once in the United States and so they are birthright citizens. That leaves only José among the siblings illegally in the country. Similarly, his parents are illegal aliens and when we talked his father was in the process of being deported. José presumes his father will return to Toluca. As far as he knows he has one uncle there, that's it. José does not know Mexico, never having returned since the family left. Now he has "the feeling of not being either from here or there. It is extremely hard to live like this."

José, of course, is not alone in this predicament. Each year some 65,000 undocumented students graduate from high school in the U.S., many of them like José having grown up in the United States regarding it as their home. Research indicates that as they become aware of the lack of opportunities that they will face after high school, morale and motivation slump at least for some students, some even giving up and dropping out of high school.(1)

In recent years a primary hope for undocumented students has been the possibility that the DREAM Act might pass Congress.(2) This would provide undocumented youths who came to the U.S. before they were sixteen and have lived here at least five years a path to citizenship that would lead through either honorable military service or completion of two years of college. Estimates of the number of people who would be eligible run from two-thirds to three-quarters of a million.(3)

Across the country undocumented students have gone public with their status as a way of putting individual faces on what can otherwise be just one more abstract issue. Among them was José, who held his "coming out" in the summer of 2010. He did it "because it was necessary to let people know of my situation . . . about the things I can not do . . . like drive, get a job . . . live like a normal citizen."

It took about a month to plan the event. He was aware of the dangers of calling authorities' attention to himself but "I didn't care any more." Afterwards he had "no more fear" and when I talked with him more than a half year later he had not yet heard from the authorities. Instead, he was gratified by the support that he received from friends and neighbors—along with their expressions of surprise, never having guessed his undocumented status.

Momentum seemed to be developing for the DREAM Act through 2010 with more and more events like José's being held, along with rallies, fasts, and marches, including one all the way from Florida to Washington, D.C. The pressure culminated with victory in the House of Representatives in early December on a vote of 216 to 198, with only eight Republicans in support. Students from all over the country packed the galleries as the Senate took up the measure shortly before adjourning for the session. José was among them. "There were so many 'DREAMers' there." But it was not to be. Although the bill had majority support in the Senate, a minority filibuster prevented it from receiving its vote. Sixty votes were needed for ending debate, the attempt received fifty-five, only three from Republicans.(4) The students were crushed. "So many were crying," José reports.

When we talked two months later, José was holding on to the hope that if he could explain to immigration authorities "these circumstances"—why his family had come to the United States and how it was his home—that "it would make the difference, that then I could stay here." He was also hoping to find a lawyer who could help him out and thinking of making a documentary of his situation and "taking it to Janet Napolitano [the secretary of the Department of Homeland Security] and getting a meeting between just me and her." She would understand and "I could stay."

Throughout our conversation José restated the same sentiments: "I grew up here . . . I have my roots here . . . I love this country." If he were to be forced to leave, "I feel like I would be able to come back some day. . . . I would want to go back to my country [the U.S.] and . . . change my country."

I learned of José from a story in *The New York Times* that focused on "anxiety for illegal immigrant students."(5) The article centered on another Wisconsin student who was three when her family arrived but it gave José the last word: "'You know, the thing is, I just don't feel welcome here,' he said. 'You cannot live as an undocumented immigrant.'"

The article generated comments from 468 readers. Some of them were sympathetic. David from Owings Mills, MD, for example, posted, "Many of these students are technically illegal, but to call them lawbreakers is highly misleading. A child brought by her parents at the age of three is not a lawbreaker." Patsy in Arizona wrote, "I'm a retired school teacher. . . . My class was filled with these kids year after year. And year after year I encouraged them to work hard in school to get ahead. . . . The business community encouraged their parents to come here so they could pay them cheap wages and now, our government is abandoning the kids. It makes me sick. To my many Mexican students: I'm so sorry."

Many other readers, though, believe the students should be deported, even though some of them are moved by the individual stories, such as Katie from Georgia who wrote, "While I may feel sorry for some of these young illegal immigrants on a case by case basis, the people they should be angry at and frustrated with are their parents . . . the ones who brought them here illegally. The sight of these young people [at the type of rallies referenced in this article] 'demanding' their 'right' to an American education, particularly an American college education, really struck me as nervy and wrong. Play the sympathy chord all you want, but don't boldly make demands on a country that already gives you K-12 education for free, no questions asked, and a potpourri of state benefits."

For others, such as Rory from Charlotte, the situation is more personal: "As an immigrant myself, I am disgusted by those within the illegal immigrant community AND the ignorant supporters of these. I fought hard to come to this country LEGALLY. I went through all the hoops, paid my bills, my fees and lived with the uncertainty that my visa could be pulled at the drop of a hat. . . . Now, I see those who want to steal from those of us who came here honestly our blessing, our pride, our honor. It makes me sick. It makes me sick that there are American citizens who feel it is ok for those here illegally to get a free ride which is what they want."

In 2011 there was no significant action on the DREAM Act at the national level. However, California passed its own DREAM Act in September, joining Texas and New Mexico as the only states allowing undocumented students to qualify for financial aid to their public colleges and universities. Between them, California and Texas have almost 40% of all of the relevant students in the country.(6)

As the year ended I wrote José to get an update on his situation. His response was short: "It's nice to hear from you unfortunately I . . . plan on leaving the United States soon."

And then he shared with me something he had written, "I grew up during a time when justice was tested to its limits. It was the time when it seemed like the world was just an unfair world but, in reality it was not up to the world to bring justice. The injustice came from species that composed the world. The species that thought they were as powerful as god, but what they didn't know was that their time was limited. The time of injustice eventually comes to an end because no oppression can be eternal. For some it will be too late when justice arrives but, it's not who benefits from it. It's the achievement of letting people go free from the cells that surround them and letting them bring their dreams to reality."

Endnotes

(1) Leisy Janet Abrego, "'I Can't Go to College Because I Don't Have Papers': Incorporation Patterns of Latino Undocumented Youth." *Latino Studies* 4.3 (2006): 212–31.

(2) The full name is Development, Relief, and Education for Alien Minors.

(3) Jeanne Batalova and Margie McHugh, *Dream Vs. Reality: An Analysis of Potential DREAM Act Beneficiaries*. Migration Policy Institute, 2010. Web.

(4) Julia Preston, "Immigration Vote Leaves Obama's Policy in Disarray," *The New York Times*, December 18 2010. Web.

(5) Julia Preston, "After a False Dawn, Anxiety for Illegal Immigrant Students," *The New York Times*, February 8 2011. Web. I am most grateful to Julia Preston, who kindly facilitated my contacting José.

(6) Batalova and McHugh.

CARL PALMER

GREEN CARD SOLDIER

seasonal migrant worker
unwed mother in Arizona
temporary work visa expires
sent back across the border

she allows her teenaged son
a chance to have a better life
than his first eighteen years
to stay and join the U.S. Army

he fights to become an American
becomes an American fighting man
offers his life for this country and
becomes a citizen . . . posthumously

SAAD NABEEL

Interviewed by Charles Brockett

I JUST WANT TO GO HOME

When Saad Nabeel was eighteen years old he was deported from the United States, the only home that he had known since he was three. He was more than a year into his exile when I talked to him, working hard to find his way back, alternating between despair and hope.

Saad spent his adolescent years in a suburb of Dallas, living a normal American teen life, happy with his friends while still maintaining an A- average at school. The foundation of this life started slipping, though, when he applied for his driver's license in 2008. Not only was he not eligible, he had alerted authorities to his family's unauthorized presence. The family was given one more year in the U.S. so he could finish high school.

Saad had aspired to studying engineering at Stanford. Under these new circumstances he instead attended a local branch of the University of Texas on a full scholarship. And then his world collapsed in late 2009. His father was deported back to Bangladesh, following his own forty-two day detention so too was Saad—"with no hope, no purpose, I had lost everything."

Life for him in the Bangladeshi capital of Dacca was a shock, and Saad went into a severe depression. The food and water made him sick. Living in a small apartment, he and his parents were assaulted by the noise surrounding them from outside. His mother in particular was "debilitated by what has happened, she will never recover." Not only had she lost the comforts of her life in the U.S. but also she was unable to find work outside the home as she had in the U.S. Nor did she have family in Dacca, instead having been raised in a small village.

Saad makes it clear that he means no insult to Bangladeshis. His website carries the disclaimer: "I do not mean to offend anyone from Bangladesh. This is simply not my country. The customs, laws, and language are all foreign to me. I am afraid of everything here. I just want to go home."

He explains to me, "Try to imagine being three years old, growing up here, assimilating, it is all you know . . . and then being told your entire existence has been a lie." The best example of his situation that he can think of is *The Matrix* "where you learn it has all been a fantasy."

When he leaves the apartment in Dacca he is overwhelmed by its unfamiliarity. "I find it impossible to assimilate. Having been raised in the First World in such different circumstances . . . it's not just the poverty but essentially people who are indentured servants . . . and the human rights abuses all around."

Neither does he speak the language, adding to his alienation. This has also put him in jeopardy. Saad tells the story of witnessing a policeman beating three street children. Quoting a newspaper interview with Saad, "People had gathered around the policeman begging him to stop but he continued. Incensed, Saad jumped off the rickshaw, and before his father could stop him, yelled at the policeman to stop hitting the children—in English. The policeman wheeled around and hit Saad squarely with his baton telling him to speak Bangla."(1)

To understand how Saad found himself in this predicament—as he puts it, "stateless and homeless"—the story goes back to 1994. Saad's father was a successful businessman in the garment trade. He travelled internationally frequently, including at least seven times to the U.S. Within a general atmosphere of political unrest in Bangladesh, his father started receiving threats to his life. Their home was the target of a Molotov cocktail. His father was interrogated by the police. Under these threats, the family decided to leave the country.

They came to the United States and Saad's father applied for political asylum. His request was denied in 1996 and by 2002 he had exhausted his appeals of that decision. In Saad's view, "the judge did not believe my father about the level of threat against him. I don't think the judge understood the reality of a place like Bangladesh." Also, the judge seemed to be thinking, "since he had visas for other countries, why did he not go there?"

Up to this point the family was living in Southern California in Burbank. "I was all set to go to magnet middle school in Van Nuys." Instead, "my life was upended." They were ordered to depart the country voluntarily. Instead, they closed out their life in California and moved to Texas—picked perhaps because his mother had a distant relative there. "My father did what anyone would do—what was best for his family."

They were now in the U.S. without authorization, though their immigration lawyer at the time had advised them to stay in the U.S. They did have one other hope still for gaining legal status. A brother of Saad's father had come to the U.S. a number of years earlier on a student visa for graduate studies. He eventually dropped out of his PhD program but rather than return home, he stayed illegally. Through the procedures established by the 1986 immigration reform he legalized, and later became a U.S. citizen. He lives and works in the New York area.

In 1999 the uncle initiated the process to gain immigrant visas for Saad's family. U.S. immigration law favors family unification over other purposes, but there is so much more worldwide demand than there are visas allocated that the wait can be lengthy, especially when it is a sibling helping a sibling, as opposed for example, to a parent or child. Saad's father finally received word in 2009 that the application for him had reached the front of the line and processing of his case could begin. It was while they were waiting for the next step in that process that Saad's father was arrested by local immigration authorities when he went to request more time on the family extension previously received for Saad's high school completion. He was deported and prohibited from returning to the U.S. for at least ten years.

Saad was studying for an electrical engineering exam when his mother called. Together they immediately left for Canada, hoping to gain refugee status there. Instead, they were refused entry and detained by U.S. authorities. Saad was separated from his mother and held in a center in Buffalo for forty-two days with what he describes as a number of "hardened criminals." In an open letter to President Obama he wrote, "I lived in constant fear of being abused. . . . When I asked for legal counsel I was threatened with criminal charges and jail time in a federal penitentiary."(2) With me he doesn't talk about his fear but instead about "being confused out of my mind by what happened. Everything went so quickly from normal life to getting arrested and thrown in detention, separated from my parents."

And then he was in Bangladesh and under the same ten-year ban as his parents. "Academics had been my whole life. How hard it is to be told that I cannot study in the U.S., shattering my dreams. My goal was to go to Stanford and now I am being told that I can't go there because of where my parents are from and what they did." Making it all the harder to bear, some of his friends with whom he had made plans are now indeed attending Stanford.

"I would not hold children responsible for the actions of their parents. Instead, there should be a program like the DREAM Act that would allow young people such as me to stay in the United States, go to college and become citizens of the country that has been home to them." To critics of the proposal he responds, "I didn't decide to come to the U.S. What do people think—a three-year-old swam across the ocean?"

Shortly after the incident with the policeman Saad left Bangladesh, both for his safety and to further his education. He went to Malaysia, which he finds more advanced than Bangladesh, living in a hostel in the capital of Kuala Lumpur. He is now starting his second year of a three-year program in electrical engineering at a school affiliated with Northumbria University of Great Britain.

Part of what stands out about Saad's story is the widespread support and attention that he has received. He was featured in at least two articles in *The Dallas Morning News*, another in *The New York Times*, as well as a write up in *The Huffington Post*. There has been a Facebook page in his behalf with several thousand members and a petition by high school classmates that gained several hundred signatures. A professor at Southern Methodist University worked to get him admitted into SMU's engineering program in hopes that this would bring him a student visa if he would commit to then returning to Bangladesh. Reporter Jessica Meyers notes, "The irony is not lost on [Saad] Nabeel, who realizes he's fighting to return to a land he calls home so that he can benefit a homeland he doesn't recognize."(3)

Perhaps most significantly, his cause was taken up by Ralph Isenberg, a successful Dallas businessman specializing in distressed-property management. Now in his early sixties, in recent years Isenberg has also devoted substantial time to assisting young people with immigration troubles. He has been particularly helpful to Saad, consulting with him daily through his first year of exile, supporting his website, and advocating his cause.

Raised in Wisconsin by refugees from Nazi Germany, Isenberg is not a lawyer but does have significant experience dealing with immigration authorities. At the time that he met his wife Nicole she was in the process of being deported back to China and he was married to someone else. Following his divorce, they married and moved to China while he commuted back and forth across the Pacific and worked on getting Nicole a visa. Fourteen months later it was issued in 2007 and the couple moved back to Dallas.

Since then Isenberg's immigration interests have expanded and he has indeed succeeded in helping a few others with their immigration problems. His interest in Saad seems to have been particularly important for keeping up

Saad's morale and hopes. But it has not been enough. At this writing Saad has still not been able to return to what he regards as his home.

When we last corresponded Saad was turning twenty-one, "more confused than ever as to where my life is supposed to go." However, his final comment is indicative of how I think of him: "at least one thing's for certain: I know how to survive."

Endnotes

(1) Marisa Treviño, "Deported DREAMer Saad Nabeel Finds Hostility and Threats In Native Country Because He Only Knows English." *LatinaLista.net*, January 18, 2011. Web.

(2) Saad Nabeel, "A Letter to President Obama: 'The Only Home I Know Is The United States of America.'" *Huffpost College*, September 21, 2010. Web.

(3) Jessica Meyers, "SMU supports deported Bangladeshi's bid to return to Dallas to study." *The Dallas Morning News*, April 28, 2010. Web; also, "Student deported to Bangladesh fights to return to life he knew in Frisco," April 5, 2010; also see Julia Preston, "With Drive (and Without a Law Degree), a Texan Fights for Immigrants," *The New York Times*, March 5, 2011. Web. I am most grateful to Jessica Meyers for her kind assistance in facilitating my contact with Saad, as well as to Ralph Isenberg.

ANNA STEEGMANN

TWENTY-FIVE YEARS IN THE SHADOWS (Mirjana)

Only two of Mirjana's friends know that she has been living in New York City as an illegal immigrant since 1986 and that, unless a miracle happens, she might be deported. I have known her for twenty years and have never been to her home. Mirjana shares her small studio apartment, a walk-up and most likely one of the last affordable flats on the Upper East Side of Manhattan, with her dog Mazzy and her turtle Katrina.

"Sent home?" she asks. "My home was Yugoslavia. My country no longer exists. My parents, my aunts and uncles are dead. I have no one in Serbia except for a distant cousin and a few Facebook friends."

"How did you end up in this predicament? How did you survive in the shadows for so long?" I want to ask. "Tell me about the Yugoslavia of your youth," I say instead.

Mirjana was raised in Apatia, a town of 30,000 inhabitants near the Romanian border in the multiethnic province Vojvodina. Serbs, Hungarians, Slovak, Croats, Romanians and Roma lived together without much conflict. Six official languages were spoken. Mirjana left Apatia to study political science in the capital. "Belgrade was a cool city. At my university we had students from the Soviet Union, Palestine, and Africa. Yugoslavia in the 1980s was a beautiful place. Tito ruled the country. We were better off than most Eastern Europeans because we could travel abroad."

Katrina, the most imposing soft shell turtle I have ever seen, dashes from one side of the huge aquarium to the other at lightning speed. Once in a while she stops, sticks out her long neck and head and turns her tubular snout and strange intelligent eyes to us. I feel as if she's following our conversation. Mirjana looks melancholy as she pours us tea. At fifty-six, she is still strikingly beautiful with curly reddish-blond hair cascading down to her waist. Her accent is pronounced. "I believed in Marxist philosophy, the united proletariat across international borders. I still do," she says.

She remembers the good life. In her early twenties she had no care in the world. "I never worked a day in my life. As a student my parents supported me and when I got married my husband did." Her good luck did not last when the marriage became troubled. Her husband left for New York and ended up staying. After one year of separation, Mirjana, at age thirty, followed him to find out if their relationship had a chance of surviving.

They lived in Kew Gardens, Queens, an area of "beautiful houses with backyards and lovely streets with old trees." Both worked illegally. Mirjana made $80 to $100 a day as a waitress. The marriage fell apart and, in 1992, Yugoslavia fell apart. Violence and hatred erupted in her homeland. Friends warned her in letters not to come home. Their perspective, their nationalism, shocked her. In New York she had learned to appreciate differences. "I did not think of myself as a Serb," she said, "to this day I declare myself a Yugoslav."

Mirjana left her husband. He moved to California and she stayed in New York. All of their Yugoslav friends turned their backs on her. Her parents were upset. Mirjana survived with odd jobs, painting apartments and working in restaurants. Today, she works in an art gallery, a job she loves, unfortunately one that barely pays enough to survive in New York City.

"How do you do it?" I ask.

"With help from above," she answers.

She fell in love with an African-American man and ended up marrying him. Her parents did not approve. Mirjana never filed for permanent resident status because her husband could not prove that he was able to support her for his fashion business had crashed. "My legal status is my fault," she says. "I made a lot of bad decisions; I had lawyers who gave me bad advice. Right now I cannot get legal help because I cannot afford it. The lawyer demands $8,000. Catholic Charities won't help me. I'm a 56-year-old white woman. I can't compete with an HIV-positive African woman, the mother of four children."

"I didn't know that I could apply for a driver's license. I didn't know I could attend a state college. I was an immigrant but not connected to the immigrant community. I wish the American spirit would have rubbed off on me. I love the history of this country; I love how they tried to create a perfect union. Serbia has a new government now but nothing much has changed."

Her eyes have lost their sparkle. "If I'm forced to go home I have no regrets. If I didn't live up to my capabilities I have no one to blame but myself." A very American sentiment, I think.

Although she loves New York, her feelings for the United States are complicated. "I can only live in New York City, San Francisco, and Los Angeles. I'm not comfortable anywhere else in the U.S. I don't fit in with popular American culture." I ask her to elaborate. "The Mississippi must have existed for millions of years, but most Americans act as if nothing existed on the continent before the arrival of the first settlers. I don't share this view."

She does like the American pioneer spirit. "Nothing is impossible here," she says. "If you have hope in your heart you can make it. You get up, brush yourself off, move to another city and reinvent yourself. In Serbia when you're doomed, you're doomed forever. In the United States you have a chance to make your dreams come true."

"And your dream is?"

"To have a life in New York."

"Would you become a citizen if you could legalize your status?" I ask.

"I can love this country without becoming a citizen," she says. "I'm not saying I won't become a citizen. I first have to understand what it means."

Once she told a friend that she was illegal, and the woman terminated their friendship. She felt that Mirjana had been dishonest and that she would never be able to trust her again. "What else is there that I don't know about you?" she had asked. Friends who told Mirjana about job openings wondered why she never followed up. Sometimes they got angry. "They tried to help and I didn't accept their help," she says, "but I couldn't tell them the truth."

Mazzy settles by her feet and Mirjana strokes his fur. She reminds me of a beautiful actress in a tragic play. Her voice is full of anguish. "I lost twenty-five years of my life. Twenty-five years of living in the shadows, twenty-five years of fear and shame. I was never part of any community. I always was an unwelcome intruder."

She is almost in tears now. "What's the worst thing that could happen?" I ask.

"Being forced to go home," she says.

Mirjana feels that her options are shrinking. "The decision will be forced upon me." Until a year ago she did not feel at home anywhere. "I have Gypsy blood," she says. "But as I'm getting older it is harder to live out of a suitcase." She is haunted by a nightmare, a foreboding vision: arriving at Belgrade airport with a few dollars in her pocket, her dog and a small suitcase with all her worldly belongings.

Taking her first steps into Serbia, her so-called homeland, she finds herself in a foreign country.

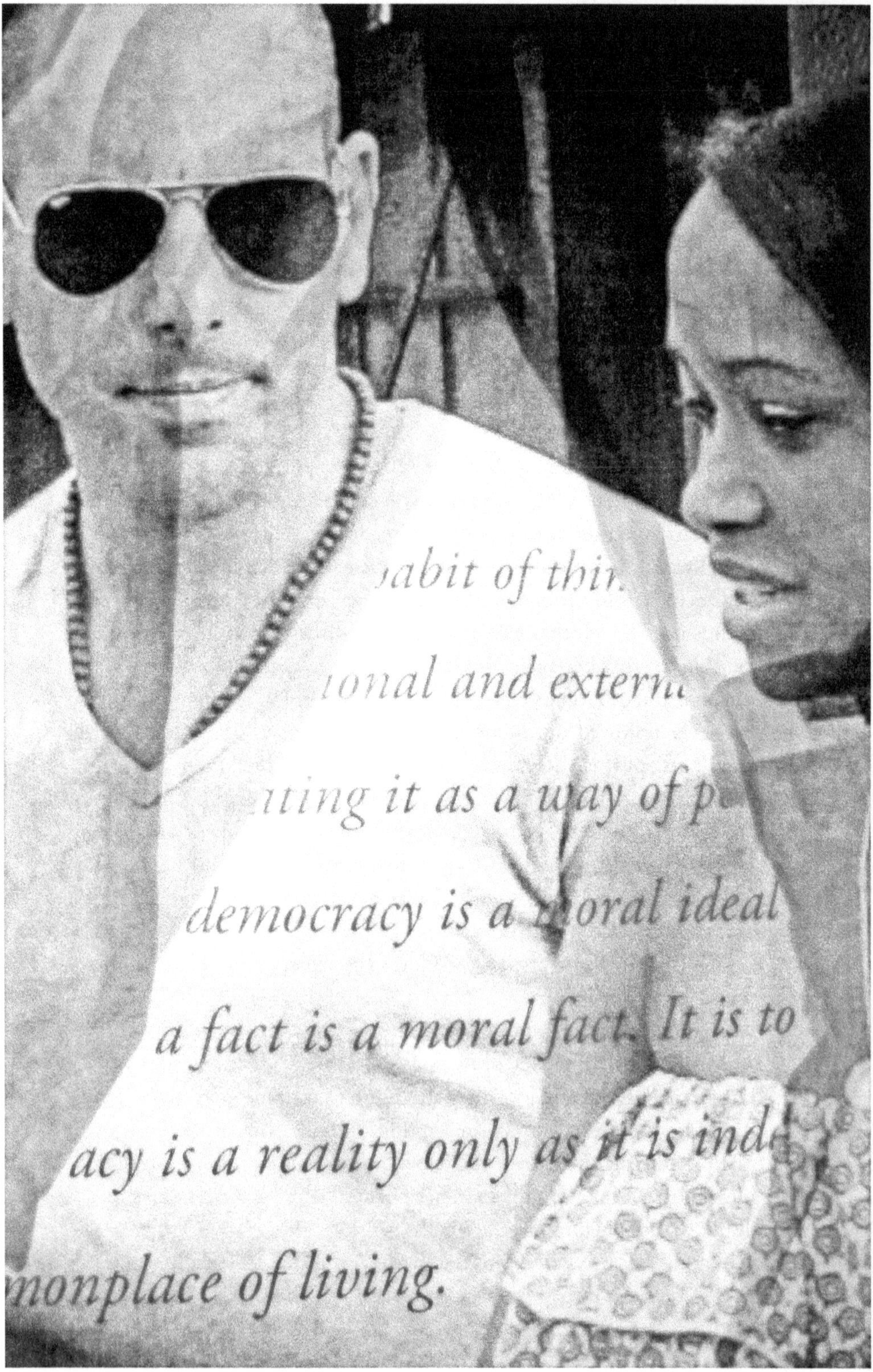

abit of thin

ional and extern

ating it as a way of p

democracy is a moral ideal

a fact is a moral fact. It is to

acy is a reality only as it is inde

monplace of living.

MARIANA FIGUERA & ANDY MARTIN

Interviewed by Charles Brockett

SO MUCH TO OFFER . . . BUT SO DO OTHERS

Mariana Figuera and Andy Martin are medical research professionals living in Florida. She is in her mid-thirties, he is in his early forties. They are married. Mariana is from Venezuela; Andy from Canada. They both have been studying and/or working in the U.S. legally for over ten years. They would very much like to stay in the United States to continue their careers, but the odds are uncertain, at best.

Mariana

"I went to the Universidad de los Andes in Mérida [a picturesque city located high in the Venezuelan mountains] for five years, which is the standard length of study in Venezuela to get a BA. Mine was in biology. Especially in the sciences there are a few things that you have to do if you want to go on in academics. You need to get a PhD but I didn't want to move to Caracas and I also wanted to experience life in another country." She first looked to Europe but found that she would have to pay her own way to study there. So she turned her attention to the United States where the resources and opportunities are more ample.

Mariana also had U.S. connections. "My mother when young came here to work so that was in the back of my mind, not with the idea of a permanent stay but staying for a couple of years. My mother came for college-level English study. She went to Minnesota for the duration of that course and then went to New York to work for a year and a half and then back to Venezuela." Part of that time she lived with "a crazy cousin" and Mariana grew up hearing stories "of the crazy things that she did in New York. . . . She had a good time, it was a good experience and left her good memories."

Mariana also heard of the U.S. from her Aunt Zöe Losada who has long lived in Caracas but was born and raised in the U.S. Zöe's two children are dual U.S./Venezuelan citizens. Mariana also has two other cousins who emigrated to the U.S., one a physician now with permanent resident status and the other an engineer and birthright citizen (William Betancourt). In contrast, her brother tried four or five times to get a visa but was always turned down, leaving him "very frustrated for a long time, wondering 'what is wrong with me, why don't you let me do it?'"

After searching, "I found a professor in Ohio who then suggested a scientist at Notre Dame. I contacted him and told him that I had read a bunch of his papers, and he offered me a research assistant position in his lab. It was an easy way to bring me to the U.S., into the lab and teach me things. And he had the money and was willing to pay. It was good luck that I was able to find this professor who was willing to pay for me. I came in November 2000 when I was twenty-three, and after ten months applied for graduate school and then started my PhD in biochemistry."

Thinking of herself as quiet and shy, Mariana welcomed "the challenge of new experience." Still, arriving in Miami was a shock. "Everybody was talking in Spanish, just like I was still in Latin America. I thought, what is this?" A different shock awaited her in northern Indiana where she arrived "in November at midnight in a little regional airport with a single baggage claim area. I was scared a little, not knowing what would happen." But good fortune was with her. Another Venezuelan she had taken a course with back home was also working in the lab, and he picked her up at the airport. She stayed in his spare room for her first six months, greatly easing her transition.

Since completing her PhD, Mariana has been employed through post-doctorate fellowships. Typically in the sciences, established researchers compete to obtain grants that then fund the fixed-term employment of younger scholars working on their research teams. Post-docs usually run for one to three years. Mariana's position at the time of this interview was scheduled to end in a few months. She is in the U.S. on a J-1 visa, which is intended to promote cultural exchange by offering professional training. When there is no position, there is no visa.

Andy

Andy was already working in the same Notre Dame lab when Mariana arrived. He was born and raised in a small town in Canada just above the border. His maternal grandfather was from upstate New York but settled in Canada where his own children were born. Andy's mother considers herself Canadian; growing up Andy had no thoughts of living in the U.S.

After graduating from college Andy spent a year in farm work. Then his computing background took him to Nortel, first working in the factory and then doing installations. His hope was to work in places "like Russia, Brazil, Hawaii, places that were developing and supposed to be expanding their telecommunications. But, at that point economics were bad and the rumor inside the company was that expansion was not going to be happening."

Coming to the U.S. and then meeting Mariana "was just a bit of luck." Andy had attended Notre Dame for his third year of college. A friend from those days had continued on into graduate school there and was getting married in 1999. Andy came down to be in the wedding party and at the reception talked with his friend's adviser, whom Andy also had had for a professor. The professor invited Andy to come back and work as a technician in his lab. "I like travel," Andy explains. "I like change. I am not afraid to just cut loose and try something so even though it was a pay cut to go to Notre Dame, it was a no-brainer."

Up to recently Andy lived and worked in the U.S. on a TN-1 visa, which was established as part of the North American Free Trade Agreement. There is no limit on the number of Canadians and Mexicans who can come to the U.S. and work as long as they meet the qualifications for the specified professions. Canadians can both easily enter the U.S. and obtain their TN visa when employed under these regulations.

For long-term stays, though, the drawbacks are considerable, especially compared to permanent resident status. The TN visa must be renewed each year. One year Andy's employer "messed it up and I was sent back to Canada." The visa must be renewed also each time you re-enter the country. "You can be turned back at the border so easily with the TN visa," Andy says, "and with the current economic situation I think the ease of getting the TN visa may be over. It is so easy for a customs officer who is processing the form to say 'no, go away.' It could be they would be trying to protect jobs for U.S. citizens."

Quandaries of Residency, Citizenship and Cultural Attachments

Ideally, Mariana and Andy would like to have green cards. Having lawful permanent residence would allow them to work anywhere in the U.S. and to travel freely in and out of the U.S. for as long as they would like. This status also is an important step toward naturalization should they ever wish to become U.S. citizens. But there are so many more decent hard-working people around the world who also would like to get a green card than the U.S.

is willing to authorize. Furthermore, U.S. policy favors granting permanent residency for family unification over other reasons such as attracting skilled workers—the opposite of many other countries, for example, Canada.

Mariana recognizes that becoming a citizen "would allow me certain things—voting, scholarships, grants, certain types of funding. Yes it would open doors but no, I have no desire to become an American citizen. . . . I feel Venezuelan, I like what I am. It doesn't mean I would change if I became an American citizen . . . . I don't have anything against Americans or becoming American but I don't see myself doing that. If I honestly look deep inside my heart, I am not an American inside."

Being Venezuelan, though, is also complicated. When younger she "was very happy with my country and my nationality but as people started to associate Venezuela with the president, with Hugo Chávez," the situation changed. "If you are an outsider it depends on what version you listen to, you can think Chávez is a great man fighting for the poor or you can think he is a dictator and a moron. So those people who associate Venezuelans and Venezuela with a dictator, poverty, poor education, dirty kids running through the streets, that bothers me a lot. . . . For the last two or three years if somebody asks, I just say I am from South America. First, because I don't want to have to explain to people where Venezuela is and second I don't want people to associate me with Chávez and their negative views of Venezuela because that's not what Venezuela is. I feel a little offended. It bothers me."

Mariana also doesn't always see herself as sharing the traits Venezuelans associate with being Venezuelan, "like being late (I hate not being punctual), speaking certain ways, liking certain things. I'm not loud. I don't play loud music. I respect personal space." Still, she likes "my country quite a bit—how close the relationships are, how easy it is to get close to people; family connections that you can keep, even if you are thousands of miles away, its like you have never left. I like the combination of cultures my country has—European influences, Black influences, Indian. I feel like that is part of me. As soon as I hear the drums from the coast of my country my blood boils, that is part of me."

Mariana has been to many parts of the United States—Indiana, Michigan, Chicago, New Mexico, Tennessee, Georgia, Florida, New York. She doesn't like "hectic cities with tons of people, traffic." Instead she prefers "the mentality of small towns. People see you and say 'good morning' to you." But, it can also be "a double-edged sword: if you go to a town that is too small, where people have never been outside of the town, have limited experience, and ask you questions like, 'have you ever had ice cream?'

"In general with the culture and people in the U.S. I am comfortable, as long as I am not being attacked. Or being stereotyped, putting all Latins in a single bag. Given the proximity to Mexico perhaps that is not unnatural, thinking all Latin Americans are Mexican. That's the only part that is uncomfortable for me. For example, when I talk with people they of course realize I have an accent, and if they see the color of my skin they put the two things together—that means I am Mexican [they think] and they treat me as if I am stupid and don't understand English. They think I'm a housemaid or tomato picker. That may sound arrogant on my part, it is not that I don't want to be recognized as a Latin American but rather it's not allowing people to have their individuality."

Mariana's workplaces have been very cosmopolitan because the scientific community is very international. Counting administrators as well as researchers, she estimates that maybe 20% of her current workplace is Latin with maybe 60 to 70% foreign born. "It has been lovely for me, allowing me to meet people from all over the world. We joke around that at our parties we have Armenian barbeque with our German friends and drink Spanish wine. Every party has ten nationalities at least. I love that, it's very easy, I feel very comfortable, everybody has an accent."

Canadian/U.S. differences, of course, are much less than with Venezuela. For Canada Andy thinks of "maple syrup and hockey whereas for Americans it is baseball. And our other national language is French not Spanish." Growing up close to Quebec, everyone in his school had to take French; Spanish was not offered. His hometown was small and homogenous so he really didn't think much about being Canadian. There was "little exposure to other cultures. Mariana teases me, 'where are the other cultures?' There was the Pakistani family that owned a lot of the real estate, but that was it. Everybody else was white bread." His parents still live in the same town, as do both his brother and sister. Today the major difference that he sees between the two countries is that "Canadians are internationally loved." He has met people even from the U.S. "who travel with the maple leaf" because of the differing attitudes toward the two neighboring countries.

Otherwise, Andy sees differences between the two countries declining. "There is more interaction between the two now with more cross-border trade, more people working on both sides of the border, many more Americans are sending their kids to Canada for college because the tuition is lower and the schools are quite good. For example, when I came to Notre Dame for my third year, the classes we were taking back in Canada were the same ones that American graduate students were getting."

Still, there are the opportunity differences. To Andy pure research just isn't funded in Canada like it is in the United States. He is clear that especially in the sciences and engineering "there are many more Canadians coming to the U.S. rather than the other way around." Indeed, he has many Canadian friends living in the United States, most of them on permanent visas either by marriage or through the efforts of their employers. Altogether in 2000 there were about 820,000 people born in Canada living in the U.S. According to one scholar, "highly educated Canadians living in the U.S. have little interest in abandoning either Canada or Canadian citizenship."(1)

Certainly permanent resident status "would make getting a job so much easier," Andy explains. "Right now we are looking for jobs and so many of the forms that we fill out online ask whether you have a visa or will you need to get one, so we know that we are going right to the bottom of the pile—not to mention all of the U.S. citizens who need jobs. We have already talked to an immigration lawyer and we would have to be so highly decorated and well published and getting our own grant monies to be considered for a permanent resident visa just based on our scientific prowess. But, that immigrant lawyer said 'you know you guys just aren't good enough and I wouldn't even take your money to undertake the process.'"

Andy's job at the time of the interview had ended and with it his TN visa. Accordingly, he had to go back to Canada and then reenter the U.S. as a Canadian visitor. He has resumed his job search. When he finds a new job he could then get a new work visa.

Mariana considers the best option for her to be another post-doc "but the situation is, I am under-qualified for senior positions but over-qualified for entry-level positions and basically there is nothing available in between." Her hope is that if she could get one more post-doc for another two or three years that it "would hopefully open the doors for a senior position."

She will also continue to pursue an even longer-shot possibility, the Diversity Visa Lottery, a small program meant to give better immigration chances to residents of countries underrepresented in contemporary immigration flows. Mariana has entered the annual lottery three times and intends to continue. The chances of someone from South America gaining a U.S.

green card through this program are under one percent (2).

If they are not able to stay in the U.S., it is clear to both of them that they would take their marriage to Canada because there would be no language barriers and there would be more career opportunities for both of them. Mariana says, "It would be crazy for me to return to Venezuela. It would add a lot of stress to our lives, maybe to our relationship. Something would have to change dramatically for me to consider going back."

However, Canada has its challenges. "It's just so cold in the winter!" Andy exclaims. They are both big outdoors people, as indicated by their fit and tanned bodies (Mariana regularly competes in triathlons). Andy's mother "has been begging us to come back for years, she doesn't like that we live so far away. But, we like the weather, we like living below the snowbelt [actually, so do his parents who winter in Florida] and have been looking for jobs in places that we would like to live so that we can have a life outside the job. If we can't find work, though, we will have to start looking further and further north."

Legally there would be no problem in Canada. Mariana "could get permanent status very easily," Andy says, and both of them "could work in anything," unlike in the U.S where they are both highly restricted. In Canada, Mariana adds, she could "even work at Starbucks or on the farm." As a biochemist whose research has been focused on human diseases, though, her hope is that she will be able to continue with this work. "I would be happy working anywhere as long as it was work related to that, anything dealing with the way proteins work in diseases but it could be any disease, working at a university or at a pharmaceutical firm."

Resourceful and optimistic, both see no issues for their marriage if they were to move to Canada—or perhaps someplace else. Mariana says, "I think personally I would adapt very easily if we moved to Canada although there would be career uncertainties. But I would do anything. I'm not afraid of flipping burgers if I have to, it would just be a stage of life. We like to travel and we are at a stage of life where we can make it work."

Endnotes

(1) Donna R. Gabaccia, "Canada." *The New Americans: A Guide to Immigration since 1965*. Eds. Mary C. Waters and Reed Ueda. Cambridge: Harvard University Press, 2007: 325.

(2) *Wikipedia.* "Diversity Visa Lottery." Web.

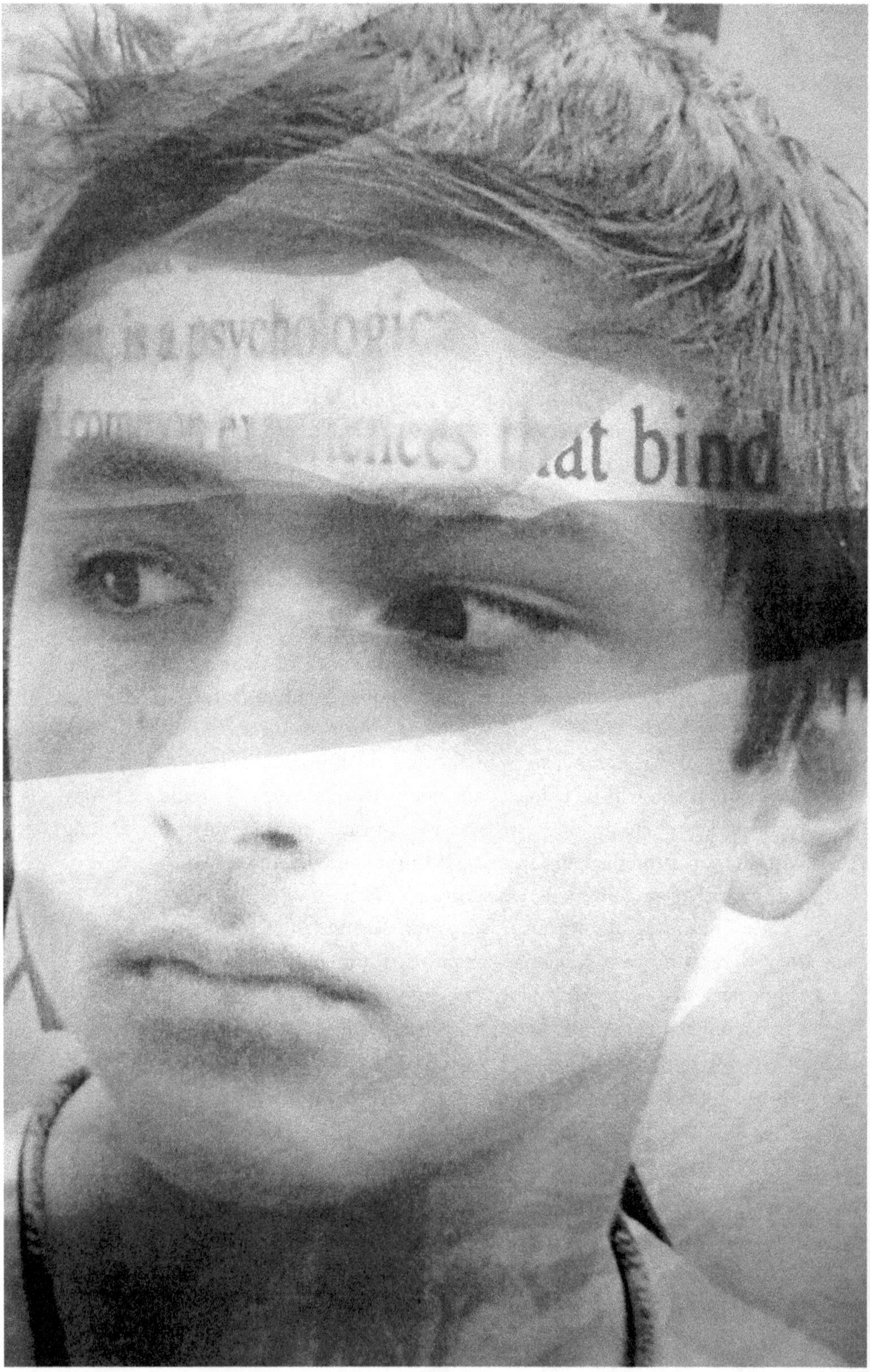

is a psychologic

at bind

V

WHY DO WE COMMIT?

ANNA STEEGMANN

THE NEW (TORN) AMERICAN

"The naturalization ceremony is a solemn and meaningful event," the letter said. I was to dress in proper attire to respect the dignity of the occasion, "no jeans, shorts or flip-flops." It was Friday, December 19, 2008. WQXR predicted heavy snowfall, hazardous driving conditions, a possible blizzard. Flip-flops were out of the question. I settled on my interview outfit, white turtleneck, navy pant suit, and moon boots.

The morning host on the radio announced "A Lincoln Portrait" by Aaron Copeland. As the music floated along, solemn and mysterious, the wailing contrabassoon transported me to my homeland, the poor blood-soaked continent of Europe. I thought about rape camps and ethnic cleansing during the Yugoslav wars, the millions killed during two world wars and the constant threat of nuclear war during the Cold War. Gruesome pictures of nameless horrors flashed through my mind. The brass section soared toward a dramatic climax and the pounding tam-tam sent tremors through my body. A male voice rose above the orchestra. *Fellow citizens, we cannot escape history.*

This music, these words are no coincidence, I thought. *As I would not be a slave, so I will not be a master,* the voice proclaimed. I thought about our European emperors and kings, our counts and rulers. Being born into the right class guaranteed wealth and success; being born into the wrong class guaranteed the life of an uneducated laborer. My grandparents, my mother and father had to leave school at the end of eighth grade to work in the fields. My mother-in-law came to the U.S. in 1950 with her young family. A refugee from the Soviet Union, she had ended up in Germany at the end of WWII, one of millions of displaced persons stranded like flotsam and jetsam all over the continent. In the Ukraine they had told her: "You were born in a basket; don't try to fit yourself into a suitcase." She loved the United States, the "greatest country on earth." In Irvington, New Jersey it did not matter that she was born in a basket; she could aspire to a suitcase or even a steamer trunk.

Words were twirling in my head: *Heimat, Mutterland, Vaterland. Heimat is untranslatable*, I thought. *It is not the same as homeland. Heimat is deeper, graver. Heimat carries the weight of a profound attachment; it holds centuries of German consciousness.* Wasn't I forever bound to my *Heimat* by my birth, my childhood, my experiences, my way of looking at the world? Could I truly become a citizen of another country? Was I betraying my *Heimat* by becoming an American citizen?

The A-train was crammed with early-morning commuters. Students were horsing around and banging into each other with their backpacks. An older woman with a Caribbean lilt warned us that the world was coming to an end. We were all going to perish unless we turned over our lives to the Lord. She was competing with a homeless veteran rattling a paper cup and asking for donations. I overheard snippets of Urdu, Creole, Spanish, and Russian. David Dinkens, New York's first African-American mayor, had called our city a "gorgeous mosaic." I felt proud to be a New Yorker, proud to belong to such a racially and ethnically diverse metropolis and country. I would never find this mix of people on any German bus or subway.

I pictured the faces of my students at The City College of New York. Razwan, Mohamed, Nor, Selah, Daler, Chukwudi, Adelina and Agnieszka expected a bright future in America and were willing to work hard to get there. Our classroom full of immigrants and children of immigrants was a miniature United Nations where white students and American-born students were the minority. *It is impossible to find such a college class in Germany*, I thought, *impossible to find such a class in all of Europe.*

During my last visit to Germany my nephew had invited me to visit his English class. The students in his *Gymnasium* (high school) were all German with the exception of one Turkish student (the proper German term is "a pupil with migration background"). His father owned a *Döner Bude,* a kebab stand. I wondered if his father had been denied better work opportunities. My nephew lives in Duisburg, a city of 500,000 inhabitants, where 16.5% of the population are foreigners and in some districts 25%. I have met plenty of Turkish taxi drivers with graduate degrees in Germany, but I have not found Turkish doctors, teachers or policemen. No doubt, this is the result of an educational system that separates the wheat from the chaff at the end of fourth grade.

I came to New York on a tourist visa in 1980. Smitten with the city, I cashed in my return ticket and stayed on as an illegal immigrant. The pre

9/11 U.S. Immigration Office did not hold this against me and allowed me to become a permanent resident after my marriage to a naturalized American citizen. My husband and I had to line up in different queues whenever we returned to JFK airport from vacations abroad. This was a minor inconvenience but no reason to apply for citizenship. I had no desire to become an American citizen, and my husband did not encourage me to do so. I had the best of both worlds: a green card, a German and, a few years later, an E.U. passport. My passport was my security blanket. If I fell seriously ill, lost my work and found myself unable to pay the exorbitant Manhattan rent, I could return to the bosom of the German welfare state anytime. Or I could try my luck in Italy, Latvia, Greece, or Spain. All that separated me from the continent of Europe was a seven-and-a-half hour plane ride.

After 9/11, I considered U.S. citizenship for the first time. I sang along with the "Star-Spangled Banner" at the graduation ceremony in the high school where I worked as a counselor. I had never done so in the past fifteen years. I bought a miniature American flag and a flag pin. This was my city, my country, and I wanted to show my gratitude and my pride as the country was so viciously attacked. I surprised myself, for in Germany the display of patriotic feelings was frowned upon. In Germany, I had never felt patriotic. School children did not line up in the morning to pledge allegiance to the flag. Flag waving was for Neo-Nazis and soccer fans.

In the following years the desire to become an American citizen slipped away. The wars in Afghanistan and Iraq were depressing. The country was headed in the wrong direction. To become an American citizen I would have to renounce my German citizenship. I felt like a child forced to decide between my mother and my father. Why could I not have both? Given a choice, I would have been born Dutch, Belgian, Portuguese, anything but German. After World War II, we were the most hated people on the planet. I was at least thirty-five years old before I could accept or even appreciate being German. It had been a hard-earned acceptance. But to consciously renounce German citizenship (for the U.S. does not formally recognize double citizenship), the country of my birth, my schooling, my mother tongue, my parents, my relatives, and the most loyal friends on the planet, felt impossible.

The German government passed a bill allowing double citizenship. I procrastinated three years before I sent in my "Application for Granting Permission to Maintain German Citizenship" with the € 300 check to the German Consulate. I was questioned about my continuing ties to Germany, the reasons why I wanted to become an American citizen (my main reason, the right to vote, was not considered a valid reason), the disadvantages and drawbacks I might be facing if I did not become an American citizen (I could not think of any and had to make them up.) I argued that after living twenty-six years in Germany and twenty-six years in the United States I was neither German nor American, but both. Therefore I needed both citizenships. After six months of waiting I was approved. The *Bundesverwaltungsamt* gave me a deadline: The "Permission to Maintain German Citizenship" would no longer be valid if I did not apply for U.S. citizenship within two years.

I hesitated for another year before I applied. To help Barak Obama win the election, I had to become a citizen. *No more sitting on the fence,* I said to myself. *It's time to join a community board, vote on the local and national level, and make my voice heard.* The U.S.A. had treated me well. I had been an illegal immigrant for six years. I had been given many chances: the chance to fail, the chance to change careers in middle age, the chance to go after my dreams. Perhaps I could become an American citizen and stay true to myself at the same time. I did not have to give up my mother tongue, my way of looking at the world.

For three hours I sat in Room 160, the Jury Room of the U.S. Southern District Court, one of three hundred eager immigrants. There were naturalization ceremonies taking place in the courthouses of the other boroughs at the same time. On average 70,000 New Yorkers became U.S. citizens each year; many like me had lived in the city for years. I watched Chinese and Spanish translators direct the immigrants. Parents depended on their children to be their interpreters. I read *The New York Times* back to back. Bernard L. Madoff had committed a multibillion-dollar fraud. Rockets and mortars had been fired in Gaza. The Iraqi journalist who had hurled a shoe at President Bush during his visit to Baghdad was applauded in the Arab world.

When I had to surrender my green card I panicked. My stomach felt queasy—a sensation of losing my footing, getting seasick. Once I left the courthouse I would not be an alien resident, a detached observer, any longer, but a citizen. I was taking this step at a time of rampant anti-Americanism. My new homeland was vilified everywhere. As an American citizen I would not win any popularity contests unless I went to Kosovo.

As a European living in the United States *by choice*, I had been attacked numerous times travelling abroad. How could I live in such a primitive country? Americans were imperialist warmongers. Schools forbid the teaching of evolution. The Christian fundamentalists ruled. All civilized countries had abolished the death penalty, why not the U.S.A.? A group of Dutch information technology professionals I met on a high-speed train from Amsterdam to Berlin made me feel as if I was personally responsible for invading Iraq. I fought them tooth and nail. At work in New York, I was often criticized by my colleagues for being too critical of the United States. In Europe, I defended America with all my might. The critics were right about the death penalty and the anti-abortion movement. But Europeans were ignorant and narrow-minded just the same. Their high-cultured citizens dressed in Levis, ate at McDonald's, listened to hip-hop and watched American blockbuster movies. Europe was not altogether different; it was just limping behind. My attackers reminded me of teenagers rebelling against their parents: all hat and no cattle. It was much easier to take the moral high ground, protest the inhumane treatment of Guantánamo Bay detainees, than find room for them in European prison cells. My attackers overlooked the injustices in their own country. There was not one person "with migration background" among them. No child of Turkish or Moroccan parents would become president of Germany or the Netherlands anytime soon.

An employee of the Department of Homeland Security stepped onto the stage and took hold of the microphone. Like a cheerful kindergarten teacher he seemed thrilled to practice with us. "No not like that. Louder. More enthusiasm." We had to trumpet the Pledge of Allegiance several times until he was satisfied. Finally, the judge came. "This is the most favorite part of my work," the Honorable Deborah A. Batts said. She told us about her grandfather, the first in the family to come from Ireland. He worked hard for three years before his wife and children, the judge's father among them, could join him. Judge Batts was the first in her family to attend college and law school. The family was proud of her. "My story is not that different from yours," she said. "Make use of the opportunities given to you by the U.S. citizenship. Get involved in your children's school; help to improve your community. Success is yours if you want to work hard for it."

I was willing to work hard and make a difference in my community. I was fine with declaring, on oath, "that I absolutely, and entirely, renounce and abjure all allegiance and fidelity to any foreign prince, potentate." But I wasn't willing to renounce all allegiance to Germany, "the state of sovereignty of whom or of which I have heretofore been a subject or citizen." I could not bring myself to speak the words *I will bear arms on behalf of the United States when required by law.* As a pacifist, I wasn't going to bear arms on behalf of the United States or any other country, not even my *Heimat.*

I was handed a big envelope. Inside I found my naturalization certificate, two booklets—*The Declaration of Independence and the Constitution of the United States* and *The Citizens' Almanac*— and a welcome letter by President George W. Bush. He called me his "Dear Fellow American" and congratulated me on becoming a U.S. citizen. "You are now a part of a great and blessed nation. Americans are united across the generations by grand and enduring ideals. The grandest of these ideals is an unfolding promise that everyone belongs, that everyone deserves a chance, and that no insignificant person was ever born."

I didn't like Bush, but I liked his letter. "Our country has never been united by blood or birth or soil. We are bound by principles that move us beyond our backgrounds, lift us above our interests, and teach us what it means to be citizens. Every citizen must uphold the principles." President Bush asked me to serve my new nation, beginning with my neighbor. "Americans are generous and strong and decent not because we believe in ourselves, but because we hold beliefs beyond ourselves." *He must have a great speechwriter,* I thought.

We sang the "Star-Spangled Banner." I cringed during the part about "the rockets' red glare, the bombs bursting in air" and got teary-eyed just the same. In spite of myself, I felt proud to belong to "the land of the free and the home of the brave." *Ich bin hin-und hergerissen,* I thought. I am torn. The German expression felt so much stronger: being yanked this way and that, back and forth between rapture and doubt. I remembered an essay by Gloria Anzaldua. "We are not crossing the bridge from one culture to another," she said, "We are staying on the bridge." The back and forth, the *hin-und hergerissen* would be my permanent home. I was a *Zwitterding*, a creature with an American brain and a European soul. Inside of me, American optimism and eternal trust in the future lived a peaceful coexistence with European pessimism and wariness about our long and bloody history.

A citizen for just a few minutes, I felt different already. The court employee gave me a conspiratorial smile on my way out as if saying "Now you're one of us." I felt different once I left the court building. Outside the first white wallop of winter was turning manic downtown Manhattan into an oasis of calm. The snow made everything look pure and pristine. The people in the street, the deli clerk, the token booth attendant, the pharmacist at the Duane Reade store, were my people now. I could no longer say, "The Americans are ignorant. They don't know anything about history or geography." I would have to say, "We Americans need to educate our young people, so they learn about the rest of the world, so they learn from the past."

America's problems had become my problems. I was responsible for making America a better, fairer home for all of its inhabitants. Something had shifted. No more *them,* only *us.*

MURALI KAMMA

BEING INDIAN, BECOMING AMERICAN

In the summer of 2011, two decades after getting my green card, I became a U.S. citizen.

Why did it take so long? Yes, I've been asked that question—but rather than look back fifteen years (when I became eligible for citizenship), I'll go back ten years (when I grappled with this issue in the wake of 9/11). Is it necessary to acquire U.S. citizenship in order to become Indian-American? I asked.

In response, I wrote: "Although not absolutely essential, I think it's a good idea and I am all for it. Nevertheless, for a long time I was reluctant to become one, since I have never ruled out the possibility of returning to India one day. Despite my enduring admiration for America, I recognize that I have two homes. Like many other immigrants who grew up in India before moving here, I have strong family ties in both countries. Over the last few years, however, I have slowly realized that I cannot become a full-fledged Indian-American until I acquire U.S. citizenship. One cannot participate fully in this society unless one accepts that honor. For instance, looking back, I regret that I didn't have a voice in the last presidential election."

I was referring then to the contentious Bush-Gore election of 2000. But more than that year or even 2001, it was 2004 that tipped the balance for me, turning an expatriate into a patriot. My son was born here in 2004, cementing my emotional ties to America like never before. Still, given that my son is now seven, the question arises: Why did I wait so long? The answer, not praiseworthy, can be summed up by one word: Procrastination.

But finally, just as my green card was coming up for its second renewal, I filed my citizenship application—and hoped that I'd be sworn in before the tenth anniversary of 9/11. Which did happen, but until the day of my interview I wasn't sure if I'd meet my self-imposed deadline.

"Maybe now you can write about this," the immigration officer said as that interview ended. I'd just shown him a copy of the magazine I work for.

What followed first, though, was my inevitable post on social media, leading to a flurry of "congrats" and "good wishes." But one response—a short, curt "why now?"—felt like an unripe holdout in a basket of sweet apples.

Perhaps I was overreacting to the two-word question, sent hastily from a mobile device by my cousin in India. Blame it on the digital age. Written communication has never been easier, but that sometimes means deciphering messages is harder. Soon, I realized my cousin was referring to the turmoil here in the wake of the Great Recession, which had greatly altered his perception of America. The financial meltdown, a paralyzed capital in a polarized nation, the debt debacle, staggering job losses, a backlash against immigrants—it was all adding up to paint a dismal picture.

Meanwhile the two Asian giants seemed to be on the ascent.

When I became eligible for permanent residency in 1991, a crisis that would lead to war was brewing in the Persian Gulf. My green card came through family sponsorship, not a lottery. Nevertheless, it felt as if I had hit the jackpot. Euphoric, after my interview, I emerged from the quietly imposing U.S. consulate and walked for hours on the noisy, bustling streets of Madras (now Chennai), before rushing to the station to board my train at the last minute for an overnight journey. Now I became a little melancholic, wondering when I'd see India again. A woman on the train asked to see the brand-new seal of residency in my passport, making me a minor celebrity in our cabin.

That year, after I landed in the U.S., turned out to be extraordinary, with victories in the Gulf War and the Cold War—following the Soviet Union's collapse—acting as bookends. America became the world's only superpower. Sure, there was a recession, but what followed was one of the most prosperous decades in living memory.

Fast-forward two decades—and the U.S. seems a very different place. Demoralized. Debt-ridden. Declining. But you wouldn't have thought that if you had attended my naturalization ceremony. I'd waited many years to become a citizen, and when the day finally arrived in Atlanta, it felt as momentous as that morning at the U.S. consulate. Standing between a South African and an Iranian, I was sworn in along with 140 others from sixty-six nations. What about the remaining nationalities, I couldn't help wondering? As we found out, a naturalization ceremony is held at this office almost every working day.

On my trips to India, I'm sometimes asked why I chose to settle in a country where I have no ancestral ties. Blood and belonging are inextricably linked in many parts of the world, but the idea of America has long been . . . well, an idea. Anybody can be an American, I say, despite the considerable obstacles to becoming one.

Not surprisingly, even here I've been asked why I came and why I stayed. What was the big draw, in other words? Mainly, at first, it was my family. And yes, America's opportunities, especially for a young person from a country that's more crowded but less prosperous, did count for something. Still, I saw my sojourn as an exciting adventure—a passage through America, as it were—rather than a permanent stay in this country. That changed over time as I put down deeper, more substantial roots. Besides "opportunity," many immigrants would mention "freedom" and "variety" (or "diversity") as determining factors when talking about their attraction to America. All true, and they are applicable in a range of spheres: economic, social, cultural, spiritual, intellectual, political. But I believe there is a fourth characteristic—"acceptance"—which tends to set the U.S. apart from other nations with immigrant populations.

If we leave out India, I can think of no other country where I'd feel more accepted than I do here. Indeed, even in this gloomy climate, polls seem to bear this out. "Although Americans are most likely to say immigration levels should be decreased, 59 percent still believe immigration is good for the country today," noted one this year, adding, "In the 10-year history of this Gallup trend, a majority of Americans have consistently believed immigration is a good thing, with a high of 67 percent in 2006." Despite the stress and strain of recent years, America's capacity to absorb foreigners remains formidable.

At the same time, as my fellow immigrants would attest, particularly if they have U.S.-born children, there is no contradiction between being Indian-American and being American. Some would disagree. Following high levels of immigration from non-Western countries, they might argue, America is undergoing such drastic shifts that it's no longer a melting pot in the traditional sense. But even if the U.S. today is more of a salad bowl made up of diverse ingredients, the metaphor only goes so far. The centrifugal forces pulling us in various directions are balanced by, I believe, centripetal forces rooted in the intertwined legacy of citizenship and assimilation, a legacy that becomes more pronounced as we move down the generational chain. A second-generation citizen is, naturally, more 'American' than a first-generation immigrant. So while Americans are individualistic (i.e., I-centric), they also have a national identity that's anchored by constitutional and cultural rather than communal ties.

Of course, it's not as if race, ethnicity, and religion don't make a difference. They do. But the idea is that, given enough time, the impact of such primordial ties can dissipate, as it tends to in the U.S. when compared to most other places. And that's because of this shared national identity—though, certainly, one hopes the nationalism is always tempered, not jingoistic. Such benign (as opposed to bellicose) nationalism has no room for American Exceptionalism, a concept that doesn't sit well even with our friends. Not to forget, we have had an ugly past in which groups seen as undesirable and unassimilable were ruthlessly excluded. That's history now, fortunately. Progress comes with a capital "P" in this ever-evolving nation, and the light on the horizon is always brighter. "Novus ordo seclorum," says the one-dollar bill. Translation: "New Order of the Ages."

Since 1980, as per the Pew Research Center, intermarriage rates in the U.S. have more than doubled; moreover, as the Brookings Institution points out, close to 25% of Americans under the age of eighteen have at least one immigrant parent. Just one generation can make a huge difference, it seems, bringing swift change that could end some of our rancorous conflicts. "E Pluribus Unum," meaning "from many, one," referred to the way the federal state was created from individual colonies. But this motto is still relevant, for it encapsulates how our disparate I-selves come together to form a We-society.

As a youth in India, I was drawn to the works of author Aldous Huxley. His death on November 22, 1963, was overshadowed by the assassination of President Kennedy. But growing up, Huxley seemed as noteworthy as Kennedy, and after I got my green card, I was pleased to remember that Huxley, too, had been an American immigrant. While visiting New York on his first trip to the U.S., Huxley noted, "What I should write under America's flapping eagle would be: Vitality, Prosperity, Modernity."

The Statue of Liberty remains the most iconic monument for immigrants. In 2011, which marked the 125th anniversary of its dedication in New York Harbor, I also came out with my American motto—although mine is alliterative rather than euphonious. As I would tell my cousin, for an immigrant like me, America represents "Hope, Happiness, Home."

NIKOLINA KULIDŽAN

MARGARITAS AND GUACAMOLE

By 8:15 a.m., Jelena is wondering what might have happened. We've been officemates for two years and it's not like me to be late to work without calling. By 8:30, she is worried. By 9:00, she is calling my cell phone at three-minute intervals. The phone is off. At 9:30, she dials my fiancé. Twelve hundred miles away, he is the last person to have seen me. Alarmed by her call, he tells her that he spoke to me around eleven the night before and that I was still driving from the airport. He hasn't heard from me since. By 10:00, Jelena is in tears.

That's when she starts a full-blown investigation. First, she calls every hospital on the Monterey Peninsula, and when she finds no record of my name, she dials the police and reports me as missing. She then summons our friend Sandro and together they go to meet a detective at the house where I am renting a basement apartment from a man whom Jelena has heard me refer to as mentally ill and in the habit of talking to himself in two distinct voices. When questioned by the detective, my landlord states that he believes he saw my car arrive late the night before and leave early this morning. The unopened suitcase they find in my room corroborates his account. The detective seems pleased, but Jelena is still suspicious. She eyes the landlord, plotting how to invite herself into his house. She imagines me tied to a chair, my mouth taped, my face red from struggle. She grows more and more upset.

Just about that time (it was getting close to noon) less than two miles away, I am walking out of a workshop on task-based instruction, trying to decide whether to go out for lunch or return to my office to check email. I decide in favor of a leisurely meal and am switching my phone on to see if any of my friends might want to join me, when I realize I have five messages. This would have been unusual at any time, but on a Monday morning it's alarming. I overcome my usual inclination to ignore voicemail, only to hear my fiancé's teary voice telling me to call him back and then some other stuff I don't quite understand. By the time I get to Sandro's message I am very confused. But I gather that Jelena and he are at my house, along with a police officer, interrogating my landlord about my whereabouts.

I call Sandro right away. I am laughing my ass off as I explain to him that I was in a workshop and that I had told Jelena about it. When we meet for lunch fifteen minutes later, I fully intend to tease Jelena about her forgetfulness but her eyes are bloodshot and she looks exhausted so I save the teasing for later. She keeps touching me as if to assure herself that I really am alive. I feel bad to have caused my friend such grief, but a part of me feels very happy. It's a relief to know that someone would notice if you disappeared.

Now let me clarify something: I am a Bosnian Serb. Jelena is a Croat from Croatia. Sandro is a Bosnian Muslim (or to be more politically correct, a Bosniak). Or at least, those would be the shorthand labels we'd use to define ourselves. The reality, of course, is messier. One of my grandparents was a Croat and I am from Herzegovina not Bosnia. Jelena's mother is actually Macedonian, and Jelena attended college in my hometown. Sandro's parents were so determined to avoid ethnic categorizations that they gave their first-born son an Italian name, and I didn't really know what his ethnicity was until I asked him about it when I started writing this essay.

We were each born into a multicultural utopia, a place where relationships were forged based on character, sensibility, sense of humor, and shared interests rather than some misguided notion of ethnic identity. We each saw that utopia dissolve into chaos and madness, our lives suddenly shaped by animosities we never held, our paths veering off to unknown terrain. We each traveled great emotional and physical distances, to meet at an unlikely place, a picturesque coastal town in central California, where we unwittingly recreated the paradise we were born into, becoming not only each other's friends but a family.

So what had happened in between?

Mine was a charmed childhood. My parents were loving and present, my older brother the right balance of protective and tough, my hometown tucked into a valley, sun-filled and safe. I was a teacher's pet, yet my peers didn't seem to resent me for it. My family spent a month each summer at the Adriatic, the weeks melting away while I chased around with my cousins, dived off wharfs, picked wild blackberries, and napped in a hammock.

At the age of nine, there were still challenges to overcome and at the time, I am sure they seemed insurmountable. I was a late bloomer in reading and had to endure countless hours of remedial activities which did little to improve my abilities but inflicted a great deal of suffering. There were also the dreaded piano lessons, my ineptitude and utter lack of talent apparent to everyone but my parents. And then, of course, there were the stupid boys.

By far the worst was Žućo, an obnoxious blond kid relentless in his attempts to lift up my skirt and touch my butt. This wasn't his affliction alone; all the boys seemed at one point gripped by the same uncontrollable urge, but Žućo stood out for his brazenness and nerve. It was probably because I would chase him the longest after his offense that I was Žućo's favorite victim. He always outraced me so it was a while before I finally took my revenge. My opportunity came the day I spotted him riding his bicycle around a parking lot, weaving in and out of imaginary obstacles. I watched for a while and at an opportune moment, I ran to him and pushed him with all my strength. I watched him crash and then took off as fast as I could. From that day on, Žućo stayed out of my way.

Then, there was Veca, my first boyfriend. One autumn evening when I was about ten, a bunch of my friends dragged me out of a pool hall and led me to a shadowy spot in the parking lot. There stood Veca. I had seen the boy around, knew that he was three years older than me, that he played soccer with my cousin, and had a younger brother, but that was about it. I had no feelings for him one way or the other. But when he asked me whether I would "go with him," I felt like I had no choice but to say yes. I didn't want anyone to think I was too timid to have a boyfriend. Veca and I were together for four months. During that time we spoke exactly one other time. He had invited me to come for a walk with him, but the moment we stepped out of the pool hall he stopped and turned to face me. I had never had a chance to study him from up close and I enjoyed this opportunity to get a better look at my boyfriend. He had a round face and pretty blue eyes set perhaps a little too close together. His upper lip was so thin it made him look strict even when he smiled. And he was smiling now.

"What do you need to take with you when you go to the market?" he asked, a smile quivering in the corner of his lips.

"Huh?" I looked at him confused.

"A basket," he said. "You take a basket."

"A basket?" I thought. What the heck was he talking about? And then it dawned on me. He was giving me a basket! He was breaking up with me! Thus I tasted humiliation.

But it was all for the best. Soon after this episode I met Marko. We had met through a mutual friend, but our instant attraction required no external prodding. The first time our eyes met, they locked and wouldn't let go. We kept looking for opportunities to cross each other's path. Life was on our side. One day I was walking back from my piano class, about to cross the street toward the railroad tracks, a shortcut to my house, when a kid on a skateboard came flying down the hill, stopping just barely short of me. Just as I was about to curse the careless hoodlum for giving me a scare, I realized this was Marko. We froze in our spots, neither of us saying anything, our eyes expressing what we had no words to articulate. Was there anything greater in the world than liking someone who liked you back, I must have wondered.

What I didn't know when I pushed Žućo off his bicycle, when Veca gave me a basket, and when Marko and I stood speechlessly in the middle of a well-trafficked road, was that the obnoxious blonde was a Bosniak, the tactless macho kid a Serb like me, and the boy whose friendship and affection would lay permanent groundwork for the sense of self-worth I would carry throughout my life, a Croat. Up to that point, I had derived my sense of identity from being a good student, from loving to climb hills with my dad, from being courageous and daring, from loving sweets and fairy tales. No single label could contain who I was. I loved my neighborhood, I loved my town, and I loved my country, and the complexities of the pluralistic society in which I grew up utterly escaped me. At what precise moment my blissful ignorance dissipated and I assimilated my surrounding's ability and need to label things, is hard to tell. But I think it began with graffiti.

Graffiti was nothing new to Mostar. For as long as I can recall, spray-painted signs were a normal part of the town's urban landscape. They were everywhere: facades and pavement, dumpsters and kiosks, stairwells and elevators. Forza Velež or Velež do groba, perhaps the two most common graffiti of that time, served the same general purpose most other graffiti did – to assert loyalty and devotion to a group or an idea, in this case, to our town's red-clad soccer team. Other common graffiti did a similar thing. Valley of the Greeks, Chicago Bulls, Radića Bronx, were all neighborhood wanna-be gangs who marked their territory with spray paint.

But in the fall of my ninth year these familiar signs were being replaced by ominous three-lettered acronyms. HDZ was short for Hrvatska Demokratska Zajednica (Croatian Democratic Party), SDA for Stranka

Demokratske Akcije (Party of Democratic Action, the most prominent Bosniak party), and СДС for Srpska Demokratska Stranka (Serbian Democratic Party). Whereas once the graffiti united those in our immediate surrounding, in 1989, at the eve of the first democratic elections to be held in Yugoslavia in fifty years, they became divisive. Everything that had once defined us—the style of music we listened to, the type of clothes we wore, the soccer team we supported—now became secondary to this new system of classification.

It turns out, democracy, like mini skirts, is not for everyone. For a place like Bosnia and Herzegovina, the land which had, for hundreds of years, struggled to maintain the fragile peace among the ethnic groups who defined themselves not so much by any intrinsic quality they possessed as by their mutual differences, an attempt at democracy was doomed. What I didn't realize as a child was that the multicultural utopia I had grown up in was a rare moment in history when my tormented homeland enjoyed harmonious existence. For all its failings, communism had accomplished one great feat—it brought what seemed like genuine harmony to a historically fragmented society. As the system crumbled so did the harmony it had helped introduce.

Along with the political acronyms, other nationalistic symbols came off the dusty shelves of history—flags, coats of arms, songs. One morning, a brand new red and white checkerboard (Croatian coat of arms) would appear on a school wall, the next morning a star and crescent popped up. Not long after, a Serbian royal cross materialized. Above it was a name written in Cyrillic. It belonged to my very own brother.

This caused uproar in my house. What had compelled a sixteen-year-old kid who had never once heard a nationalistic sentiment expressed in his home to resort to such a public display is hard to tell. It could have been an act of rebellion against our father or an act of rivalry with his friends. Whatever it was, this simple action illustrated how easy it was to fire people up. From an aloof teenager to a sworn nationalist, my brother had made his conversion in a matter of days. Many others were undergoing the same transformation.

Although it would be a long time before I would appreciate the full implications of these changes, I wasn't unaffected. Like everyone around me, I had learned to label and categorize people. All Ivans and Ivanas were Croats, I figured out, all Dragans and Draganas Serbs, and all Samirs, Emirs, and Adnans Bosniaks. Croats crossed themselves with their left hand, Serbs with the three fingers of their right, and Bosniaks didn't cross at all. Soon, many

Serbs started cheering for Belgrade's Crvena Zvezda and Croats for Hajduk and Dinamo. That left only Bosniaks loyal to our local Velež, a team less accomplished than the others but one that had united us for so long.

But even as I lost my innocence and grew more aware of the forces tearing my town apart, I was determined to ignore them. I desperately wanted my world to stay the same. I wanted to fit in. So when my friend Darko asked me during recess one day what my ethnicity was (my name being international enough to defy easy classification), without thinking, I gave him the answer I thought he wanted to hear: that I was a Croat. My deceit was rewarded. Darko looked at me conspiratorially, lifted his leg cuff, and revealed a red and white checkerboard embroidered ankle high on his sock. Flattered as I was to become Darko's confidant and ally, the incident also made me uncomfortable. Not only did I lie, but I made a pact which hinged on excluding others. This arrangement was not sustainable, I realized. It was only a matter of time before someone else asked me the same question and my friends started comparing notes. It was much easier to ignore and deny that seismic shifts in mentality were taking place all around me and to assume that this over-focus on ethnic identity and nationality was a temporary fad just like leggings and tall hairdos. So for a while I became the most fervent proponent of the view that nothing strange was really happening in Mostar, that the rumors were baseless, fear unjustified. Our life would go on as it always had.

But ignorance is bliss only to a point. In late March of 1992 my friend Ivana told me not to sleep in my bedroom. The bedroom looked out onto the military barracks right across the street where, according to Ivana, "something bad" was soon to happen. The rumor had it that Ivana's mom was dating a Croatian military officer which explained how a twelve-year-old girl could be in possession of such potentially life-saving information. But to take Ivana's advice would have required me to admit that war was coming to my hometown. That I couldn't do. Instead, Ivana and I placed a bet. Nothing would happen in Mostar, I said. A week later, our life was still as it had always been and my friend had to buy me lunch. Less than a week after that, a 20-ton tractor-trailer exploded exactly where Ivana had said it would, wiping away the entire western side of our building, my bedroom wall included. At the time this happened, I was climbing stairs to my apartment, and would have already been inside if not for the fact that someone had disabled the elevators and it was a long way to the eighth floor. I never saw Ivana again, but if I ever do, I will buy her the lunch I owe her.

As little as my parents seemed to care about national identity, once the time came to leave Mostar, there was really no debate as to where we would go. Within two weeks of the explosion, we were on our way to Serbia. Whereas I had spent every summer of my life up to that point in Croatia, I had been to Serbia exactly once before. A year earlier, I had accompanied my mom on a business trip to Belgrade, mostly to fulfill a lifelong dream of flying in an airplane. I took Belgrade's grandiosity with a child's matter-of-factness. I saw big city squares and fancy stores and fuming buses and street cars and a restaurant called McDonald's where young people in clean uniforms stood behind a counter, took orders, and delivered the neatly wrapped food like Christmas on a tray. Because my life was waiting for me unthreatened five hundred miles to the south, I felt no need to judge this place. But when we arrived there in May of 1992, this time to stay, Belgrade became a proxy culprit for my loss. Finding flaws with the city and its people became my way of reasserting loyalty to my war-torn hometown.

The unchallenged ethnocentrism of a largely mono-cultural society soon surfaced as the most unforgivable of those flaws. Ignorance had bred misunderstanding. Otherwise intelligent, kind, and well-meaning people lived with inexcusable stereotypes simply because they had never met the objects of those stereotypes. Ethnocentrism was a default setting, a set of assimilated views unchallenged by either experience or deep thought.

But there were also those whose nationalistic views seemed the centerpieces of their existence. One such individual was my high school homeroom teacher. On the first day of class, she came in and announced that she would be teaching the following subject areas:

1) Serbian language and literature,
2) Cultural history of the Serbs, and
3) Humane relations among the sexes.

Serbs, our teacher would have us believe, were the oldest living organisms on earth. Her zeal quickly became a class joking matter. "Remember, amoebas, then Serbs," my friend Miloš would say. "That's right! While our peasants ate with forks and knifes, those savages in English courts were still stuffing their faces with their hands," someone else would chime in to keep the absurd comedy going.

Inciting nationalism was clearly my teacher's goal. Toward this end, she endeavored to portray Serbs as a people: 1) inherently and uniquely worthy—fearless, heroic, and defiant in the face of oppression, 2) victimized throughout their history, and 3) unjustly demonized by the West in recent times. The facts to support these points became pillars of every class hour: our medieval state was a model European monarchy; our fight against Ottoman invaders valiant and unprecedented; our resistance during five hundred years of cruel Turkish rule courageous and remarkable; our suffering in the two world wars tremendous; our wholehearted devotion to the idea of Yugoslav unity utterly naïve; our demonization in the latest war uncalled for and unjust.

To forgive and forget, according to our teacher, meant to betray the sacrifices of our ancestors and to allow history to repeat itself. I adamantly rejected this conclusion. My childhood was all the proof I needed that to forget was the perfect solution. Because my parents never did anything to perpetuate the narrative of Serbian victimization or superiority, I grew up without stereotypes, grudges, or a misguided sense of pride. My parents had forgotten so I grew up never having known. And others did too. But then we were reminded. The likes of my teacher took it upon themselves to perform this valuable community service. Nationalism gone amok, merely unhealthy in the case of a homogenous society like Serbia, proved tragic in a place as multicultural as Bosnia.

My entire being rejected my teacher's indoctrination attempts. I did everything I could to rebel against them. I refused to write in Cyrillic. I mocked epic poetry and the self-reinforcing myths it perpetuated. I rejected religion as just another tool used to draw false distinctions among people. I spent hours formulating counterarguments to my teacher's eloquent diatribes against the West and the New World Order which the Serbs were so courageously resisting.

But the power of propaganda should never be underestimated. You can only hear something so many times before you start to believe it. Somewhere along the way I got baptized in the Serbian Orthodox Church (something my parents had never bothered to do when I was a kid), started writing in Cyrillic (so much so, that to this day my U.S. passport and driver's license are signed in Cyrillic), and believing that being a Serb was an integral part of my identity. I still harbored no resentment toward any of my south Slav brothers and sisters, but I had internalized the distrust for the "West" I had been fed.

Such, approximately, remained my mindset when I came to the U.S.

as an exchange student in 1998. The stated objective of my trip was to finish high school and improve my English, but my parents and I both understood that this was my one shot at a better, more stable life and that I would do my best to find a way to stay. As I prepared for the trip, I received many words of warning about the prejudice and stereotypes I would face in America. The Western media had portrayed Serbs as ruthless savages who had plundered and pillaged their way through Bosnia and I would surely be asked to answer for my compatriots' alleged crimes, was the gist of what I was told. I came to the U.S. with my guard up.

Whether or not these words of warning had had any basis in reality, whoever was putting them forth had greatly underestimated the short memory span and general obliviousness of the American public. Three years had gone by since the war in Bosnia, and whether my hosts remembered or believed what they had heard on CNN, they treated me with complete open-mindedness. They didn't seem to care where I came from, as long as I was willing to embrace American values of hard work, self-reliance, and integrity. Because those came naturally to me, in some ways the U.S. felt more like home than Serbia. Six months into my stay, the culture shock I felt when I first arrived was starting to wear off, and I was getting accustomed to my new environment. That's when NATO's military intervention in Serbia became the front and back of every news broadcast.

The way CNN presented it, the U.S. had to act out of a moral imperative to preempt what-wasn't-quite-yet-but-would-soon-most-certainly-become genocide in Kosovo. Milošević, still remembered for his role in the atrocities committed in Bosnia, was accused of planning an ethnic cleansing campaign in Serbia's southernmost region with a majority Albanian population. He was given an ultimatum: either withdraw all security forces from Kosovo or NATO would commence its campaign to protect and safeguard the vulnerable Albanian population.

The way Serbs saw it, NATO's military intervention was not only unjust, it was criminal. The Kosovo Liberation Army, a militia regarded by the U.S. as a terrorist group only a year earlier, was now being relabeled as freedom fighters. Without the vote and approval of the United Nations Security Council, NATO had taken it upon itself to settle a territorial dispute in a sovereign country. Given how many similar disputes were being waged the world over, many of them far bloodier, it was hard not to concede the point my teacher had been making all these years—the West clearly was against the

Serbs.

The three months that ensued were some of the hardest in my life. While my family and friends were in harm's way, not only was I safe, but I was safe in the bosom of the aggressor. As the show of brute force continued, with another part of my country going up in flames every day, animosity and anger were growing in my heart. What bothered me most was the disingenuousness of the politicians who were selling the campaign as a moral necessity and the media that unquestioningly went along. Day in and day out, the media aired pictures and stories illustrating the plight of innocent Albanians, neglecting entirely to show the human face of Serbian suffering. The bombing was aimed at the evil regime, not the Serbian people, the message was repeated, but bombs kept falling on regular folks and not a single corrupt official. Collateral damage was mentioned only briefly in the news, and even when it was, it was treated more as an aside than a tragedy in itself. No hard questions were asked: What constitutes genocide; was it really taking place in Kosovo; is every group who desires independence entitled to it; what rights and responsibilities does a sovereign country have to protect its borders from the inside and out; when is the international community justified in intervening?

These three painful months showed me two faces of America that twelve years later I still struggle to reconcile. I saw America as a self-righteous, hypocritical bully, who under the pretense of justice, human rights, and well-being for all ruthlessly pursues its own interests and agenda. This America stretches the truth, simplifies, applies different standards to different situations, sometimes even lies outright, counting on the public to think little and forget fast.

But I also saw the humane and kind America willing to interrupt its self-absorbed existence to offer a helping hand to those in need. This America is both naïve and courageous, idealistic and pragmatic. It believes in the intrinsic value of every human being and in the ability of each individual to make a difference. I have seen this America act countless times in my thirteen years here, but never as much as during those months when I needed it most.

In the spring of 1999, as I struggled to justify to myself how I could still live in a country that was putting in danger the lives of those I loved most, it seemed like everywhere I turned people were only looking for how to help me cope. Kids who never spoke to me before now invited me to do things. Teachers called on me to tell my side of the story. An Orthodox church was located. A Serbian exchange student at another school was summoned. Even a fund-raising campaign to send me to college was kicked off. The way people around me acted during that time humbled, inspired, and indebted me for life.

Though I still keep my old-world nihilism, loudly stating that we are nothing but meaningless specks in a meaningless universe, it's mostly for show now. Deep down I have adopted this uniquely American belief that each person can truly make a difference, and that each person must be judged on his or her own merits regardless of the narrative of their past or the system that has shaped them.

The NATO intervention cemented in me the link between my identity as a Serb and the disdain I felt for the hypocrisy of the powerful and mighty. But it also did something far more positive—it planted the seed of tolerance. It led me to understand that tolerance does not require agreement or even acceptance. All it requires is the recognition of another's humanity. It requires an understanding that all our beliefs are external to who we really are, imparted to us by our environment and either reinforced or challenged by our life experience, but that underneath those beliefs is a much deeper level of humanity—and on that level we are all brothers and sisters connected by our shared experience of suffering and joy.

Many years later I am in Arlington, Virginia. It's a Thursday night and I am having margaritas with an Air Force colonel. When he asked me out for a drink all I knew about him was that he was handsome and that he had a kind smile. For the time being that was enough. Soon after we sit down, however, I learn that my companion has spent most of his career as a bomber pilot. That gives me pause.

"Did you . . ." I hesitate, looking for an appropriate verb. "Did you fly over my country?" I ask.

"No," he shakes his head slowly. It's an inconclusive "no," as if he would like to add that this was a grievance he would take up with fate the first chance he gets. But he doesn't say anything like that, not this first time we discuss it anyway, and I sigh with relief.

"So how does it work?" I ask after a brief pause. "You just press a button?"

"Pretty much," he nods. He wears a half-apologetic-half-mischievous smile. "The bombs are pretty smart these days. They have navigation devices. They are precise. If this restaurant was my target, I could be pretty certain I'd hit somewhere between these two tables." He stretches his hands. "You want to get it right the first time. You don't want to have to go twice."

I say nothing. A few years back and I would have judged him. But the black and white have long since seeped into each other. I am just processing it all.

"The idea is that you are getting the bad guys, right?" he says. My silence must have made him feel like he needed to defend himself.

Normally, this would set me off. But my companion's gentle demeanor has a calming effect on me. So when I speak, I speak softly too.

"But sometimes you miss the bad guys, right? You hit innocent people."

This conversation will never get anywhere, of course. So many layers of belief stand in our way. After twenty-six years in the military, my new friend must at the very least believe that war is sometimes necessary; that killing bad guys makes the world a better place. It's not an outrageous belief by any means. But it's not the one I hold. What I believe is that many, if not most wars are avoidable and that the world would be a better place if people had the wisdom to avoid them, that any good that comes from violence is tainted, that force self-perpetuates, that most of our leaders are flawed and short-sighted even if they happen to be well meaning, that more important than being an American or a Serb is the fact that we are human, that the interests of humanity as a whole should supersede the interests of any nation state, and that bombing is very rarely in humanity's best interest.

It's all too much, of course, for the first drink so I don't share any of these thoughts. Instead, I listen to my new friend tell me about a buddy of his who didn't make it back from his last tour. About a little boy and the young widow. It's hard to make any political points after that.

So we move on to talking about life instead. As different as our paths have been, on this hot August Thursday we find ourselves in similar predicaments. We are both going through divorces and dealing with guilt, uncertainty and fear of loneliness. We are trying to find peace with our families, looking for apartments, filling out and filing paperwork, and considering the practical and philosophical implications of our decisions. We may or may not at some point dissect each other's beliefs and find flaws with them, but right now that's secondary. What comes before is empathy. And attraction. And curiosity. And a need for touch. And a desire not to be judged. And so many other human emotions that have nothing to do with beliefs and labels each of us has acquired in our lifetime.

So we dig into guacamole and clink glasses and for the moment at least there is nothing that divides us.

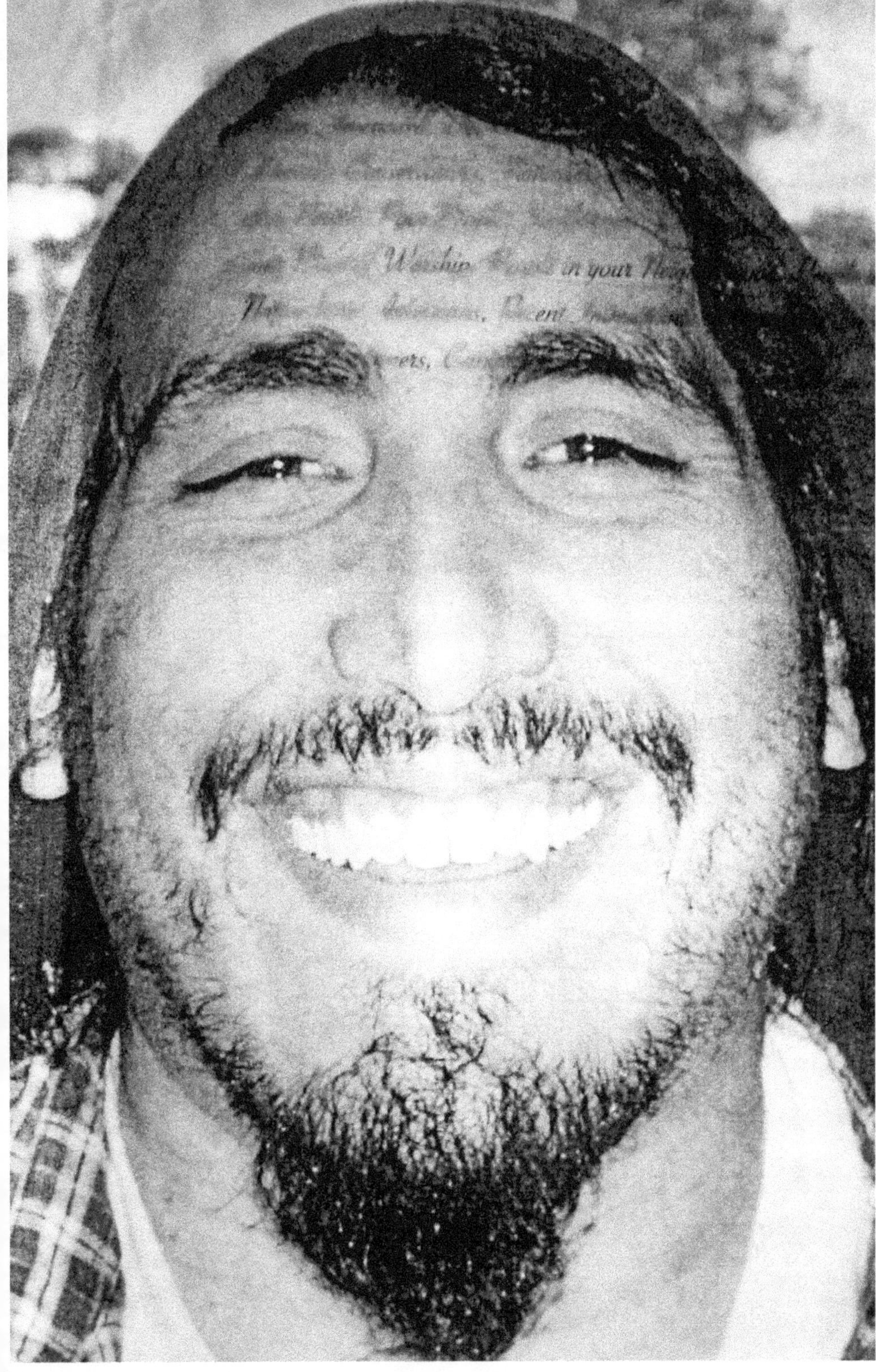

BARB TOEWS
Interviewed by Debra Gingerich

IT IS MY HOME, BUT ONE THAT SOMETIMES ACTS IN WAYS I DON'T LIKE

I first met Barb Toews in 1994 while we were both working for the Mennonite Central Committee, a relief and development organization with its international headquarters in Lancaster County, Pennsylvania. As an international organization, our co-workers and friends came from many places including Germany, Paraguay, Switzerland, Canada and states throughout the U.S. Barb was one of only a couple people in our circle of friends who had roots in Lancaster County. At that time she had lived there since 1977, only living elsewhere for her undergraduate studies (which she attended in Canada) and a couple years working in Fresno, California.

At first look, Barb was the typical Lancaster County resident, knowing the back roads around Ephrata as well as the tightly organized streets in inner-city Lancaster. She hung out with friends from the area and effortlessly built professional relationships with community leaders for her work as the director of a victim-offender reconciliation program. Barb still lives in Lancaster, with just one more brief time away to attend a master's degree program in Virginia. She is in the dissertation phase of a PhD, doing cutting-edge research related to the incarceration experience in the United States. Still, she makes time each week for a variety of reality TV shows and crime dramas. There is no denying that much of Barb's life experiences are intertwined with American culture.

But that is only a first look. A deeper look discloses much more. Barb is a Canadian, both by citizenship and at heart. A significant part of that identity is in her Mennonite roots. Known as Russian Mennonite, Barb's ancestors migrated to the plains of Canada in 1874 and developed customs that reflected their time living in colonies in what is now Ukraine as well as their Canadian existence. When Barb's family moved to the U.S. they lived and worked among Mennonites known as Swiss-German Mennonite, who had different traditions because of a different migration history. While growing up in the United States, her parents continued and encouraged the Russian Mennonite customs established in Canada and instilled in her an identity that persists through years of American life experiences.

I caught Barb by phone on a Sunday afternoon while she was grading papers for a course she teaches and making chicken broth from scratch. We talked about her identity as a Canadian citizen as well as United States resident.

Where were you born?

I was born in Thompson, Manitoba, Canada in northern Manitoba. My father had received a Master in Social Work with financial assistance from the Manitoba government that required him to work in a rural location for a couple years. After completing his work in Thompson, about a year after I was born, we moved to Winnipeg, Manitoba, which was the area where our family lived.

When and why did you come to the United States?

We moved to the U.S. in December 1976 when I was in the second grade. My dad was working for Mennonite Central Committee (MCC), an international relief and development agency. He was transferred to the U.S. to fill a senior management position. Soon after moving, my parents applied for green cards for the family. My green card is dated 1978 so I have had it, and essentially have called the U.S. home, for thirty-five years. My parents stayed in the U.S. for nearly thirteen years. My older sister only lived in the U.S. for nine years, at which point she moved back to Canada for college and has remained there ever since.

What were some of your first impressions of the U.S. once you arrived?

The first impressions I had were based on a child's perspective. Since my father worked for a global institution, we had a global viewpoint. We moved from central Canada to the eastern U.S., so I remember feeling that we were moving closer to the rest of the world and told people that we were going to be living across from Africa.

There are several impressions that come to mind once we moved to the U.S. I recall people having very strong reactions to cold weather, which, coming from Manitoba, was no big deal to me. While walking to school the first few days, I noticed that people were bundled up in winter coats and I was only wearing a sweatshirt. I also remember that people talked funny and used different words. For example, I called a zip-up sweatshirt with a hood, a "kangaroo" while people here called it a "hoody." Even now, I usually call it a kangaroo. I also remember feeling proud in school because I could write cursive when my classmates were just beginning to learn, the one difference in the education system that I noticed at that age. They used paste (glue in solid form) that was kept in a Tupperware container in their desks. I had only seen liquid glue coming out of a bottle.

In Canada, were you a part of a defined cultural or ethnic group? How did that influence your relationship with that country?

I am part of the Russian Mennonite community in Canada. My identity as a Canadian is intertwined with my cultural and religious identity as a Russian Mennonite. I am not able to separate the two and that likely has to do with how both of those identities developed for me.

How did you develop a sense of yourself as belonging to a country?

My identity as a Russian Mennonite and Canadian was developed by both what was present and what was missing in my life growing up.

One of the main events that influenced my identity was dinnertime. We regularly ate dishes ancestors had brought with them from Russia such as *borscht*, *halubschi* (cabbage rolls), *verenicki* (cottage cheese *perogies*) and *keilke* (homemade broad noodles). This was obviously different from the foods eaten by my friends and neighbors, including other Mennonites. Even the ingredients we used were authentically Canadian. Manitoba sausage and New Bothwell cheese were habitually in our fridge. My dad brought these foods back from his frequent trips to Canada.

Our family regularly had Canadian employees and volunteers of MCC to our home during holidays and for events appreciated most by Canadians, such as the National Hockey League final playoffs for the Stanley Cup. It is because of hosting this event that we even had a color TV and cable. I remember my mom making huge amounts of *verenicki*, my dad grilling Manitoba sausage and the backyard full of people "like us" who salivated for this taste of home. These and other types of gatherings influenced my Canadian identity also because of who was not present. When others spent Thanksgiving dinner with their local family, we spent it with Canadian friends and acquaintances because our families were too far away. The absence of regular family get-togethers was a constant reminder that I was Canadian, or at least not from here.

In my peer group, I rarely felt different though I did receive some friendly teasing from classmates that I was not American, "should go back to where I came from," "stop breathing their air" and "stop living off their taxes." Sometimes people knew the term "alien" in reference to non-citizens (as a green card carrier I am a resident alien) so I got some ribbing about being an alien. It never felt malicious, though. It was one of the few areas of difference in my life that I liked and was proud of.

What experiences have caused you to feel American and challenged your sense of being Canadian?

These are not specifically experiences, but there are several characteristics I have that seem American. I feel that I fit the stereotype of the ignorant American populace. For instance, I don't have interest in topics that I don't need to know for my everyday life, like geography or international current events. While dining in restaurants, I expect quick and friendly service. I also like Howard Stern. Canadians are stereotypically more informed, polite and couth than Americans so I feel like I am not all that Canadian with these traits.

Admittedly, I have identified more negative stereotypes of Americans and counter them with positive Canadian traits. I know that I also should acknowledge the positive things about being American and negative Canadian traits. This sense of negativity probably stems from the fact that I have always had a strong sense of social justice and typically side with the underdog. As a result, I experience tension in my relationship with the U.S., a global superpower. It is my home but one that sometimes acts in ways that I don't like, so it is nice to be able to identify as Mennonite and Canadian. I was an undergrad in Canada when the first Gulf War occurred. I remember threatening, quite loudly, to burn my green card if the U.S. went to war. They went to war but I never followed through on my threat. I wanted to speak from my perspective, as a Mennonite and Canadian, against the U.S., my other home. But, I wasn't prepared to go so far as to let go of my U.S. home by losing my legal status.

In terms of my political views, I am more Canadian than American. I also don't identify with mainstream religion in the U.S., and definitely not with the Christian right. In other cultural areas, I am a fairly typical American. But Canadian pop culture is quite similar to the American culture of movies, music and TV.

Have you considered becoming an American citizen and why did you decide against it?

When I got married, I changed my last name from Toews to Toews Shenk (but without a hyphen). I updated all of my Canadian and U.S. documentation to reflect this name change. In some ways, this combined name reflected an inter-cultural marriage as Toews is a common Russian Mennonite last name and Shenk is a common Swiss-German Mennonite name.

Since I had not hyphenated the two words of my last name, people started calling me by Shenk alone. I quickly realized that I was uncomfortable being called this because it did not represent my Russian Mennonite identity and thus seemed to deny my familial and Canadian roots. To call me Shenk was to identify me as Swiss Mennonite and American, even though the person calling me Shenk may not have known this. I was uncomfortable enough with this that I decided to return to using just my maiden name.

Changing my Canadian documentation was quick and easy. I only needed to submit my birth certificate that showed my birth name. Making the same change in the United States was more complicated, especially as it related to my green card. Changing the name on my green card upon marriage simply required showing my marriage certificate and completing the appropriate paperwork. To change it back to my maiden name, I had two options. I could provide legal documentation of a name change, which required hiring a lawyer and appearing in court, with a cost of about $1,000. Or I could become an American citizen and change my name in the process, with a cost of about $300.

Since my Russian Mennonite and Canadian identities are so connected, becoming an American citizen in order to change my name back to just Toews seemed in conflict with my true intentions. If I felt like people were calling me Swiss Mennonite and American when they called me Shenk, I wondered how I would feel actually being American. I chose to spend the extra time and money to change my name back to Toews in the courts and keep the green card.

I am now considering going back to Canada for work. If so, I would have to give up my green card and thirty-five years of connection to this country. So I am now pondering becoming a U.S. citizen in acknowledgement of my connection to this country and to have the freedom to go between the two countries. It is in the process of leaving the U.S. that I have become most aware of my attachment to this country. I must admit that I am only considering citizenship now that it brings a benefit to me. That very perspective seems like a stereotypically individualistic American response in itself.

I have a certain amount of fear when thinking of a possible return to Canada. I know how to be in the U.S., but I am not sure how to be in Canada. I'm afraid that it will be obvious that I have lived many years in the U.S. My parents assure me that after the normal adjustment, I will feel like I have come home. They also say that I'll quickly discover the Canadian "warts" and that I'll still be able to listen to Howard Stern.

What responsibilities do you feel you have to the U.S.?

As a long-term resident, I believe that I should be responsible for everything that a citizen is. But since the law has determined that I can't do certain things, such as vote, run for office or serve on jury duty, I have not gotten involved when I should have. Even though I can't vote, I could influence the political process by volunteering for a political campaign, for example. I must admit that as a non-citizen, I allow myself to be relatively indifferent about civics in the U.S., which means I am actually shirking my responsibilities as a long-time resident.

What responsibilities do you feel you have to Canada?

Since I don't live in Canada, I don't feel like I have practical, everyday responsibilities to Canada. In a broader sense, I do feel responsible for promoting a liberal political worldview that has dominated the Canadian government system and my family's perspective, especially as it relates to being Mennonite. Through my studies and work, I try to encourage a liberal, common-good, "we're all in it together and should get through it together" point of view.

Do you see a difference between being an American citizen and being American?

Yes and no. I think it depends on one's experience living in the U.S. For instance, it is possible to be American without being a citizen. A person who lives in the U.S. for a long period of time is influenced by the culture and values of America, even without having citizenship. I am probably as much American as Canadian. To this point I have talked about my dual identity of Russian Mennonite and Canadian but in reality, I have a triple identity that also includes American.

There are citizens by birth who have never lived here. They can be citizens without being "American." But I think it is unlikely that a person can be an American citizen without being American if they have lived here. Anyone who has lived in the U.S. long enough and gone through the process to become a citizen has been connected enough to the U.S. system and culture to be American.

D. ELWOOD DUNN

Interviewed by Heather Tosteson

I LOVE THIS CATEGORY OF PERMANENT RESIDENT ALIEN

D. Elwood Dunn has taught political science for thirty years at the University of the South. He began his career as a professor and diplomat in Liberia, rising to be Chief of Staff in the Office of the President. He is a permanent resident; his wife, an Episcopal priest, and four children are U.S. citizens.

Early Life in Liberia

I was born in the city of Lower Buchanan, the capital of the county of Grand Bassa. Now it is the second largest city in Liberia. An iron ore company started up when I was leaving high school and contributed to its growth, but when I was growing up it was a small town. It was a safe and secure place and I had a safe and secure childhood there.

I had a loving family that took good care of me. I had very little sense of a world beyond that place. Monrovia felt very far away.

I was not born in wedlock. I had many half brothers and sisters (although in Liberia there are no halves). On my mother's side, we were four—I have three sisters. On my father's side, there were in excess of twenty. I define my family by my mother, in particular by my maternal grandparents. That is the world I grew up in and to which I have a strong attachment.

My father was a politician. He was the superintendent of Grand Bassa County, which is like being the governor of a state. I was always identified as his son. When I was born, he had ceased being superintendent, but he was well known. I admired him because he looked successful and prominent in Liberian terms. He was somewhat wealthy. I aspired to being successful and financially comfortable, those were things about him that I did want to emulate.

My mother's parents put a premium on educating their children. They sent their girls to Roman Catholic schools for a very solid primary education. They became a schoolteacher and a secretary. My grandparents raised us exclusively. My mother left us with them. For me, my grandparents were everything, *everything*. I don't feel I missed anything. They supplied me with everything I needed, brought me a sense of security and a sense of belonging and purpose.

College and Development of Sense of National Identity

When I went to college, few in my immediate family had gone. I went to college far away, to an Anglican college, Cuttington College, in Suacoco, Bong County, in central Liberia. The experience was transformational. I liked what I walked into. I felt good about what I discovered.

It was the first time I had come into contact with Africans from other countries. This was in the early 1960s and there were scholarships to the school from international organizations to help prepare people for the day when their countries would be independent. There were Kenyans, Tanzanians, Ethiopians, Somalis.

My awareness of myself as Liberian came from my relations with other Africans. Ghana was becoming independent at that point. There was such a strong sense of the importance of African independence. I was seeing myself as more than a Liberian. I was beginning to see myself as African, in an Africa on the verge of becoming self-governing. There was such a sense of excitement. At holidays we would go home and during those holidays, one country after another would become independent. We would be celebrating all the time.

I felt I was becoming part of an exciting future. I thought, "I'll complete college and go to graduate school and I'll contribute to this new Africa." I toyed with the idea of doing this from the pulpit, studying theology as social gospel. I didn't go on with it because I had some problems with the church infrastructure. It felt problematic. There was an American missionary mission that headed the church. I had seen people ahead of me run into problems with the bishop. One man spoke up and the bishop told him, "I will not recognize you. This is none of your business."

The man replied, "This is my future. Why isn't it my business?"

I didn't want my future to be foreign controlled. One could say that my new African awareness helped in my resistance. I saw the limited resources available to clergy and decided I didn't want that. However, there were internships available at the Liberian Department of State, and I had an interest in diplomacy. I saw myself in graduate school, preparing for being a diplomat. I didn't see it as a surprising development. It was part of a natural process. I was being educated for a *purpose.* There was a charge to students to serve the church and to serve the state. Service to the church meant being active in it in some form. Serving the state meant, if called, you are ready. Otherwise, you must acquire a profession. This attitude was extremely strong in my time in the early 1960s.

Class-Ethnic Stratification in Liberia: Indigenous and Settler-Liberians

Growing up, I had no sense of this stratification. I didn't see this as a problem that needed to be fixed. There was a way of life. The people in the coastal areas were seen as "civilized." Those in the central area were seen as "uncivilized." The problem was civilizing and *Christianizing* the large indigenous population. I saw this in action.

There was a ward system, where my family, my grandmother and grandfather, would invite interior people to come live with them, become part of the family, and go to school like us. It did not occur to me there was a system of gross inequality in this until I went to college and my exposure broadened.

But the largest revelation came while I was in Washington, D.C. in graduate school. Because I was learning about Liberia in a different way then. I was in a position to compare Liberia with other African experiences. I learned about my country in a profound way in graduate school when I was away from my country. It transformed my thinking completely. Once I got here, my study showed me the sense of denigration of things of indigenous Africa and the substitution of things Western. Everything Western was on a pedestal.

I was seeing these two sides of myself for the first time. My struggle to reconcile those two parts of me was important because it was *defining* me. It was not a simple conversation. I was challenged in terms of making a choice about what direction this struggle should take. It led me to begin a long journey of trying to imagine a *hybrid* Liberia, combining elements of indigenous and elements of imported values.

There were clearly value systems of both sides that one wanted to keep and blend. The West had something to offer. For example, I accepted Christianity coming (but not necessarily in Western garb). But indigenous values also needed to be redeemed. The important indigenous values to keep were the ones farthest from me, things having to do with language and culture. I regret that though I understand an indigenous language, I can't speak it. I used to speak it. I regret the loss because language is an expression of culture.

Coming to the U.S. to Study

Given the orientation of Liberia, the study of law and religion you could do in Liberia, but for everything else you needed to go out of the country. Going to the U.S. was natural if you wanted an MA in Diplomacy.

However, my first opportunity to study abroad was in France. It was a *wonderful* experience. I learned another language and that language opened up the Francophone African world for me. I had learned about the Anglophone world, but in France I met Francophone Africans and had an entree into that world.

Whether going to school in France or the U.S., I always see myself as a sojourner. I'm always passing through. I'm coming for something and I'm focusing on that something, and then I'm through and I'm focusing on something else. I think this attitude is intrinsic to me. My home was my anchor, my rock. It defined everything for me. I still live by their precepts and examples.

I left France in part because I found that it would take me longer to earn a degree there than in the United States. I earned my MA at American University in Washington. My idea was to do a master's degree and then return to Liberia. The idea of studying for a doctorate came later. I was encouraged to apply and that made sense to me. Liberia's president at the time was a very autocratic president. He had not worked well with my father. He had marginalized my father. So I decided I needed a profession. A doctorate was my fallback position if I could not be a diplomat. My life has always moved back and forth between teaching and government service.

I met Matilda and married her while I was in Washington. She was a student at Howard, studying biology. I am someone who keeps lists, who says, by this age I must do this. So on my list was that before I turned thirty I must have a doctorate and be married. So, at age twenty-nine, I met Matilda through the Liberian and African community, which, on the weekends, socialized. We danced to songs like *R-E-S-P-E-C-T*. Matilda came from a very similar background, but she didn't go through such a revision in her thinking as I did.

After I completed my course work for my doctorate, I took a job at Wesleyan in New Jersey and I finished my doctoral degree in 1972. Our first son was born in the U.S.

Returning to Liberia

In 1974, we returned to Liberia. I had no real idea what I was going to do when I went to Liberia. One president had died, another was in power. I wanted to earn some money to begin. Our second child, a daughter, was born in Liberia.

I had a good feeling about returning to Liberia. I was ready now to be back home and do my life work. I had two jobs to choose from, one at the University of Liberia as a dean of the college and the other at the Ministry of Foreign Affairs as an assistant minister. I opted for Foreign Affairs. Working in the government was quite an experience. I spent three years in the Ministry of Foreign Affairs.

Then I joined the president's staff in the presidential mansion for another three years before the coup. Every place was an opportunity to serve. I felt so. The president had a sense of purpose that I shared.

We faced a crisis in 1979. When that crisis came, I think that I found out that my president was a little indecisive in the midst of the crisis. I didn't know what was coming next. They set up a commission to study the crisis. I had a hand in its composition. Then they added me as secretary to the commission. We did the work and submitted the report. Then the politics started. It was a radical report in many ways and people in the President's family and in the government felt I shouldn't sign it.

The report covered many things, in particular the need for the perceived minority governing Liberia to open political space so the majority would have the opportunity to participate. There was controversy in the society about this. But I was not alone in these ideas. In the 1970s there was a lot of conversation about these things. Those of us in government shared the views of those outside the government in many ways.

The president sensed this but felt pressure from the old guard. I felt the pressure and said it was time for me to go back to academia, but he wouldn't let me go. He was caught between change and the status quo. I think he was struggling, and he felt he could continue the struggling until the end of his term. (This was 1979 and the end of his term was 1983.) I think he intended to throw his weight behind significant change when his term was over and the question of his successor was raised. But he did not know that he didn't have the time. The following year he was assassinated.

I did not see the assassination coming. I saw that there was going to be significant upheaval under our watch, that people of my generation would be in senior positions then and their house would tremble. But it all happened before that.

Coup

The week before the coup, I'd been sent as a special envoy to Zimbabwe. I'd done my mission. I'd gone to catch my plane for Nairobi. In Kenya, I got the news. The borders were closed. No one could enter and no one could leave. I had to stay out until the borders were open. I returned ten days after the coup.

Matilda and the children had to go into hiding. I could communicate with her, so I knew she'd gone into hiding. People had called her and told her to tell me to stay put, but I returned. I did not return with the intention of leaving. I returned with the intention to teach, which is what I did.

I left at the end of the academic year. I left because I got a very clear sense that a political explosion was about to take place among the new military leaders. Liberia was going to become an unfavorable place. Even then civil war was on my mind.

Matilda doesn't have a political antenna. All the time, she was reluctant to leave. We sent the children first to stay with American friends in Virginia for a few months. We had friends in New York, so from there I began looking for employment—and somehow ended up in Sewanee, Tennessee! I went to the headquarters of the Episcopal Church in New York. I looked up Episcopal colleges. There were seven or eight in the United States. My CV reached the chair of the political science department at the University of the South. I had never heard of Sewanee before. This professor called me and he said he'd like to invite me for an interview.

So, in 1981, I came to Sewanee. I felt like I was sojourning in Sewanee. Clearly. Clearly. I thought at most I would give it four years and then I would be back on a plane to Liberia. But in 1984, there was a serious clash between the military and students in Liberia; in 1985, there was an attempted *coup d'état* against the military government; in 1989, civil war started. Experiencing all these events, you ask yourself how you are going to recalibrate. *Events* changed my plans. I never had a point where I felt I would not go back.

I always felt I could serve Liberia. Even in my research, I felt I was serving Liberia. In the archives of the Episcopal Church in Texas, I was reading through papers on the Liberian and U.S. Episcopal churches. Writing the first non-church history book was serving Liberia. Helping mediate between warring factions in the U.S. could serve Liberia. Even in my consulting at the State Department, I went to talk about Liberia.

On that list of what I must accomplish, serving Liberia was always the most important thing.

Citizenship

Three of my children were born in the U.S. and the daughter who was born in Liberia became a naturalized citizen. My wife is also a naturalized citizen. For both her and my daughter it was a practical decision. My wife became one because it made it easier for her to take care of her parents, and for my daughter it made life easier when she went to high school and college. They certainly didn't have the hang-ups I had about becoming a citizen.

I am a permanent resident. My family puts no pressure on me to change my status.

My children consider themselves Americans, but they have grown up in our home, so they have received a heavy dose of Liberia, its food and language and other features of culture. It has led them to a place where they are straddling two worlds. When Ellen Johnson Sirleaf won the Nobel Peace Prize this year, my kids were the first to call. They were jumping up and down with excitement.

My younger children, who are just starting their careers, are excited about going back to Liberia. They don't intend to give up their U.S. citizenship, rather they would like to straddle two worlds. My second daughter is a lawyer and works in a law firm. She and I were in Liberia during the Christmas holidays.

But I don't see that I could become a U.S. citizen. I love this category for permanent resident alien. I would find it very difficult to vow allegiance to another country, I feel so strongly identified with Liberia.

Cultural Identity

I suppose my strong identification with Liberia is because I was *born* there. I experienced life there up to adulthood. My navel string is buried there. I feel strongly passionate about the place. My mission in life is to make the place better for the next generation. I see it as part of a larger project: the regeneration of Africa. Talking about the degradation Africa suffered through the slave trade and colonization and marginalization, my question is what can we do to *lift* Africa. That question is deeply mine. Perhaps my younger daughter and son understand me best, understand what gives rise to this sense of loyalty in me.

It is extremely important to me. Right now, I'd like to die in Liberia. We built a house in Liberia in the 1970s. It is a concrete structure that is still there. Whenever I go to Liberia, that is part of what I do, I work to restore that house.

Contributions to the U.S.

I think I meet my responsibilities to the U.S. as a permanent resident. I pay taxes, I am law-abiding, and I am raising contributing citizens. I think people here have all the answers they need for this country. I don't know if there is anything I can bring. I do see the world as a global village.

This sense of alienation that is part of being a permanent resident appeals to me. I don't feel myself anchored here in a *soul* sense. I define myself, my role and my place, in very narrow ways. I see Chattanooga as a place where I go to bed. We have a house, we pay taxes, but I don't see myself as engaged in community activities. I have trouble with churches. I attended for the first five years, but not in the last ten or fifteen. I feel another sense of alienation when it comes to church. A feeling of being displaced. A feeling of wanting to reconnect to institutions in Liberia. I have a deep sense of alienation. It leads me to wonder how some people can become part of two places.

When I go to Liberia, I *feel* a connection. It's not to say I don't sense changes in neighborhoods and generations. There is a new set of neighbors and a big generational change. It is a very youthful population.

There is a difference between diasporan Liberians and those who stayed. For those who stayed, their sense of Liberia is not all rosy. There are people who will feel very loyal to Liberia. There are others who are poor, whose focus is materialism. There are people in Liberia *dying* to come to the U.S. They think, I just want to better myself. If they were able to stay there and go to high school, for some that would be enough. For others no.

But a feeling comes over me when we walk down the stairs of the plane in Monrovia and I look over at the immigration people. Someone knows my name. People help me. They say to each other, "This is Dr. Dunn." "You mean, Dr. *Elwood* Dunn."

Teaching—Political Consciousness and Social Commitments

I *observe* life in America. I'm not a participant in this life in America in any way other than that in America you have a role and that role for me is called education, and I am called to do that to the best of my ability. I am engaged in the business of education.

In 1968 on the campus of American University, anti-Vietnam War demonstrations were held and my African colleagues from The Gambia enthusiastically joined. I couldn't bring myself to join. I had sympathy. But I saw myself as an alien observing and not someone whose *place* it was. I suppose that attitude has just been transposed to living in Tennessee all these years. I see that it is potentially costly to me emotionally but I don't think that has happened. Hopefully I will be finished teaching before that happens.

In terms of teaching my students, I tell my native-born students that they should join the world, pursue their passions. We sit in my office and we help refine and define their passions.

When I have to do this with African students, I tell them, "Africa is waiting for you. Never forget Africa." I have students from Rwanda and Southern Sudan and we talk about these places. I encourage my African students to go back.

With my non-African students, I don't see it as my place to encourage them one way or the other except to help them find for themselves their purpose in life.

nts and Americ

al forces. One is the

of American national ide

al attachments in favor of a more

hould allow and even encourage thi

civic suicide.

nsibilities that become attached t

ing about, is a psychological ter

d, and common experiences th

e rights of a citizen, but feel li

VI

WHAT DOES *AMERICAN* HAVE TO DO WITH IT?

JODI HOTTEL

"GOD BLESS AMERICA"

At seventy-eight,
bound to a wheelchair
by stroke and dementia,
my mother weeps
while she listens to the anthem
on the nightly news,
cherishing this country
of her birth, but no longer
able to repress
the shame of internment.
The only crime—
her Japanese face.

At sixteen,
wearing a smile
and saddle shoes,
she left behind
her best friend Mary
and her new pump organ
to live in the barren
Wyoming desert behind
barbed wire.

And now,
I have a hole
where her pain is planted,
watered by the tears salting
her lips as she mouths the words,
"my home, sweet home."

EVACUATION DAY
—June 5, 1942

At an empty station, beside
the train tracks' quiet gleam,
it's dusk, the in-between time
of a warm June evening.
With brakes screeching, a truck
skids to a stop at the platform,
spilling out young soldiers,
rifles slung over their backs,
drunkenly shoving each other,
shattering a windowpane in the station.

With a hiss, a black train creeps in.
Silent, the Japanese families approach,
dressed in their Sunday best.
Numbered and tagged,
they line up to board, heavy
with what they are allowed to carry.

Throughout the night, the train carries
its freight from their Yakima Valley homes
to an unknown future. Soldiers order
shades drawn, parade the aisles, point rifles,
as though their weary prisoners could escape.

Pulling into the stockyard,
the train's shriek signals arrival,
but still in darkness, the cargo
hears only the clang of the closing gates.

UNWRITTEN NOTE

The news is on everyone's lips
like flies gathering on excrement:
President Roosevelt has ordered

our removal. Will we be
taken from our homes like vermin?
I know it must be a misunderstanding,

gossip spread in these
harsh times. I choke
on acrid laughter.

It is not possible.
After all, I served
my chosen country in the Army,

in the Great War. So I go to see
my longtime friend and sheriff
of Monterey County.

It is no joke, Hideo. You'll have to go.
He can't look me in the eyes.
When he finds my body hung

in this rented room, with
my certificate of honorary citizenship
expressing *honor and respect*

for your loyal and splendid
service to the country,
he will understand why

I could not allow
this noble country to tarnish
its honor, or mine.

*Hideo Murata, an Issei veteran of the U.S. Army in World War I, committed suicide rather than enter an internment camp during World War II. He did not leave a note.

JULIJA SUPUT

THE RETURN HOME

"Are you going home for vacation?" a flight attendant asks, bending toward me, offering a glass of water. Puzzled, I look at her, shake my head.

"Work," I mumble. I take a plastic glass from the tray she balances on one hand with the dexterity of a circus juggler. As I move the book I was reading, Homer's *Iliad*, to make room for the glass, she glides away.

Her question floats in my head, though. "Can I pass for Korean?" I wonder, touching my face, my high cheek bones. I play with the idea that in Korea where I am heading for a couple of days of work, I could walk the streets and blend in, be considered a native. "Why not?" I wonder. Then I look at my colleague sleeping in the window seat. He is Korean, and we definitely do not look anything alike. However, the possibility of a new identity germinates in my mind. I soon forget Achilles and his wounded pride and my determination to finish reading the book during the flight. I turn the light above my head off and close my eyes.

But I don't think about a Korean identity. Instead, memories of my past swirl in my head, and I think about how I ended up on this plane, boarding it with an American passport. I think how, when somebody in California where I have been living for the last ten years, detecting my foreign accent, asks me where I am from, I say, "Croatia." In response to my interlocutor's baffled look, I explain that Croatia was a part of the former Yugoslavia. Few know about Croatia but many are familiar with the Yugoslav civil war. I quickly add that I was lucky; I and my family were not harmed in that war, at least not physically. But I did suffer loss, too. I lost my Yugoslav identity.

My childhood memories are a collage of happy images in which, year after year, I am a part of every school celebration of our Socialistic Federal Republic of Yugoslavia and our President Marshall Tito. I am his pioneer, his follower, and I feel special while I recite poems dedicated to him and to our country, dressed in the pioneer's uniform: white blouse, blue skirt, red kerchief tied around the collar of my shirt, and a blue cap. My mother makes sure that the cap does not slide off my head and secures it with hairpins. My performance is rewarded with loud applause. As I exit the stage, I glance at the audience and, in the back, I see my mother, her eyes shining with tears.

After the ceremony is over and the tribute to our grand nation has been paid, I play hide-and-seek in front of the school with my schoolmates, while my mother chats for a while with other mothers and listens to the praise for my performance. Everybody is proud and happy. I don't understand exactly why but later I will learn about the greatness of our President Tito who said no to the Soviet Union. Yes, we are a communist country because we care for our citizens, but we are a nonaligned nation, not a satellite nation of the Soviet Union as the rest of the East European countries are. We do not even geographically consider ourselves Eastern Europe. We are South Slavs as the name of our country clearly indicates.

I learn about the geographical and political structure of my country in school. It has six republics and two official alphabets, Latin and Cyrillic, and three official languages, Serbo-Croatian or Croat-Serbian, Slovenian, and Macedonian, and we are all Yugoslavs. I grow up in my neighborhood feeling happy and safe. I live with my mother and two brothers in a little apartment much like all the other children I know except that most of them have also a father, absent from my life. But since I don't know what it means to have a father, I don't miss him. I have everything else. I deem my mother the most beautiful and the best mother of all mothers I know. I am an excellent student and the teachers predict a bright future for me.

In the late 1960s, I am about thirteen when I travel for the first time to play in a tennis tournament in Subotica, a city in Serbia, close to the Hungarian border. My mother accompanies me. She wants me to meet some relatives from my father's side. They don't live in a small apartment as we do, but in a big house, furnished with antique furniture. Oil paintings decorate the walls and I think how real the lemons and apples on one painting seem to be. Other paintings are of some people and they are not interesting to me. Later I find out that the faces from the paintings are all my father's family.

My father's uncle and aunt are old, their hair silver, their movements elegant and stiff, and I feel intimidated. They complain about my father, the black sheep in the otherwise successful family. The aunt sighs as she complains about our President Tito who took away everything they had, and left them with so little. I look at her and at the carved massive furniture I have never seen before, and I don't understand what she means by "everything," but I am afraid to ask. Later in the street, as I feel the summer breeze on my face, I clutch my mother's hand firmly, relieved that we left that stuffy house with those people who don't like our President Tito. I can breathe again.

Every summer after my visit to Subotica I spend traveling from one tennis tournament to another all across Yugoslavia. I have friends in each republic, in each city I play. In Belgrade, our hosts never tire of taking us around, and every year I look forward to going there again. The same happens when I go to Sarajevo, or Ljubljana, or Skoplje. The people are warm and hospitable. They charm me with their sense of humor. I end up having a pen pal in each of the republics, and when my school starts in September, I check our mail box every day. I like living in Yugoslavia. It's a beautiful country.

On a sunny day in May, 1980, Tito dies, and I take my four-year-old son to a small park by our skyscraper. He plays in a sandbox alone. I sit on a bench alone. The silence is unbearable and the streets are empty. I am not aware that is the day Yugoslavia starts to disintegrate. Yugoslavia does not have a president any more, but a presidential body with the members from each republic. For a while, it feels strange living without Tito, omnipresent since my birth. I feel as if I have lost my grandfather. I am young though, and I am more interested in foreign languages and love than in politics. Only from time to time I hear about accusations that new political figures have made about Tito's regime. It seems that "my grandfather" Tito was putting everybody who was against his ideology into prison on a remote and desolate island. I think about my serene childhood, I remember the poems I recited for him, and I refuse to believe these stories.

"They predict war within Yugoslavia in a year," my friend Ana tells me as she inhales the smoke from her Marlboro cigarette and takes a sip of Turkish coffee. I look at her long red nails. It's 1989, and I have just returned from Italy where I had lived for six years.

"Who are they?" I ask.

"The Americans," she says.

"Why? How would they know?"

"They know everything. Yugoslavia will disintegrate," she says, with the voice of an expert. I am ignorant as I could be. I have three kids by now, and they are my only concern. I again refuse to believe until the first skirmishes, and then war when Croatia declares its independence. Soon the war in Bosnia starts. People who have lived together cherishing the same values for more than fifty years start killing each other. Thousands of men disappear.

Their bodies are never found. Hundreds of thousands flee and live as refugees all around the world.

I cease to be a Yugoslav citizen. I am Croatian now. I have to change my ID, my passport. The new Croatian president celebrates our freedom promising everybody a better life in a democratic Croatia. Everybody seems enthusiastic; everybody suddenly becomes proud of their Croatian origin.

"We have been Croatian for the last four hundred years," my childhood friend tells me as I visit her at her office. I look at her dark skin and hair, and think that, as her family comes from a small village on the Adriatic coast, some pirate from the shores of Africa must have stopped there leaving his seed. But she does not seem to have any doubt. I feel embarrassed as I cannot claim the same. I think about my absent father and his Serbian roots. Does it make me less Croatian? Now that I have lost my Yugoslav identity, what other than Croatian can I be? I was born in Yugoslavia, and raised in Zagreb, the capital of the republic of Croatia.

The euphoria of the new Croatian identity subsides to fears of war and survival. I move to a small island, outside of the war zone, where the climate will benefit my son's health. For five years, the beaches in summer are left to the island's inhabitants and refugees as foreign tourists are advised not to come. The summer houses that once belonged to Serbs are sealed. Refugees from the war zone live in the hotels. Most Serbs who used to reside on the island have left overnight. I try to focus on my children, but when I see students from the war zones in the school where I teach, my chest hurts. How could Yugoslav brotherhood and unity have turned into one of the cruelest wars in recent history? I think about Czechoslovakia and the peaceful separation of that country.

The war ends in 1995, but Serbs do not come on vacation to the island any more. I miss their humor. Life on the island goes on. The tourists slowly start coming back, and on summer evenings music and foreign languages resound in the main square again. The school children do not learn Cyrillic in school as I did. The state school curriculum has been changed to fit the new Croatian history. But for the Croatian citizens, a new identity is not enough any more. They count on a better life in independent Croatia. They hope that a transition from communism to capitalism will benefit all of them. But the frustration they experience as they realize that this is not going to happen is equal to the euphoria they felt when, in 1991, Croatia's independence was recognized, first by Germany and then by other countries. The transition makes greedy and corrupted politicians rich over night, while the rest of the population struggles to survive. In a new democratic and capitalist country, old people rummage through garbage bins. Such scenes were absent from my childhood memories.

In 2001, I came to the United States and started working as a language teacher at a language institute in Monterey, California. I looked forward to learning and speaking English. Instead, I found myself working with colleagues from what is now called "the former Yugoslavia." Some of them came to the States before the war to get their degrees; some, especially those from Bosnia, came as refugees and rebuilt their lives from scratch. Rarely do they talk about the war, but I saw the fear in the eyes of my colleague from Sarajevo when, on September 11, we watched on TV as the towers in New York, engulfed in the flames and smoke, collapsed into a mount of rubble. I felt as if I were watching some action movie, so unreal it seemed. She trembled.

Our foreignness to the States is what unites us. I recognize in my colleagues the generosity of my Serbian and Bosnian hosts from my youth. Whenever I need help, I can count on them. When I moved to a new place, Jelena and other female colleagues made sure I had utensils for cooking. As I gradually furnished my small apartment, there were Zdravko and Radovan who offered to help carry a new mattress or a TV stand. When I found myself in a precarious financial situation and was not eligible yet for a credit card, I knew that I could ask my young colleague Sandro for help. Since they all had gone through the immigration process, they never tired sharing with me what they knew about it. Even today we never talk about the war. We live in the present.

As I laugh with Emina from Belgrade who became my most intimate friend, I realize that had I stayed in Croatia, I would have never known her exuberant beauty and love for life. I cherish my friendship with her as a rare jewel. When Nikolina joins the department, I am ready to move on to work in another department. The only thing I know about her is that she is beautiful and very young, and originally from Bosnia and Herzegovina. Her mother, she tells me, works for the Bosnian Embassy in Zagreb, and is in love with my native city. Nikolina is in love with Belgrade though, where her family moved during the war.

We become close friends a couple of years later, when we both move on to different positions. Our offices are not in the same building but close enough so that we start walking together during our lunch break. We share bits and pieces of everything: our past, our present, our future. And while I hop by her side trying to keep up with the strides of her long legs, I wish she were my daughter. She is smart and diligent. She has very specific goals in her life. I think about myself at her age, and realize how different I was. I wonder now whether growing up in a country with limited options had something to do with the skills I lack and she abounds with.

"Soon, America will be the place where I have lived longest," Nikolina says one day. I can see how confident she feels when she speaks English, and how she defends American values when sometimes I question them.

I think about my two sons as their English becomes native-like, while their Croatian deteriorates. But it is not only their English; it's also the way they move; the way they wear their pants; the way they feel.

"Our basketball team won," I say one evening while my boys and I sit at the table and eat dinner. It's summer and the summer Olympic games are aired on all of the sports channels. My son gives me a strange look.

"What team?" he asks.

"Croatian," I say, shrugging my shoulders. "Who else?" I think to myself.

"Mom, I am American."

While I look at my American son, I start thinking that I might have made a mistake by coming to the United States. My boys will forget who they are. Soon I realize how silly my thought is. They are in the process of forming their identity, and the place they live in, the people they are surrounded with, the education they will receive certainly will have roles in it. That is what I wanted for them after all. I wanted to give them a broader perspective, more options. I wanted them to be the citizens of the world. But now, even though an ocean and a continent away, I want them to feel Croatian. They will be whomever they want to be. They will discover their own place of belonging.

I did not realize the extent of my own change until I visited Croatia for the first time after four years of living in California. As I sat and gazed around in a tramway crowded only with Croatians, a thought hit me: "I do not want to be only Croatian any more; I want to be a citizen of a larger world, a multiethnic world, similar to but much bigger than the one into which I was born." So, when I returned to California, I applied for American citizenship.

The pride of belonging I felt as I recited poems to President Tito does not exist any more, but I know that my new identity is a result of my own choices, not an accident of birth. I realize that I could change again. I could possibly move back to Europe, work in Germany, a country I have never lived in, but only visited in the 1970s. I can imagine myself as a student and user of yet another foreign language. I can imagine myself learning and adopting the German way of life.

While I am lost in these thoughts, the pilot of the United Airlines jet skillfully lands on the tarmac of the Seoul airport. Outside, it's hot. While I wait for the bus that is going to take me to the city of Osan, my final destination, only about an hour from the capital Seoul, I look at the crowds of mostly young boys and girls coming in and going out of the airport terminal with unusual speed. The girls are small and slim with black shiny hair, all beautiful, all in shorts or summer dresses.

I notice the same scenes as I stroll in the streets of Seoul the following afternoon after I have finished my work, and on the weekend, when I visit Sokcho, a port city on the coast of the Sea of Japan. All Koreans seem very beautiful and walk very fast. I am alone and it suits me not to talk to anybody. I wonder whether the crowds of people I pass notice my foreign look or whether I can blend in with them. For a while, as I pass by fancy clothing stores very similar to those I see in the States or in Croatia, I imagine that I am one of them. But a little later a boy of about twelve walking beside his mother and sister bows to me, and I don't know whether he bows because I am an older person or because I am a foreigner.

I am not sure how the Koreans feel about foreigners. I don't see any. I walk for hours looking for a tourist agency. I find none. When I try to ask somebody on the street for help, nobody speaks English. Maybe the Koreans do not like foreigners, after all. As my hip starts hurting from all the walking, I think about the Ancient Greeks who considered foreigners barbarians and treated them badly. Finally, when I reach the end of a street, I see a little kiosk with tourist brochures. My feet burn, but I am relieved as I discover that a young lady speaks English. She informs me about some places to visit, and when I ask her to give me a brochure, she says they don't have them in English, only in Japanese and Chinese.

I see and learn as much as I can about Korea during my free time and in the evenings, I continue reading the *Iliad.* The images of landscapes and people of this peaceful country alternate with the images from the book: the multitudes slain on the battlefield, parents grieving for children, wives mourning their husbands. And while I eat a Korean dessert, a green tea ice cream with beans, I think about the grief and suffering of my Serbian and Bosnian colleagues, about the Yugoslav conflict in which all parties suffered irreparable loss. There were no victors in that conflict, only vanquished. Only later do I realize that I have been so intent on the people in front of me, that I have not considered Korea's own bloody and tragic past.

The last morning, I rush to the market to buy fresh rice noodles and I savor them in the bus that takes me to the airport. It's drizzling outside and as we pass across a long bridge, I can see a row of rusty fishing boats bobbing up and down on the sea. I ponder whether I could spend a year or two living here. A couple of hours later, on the plane, as the pictures of pristine Korea and its perfect looking people fade from my memory, I think about what it was I was missing there.

The answer pops up as soon as I step into the San Francisco International Airport. An Indian looking lady walks by in a long sari, a pink cell phone glued to her ear; two Asian girls hop around their parents while their father cranes his neck toward a big blue screen to find the gate number for their flight; an overweight Caucasian lady in white sweat pants steps onto an escalator; a black man rushes by me. I am home.

ation/Illegal aliens

Crime

Jobs/Economic growth

xes/Government spending

Health care

Poverty

War/Terrorism

Moral Decline

Other

DEBRA GINGERICH

A HALF-AMERICAN IN PARIS
(Zvonko Smlatić)

Zvonko is a pescetarian. He eats no meat except for seafood, and he follows this as though it is law. I tried to explain this in my lousy French to the clerk at the pastry shop near our hotel in Paris. After paying for our quiche and settling into seats next to the window, I noticed a substance between the eggs and cheese that looked suspiciously like chicken. One taste confirmed this. Zvonko's irritation was unmistakable.

"Why doesn't she speak English?" he muttered and suggested that we return the quiche and request a refund. I knew my French was at fault for the first misunderstanding, and I certainly couldn't come up with an explanation for a refund. I ate two breakfasts while Zvonko sought out another pastry shop with an obvious vegetarian option (and English speaking clerk).

After eleven years of marriage, my husband Zvonko and I were taking our first trip together to a country other than the one where he grew up. Having watched Zvonko struggle to adjust to American culture, I have never defined him as American, even though he carries an American passport. I feel most American when I am travelling abroad. Sometimes I think I have little in common with many Americans, but the cultural differences I experience when I am outside of the country force me to acknowledge how American I am. In France, I was made aware of how American Zvonko had become. I watched with amusement as Zvonko showed stereotypical American tourist traits, like complaining about the service in the grocery store or his pastry shop reaction. Nevertheless, as we enjoyed our quiche and croissants before another whirlwind sightseeing day of Paris, Zvonko reflected on this by calling himself an American tourist, but then quickly adjusted that label to half-American. He was still not able to fully embrace the American identification.

As is true of all of us, Zvonko's story started before he was born. A handsome Bosnian Muslim man moved to a mining town in the Serbian mountains near the border with Romania. He was a strong, hardworking man who believed in a unified, communist Yugoslavia. Work brought him to Majdanpek but love kept him there. He met a local teenager with the ability to instantly love anyone she met, whatever their ethnicity, nationality or mother tongue.

Zvonko's brother was born in Majdanpek. Two years later, Zvonko was born in Tuzla, Bosnia-Herzegovina, former Yugoslavia. When he was about two, the family moved from Tuzla to Zagreb, Croatia. He was three or four when they returned to Majdanpek, where he grew up. Many people emigrated there for work at the mine and coexisted with the Vlach, a Romanian minority group in Serbia who inhabited that area. The town has boasted thirty-five nationalities: German, Greek, Bulgarian and more. It was in that multi-ethnic environment that Zvonko shaped his identity. When very young, he played under the kitchen table while his mother and her friends drank Turkish coffee and gossiped in Romanian. Once in school, he studied alongside students with last names like Kobau, Fogl, and Stojavski.

Another significant influence on his identify was his family. Since his parents were of different ethnic groups, they taught him that he was not Vlach, Serb or Muslim; he was Yugoslavian. Being Yugoslavian meant embracing the different ethnic groups in the country. They taught him that people from the different ethnic groups were equal and should live together. He spent summers with his cousins in Croatia and visited family in Bosnia. Many of his aunts and uncles were in mixed marriages. His family was a microcosm of the multi-ethnic Yugoslavia.

Our trip to France was not for sightseeing alone. Now a microcosm of the fragmentation of Yugoslavia, Zvonko's family has been separated by country borders. His parents remain in Serbia while his brother, Ivan, is a resident of France and Zvonko has become an American citizen. We travelled to France to spend time at Ivan's home in Normandy along with Zvonko's parents who flew in from Serbia. During those days, the cultural differences mixed together like vegetables in stew. We ate Yugoslavian food that his mother adapted as best she could using French ingredients, drank French wine and sampled pâté that Ivan made himself. Ivan spoke comfortably in French with his neighbors while Zvonko switched between Serbian and English at such speed that he sometimes didn't realize which language he was speaking, needing to be informed when he spoke the wrong language to his parents or me.

The two of us alone in Paris after the Normandy excursion, Zvonko reflected on another farewell with his aging parents. "My family knew that I always wanted to explore. My decision to move away from Yugoslavia did not surprise them." He said, "Of course, my parents would like me to live close to them but they sense the freedom I have found in the U.S. They understand this because of the difficulties they have experienced in former Yugoslavia as a mixed couple."

He looked out the window onto the Paris cobblestone street and revealed, "In the U.S. if you don't want to talk about your private life, people respect that. In former Yugoslavia, even strangers feel they have the right to ask you personal questions."

In Serbia, Zvonko was required to carry documents that listed his father's name. When his father's name was seen, he was treated differently because it identified his father as Muslim.

As is typical in his culture, he told me a story to explain. "I ran into a guy once at the library who I noticed was reading a book about Tito, the former dictator of Yugoslavia. He said that he liked the time of Tito because he was Muslim and no one saw him as different during that time. This is why many people from Yugoslavia say that they will never go back. It is really difficult after living in the U.S. for a while to return to where they grew up and live and work there. They don't want to be judged that way again." He said, "We have a saying, it is like jumping from a horse to a donkey. You get used to the freedom of speech, freedom of religion and privacy."

Zvonko did not plan to stay when he first moved to the United States in September 1999 at the age of thirty-four. He had been hired to work as a volunteer for an international relief and development organization. He had met some people at a conference in Austria from that organization who were working in Bosnia. He was impressed by their work, and after continued contact, he was offered an opportunity in America. He thought it would be a good experience to come to the U.S. for a couple of years and improve his English. Like his father in Majdanpek, Zvonko met a woman in this new place and fell in love.

He may have stayed in the U.S. to marry me but the freedoms of speech and religion were especially important to him as well, being from a country where religious identity and ethnic loyalty turned into war. His first impressions coming to America were that people smiled a lot and offered a warm welcome. He felt a sense of freedom right away.

But there have been times when he also has felt uncomfortable in the

U.S., especially when watching the increase in patriotism leading up to the wars in Afghanistan and Iraq. In Yugoslavia, patriotism was used to influence people to support the wars against the other Yugoslavian states. Serbs raised their flags high as they pushed for war.

"Being proud of your country is fine," he said. "But it can be dangerous when it includes seeing other people as less than you. I saw this happen in Yugoslavia between the different ethnic groups."

The civil wars and breakup of Yugoslavia have not changed his national or ethnic identity. He still believes that all three ethnic groups (Serb, Croat and Muslim) can live together in former Yugoslavia.

"I don't like to say I'm Serbian. I don't identify with being a Serb," he mused. "I have to say it sometimes, because Yugoslavia no longer exists, but my identity is still Yugoslavian."

This identity has influenced his religious practice. He was not religious growing up. There was no religion promoted in his home, but his mother's family celebrated their Slava (family's saint's day), which is a part of the Orthodox tradition, and he enjoyed those celebrations. He started practicing a religion as an adult when he became friends with people who were active in the Orthodox Church.

When we toured Catholic churches in France, I took snapshots of the artwork while Zvonko crossed himself in front of the statues and icons just as he would in an Orthodox church.

"I am Orthodox Christian because the people where I grew up and lived for much of my adulthood are Orthodox. For the most part in Europe, people's religious identity is based on where they live." He said, "I could have just as easily adopted another religion. If I had grown up in Bosnia, I could have been Muslim. If I had grown up in Croatia, I could have been Catholic. If one concentrates on the moral values of these religions, they are all good religions. I feel connected to all three because they are the main religions of the country in which I grew up."

Zvonko's search for a multi-ethnic, multi-religious society that lives in peace has settled him in the United States.

"When you move beyond ethnic identity, you open your mind to the world, to the environment, to democracy." He explained, "Living together is the solution."

But that hasn't erased the influence of where he grew up.

"So, if you are only half-American," I asked him. "How do you describe yourself?"

"I am a guy from former Yugoslavia." He said, "I am a European American with the Orthodox religion."

It's as simple as that.

JANET & JOE KIM

Interviewed by Heather Tosteson

FOR TWO OF THE BIGGEST DIFFERENCES, THERE ARE NO WORDS IN ENGLISH

Janet Kim was born and grew up in Korea, while her husband Joe, the child of Korean parents, was born and raised in the U.S. They are both in their mid-thirties. They live in Brooklyn, where they have two clothing stores. Joe works as well as a computer consultant.

Coming to the U.S.

Janet: I grew up in Seoul. Most of my mom's family lives in Canada. I saw them often. But I didn't think about going to Canada or the U.S. myself until I was in college. I saw my friends going out and I wanted to do something similar.

I was studying drama and wanted to be a musical actress. Because music is not really a Korean thing, I asked my parents to send me somewhere. They suggested Canada because all my family was there, but that was the only reason why. I knew about L.A. and Washington and New York, of course, but I had no real idea about the world outside Korea (and in that way was not like many Koreans my age). One of my friends moved to New York in middle school and she told me she would be a social support if I went there.

So, in 1999, I went to New York for a year and a half. I studied at a language school for three months. I was supposed to go for a year but I felt I was wasting my time. I found a small dance school and studied there.

I met Joe during this time. I was working in a small store in Korean Town. I knew several people from NYU's Tisch School of the Arts, Korean friends studying drama there. There was a Korean student club and Joe's cousin was hanging out there and brought Joe with him. Joe's company was near the coffee shop, so we began seeing each other.

My English was nothing. I couldn't say anything. I had a horrible experience once at dinner. I ordered fish, but when I went to pay, my credit card was declined. They were accusing me, and I was afraid I couldn't explain I could go to an ATM and get the money. I gestured to try to tell them. They told me to put my coat and purse on the counter, and then I was allowed to go out and get cash.

I didn't learn English in language school. I began to learn it at dance school with native American speakers. Sometimes using English is easier than using Korean. My friend Choon-yei and I find occasions when it is easier, especially with older people. In English there is no difference in how you address them. That isn't true in Korean. So, on some occasions English would be less complicated. In Korean it is also hard to say no or negative things directly. You have to talk around it.

In Korean, Joe talks like a four year old, so we use English for our relationship.

Growing Up in the U.S.

Joe: My dad came to the U.S. in the early 1970s for a few years, then he brought over my mom and my sister , who was six months old. We spent time all over the New York area.

Janet will mention that I'm more sensitive to being Korean in body than she is. More sensitive to anything Korean or Asian-related socially or politically. I don't know that I'd identify as Korean. I remember wishing Bruce Lee was Korean. There was this idea I was different. It wasn't such a big deal in Queens because there are so many different races. People would just ask are you Japanese or Chinese, and I'd say, Korean. Five years later there were many Koreans living there.

In Long Island, the difference was more pronounced, especially at first. But then Koreans moved in and created their own community by the time I was in high school. But in elementary school, there was one Japanese student and me. There was an element of racism in my growing up.

For me understanding of my feelings came on a trip to China in college. The group was all white except for me. Unlike in Shanghai, much of China is not used to Caucasians. Chinese people would surround the white people, and after awhile, it began to annoy them. I thought everybody should travel to someplace where they weren't normal.

Janet mentioned early on in our relationship how many things were driven by my sensitivities about this.

Naturalized & Birthright Citizenship

Joe: My mom got her citizenship ten years ago, with my sister. They had green cards most of the time when I was growing up. I went into another line when we came back into the country. My mom was very excited to vote in local elections. I thought it was endearing. It has been great for my sister to become a citizen.

I often think of myself as an American who happens to be of Korean heritage. My neighbor is fifth or sixth generation Chinese. There were only two Chinese people in his high school in Florida. He has no concept of Chinese culture outside of what it is in Flushing. He's like me but even farther removed. He wouldn't even have thought of himself as Chinese unless there was an outside reminder.

I went to a small liberal arts college where there were a total of four Korean guys. My friend Jake and I almost felt we shouldn't hang out together, even though we had friends in common. We didn't bond until we both came to New York. I don't know if I can describe the complexity or silliness. There were some other things involved, but the Korean part didn't help. We had this feeling that others didn't view us as regular blokes. It was a diminishing role.

Nationalism

Joe: I am mystified by truly nationalistic Americans. Maybe it is my Korean background or my middle-class background. I went to public school in a very affluent neighborhood. Most of them wouldn't have *gut* nationalism.

Janet's nationalism as a Korean pops up. She has a sense of pride that comes out. I can see it in my family, Janet's family, and other people. And a small part of me *does* find joy in Korean accomplishment.

Nationalism can make you a fan of your own country, but I think you can also laugh at it. But I would be offended if someone else did.

Janet: I never thought about it much. In elementary, middle and high school, the schools are trying to make sure Korean kids have pride in their country. They are meant to hate North Korea and Japan. In elementary school we had to make a poster about how much we hate North Korea and how we need to defend ourselves—and *creatively* draw it. That was in my art class. That gave me the idea that North Korea was the enemy, dangerous. And we were supposed to say we wanted to be reunited after Kim Jong-il.

In history class they would talk about the long history between us and Japan and that gave us a hatred of Japan. It was built into all our generation.

We were also learning lots of good things about Korean history so we should be proud.

I never thought much about it. It was *normal* to be Korean. But when Joe and his sister visit, they will say, "Oh my god, there are so many Koreans." To them it is really amazing.

Courtship

Janet: We dated for eight months. I had to go back to Korea to finish college. We had a long distance relationship for four years. Then I returned to New York and I moved in with him. This was after a huge engagement party in Korea—my parents would not have been comfortable otherwise. We had a City Hall wedding a few months later and then two years later we had a Korean ceremony in Korea. I felt married when we moved in together, just to do that meant that we were, not like here.

My parents didn't like the idea of my having a boyfriend in New York, and no one believed me when I said we'd end up together. I didn't know if it was going to be a rest-of-my-life thing. All my friends and my parents didn't take it seriously until he began to visit me two times a year.

When I told my parents I wanted to go to New York to visit him seriously, there was fighting. Lots of drama. My parents were insisting that I find another guy in Korea. When I finished college, I was starting in some plays as an actress and building my career. It sounded like getting married in another country was not right, but we needed to decide. We had been together four years. My parents were still bothering me about it, so we made a decision.

Joe: As a typical male in the U.S., I had no thought of marrying—or dating internationally. I was twenty-two when I met Janet, and she was twenty. But it was our only way to be together. I *know* how her family took it, but this is how I *want* to see it, like *My Big Fat Greek Wedding*, where the father explains why he objects to her marrying outside their culture. He doesn't know how to verify the suitors.

When my parents met Janet's parents, their response was, "Oh, you're very similar to us." Both our dads fought their way up the corporate ladder. Like her dad, they are CEOs. They all come from the southern part of Korea, not Seoul—sort of like the difference between typical New Yorkers and Southerners here.

It was a relief. Things went more smoothly after that. But it is a very typical Korean drama, this meeting between families. It can make or break a relationship.

Janet: His family didn't like me. I was not a typical Korean. I was trying to be an actress. Koreans of an older generation have a negative assumption about artists. There are social expectations that we are expected to meet. My sister did. She is the girl all Korean parents want. Went to a good school and studied a lot and got a nice job and has the right attitude—she has a Korean manner toward older people. I was always the little weird child. I would fight with my parents because I had different attitudes.

Changes After Coming to the States

Janet: I don't think that I'm that different. My main goal is the same. I want to have a happy life and to accomplish something more than just being a woman with a man. I want to do lots of stuff and to experience lots of stuff.

Joe: I think there is a huge difference. Like your views on religion—

Janet: In Korea, we are Christian. All my friends are Christian. I *converted* to Christianity, and then made all my family Christian. I was never a crazy Christian. I enjoyed the singing and the socializing. I never read the Bible. I went every week because I was supposed to. My family and my friends' families came too.

When I came here, I had heard that the U.S. was a Christian country. But I married someone who is cynical about religion and was trying to convince me it is all fake. We had a lot of fights about religious issues. It offended me that he kept poking me. But after three years of marriage, I found myself like him. I wouldn't say I am atheist, but, what is the word—agnostic. My parents and all my friends are very sad that I'm not Christian anymore. We have had big fights about it, so now we avoid the subject.

I never liked church. I didn't like the service, didn't like the sermon. I went because I *had* to. I really believe that there is a God. I am praying, I talk to Him all the time. I have a strong belief there is something. Church is where that can happen.

In America, I had a big shock. I never knew people had different religions. I met Roman Catholics, Jewish, and Muslim peoples. I knew the religions existed but I never had met people who practiced them. Now I actually saw people who were different faiths. It made me realize there is something up there, but that people have different ways of meeting this God. So in the end, all these rules, *people* made them. Joe is sort of right. But I still think there *is* something.

Cultural Differences Between Korean and American Born

Janet: I always tell Joe he's a banana. Yellow on the outside, white inside. It's different for Travis [her friend Choon-yei's Caucasian husband]. Joe understands Korean culture more, but there isn't more Koreanness in him. He is more familiar than other white people, but it is true that the inside of Joe is white. Every time we talk about news from Korea, he always says, "*Your* country." When he talks about America, he says, "*Ours* or *my* country." That is the way you can tell what he really feels.

Joe: When did I say—

Janet: Always.

Joe: I wouldn't even have bothered to understand more. The opinion of my family and my extended family, what was *their* way of doing things was always described to me as the way *all* Koreans did things. But when I met Janet and her friends, I understood that some of what they said was true, some wasn't. I had off-the-cuff ideas about Korean culture, now it is more complicated.

I would say that some of the American values I have are a sense of privacy, entitlement, less of a sense of obligation to family or to the Korean race. I am more American in that regard. Living with Janet didn't make me more Korean but it did make me understand what being Korean was more. After the shooting at Virginia Tech, Janet felt shame. But I think most people have a view of Koreans as being responsible. I remember being puzzled at the reactions of Koreans as if the behavior of this one person was somehow representative of them.

Janet: I have definitely changed a lot. I spent most of my twenties with Joe, so I am definitely different from who I was when I met him. I still have a lot of Koreanness. I am still struggling to adjust in this culture. Whenever I talk to my sister or friends in Korea, that is the only time I feel we are very different now. They don't really understand me. My not having children, for example. Although a lot of people in Korea are not having children, they are scared of getting divorced or are focused on their career. But my sister and my friends feel you get married and then have a baby. I married earlier than them, but I'm not having a baby. I was never like I *need* to have a baby. As we get older, Joe is more the same way. We are fine with or without a baby.

I did have some craving for a baby last year. But in order to get pregnant, I have to do something. I didn't want a baby enough to do that process. I'm not willing to do that right now. But last year was the first time I felt I really wanted a baby. I talked to Joe and said, "We're in our middle thirties, this is our last chance. If you want to have a baby, you'll have to tell me." Joe still said no, so I made the decision I'm just not going to do anything one way or the other.

I feel that this is an American decision on my part. I think of having children as my decision. But my family doesn't see it that way.

Green Card or Citizenship

Janet: For me, there was no reason to get citizenship. Now that has changed. Before if I got U.S. citizenship, I had to give up Korean citizenship. Now I can have dual citizenship. We're now thinking, why not get U.S. citizenship. I'm really hoping I could bring my sister or brother. Recently my friend Choon-yei and I have been talking about it. For me my resistance has been more about not wanting to relinquish Korean citizenship. I'll *never* give up Korean citizenship. I know that.

Another reason I was hesitating was that you have to take a test. I would have to study. But Choon-yei said, "Let's study together. It would be fun." For her maybe. I couldn't pass the driver's license test. And you have to spend a lot of money. It is unnecessary spending for us—$700-$800.

Joe doesn't feel strongly either way.

I just went to Korea for my sister's wedding for a week. I hadn't been there for four years. They found out I was a permanent U.S. resident, and they moved my identity to somewhere else. I lost my national healthcare. I don't belong to an address anymore. In Korea, if you get married, they move a woman's identity to the guy's family. But Joe didn't have Korean citizenship, so they had nowhere to move my identity. I am still single in Korea. I'm up in the air in Korea. They rejected me when I applied for a credit card in Korea because they couldn't find my identity. I felt really bad, really scared.

Maybe U.S. citizenship would balance that. The only difference is you have to go to jury duty and vote. It is not as if people are going to treat me like an American. They are always going to ask me where I'm from.

I don't know if I want to settle here forever. I may want another adventure with Joe—to live in Japan, Europe, or Canada (my wish list). I want to float awhile.

But as long as I can keep Korean citizenship, I don't mind getting another citizenship.

Birthright Citizenship and Illegal Immigration

Janet: I know Korean girls who when they get pregnant they go to the U.S., to L.A. There is a big apartment building where they stay for six months. It is purposefully made for Korean women. A male baby, if he has U.S. citizenship, doesn't have to do military service in Korea.

I didn't even know that the U.S. government allowed that. It can be unfair, but on the other hand, why not?

Joe: There's a natural limiter to who can do this. You have to be able to afford not to work for six months and be catered to. From the U.S. point of view, people whose children can afford this may be people we want as citizens. If we allowed illegal immigrants who have lived and worked here for three to five years to become legal, that would have a major impact. But this is a much smaller effect.

Janet: But it's just for rich people.

Changing Gender Expectations—Korea, America

Janet: In our parents' generation there was a lot of dismissing of women. But for my generation, it is all about what kind of family you're raised in. My family is more like *all* about women. My mom has a very strong character. She has been working as a career woman and made more than my dad a lot of times. Hers was the voice we had to follow. We loved our dad, but it is natural for me to put women above men, the women's voice is louder in my family.

My mother's mother-in-law treated her badly. My mother had to obey, to sacrifice her life a lot for that. She couldn't reject or say no. There was a lot of trauma between my mom and my grandmom. Within *our* family, my mom is the strongest. There are three children in our family, two daughters and then a son. My sister, my mom and I all have strong characters. My dad and brother are quiet and smile. They don't mind. Many Korean families keep having babies until they have a son. I think my family did the same.

Korean-American In-Laws

Janet: I tell other people who have been dating a Korean-American guy, "Don't do it!" In any Korean-American immigrant family, the parents are difficult to deal with. People living here, it is not as if they are communicating with the American society. They are working inside a closed culture with other Korean immigrants. They are stuck. I notice that my aunt on my mother's side has lived in Canada for thirty years, but I feel like they are living in the past. They are more traditional than Korean people in Korea. That's why I don't recommend it. Also, they are always struggling with their children. They have *big* expectations of their children. And their expectations toward their daughter-in-law are very strong. They ask their children to be doctors and lawyers so they can be proud of them and justify their sacrifice. But they can't really communicate with their children. There is a language barrier and the children have another culture. They fight or don't communicate.

Then their son has a traditional girlfriend who *speaks* Korean. They think, *Finally, I have an interpreter for my son!* The daughter-in-law will always be in the middle.

Before Joe met me, they never asked him anything. Now, they're hoping that they can do things together—through me.

You have to understand that the Korean expectation is that younger people can't say no to older people. I know this because I was raised in this way. They ask me to do things because I can't say no. This happened a lot and Joe and I began to fight. We had a lot of drama about it. Trying to figure out how to handle it. It is a very big issue. I have talked to other women like me, and they all have the same problem. Joe knows I'm not a traditional girl, but I *am* a girl who grew up in Korea and speaks perfect Korean.

However, Joe's parents are better than other immigrant parents because they are going back and forth all the time between the U.S. and Korea. They have this immigrant parent intensity, but it is better than that of those who are stuck in the U.S. or Canada forever. Living in Korea, they can see it is changing.

Joe: I think my parents are better than some immigrant parents because they have higher education. Many immigrants who came in the 1960s and 1970s wanted another life. They started from the bottom. That's why they have intensity.

Janet: Joe's parents are a rare case. They moved to the U.S. because his work sent him to America. His father still has a green card and is doing business in Korea.

Joe: I don't think my mom has changed by living again in Korea. They fit in well. They want to come back, but they are comfortable living in Korea. The first six months were difficult, but afterwards it was OK. They have family and friends.

Now there is forgiveness for foreigners. Janet's family is forgiving of how I speak to them. I don't use honorifics. But for many, it confuses them when someone with an Asian face doesn't do this. I think it would be easier for me to live there over time. But there are negative pressures toward foreigners that are insistent. I was on a bus where the bus driver purposefully closed the door on some Brits. I imagine that would get tiring after awhile. I have had cab drivers brush me off when they hear me speak.

For a Korean, there is a difference between marrying an American and someone from Brazil, for example. There is definitely a respect afforded America that Koreans wouldn't give others. It is tied to the Korean War, to the idea that the U.S. is on top, a feeling of being under a giant's shadow. This was true for Japan as well (odd for such tiny nations). China has a different relationship just because of its size. Chinese feel they are the next big step.

Starting a Business

Janet: I studied drama, acting and dancing. I had no other skills. It was clear to me I had to find another career when I came here. Joe's sister got me an internship at a magazine company once I had a work permit. Then I went to work at Urban Outfitters, working with other college students. Finally I quit and found another job at a company working for the government. I was an information broker, handling calls from Medicare patients looking for information and making complaints. I got the job because I speak Korean and there are a lot of Koreans here, but I didn't talk to that many of them.

After seven months I had to quit, there were so many stories and they were so depressing. So I asked myself, What should I do now?

I like bright colors and like to wear noticeable clothing, hats and shoes. They are not always expensive, just what I like. When I lived in Korea, my Korean friends said it was unbelievable to them that I would wear clothes like this—so colorful. Some thought it was fun, but many were judgmental. But when I moved here, lots of girls on the street, and even older ladies, would stop me and ask, "Where did you get this?" It could be my cellphone or something I was wearing. Because I was very lonely (Joe was always working), I got depressed and would entertain myself by going out shopping. I wasn't necessarily buying things, just looking and liking the company talking with the girls in the stores. I thought maybe I should be a buyer. I'm bad at art so I couldn't be a designer. I never had a specific plan, but one day walking with Joe, it hit me: Joe is a programmer. I can start with a very small thing. I can ask Joe to make a website, and we can see if I can sell. Joe was supportive.

Six years ago we started the website. Because I didn't have any expenses, and I didn't even know anything about budget, I just bought. We got a lot of debt. I didn't know how to get traffic on the website. Many designers wouldn't sell to us because they didn't know me. I needed to find new, smaller designers. After a year, I found a lot of designers that I picked became bigger designers (sixty to seventy percent of the designers I picked did well). There was not a lot of profit, but we survived. One website and two people—and Joe had a full-time job.

Then we had this inventory to get rid of. So I looked for space to rent for three weeks to get rid of the inventory. It was hard to get a spot, but I kept looking. I saw an ad about renting part of an office, its storefront. It was a decent place and the price was reasonable. They were fine with our renting it for one week, three weeks, or month to month. I was scared but we decided to try and signed for three months. It was what they call a pop-up store. When it was time to close after three months, we were all of a sudden getting all this press. This was interesting to people when many retail stores were closing. We had such a good response and a good reputation after three months, so there was no reason to close down. We thought, let's just kept the store. We're still running that store. We recently opened our second one.

I never feel like I succeed at anything. I never force anything. I do what I have to do at that moment. When we got written up, I didn't realize it was a big deal for a big national paper to write about us. People think it was a success, although nothing changed for us.

That's how I feel now. I still feel I'm struggling. But from other people's point of view, they feel I am doing very well and am very successful.

Joe: We're OK. It's interesting the perceptions we have from other Asians when they understand we're the owners.

Language and Culture

Janet: For two of the biggest cultural differences between Joe and me, there are no words in English. And that is part of the point. They are hard to explain.

The first, *hyo,* is based on a Chinese character. It is a feeling for your parents that combines appreciation and big guilt and paying back and respect.

Joe: I think it is called filial piety in Chinese culture.

Janet: It is the number one thing your parents and school teach you. They are making sure that children have *hyo* in mind. It is more important than anything. It is directed toward parents and in-laws. A lot of it I don't necessarily agree with, but it is inside me and it gives me a lot of struggling. I am kind of brainwashed this way. Every time we get in an argument, I feel Joe will never get this feeling.

Sometimes between him and his parents—because his parents have this thing but *he* doesn't—for me that is very sad. I have sympathy for his parents. I feel if I had a child and they didn't have this feeling toward me, I would be very sad too.

I feel this way about my own parents too. I can ask Joe to do something for them, but he doesn't really get it.

The other word, it sounds like *tjung,* is not in English either. It is different from both love and friendship. It is a feeling toward anyone you feel attached to. You can have happy *tjung* or hateful *tjung.* There is a Korean quote, "I have been with you for a long time. I have happy *tjung* and hateful *tjung.*"

That *tjung* is not just with family and friends. It is also toward society. There is a famous Korean snack—*chokupai*—that is sold in a big box. They always write the Chinese character for *tjung* on top of the box and give this snack to everyone. It is sharing *tjung.*

I have this thing about *tjung.* Joe doesn't have it. That's not a bad thing, but it makes us very different. I'll be very pissy if Joe eats cake without me. My friend Choon-yei and her husband Travis have the same argument. Travis will ask, "Why do we always have to share food?"

Koreans have to think about other people all the time, share things with other people all the time. I want to be less *tjung.* Joe asks me to be less that way—he thinks I am too sensitive to other people.

What do you think is the most important problem facing this country today?

Immigration/Illegal aliens

Crime

Jobs/Economic growth

Taxes/Government spending

Health care

Poverty

War/Terrorism

Moral Decline

Other

Don't know

DIANA ANHALT

GROWING ROOTS

Mexico City is magical, and I was eight years old. I had lived in New York from the day I was born, and I doubt anyone could have prepared me for a place so foreign with its palm trees and street corner musicians, its florid colors, and markets redolent of mangos and tortilla dough, its *burros* carting wood down the *Paseo de la Reforma*, the *charros* on horseback, lottery tickets, second-class buses, and car watchmen, the handshakes and cheek kisses, Spanish.

In any case, no one ever tried. My family fled the Bronx on November 15, 1950, the day I was supposed to be the apple blossom in our school pageant. I cried all the way to the airport and so did my four-year-old sister, though she didn't know why. "Why didn't you tell me? I had a singing part." My mother ignored me. My father plied me with chocolates. But once on the plane—I had never flown before—I stopped crying. The flight attendant pinned a Junior Stewardess pin to my chest and allowed me to follow her down the aisle handing out chewing gum. (Air travel was far more gracious in those days.) When a woman looked up from her knitting to ask, "Where are you going little girl?" I gave her the same answer my parents had given me. "I am going to California." "Well, dear, if you are going to California, you are on the wrong plane. This one is going to Mexico." I ran back to tell my parents, in case they didn't know.

Only years later would I question, and only years later would I realize that we had left the Bronx so precipitously because we had to. It was the height of the McCarthy era, and my father had run for public office on the American Labor Party (ALP) ticket. (By 1950, the ALP, a political pressure group, was accused of being a communist front and was under investigation by the FBI.) Mexico, I discovered, was one of only two countries that permitted the entry of U.S. citizens without passports—Canada was the other one—and the State Department routinely denied travel documents to the politically suspect.

When we first arrived, I was inconsolable. I missed my extended family, my friends, P.S. 106. "She'll be alright," I heard my mother tell my father. "Once you live long enough in any place, you grow roots." (Today I realize she was probably addressing her own apprehensions as well as mine.) But she was right. In the way of children, I adapted to the enormous changes taking place in my life within months.

No doubt adaptation had to have been far easier for me than it was for my parents. They were running scared. My mother instructed me: "If anyone asks what we're doing in Mexico, don't tell them." But even if I had wanted to, I couldn't, because no one had informed me. I was, they told me, to write "Zyke" in my notebooks rather than Zykofsky, our real surname. (They subsequently told me to change it back.) No doubt they feared the Mexican authorities, hand in hand with the American Embassy and the FBI, were keeping an eye on us along with the more than seventy families who had immigrated to Mexico in the late 1940s and throughout the 1950s for political reasons. My parents were right to be cautious. We were under surveillance. However, they probably felt more secure knowing that in Mexico, unlike Canada, the rules could be bent and often were.

In spite of their fears, they sent me to the American School, closely allied with the U.S. government, where many of my classmates were the sons and daughters of embassy personnel or employees of large American companies. Half my school day was in English, the other half in Spanish. At the beginning, I understood little in this new language, but I remember learning a song about *la gloria de America.* Upon returning home, I told my parents how nice it was for Mexico to write a song praising the country of my birth. They explained to me that "America" included an entire continent, and the word was not synonymous with United States. (To this day, I grow impatient with using the two terms interchangeably and believe it says a great deal about the United States and its sense of self-importance.)

By the time I left Mexico for Michigan State University (MSU) in 1959, I had learned to kiss my friends hello and goodbye, to roll my tortillas around just about anything, and my Rs around words like *ferrocarril.* I knew the Spanish lyrics to the *corridos* and love songs, addressed my elders as *Señor* and *Señora,* had grown accustomed to three-course lunches, to *salsa* with every meal, to reading, writing and speaking Spanish, to having servants. I had become thoroughly adapted to Mexico.

True, much of what I had learned about Mexico disturbed me. I was well aware of the corruption and contributed to it: My driver's license cost me fifty *pesos*; when a policeman stopped me for going through a red light and I asked him to give me a ticket, he refused and suggested, instead, that I join him for a Coke. I could never understand an election process where the president in office designated his successor. (My father called it the perfect dictatorship.) Political power was in the hands of one party, the *Partido Revolucionario Institucional* (PRI). Religious life was dominated by one church, the Catholic Church. And it was impossible to be impervious to the poverty, the sense of rank and entitlement by a small minority, the injustices and enormous social inequalities. I found it impossible to avoid feeling guilty for living as well as I did.

It wasn't until I arrived in East Lansing, Michigan to attend MSU that I realized how Mexico had seeped into my life, like water into my shoes, and only then did I become aware of how different I was from my classmates. When they asked where I came from and I replied, "Mexico," they'd say, "Oh, New Mexico." Most were incapable of comprehending that they were actually speaking to someone who had lived in another country. So many of them seemed impervious to anything happening beyond their city or their state, and few understood when I tried to explain the enormous disparities between the two countries. (And few of them cared.) I realized that I had become far more sensitive to what inequality really meant and, at the same time, had developed a greater sense of proportion: What things are truly significant in the scheme of things? What things aren't? Consumerism disgusted me, as did many of my schoolmates' disregard for politics, for registering to vote, or serving on a jury.

When I returned to Mexico in 1962, some three-and-a-half years later—I would earn my BA and a degree in education at Mexico City College—I felt completely at home. Even though I recognized that I would always be a *gringa*, a foreigner, and on top of that, a Jew, in a country where anti-semitism still lingers, I had a tight-knit circle of friends, mainly Americans, former classmates or faculty at the American School, where I taught. Mexico was home. I was determined to remain there, and I did. I married Mauricio, the son of European immigrants, with whom I shared much in common, and we had two children, children who were fortunate to be surrounded by family on both sides: They had cousins and grandparents, uncles and aunts. Mauricio's family was an extended one and, true to Mexican tradition, much of our daily life rotated around his family and mine.

Although I was well adapted to life in that country, I could not help but feel strong ties with the United States. While at MSU I had had the opportunity to witness the social and political changes taking place in the early sixties. (Most likely my parent's politics had had a profound influence on me.) Integration was a central issue and a number of students at MSU rode the freedom buses headed south during summer vacations. U.S. involvement in the Vietnam War was underway, although the controversy surrounding it would come later. At the same time, the Women's Movement was coming of age, and I became aware that inequality between sexes was, and continues to be, far more dramatic in Mexico than in the States.

In 1972 American citizens residing abroad—and that included me—were given their first opportunity to vote by absentee ballot. I campaigned for McGovern. When some of us were denied the right to vote due to misinterpretations of the newly implemented law, we protested, and our plight was printed on the front page of *The New York Times*. My Mexican friends and family had a hard time understanding why the need to vote had become such an overriding concern for me. (I wasn't even living in the United States.) They had an even harder time understanding why, sometime later, I became so incensed by the Watergate scandal. No one, in a country as autocratic as Mexico, could make head or tail of it. How was it possible for the people to demand that a president be held responsible for his actions?

By then, I knew that intellectually and politically I was more American than Mexican. But it wasn't until last year that I recognized how subtly, but effectively, Mexico had worked its magic on me. Over the years, my sister, my brother born in Mexico, and, subsequently, my parents, had returned to the States. Both my mother and father died shortly after. Mauricio lost his parents and two brothers. Our two children and our nieces and nephews, all of whom were bilingual, well educated and, as a result, prepared to live elsewhere, also left Mexico for Canada or the United States in the belief they would enjoy greater opportunities there. My husband sold his business and retired. The roots we had laid down were beginning to languish.

And we had grown older. What support system we had had was gone; life in Mexico was growing more conflictive. If we settled in the United States I could apply for Mauricio's green card. (I was afraid, should something happen to me, it would be more difficult for him to establish residence in the United States, where he would be closer to his children.) Once we had made up our minds—it took us three years—we moved to Atlanta, where our son and his family live.

Although I have always been an American citizen, I had not lived in the United States since college, and the United States had changed. So had I. Only after I had settled here for good on July 31, 2010 did I begin to recognize the foreigner inside me. At my granddaughter's birthday party I wandered around the room introducing myself to all the guests. My son approached and whispered, "We don't do that here, mom." I did it anyway. I had never cooked a meal in my life, worn blue jeans outside the house, read the fine print, followed the rules, made reservations by computer, been careful about expressing my feelings. At the same time, I had developed a talent for extricating myself from sticky situations. (But if I had been stopped in Atlanta for driving past a school bus unloading passengers, it wouldn't have worked.) As for expectations . . . I had never had them because in Mexico you never knew what was going to happen in the course of a day. Life was full of the unexpected, and I had become fatalistic: What is meant to be will be.

Yet, as much as I admire the United States, in particular its democratic system, its orderliness, efficiency, access to information, and its ability to implement change, another side of me, the emotional side, will always yearn for Mexico. I still tear up when I hear a Mexican song on the radio, eavesdrop on a conversation in Spanish, or eat a perfect guacamole.

My mother was right. I laid down roots of my own in a place where corn and tomatoes grew in vacant lots, where cilantro and basil thrived on window sills and in a city balanced on the bones of civilizations long gone. Thus, it comforts me to know that roots are hardy travelers, adaptable: they float on water, cohere to wood, burrow deep beneath foundations, buckle floorboards. In some magical way I will lay down my own in this my new, my native country.

HEATHER TOSTESON

A FEELING OF BELONGING

A psychological sense of community is "the perception of similarity to others, an acknowledged interdependence with others, a willingness to maintain this interdependence by giving to or doing for others what one expects from them, and the feeling that one is part of a larger dependable and stable structure."
Seymour B. Saranson, *The Psychological Sense of Community: Prospects for a Community Psychology*

Diversity does not produce 'bad race relations' or ethnically-defined group hostility, our findings suggest. Rather, inhabitants of diverse communities tend to withdraw from collective life, to distrust their neighbors, regardless of the colour of their skin, to withdraw even from close friends, to expect the worst from their community and its leaders, to volunteer less, give less to charity and work on community projects less often, to register to vote less, to agitate for social reform more but have less faith that they can actually make a difference, and to huddle unhappily in front of the television.
Robert Putnam, "E Pluribus Unum: Diversity and Community in the Twenty-First Century"

In the United States, two distinct migratory formations are taking place that have different causes and generate divergent outcomes. One migratory formation is made up of highly educated, highly skilled workers drawn by the explosive growth in knowledge-intensive sectors of the economy. . . . These immigrants come to thrive. . . . The other migratory formation is made up of large numbers of poorly educated, poorly skilled or unskilled workers. . . . Poorly educated and unskilled immigrants come to survive—some are escaping economies that went belly up during global restructuring, others violence or war. These immigrants tend to settle in areas of deep poverty and racial segregation. . . . When poverty is combined with racial segregation, the outcomes can be devastating.
Marcelo M. Suárez-Orozco, "Everything You Ever Wanted to Know About Assimilation but Were Afraid to Ask."

Immigrant resentment, like racial resentment, combines an adherence to traditional norms and values associated with American national identity with the belief that minority groups fail to live up to them. . . . Whereas racial resentment involves viewing minorities as violating the liberal norms of self-reliance and hard work, immigrant resentment involves viewing Latinos, Asians, and recent immigrants as not being concerned enough with the public good, placing too much of an emphasis on particularistic ethnic concerns, and rejecting the civic duty of assimilation. In this example, immigrant resentment involves disparaging immigrants for taking advantage of economic opportunities in the United States while shirking the responsibilities of citizenship. . . . Other resentments stemmed from the concern that immigrants today have no interest in thinking of themselves as American or becoming part of the community in which they now reside. Instead, they keep their attention focused on their own culture and on the happenings in their country of origin.

Deborah J. Schildkraut, *Americanism in the Twenty-First Century: Public Opinion in the Age of Immigration*

I have lived in very diverse settings at many times in my life. Until college, my son rarely went to a school where as a Caucasian he was an ethnic or racial majority. However, unlike Robert Putnam's description above, I would describe those experiences as having a sense of social vibrancy even if the ethnic groups didn't necessarily interact much beyond the public schools. Here on the outskirts of Atlanta, the area we live in is one of the most racially and ethnically diverse in the country. But it is also an area where the situation is far closer to Suárez-Orozco's description of dystopian immigration and Putnam's description of highly diverse communities depleted of social capital. People are struggling, especially with the housing crisis and recession. But they were struggling before that. One young woman working for a refugee association blithely described the area as a suburban slum. I think this might be a harsh over-generalization, but I would say that most people are trying hard to hold on to their jobs, their houses, the tattered hem of the middle class. Many are less than a paycheck from disaster.

The ethnic mix here is fascinating to reporters from *The New York Times*, the *Christian Science Monitor* and to local and international NGOs, especially refugee agencies, the United Fund and other local foundations. But I'm not exactly sure what people are seeing. Are they focused solely on the refugees or equally on the endemic poverty, the resentment of the

African-American community, the sometimes prissy disapproval of the remaining elderly white residents? This area seems far from the utopian immigrant dream, but it is not as bad as the dystopian vision of Suárez-Orozco. However, the refugees who stay here for years are, in general, the ones without resources or education or language to get away.

Both these immigrant realities, utopian and dystopian, get played out for me whenever I walk two blocks up to the main road. On the corner to my right is a CVS pharmacy which, along with the local branch of the county library, embodies my dream of diverse community. There are two warm and competent Nigerian-born pharmacists, Mba Kalu and Ann Oyundale, and a beautiful and amazingly efficient and sociable lead pharmacy tech, Meyosha Stanley, known to all as Mimi. The whole world comes there, refugees for isoniazid or antibiotics, older African-American women and men for blood pressure meds and insulin, I for pancreatic enzymes. We take our blood pressure, try out reading glasses, or page through *Self* magazine, talk with a companion, or text as we wait for our prescriptions to be filled. There are no secrets here, especially from Mimi, who knows all our dosages, our physicians, our insurance companies, and our names—which she sings out, always prefaced with Miss or Mr., when we're still several yards from the counter.

Mimi's daughter is ready for college. Mimi is thinking about going back to school. Pharmacy? I ask her. But I have a feeling this woman can do anything she wants—and that it should have something to do with being able to build, so naturally and intuitively, a cohesive social world where one did not exist. Anyone walking in here fits. No questions asked. And they feel it. This is, I want to tell her, a rare gift. She should bank on it.

Walking up the same street I very occasionally choose to turn to the left into the small down-at-the-heels plaza that is populated almost entirely by Somali businesses. I happily, pluralistically, give people instructions to our house that include turning just before they reach the Halal Pizza joint—but I don't actually dare frequent the Halal Pizza joint. To do so I would need to make my way through a large crowd of Somali men since this is where all the Somali taxi drivers hang out between rides. This is not a place where Caucasian women with short, bare hair, however committed to diversity and ethnically practiced they may be, feel welcome. On principal, early in our time here, I insisted that my husband come with me to explore the shops in the hope that I would overcome my discomfort. So now we do buy cardamom seed, injera, and Bosnian bread at the one market where people don't scowl or fall silent when we enter. This is a busy plaza, especially on Fridays after services at the mosque down the street. It has a grocery store where they sell camel meat, and several dress stores with hijabs, Somali saris, Middle Eastern caftans, and the floor-length, hip-hugging flared skirts popular with the Muslim high school girls. It also feels both exotic and insular, intimidating, indifferent if not hostile to American values and virtues.

If it feels this way to me, I wonder what it feels like to the elderly white women, many widowed, who have lived in this little neighborhood for over half a century, raised their own children in these schools, and still try to collect from vacant lots and the yards of foreclosed houses the trash that accumulates as extravagantly as it does in Guatemala. Or how it feels to the African-American families and single women who bought their houses here in the seventies and have been carefully building equity ever since.

How is this rapid and large influx of refugees, the least prepared and committed of immigrant populations, affecting the sense of community of people who have stayed loyal to their houses and their little neighborhood through integration and several decades of refugee resettlement, when as they turn down into their neighborhood they pass a strip mall that seems oblivious to all the social capital that commitment has required?

My ambivalent responses to my neighborhood have always troubled me given my deep commitment to pluralism, have felt, actually, unspeakable. But brooding over Robert Putnam's article in the last few weeks, I felt a sigh of relief. This wasn't just about our little unincorporated corner in Stone Mountain, Georgia. It wasn't actually about me. It was about diversity itself. And this uncomfortably familiar immigrant resentment that I read about in Deborah Schildkraut's *Americanism in the Twenty-First Century*, seen in another light, could also be understood as a commitment to belonging.

A month ago, on a whim I attended a meeting of a long running, very well-intentioned, often sparsely attended community health collaborative in this area, which on my visits has always seemed remarkably low on community and high on tired agency representatives. There are often complaints that no one lets anyone else know what they're doing, which feels a little odd since clearly there is more than enough basic need to go around. The day I was there, the group was trying to decide on their next year's goal.

That evening I was still reeling from a conversation I had recently had with a man starting up yet another little community nonprofit whose focus was on refugees, indeed who defined this area, its "community," only through them. He excitedly described his idea of inviting down wealthy people from Buckhead, the wealthiest part of Atlanta, to provide refugees with models of successful (did he mean white and rich?) Americans with the hope that perhaps the refugees might find some job opportunities. I thought of all the African-American young men in these same apartment complexes and said, "Isn't it interesting that they would come to meet the refugees, but would never consider coming to meet those poor African-American teens who are probably even more in need of a job, a positive model." He looked at me a little blankly, then said with a shrug, "Of course not. They aren't exotic enough." I wasn't just asking him, I was asking myself the same question: We weren't, were we, creating anthologies about endemic poverty and unemployment in the major minority population here? But the image haunted me. All these young African-American teenagers watching wealthy (white) businessmen coming only to speak to the Bhutanese, the Burundis.

So when someone in the group made the suggestion that perhaps the focus should be on creating a welcoming committee for immigrants, perhaps giving them shopping bags since everyone walks around here, I heard myself say, "It seems to me state agencies and foundations have been contributing money and effort to this city from the top down for years to try and build community. But that isn't where community comes from. It starts from the ground up. How can anyone welcome someone else when they don't feel welcome themselves? And why would you want to welcome someone who doesn't welcome you? The immigrant populations that come here need to welcome too." The African-American facilitator and the African-American social worker nodded energetically.

"They connect with their case workers, but not necessarily with their neighbors. It's a two-way street," I went on. "This is a question we have been asking recently in our citizenship project. What are you giving back?"

"And what do people say?" a young woman from the county health department asked.

"People are usually floored. They have survived immigration, survived being a refugee. They can't imagine anyone could expect more."

"You mean there is some resentment of the refugees?" an earnest second-generation Asian nature activist (who comes from somewhere where they don't speak with a southern accent) asked ingenuously. A late arrival, he had missed the man from the YMCA talking about how he had tried to negotiate between rival gangs of African-American and Bhutanese teens.

The facilitator and the social worker paused, obviously reluctant to tarnish his gleaming idealism.

"On occasion," I said gently. "What if we focused on belonging instead of welcome," I suggested. "That would apply to everyone. Why don't we talk about reciprocity?"

To my surprise, the idea resonated and it was chosen for one of their year's goals. I couldn't believe it. In the five or six times I have come over the years, I never before felt a word I said had registered there. I felt a need to return at least once more just to see if I was dreaming.

The next week, I woke up one morning filled with a clear resolve. I was going to take a Deweyan approach to these troubling questions of reciprocity. I called my friend Diane for encouragement.

"I've decided to go up to the Somali plaza today and to walk into all the stores by myself and see if people are really as resistant to my presence as I imagine they are," I announced.

"Why are you going to do that? They don't want you there."

"I know. But these are public businesses. I should be able to go into them."

"But they don't feel that way. They feel like they're back home. They want to act like that too."

"I know. But it is only two blocks from *my* home. Besides, it is so different from the experience at the CVS, I want to pay attention to it. If I feel afraid, what do you think others feel?"

"Are you going to wear hijab?"

"Of course not."

"Well I guess you better have your questions then." Diane, ever pragmatic, sounded resigned. She has known me for almost twenty years now. "How are you going to begin?"

"What about, 'Are you an American citizen?'"

"They'll think you're spying!"

"Just by asking that? Since when was that a dangerous question?" Had I forgotten we are in Georgia, that we have a law now, H.B. 87, that mirrors Arizona's? Since when indeed.

Diane just reminded me of our friend a Turkish physician who feels that there is great prejudice against immigrants these days, especially against Muslims. "You know how she would react to that question. This will be even worse."

"But that's crazy."

"Not crazy. Just conspiratorial. Everyone is conspiratorial these days. Look at us."

"What if I ask them about belonging?"

"They'll ask you why you're asking."

"I'll tell them I'm a writer."

"That will make it worse. Whatever you do don't take a notebook."

"Or my camera." This was all beginning to feel overwhelming. Then I thought about the grocery store, how the cashier there once smiled at me. I could start there.

"Well you better get prepared for the pushback. Now that I think about it, that will be interesting. Pay attention to the pushback, when it comes and why."

"Listen, I agree with everything you're saying. But I want to know if what I feel is actually true. Because if I believe it is, it is true in its consequences. I do feel they don't want me there, feel I have no right to be there, feel they've made a world unto themselves."

"Be careful."

"I have my phone—and my best friend on speed dial."

As I walked up the hill, I realized that of course I would start by buying something and let things develop from there.

As I turned into the plaza, I noticed there weren't so many men around today. It was a warm but gray day, a little lethargic. I found I could comfortably stand still and take in all the stores—the Halal Pizza advertising Philly steak and hot wings, the signs and shops for money transfers, for mobile phones, for Western Union, for tax preparation.

There was a fair amount of foot traffic, almost exclusively male, in and out of every doorway. An older man, with a Middle Eastern face, broader, paler than the Somalis, smiled at me as if he were waiting for me to approach. I smiled at him but kept on walking. I decided my first stop would be the dollar store, It's Amazing.

Abdi

I pushed open the door and went in and looked around, then looked at the man inside the cashier's desk and announced with a smile, "I live nearby and thought I would come by and see what you have."

The man, slight, in a plaid button-down shirt, nodded. There was no one else in the store.

I walked over to the religion section. Many of the books were in English. *The 99 Names of God. The Prophet Mohammed and His Wives. Attachment and Aversion.* There were many children's videos on Mohammed. *Instructions for Women.* Beyond the books and videos, there were sewing kits, slip-on plastic slippers, many brooms, copper scrubs, tea kettles, an entire aisle of white porcelain plates of different patterns, teapots, tea sets, casserole pots.

Standing in the middle of the aisle, I commented on the good quality of the pots. Approaching the counter, I observed they had many books in English.

"All religious books," he said looking a little dubious.

"Yes, but many are in English as well as Arabic."

"And my language."

"Somali?"

"Yes."

"How long have you lived here?"

"Three years." He spoke easily, without accent.

"And you learned English before you came?"

"I never learned English."

"But you speak so well."

"I never learned English. I worked."

"But in the last four years, how have you learned to speak this well?"

"I only talk with people. I don't speak well."

"You speak very well. I speak Spanish but your English is better than my Spanish—and I've studied it and also lived in other countries." I segued from there into a discussion about my sisters, who have both lived their adult lives in other countries, and how we had recently been talking about belonging, how long it takes to feel you belong in a different country.

"Do you know that word—'belong'?" He nodded. "Do you have a word like that in Somali?" He shook his head. "You came here three years ago. Do you have moments when you feel like you belong?"

"Oh no," he laughed loudly. "I have never left Somalia. I am still there. Everyone I see here is Somali. This is all Somali plaza. And in my apartment building, everyone is Somali too. Maybe someday if I move somewhere else, I will finally be in America!"

I told him that I had been thinking a lot about belonging and that today I had decided I would come here because it was very close to my home but a place where I didn't feel I belong. He smiled with a gentle, understanding smile, glancing out at the parking lot, the streams of men on the sidewalk. I looked out with him and laughed, "I don't feel I belong because it feels like I too am in Somalia. A Somalia that is only for men. But I decided I would go and talk to people, individual people, because it is the *group* that feels so different. When I talk to you, I don't feel that way."

I told him I was a writer and was writing an essay on citizenship and belonging and that I was going to mention him and this experience. We exchanged names. He eagerly wrote his on a piece of paper and pronounced it for me. I gave him a business card. I pronounced my own names. "I will bring the book and show you when it is published." Abdi looked very pleased. We both glanced over at the display of books, decided better. "I'll come again and we can practice English more."

Ahmed

At the grocery store I headed over to the spice section as I usually do when I visit. There was fenugreek, plain and ground. What do you cook with fenugreek? I imagined asking. Cumin. Fennel seed. Ground fennel. Ground ginger. Tea set. Kettle. Lots of animated talk was coming from a small room the size of a walk-in closet where an old man stood behind a desk elevated as high as a pulpit, gesticulating like a Pentecostal preacher. It was all very intense but didn't sound argumentative. It was an express delivery service.

The cashier's desk was also raised. To its right was a small counter and narrow window, above it a white board with all the meats available, including goat and camel (which I learned on a previous visit was shipped in from Australia). I selected a bag of green cardamom seed and brought it to the counter. I asked the cashier how long he has lived here. Since 1992, he told me. He has been a citizen since 2000.

"Did becoming a citizen make a difference to you?"

"It makes it easier to travel."

I mentioned my sisters and the conversation (as yet fictional) we had recently had about belonging. I asked him about whether he felt a sense of belonging here.

It seemed self-evident to him. "Of course. All my children were born here. This is where I am." We talked about the camel meat, how people coming in there must feel at home, have a sense of belonging, when they found a familiar food.

"When we started in 1996, we were the first store here. We were very small. Just the front. Now we have taken up more and more space. But it is not just Somalis who come here. We have people from West Africa, from the Middle East." He kept encouraging me to visit the Somali Association on the other side of the plaza. There was a woman there who taught English. "Here we just do business."

A man came in and went to the meat counter, then came to the counter and held up a plastic bag with a price written on it in blue magic marker. He read the numbers off in English and glanced at me and smiled. The cashier took the money he handed him, then looked up and the man with the bag, quicker in his math, gave the change, speaking again in English and glancing over to make sure I registered it.

"He has a store too," said the cashier who I now understood to be the owner. The other man, leaving the store, smiled.

"And is very good in math," I said loudly. He waved calling out something to the owner in Somali as he pushed through the door.

I gave the owner cash and my business card, saying my name as I did so. When I asked he shared his name—after a hesitation long enough for me to wonder if he was choosing a pseudonym: Ahmed. I told him what I'd told Abdi. He had the same sympathetic smile as Abdi, but there was also some amusement, a sense that perhaps he didn't mind the discomfort. I told him how Abdi next door has said that this was really Somalia, that he had yet to arrive in America. Ahmed really laughed then. I told him I would mention him in my essay, and he too looked pleased.

Karim and the Mystery Woman

Looking at the row of clothing stores, I stood still trying to decide which one to go into. In one, the man with the ready smile, clear English, and unknown meat stood behind a long counter that seemed to hold perfume bottles. A woman in a black burka was there and several other people. It looked too crowded. I was trying to decide between two others when a woman looked out at me through a glass door and beckoned urgently for me to come in. As soon as the door was half open, she asked me what I was looking for. All the clothes were wonderful. On the left wall caftans in vivid colors hung on hangars. On the right wall, the saris that Somali women favor were folded into clear plastic envelopes, a little cloth spilling out here and there.

"I don't know. Something beautiful. But everything's beautiful."

"It is for a gift?"

"I don't think so."

"For yourself then." She sounded a little quizzical. She was wearing a bright green underscarf, a patterned one over it. A sweater.

"We have many wonderful things here. Look."

I couldn't actually imagine myself in the caftans, although there was one red patterned one that caught my fancy, as did an equally vivid red sari with gold trim on the other wall. "Perhaps today I will just look."

The tall serious man behind the counter looked up and nodded pleasantly.

Somehow we all glided into a talk about belonging. The man behind the counter, the woman told me, was the husband of the owner. She herself was just a big mouth. Actually, she was giving the owner's husband instructions on how to link up electronically to some validation service. "I am just here giving my opinion." She roared with laughter.

I asked the man behind the counter how long he had lived here. "Six years," he told me.

"Too long," she said.

We talked about my sisters, their feelings of belonging, especially my sister in Venezuela. "She has children, then it is all settled," the woman said briskly.

"Not really. She is there, has lived there almost forty years, but she also feels at home here."

"For me it is settled. My children are here. I am here. That's it. We go back every summer. It used to be better there. $100 would go a long way. Now it is different. But I want to stay here. I don't want to be there. Neither do my children. My husband, he would like to go back."

The man behind the counter smiled. When I asked him, he said he knew what the word belonging meant but agreed that there wasn't a word like it in Somali.

"What is it?" the woman asked impatiently. "I don't get it."

"Something can belong to you—like clothes," the man explained. "Or you can belong to a religion—"

"Or a country," I agreed. "But it is also a feeling. A feeling of fitting in."

"I don't understand," the woman said.

"Well, when you are living in a place, you don't always feel you belong there, that you fit. But when you leave, you might discover—"

She nodded emphatically. "I don't belong here. I belong in Chicago. I gave my heart to Chicago. Even with the wind chill, even though I never drove anywhere, I only took the bus and the subway, I loved that city. My children tell me I should go back to Chicago. I lived in a tower looking at the lake. We had no air conditioning, but you could just open the windows and the breeze would come in. All I did there was stay in my apartment or work or take my daughters to the playground or school, but I loved it.

"Here I drive everywhere. I talk to everyone. It is who I am. I sit on a bus to the airport and by the time I get there, the woman beside me is taking me to the frequent flyer lounge with her. Because of my big mouth. I am talking to you too, that is just what I do."

She yelled more instructions to the man who was still trying to connect through the Internet. "You'll have to use the phone," she told him.

"Where are you from?" she asked me abruptly. I tried to explain. "Military brat?"

"Something like that. Maybe that is why I am so interested in belonging. I don't feel that I am from a state because I moved so much. I think I am from America. I moved to the South in the time of Martin Luther King. I did not belong then, but in some way I do now."

"Not me." The woman vigorously shook her head, turned on her heel and walked toward the door. "I don't belong here."

"Not the old South," I said to her back, her shaking headscarves. "The one that we have now, that is mixed and changing. I feel at home with people who have moved here." She paused, appeased.

"And you?" I asked the man behind the counter. It turned out he has come to Georgia from Oakland, where he had lived for thirty years. He had moved there from Somalia when he was seventeen. Married there. They moved to Atlanta because of the cost of living. They had bought a house here. He missed Oakland. The temperature. He found it isolated here. Segregated.

I told him I had lived in San Francisco, loved it. I described riding on the Geary Express, watching all these different people board, block by block, culture by culture, language by language. "I like the mix," I told him.

The woman was listening intently again. "That is what is missing here. There is no mix."

I told them that I was a writer, about my project for the day (which at that moment I had decided was complete). The man shared a smile with me similar to that of the man in the grocery store when I described my discomfort walking through the plaza—sympathetic but also like Ahmed amused, perhaps a little vindicated. I told them I would include them in my essay.

I gave them each a business card. The woman looked at it closely. I pointed out my name and then that of my husband. "You are not married?" she asked, noting the difference in surnames. I told her we were but just had different names. "You don't live here?" she asked pointing to the address on the card. She was trying to reconcile our business post office box and my saying that I lived just down the street. I assured her that this was our business address and that I did live two blocks away in a big brown house.

"You can write, but you can't use my name," she said. "I will not give it to you." She was laughing but also meant it.

"That is not very reciprocal of you," I said. I was laughing but also meant it. "I will call you The Mystery Woman." The man behind the counter laughed loudly.

"And you?" I asked him.

"Karim," he said after a second's hesitation.

"When the book comes out, I will bring it and show you," I said.

"If he is not here, you can show it to his wife. She is the owner," the mystery woman said.

"Not everyone is like us," she warned me as I left. "Some people would not answer your questions."

But she did and because she did, and Ahmed and Abdi had as well, I would have, now, a different set of presumptions when I looked at this plaza, ones that included laughter, looks of recognition, moments of hesitation, moments of genuine honesty on my part, a feeling of being met for a moment in *my* difference.

AURORA FERRER

IMMIGRANTS GO HOME!

Today I saw the angry faces
Of grown children I had helped raise
Sporting a sign that cut through my heart
"Immigrants go home!"
Really? Don't you remember?
Don't you remember what it is to be me?
Come with me back in time
To 1620 onboard the Mayflower
Filled with people just like me.
In fear for their lives, praying for a new start,
Don't you remember what it is to be me?
I know the memory is there
The stories of struggles and hardships,
The stories of goodbyes,
Leaving your mother, father, sister and brother
Whispering, *Adios* to your final sunset
As it sinks into the only horizon you have ever seen.
Taking deep breaths as you walk away
Crafting a golden treasure box in your head
To place each smell and memory and story.
Don't you remember?
Don't you remember what it is to be me?
Knowing who you are here and now
On this land and in this language
And not a clue who you'll be there
Or what they will call you.
Knowing that the fear of leaving all you have ever known
Is surpassed only by the fear of staying.
Feeling your heart pumping in your throat

As you cross the invisible line
Of forever goodbyes to unwelcoming hellos.
Don't you remember?
Don't you remember what it is to be me?
            Looking at your reflection
In the bathroom mirror
What continent bore your line?
Your fair hair and fair skin
DNA gifted to you by immigrant ancestors.
Don't you remember?
Don't you remember what it is to be me?
            And where would you be now
If the cargo of the Mother Mayflower
Landing on Plymouth Rock
Was met by a mob of angry Americans
Of dark hair and dark skin
Sporting a sign "Immigrants go home!"
For were it not for (Native) American charity
A moot point this poem would be.
Don't you remember?
Don't you remember what it is to be me?

Tell me the number of grou... el p...

e most like you in the... interests and ...

...an Americans, Black... Hispan... White...

...ple. ~~Young People~~. Liberals, Conser...

...ple. Labor Unions. Middle Class People...

...People, Southerners, Chris...

...dhists, People at your Place of ...

...hborh... at ... Americans...

...ericans, Recent Immigrants, Naturalized ...

VII

WHERE DO WE BELONG?

BRIAN JUNGWIWATTANAPORN

ASIAN/AMERICAN

Uncomfortable silences follow questions on where I'm from, where I live, and which country or culture I feel a greater affinity for as I think through, yet again, how to reply. Sitting in exams during high school I would shade and erase the bubbles asking about ethnicity. I remember wishing for a simple classification, an identity I could mark. Before I began casually checking "other" on the various forms and documents life presents one with, I was in ethnographic fact an Asian-American. But I have credible claim on several other identifiers, some adopted, others imposed: Asian, American, the hyphenated grandeur of Asian-American, third culture kid, dual citizen, yellow, white, not really an American, the smudged AmerAsian.

People rarely realize that there are in fact two types of Asian-Americans. While you may think there are many more that fall under this umbrella as images of Chinese-, Indian-, Vietnamese-, Korean-, Pakistani- and so on Americans fill your head, from where I and the others like me sit, there are only two. There are Americans of Asian descent or of recent immigration who have parents of the same ethnicity, and then there are Asian-Americans of mixed parentage and dual nationality. While the former may use any of the charming hyphenated titles above, children of parents with differing nationalities end up with something that sounds like something less: the dreaded "half."

As half-American, half-something else we have different challenges. The first type of Asian-Americans have cultural markers for their identities. Amy Tan's *The Joy Luck Club* or Jhumpa Lahiri's books trace the conflict of being in one culture with roots in another and coming to terms with both. But within either culture, they have access and outlet to another, so they can be both, fully Asian and fully American. Being half this and half that, however, is the denial of something full. This is not to deny the assimilation challenges of American children with Asian parents, but at least they have their own books.

Growing up in Boca Raton, Florida, the world was a bubble. Learning later that it was an affluent area surprised me. As a child everything seemed normal, and I very much thought of myself as an American. I believed in our myths, knew our states and capitols, and cheered our teams in the Olympics. It never really occurred to me that I might be something else despite other children laughing and pointing, pulling the corner of their eyes, distorting them as they narrowed. As a child being an American in my community was playing baseball, speaking English, eating apple pie, and celebrating the Fourth of July. My family ate rice every day, an American mother's small concession to an Asian father. It never struck me as different. I thought everyone ate rice. The neighborhood agreed that the foreigners here were our Spanish-speaking Bolivian neighbors. Maybe it was Roberto's black hair and slightly darker skin, or just proximity, sharing our yards, but we got along with each other better than with the other kids. We never felt different though; we were always invited to the neighborhood's reindeer games. I never felt too out of place; like many children I didn't know things could be different.

I took my first trip to Thailand at the age of ten, and moved there when I was twelve. While our home in Florida was a rest stop for travelling Thais when I was a boy, going to Thailand was the first time I felt different. I felt both more American and less: I learned that my identity was flexible, a choice. Attending one of the few international schools in Bangkok, I was confronted with several emotions. I felt the boundaries that marked me as an American more surely. Living in Thailand, the land of my father's family, I also desired familiarity with it and with them. I wanted to learn about myself in a way I had lacked access to before.

Growing up away from the United States, my perspectives changed. Although I was still immersed in U.S. history, cheered U.S. sports teams, and returned for a short visit every year, I could feel a gap between myself and other American children. Reading the paper, watching news from the BBC, NHK, Deutsche Welle, and reading the local English dailies I saw my home, the United States, from the outside for the first time. It looked different. Having sold our house, we no longer had a base to return to in the U.S. We began to regard a trip to the U.S. as going home, no matter where we were headed. We no longer claimed a regional American identity, lumping the coasts together with the middle, telling strangers we were from "America" but unable to say where exactly. Living abroad facilitated this distancing while confirming a sense of place. I was an American from nowhere in particular.

Attending Boston University's urban campus, I anticipated exploring my interests and identity like many other incoming students. Returning to the United States, I began to see the gap between myself and my American friends. There were no stories to share about the American high school experience, driving as a teenager, or television. I had very little cultural literacy. Not being completely socially awkward, I could compensate, I was American enough, but I had also spent several years outside looking in. I did have difficulty relating to people, being both naive and arrogant, confident in dealing with the world, and trying desperately to find ways to engage with my home country. My studies ended up focusing on international affairs and economics. I can't remember if it was a failure of imagination or just where I felt comfortable at the time. Looking toward graduation, I applied for jobs in Boston, and while happy to call the U.S. home again after several years of studying there, I also knew that I would leave. I had grown to love much about the U.S., its diversity, its culture, the confidence I felt as an American, but for some reason it has never been enough: I knew that I would want to live abroad again.

Sometimes big changes require baby steps. After a year of living dangerously in a cubicle in Boston's financial sector, I moved to Los Angeles to become an elementary school teacher. Working in an under-resourced school district, a majority of my students were first- or second-generation immigrants. The idea of the American Dream and struggle was palpable when meeting their parents, who worked hard during the week, were assimilating into the system, but keeping their culture close to the heart. Like me, my students were American, and identified as such, though they were perceived as recent arrivals by others in the community. My father had a similar story, moving to the United States to study, he met my mother at a small community college in Rochester, New York. Like many other immigrants he worked, saved, and studied along with my mother until they could apply for better jobs, buy a house and a new car. Looking back, it seems the dream was one of acquisition, progress measured by things, but for people with their backgrounds, material goods meant security as much as success. Unlike the parents of many of the friends I was to make later in life, my father never became an American citizen. He never aspired to it, nor did he consider it for practical matters despite living on American soil for seventeen years. I wonder if he always knew he'd return home someday. He could work in the United States and that was enough. He was never ready to compromise or progress beyond his original identity.

In many ways I've felt like the black sheep of my family. My mother was never comfortable living in Thailand, having left her own professional career to live there. My father's family was urbane, many were educated abroad and spoke English, but still there was a gap in understanding them and in being understood. A similar situation existed with my mother's extended family after we moved abroad. My sisters and I couldn't relate our experiences to our cousins; we were unable to articulate our own changes in viewpoints and relationship to the country and the world. Eventually my parents separated, my mother returning to the United States, my father remaining in Thailand. Family fractured, the pull between countries became more pronounced, feelings of guilt about being in one and not the other surfaced.

After living in the U.S. for nine years, it took going to Bangladesh with the Peace Corps to truly feel American. Representing the country every day with everything that I did, being constantly identified and introduced as "the American," while teaching in a rural community created an expectation that's difficult to challenge. Being engaged in service with other Americans, sharing our experiences, confirmed the American in myself. Within such a different environment, I found solace in that identity. With people asking everyday for help, for a visa or a job in the United States, I felt incredibly lucky about the opportunities I'd had. Like many other volunteers, homesickness and loneliness occasionally descended. During those times I struggled. I felt more American than ever, but also felt that there were few places in the U.S. that I could feel comfortable enough to call home. Talking to my family, I realized where I wanted to be, that I always had a home in Thailand. However, I would never be fully Thai. I knew from my childhood I would always be perceived as foreign. Being the permanent other can be difficult, so I decided to return to the United States.

I was accepted into Johns Hopkins School for Advanced International Studies in Washington D.C. I was eager to develop a skill set which would allow me to live overseas for the long term. I focused on Southeast Asian Studies desiring to learn more about part of my heritage. With a liveliness and coziness that I hadn't felt abroad, I found a sense of home and comfort that surprised me. I noticed that many of my friends were fellow Americans with extensive experience living and working overseas or international students. I found myself in a mixed tribe of Americans who had or would live most of their professional lives overseas. It occurs to me that when abroad, when associating with fellow Westerners, I inevitably find comfort in the American sphere. There is a cultural root, a way of interacting, a perspective that I still have, which although hard to define, is very much American. More than other groups, I find this one mine. Americans who have left the U.S. or are linked to several countries grab my attention and provide comfort, a place I can fit. Upon finishing my studies, I seriously entertained staying and making my career in the United States. The nation's capital was small, but worldly and engaging. Friendships, opportunity, and the vibrancy of urban life pulled while a desire to go beyond our borders gripped me. I had found my community of people but the decision on a physical place to live caused struggle.

Returning to Thailand to work for an international charity, I realize this country grips me and the opportunity to learn more about my father remains a central theme to my life. There are a surprising number of people like me here, children of Thai and American or European parents trying to make their way, trying to find a home. I find my place with them as well while still struggling with aspects of the culture. Travelling back to the United States, I feel apprehension as questions race through my mind: What has changed? What will I think this time? Do I have a place here? Can I love and feel revolted by different parts of the culture? There is a sense of home, but I imagine it's similar to living with your parents after university, it's temporary and comfortable, not where you remain. I enjoy living abroad now, although there's still a sense that I may return, maybe for a year, maybe for five. Living in the U.S. and being an American is a theme or a recurring chapter, but as I have grown to realize, it is not my whole story.

I feel less confused. I no longer feel like I live overseas. I am home here. I am home there. My sense of place derives from a community of people. Living in either Asia or America there is tension: I feel a disconnect with both, equally at home and longing for the other. My mother refers to my sisters and me as a culture of one, our own, separate from where passports say we're from. I never took to the hyphen or the moniker dual citizen. I found preference for the slash, Asian/American, wholly both, never separate. Still, asked where I'm from, I'll mention the nationalities of my father and mother hoping it satisfies the interrogator. It often feels more tangible, the claim more legitimate, when I discuss its origins. My mother is an American, my father Thai, so I am fully both.

As a dual citizen there is a claim by both countries to fulfill certain responsibilities. While I have availed myself of the advantages of having two passports, being a citizen of two countries simultaneously and living abroad requires choices. While I vote in the U.S. national elections, it feels dishonest to vote in local or state elections while living abroad and not having to face the consequences of the electoral process. In Thailand, I have avoided some of society's expectations, monkhood as a young man and military training in secondary school. I feel less able to fulfill the cultural and societal obligations of citizenship in both countries. Being of both countries it is impossible to deny either: citizenship in both is integral to my identity. Unable to feel that I fulfill the obligations of either country though, at times I feel I've transferred my half-ethnicity into half-citizenship. As a result, I try to overcompensate. Volunteering for Peace Corps, joining Teach for America, working for charities in Thailand, my professional life has largely been about defining and defending my identity and citizenship. When I was younger I would cut off questions of identity and declare "world citizenship." It seemed unfair to have to choose, to have to question loyalties. Feeling like a discontinued toy, wondering why the company didn't make more like me, it has taken time to find my place in the world. I've found that I never needed to be so narrow. American identity is flexible: I can be different but still a citizen, and to a larger extent, a state or culture cannot wholly define my identity either. I acknowledge much of my shape has come from the United States, as have most of my opportunities. I try to keep this in my mind while finding myself fully at home wherever I may be.

Concepts not only gui

revalue life by the

vast and simpl

new feelings

interests

Idea

taken thus

etc. dwindle

Loyal in our me

abstract loyalty as

infinitely loyal to;

'momentous issu

scraps, mere

PAIGE HIGBIE

THE ROOTLESS

Nationality. A feature as inextricable from you as your last name, the color of your eyes, the language that you speak. It is a category toward which you feel the kind of intimacy you only experience when you are born to something. From the moment you leave your mother, you are caught in its cultural net. The classification is then formalized: papers are exchanged, documents signed. Then it is done, your civic baptism is complete. Out you go into the frozen parking lot air, and there it is, spread out before you like the promised land. With the casual flick of a pen, that land has become yours, and through the magic of information technology, your data is sent to a larger archive where you will become seamlessly woven into the larger web of civil kinship. Right? Wrong.

It is a beautiful vision, is it not, this image of the ascendancy to the sacred flock of the "nation"? But when has putting a stamp on anything ever made it true? You can drown me in holy water if you like, it will never make me a Christian. You can renew that passport as often as you want, it will never make me an American. But how can this be? I went through the above process. That was me in the parking lot, with the birth certificate and adoring parents. The Pennsylvania winter was the first season I ever met. Easter was the first holiday, complete with Hershey chocolate eggs and stuffed bunnies wearing the American flag for a sweater. I was the big, blue-eyed baby in the Fourth of July home video, crying because she was frightened by the fireworks. Like a good citizen, I partake in all the American cultural rituals. But no matter how many times I put my hand on my heart and speak the pledge of allegiance, it is always a lie. Here is why.

I am what modern sociologists call a Third Culture Kid. We are the children of the highly mobile international workforce that globalization has called into being. You see, I may have been born in America, but I certainly did not stay there. The TCK grows up among worlds; has access to many, but is never wholly a part of a single one. We are cultural Frankensteins, piecing together the worlds we have known to form something which we can comfortably stand upon. Now, Frankenstein may sound like a harsh term to you, but make no mistake, that is how we feel. The most hated question of the third culture kid is "where are you from?" My god, that question, it always comes. And, each time, answering it involves a long and complicated response in which we are forced to reckon with the reality of our nationlessness. That question makes us feel our fractures and highlights the fact that no one else seems to have them.

The hardest thing you can ask a TCK to do is to return "home." I know this because I have done it. A year ago I moved back to the United States to go to college. I had always been curious about America. Though I am not really American at all, my American accent often results in people overseas making the mistake. Living in Australia with an accent like mine meant that I was getting cornered into being American. If you get told a thing a certain number of times, eventually, on some level, you begin to believe it. Though I had never grown up in the U.S., I fancied I had a degree of insider knowledge about the place, the culture. After all, we still kept up some of the American traditions. We celebrated Thanksgiving. We went back every other Christmas. I had even been to an American summer camp. I had grown up surrounded by all these really American things, things the Australians always found odd. Moving back meant returning to a place in which all these odd things would be normal. How could it not feel like a homecoming?

I was wrong. It turns out that for the TCK the concept of repatriation, of returning home, is almost entirely a myth. What many other people don't quite understand is that we don't have a "home." So, returning to your passport country, flushed with the expectation of experiencing that "home" feeling for the first time, only to realize upon arrival that it feels like just another posting, is understandably disappointing. Indeed, often times it is devastating. The TCK's identity is a very beautiful but very fragile thing. We are cosmopolitans in the truest sense. We belong everywhere and nowhere.

Being unable to feel a connection to what you were always told was "home" deals the final blow, cuts you from your anchor. Never again will you feel attached to geography. You are free to float up into the ether. And those who have not developed a solid identity by the time that tether is cut, an identity that does not need contextual nourishment, should be wary. They might just asphyxiate.

It's a big task, knowing yourself without the aid of context. Who would you be if I took away your house, your friends, your pets, your belongings? If I took away your school, your job, your church? Who are you then? The third culture kid changes all of these, multiple times. I remember being seven years old. My mother took me into the toy room and sat me down in front of my toys and told me to choose ten. The rest would be thrown away. It wasn't cruelty of course, but necessity. We were moving again and there was only so much room. It's not just toys either, you lose people too.

When someone dies in a community you hold a funeral, there is a wake, casseroles are made, people grieve, maybe some go to counselling. When a child moves countries it's as though everyone in their old world dies. But there's no funeral, no casseroles, no counseling. And you can go ahead and say, "nobody's actually dead. What about emails, what about phone calls?" And all that's fine, if you're an adult. But children don't make international phone calls and you can't play Barbie over email. As I said, we lose whole worlds.

And do you know what happens to that kid after a couple of moves? She gets really good at it. It's not that she gets good at losing people, that would be inhuman. What she gets really good at is learning not to rely on people in the first place, to keep them at arm's length, always. It is the only way.

And then that little girl grows up. Eventually the merry-go-round stops and she has to get off, and get in a car and go to college and be like everybody else. But she's not. She starts having problems emotionally attaching to people because, honestly, she's forgotten how to do it. Maybe she makes lots of friends, maybe she doesn't. Maybe she sleeps around, maybe she doesn't. It doesn't matter, because when she is lying in that other person's arms all she wants to do is cry. Because, even though they are so close, bare skin to bare skin, she still can't reach them, she can't remember how. This is what happens when you don't get it right, when you drift off into the ether without knowing yourself. This is what it looks like to emotionally asphyxiate. The principle is simple: adapt or perish.

This principle made manifest looks a little like me. As a point of psychological interest, consider this. I can get up and move at any time; no goodbye party, no tearful send off at the airport. I have mastered the act of vanishing. I also don't miss people. I feel guilty about it, but I don't. In fact, I would lose more sleep over leaving behind my copy of *Wuthering Heights* than leaving behind my best friend. It is not that I am heartless. I pay for every person I lose, but with a price far higher than simple grieving and one very few will understand.

No, this is not a fable, distressing as the initial snapshot may appear. I am not here to scare you off moving your kids around the world when they're young. So long as you do it right, there should be no problem. I am actually writing this because I want to show you the lighter side, I want to clue you in to a world you might otherwise never have known existed. You see, there actually is an island for us misfit toys, a safe haven for the cultural hybrid. Indeed, it is the very place we were born. Of course I do not mean born in the physical sense, but in the cultural sense. You see, the rootless, being human beings and therefore compulsive builders of community, make their own kind of "home culture." This third culture blooms in the modern cosmopolitan zones, in what those in the know call "the bubble."

Naturally, everyone has great affection for where they grew up, and I am no different. I want to tell you about "the bubble." I want to tell you about my home, because it was so very beautiful. It is the natural habitat of the rootless. Like its inhabitants, it is totally dis-embedded from geography and can spring up wherever there is a convocation of converts. I am not being hyperbolic, I really do mean converts. When you talk to an "expat" (meaning expatriate) you will see why, for I am not the only one that is enamored with my "homeland." But let me try to explain it a little better, let me try to explain what it was like to live there.

When I think of "the bubble" I think of children, children of every color, language and creed. You see, bubbles tend to develop around international schools. My particular bubble had built itself around the International School of Hamburg in Germany. I look back at the visual heterogeneity and it staggers me, but at the time it was so perfectly normal. We did all the things normal children did, of course, but with an odd twist. We played together, but sometimes the games would be in other languages, because there was no English equivalent. We too traded food at lunch, but when we set up to barter the contents of our lunchboxes, the most strange and wonderful foods would appear on the table. My personal group of friends was an ethnic rainbow of American, British, Dutch, Japanese, African, Israeli and Iranian. (Interestingly, the Israeli and the Iranian were best friends.) What was common among us united us, and what was different was cause only for positive curiosity. Prejudice did not exist. It couldn't possibly. It was thus that when I left the bubble I had absolutely no concept of racism. I was never given the psychological tools with which to interpret different as dangerous.

So, in the bubble, the kids would make friends, and then so would their parents. In a foreign country where you don't speak the language, there really is no one else to befriend. But even though you are forced into their company, it all works somehow, because, though you're all from different countries, there is an element of commonality. For example, you're all pretty well educated, or else you wouldn't have the job that has sent you here. You're all interested in the world, in foreign cultures, or else you would never have agreed to move. You've also got a lot of available money, because whoever is paying your salary is also paying your living expenses because they feel bad about sending you out-of-country. And so all the parents quickly realized how amazingly well they all got along. Pretty soon there were book clubs and nights out and shared trips abroad. We started meeting people with the most incredible stories, borrowing aspects from their culture and incorporating them into our own. We started celebrating festivals I had never heard of, eating food I'd never seen before. It seemed like a holiday that was never going to end.

But it does end. Everybody knows it must. That knowledge was the little cloud that hung over our secret utopia. You see, if you're in the bubble, chances are you are either a "business brat" or a "diplomat baby" (the army kids tended to go to school on base). In both cases, overseas assignments typically last around three years. School was like a revolving door. It seemed like every other week one of our classmates was moving and someone new was coming in. When you leave, and you always do, you are going one of two places: home or another posting. Of the two, home is the most feared. It doesn't seem to bother the younger kids, but the idea of moving home petrifies the older ones. It's because they know. When you move postings, the party just changes venue, and guest lists. But when you go home, the party ends. Going home means it's really over.

When people get off "the circuit," one of two things will happen to them. Option One, you realize how much you missed home and never move again. Option Two, you get the itch. I have the itch. So does my mother. With the itch, everything is fine for the first year. And then you get to year two, year three, and the soles of your feet begin to tickle. By four years the itch is driving you mad. You have to change something. The itch made manifest can clearly be observed in my own life. When I was twelve we moved from

Germany to Melbourne, Australia. We planned to stay. For the six years I lived in Melbourne, we moved once, renovated twice and travelled every single holiday. In the past three years I have attended three different universities, lived in three different cities, on two different continents. It is a sickness. And I know exactly what kind. It is the sickness of longing, longing to return to that "home" feeling. You know you have felt it, or else you wouldn't miss it so badly. But you can't remember where it was that you felt it. The answer is simple, and yet it is always overlooked, because life in the bubble is life on a stopwatch. It is a fundamentally transitory space that people move through. It is a vacation, not a home. And yet, that is what they are longing for, the bubble, even if they don't know it yet. And they want that feeling back so badly that they are willing to wander the earth for the rest of their lives until they find it again. It is an old story: Adam and Eve roam the wasteland after their expulsion from Eden, desperately searching for a way back in.

All up, I have lived in the United States for about four of my twenty years. An immigrant is required to live in the country for five years before they are able to apply for citizenship. Had I not been born in the United States, to American parents, I would not even merit a passport. I also have an Australian passport. If I had to pick the one with which I most culturally identify it would be the Australian. But even then, it is not my nation. It is close, but I still can't quite call it mine. Your nationality is not determined by where your family is from or where you spend the most time. Your nationality is the nation that has most shaped you. It has been almost ten years since I lived in the bubble. But it doesn't matter. Its vision still holds me captive. And I will never be satisfied until I can return to it.

I always love to hear stories about people who were born into one culture, but, out of love, adopted another. I collect mental snapshots of these figures like baseball cards: the British viceroy to India who "went native," T.E. Lawrence, aka Lawrence of Arabia, who fell in love with the people and the region for whom he was named, Cosme de Torres, a Portuguese Jesuit priest who, in the 1600s, went to Japan and was so mesmerized by the complexity and elegance of medieval Japanese culture he never left. I take my lead from these men. It is an audacious idea: that nationality is something purchased by love and not lineage. And it is so entirely out of keeping with how the world is organized there is no hope of it ever being made a legitimate metric. Wouldn't that be interesting though? Wouldn't it be interesting if we got to choose our social contract instead of being born into one already pre-made?

What would the world look like then?

On paper I am an American and an Australian national. Don't get me wrong, I am grateful to be a part of countries as privileged as mine. But speaking truthfully, all those passports mean to me is a shortcut in the customs line. They do not speak to me of an identity but of bureaucratic convenience, a humanized dog collar. Now I am happy to keep wearing the collar so long as people are able to recognize that it does not mean that America is my owner. They have yet to make a collar that fits people like me.

MARCELLE KASPROWICZ

SO WHAT ARE YOU ANYWAY?

"Where are you from?" Because of my foreign accent, I am often asked that question. Do I say I am a Texan? Do I say I am French? Do I say I am Italian? My background is rather complex and, to a certain extent, I would be justified in giving any one of those answers. However, I would only be partly truthful. Let me explain my predicament.

I could, for example, answer that I am from Texas and I often do. After all, I have lived in Texas for more than thirty years and, in many ways, I have become a Texan. My answer is usually dictated by the situation. For instance, when I am traveling in the United States, I usually reply that I am from Austin, Texas. I am assuming that what people want to know is where I *live* so I am probably giving them the most appropriate answer. I occasionally note incredulous stares but my response is not openly challenged. My interlocutor may be too polite or perhaps lacking the time or interest to question me further. My excuse for giving, at best, an incomplete answer is as follows. Most people are not truly interested in the answer, at least not one as lengthy as needed to be accurate.

Occasionally, I run into someone with a genuine interest in the matter, or perhaps less concern about social conventions who, puzzled by the obvious inaccuracy of my reply, will retort, "Yes, but where are you *really* from? I noticed your accent . . ." In that case, I try to give a shortened version of the whole account, enough to satisfy the listener's curiosity without overwhelming him with details. I may start with, "Well I have lived in Texas for more than thirty years but I was actually born in France and lived there until the age of . . ." At that point, my interlocutor's eyes begin to dart left and right. My choice is to be either inaccurate or boring!

It would not be fair for me to give the impression that most people react negatively to my clarifications. Some people actually *are* interested and ask additional questions. Here is my chance to tell the "whole truth." Yet, I am not always emotionally prepared to tell the "whole truth" and do not always welcome such interest. Discussing my origins with U.S.-born acquaintances can be frustrating but not personally threatening. The situation is more emotional with French speakers. Sometimes I speak English with them just to avoid questions. If the interaction is very short, because my accent is slight, I am often accepted by them as a Texan. In a more lengthy conversation, we eventually switch to French exchanging personal details of our lives and finding much in common. For once I can share simple childhood experiences. I belong.

At some point, however, my maiden name comes up in the conversation. My interlocutor may casually ask if my name is of Italian origin. The question is quite inconsequential on their part. After all, so many present French citizens have their roots in another country and there is a good chance the one asking the question is such a person. Yet, I feel ill at ease, as if I had been caught in a lie. To avoid the situation, I often blurt out the information as soon as I can and often at the most inappropriate time. Since I was born in France and feel that the French culture has been the most influential in molding my identity I feel most threatened when that part of me might be challenged.

"Where are you from?" This question still troubles me yet I sense a gradual shift in the way I perceive myself. I must accept the truth. I don't belong to just one culture. It is true that French culture is an inextricable part of my identity. Yet, in a still more distant past, I also remember some of my Italian baby talk, bits of everyday Italian conversations between my parents.

I now accept those divergent cultural pulls as the core of my identity and see their interplay as a source of strength rather than insecurity. One thing is certain, had I not come to America and embraced her can-do attitude, I would not have the self-assurance to submit this writing for publication.

Calm and humor are my defense now when confronted with my title question. More importantly, I am able to answer it for myself. I am just the typical immigrant with her identity crises but an immigrant lucky enough to have leisure to spend on such a personal quest. In the end, perhaps I too can add something to America's constantly evolving "cultural symphony."

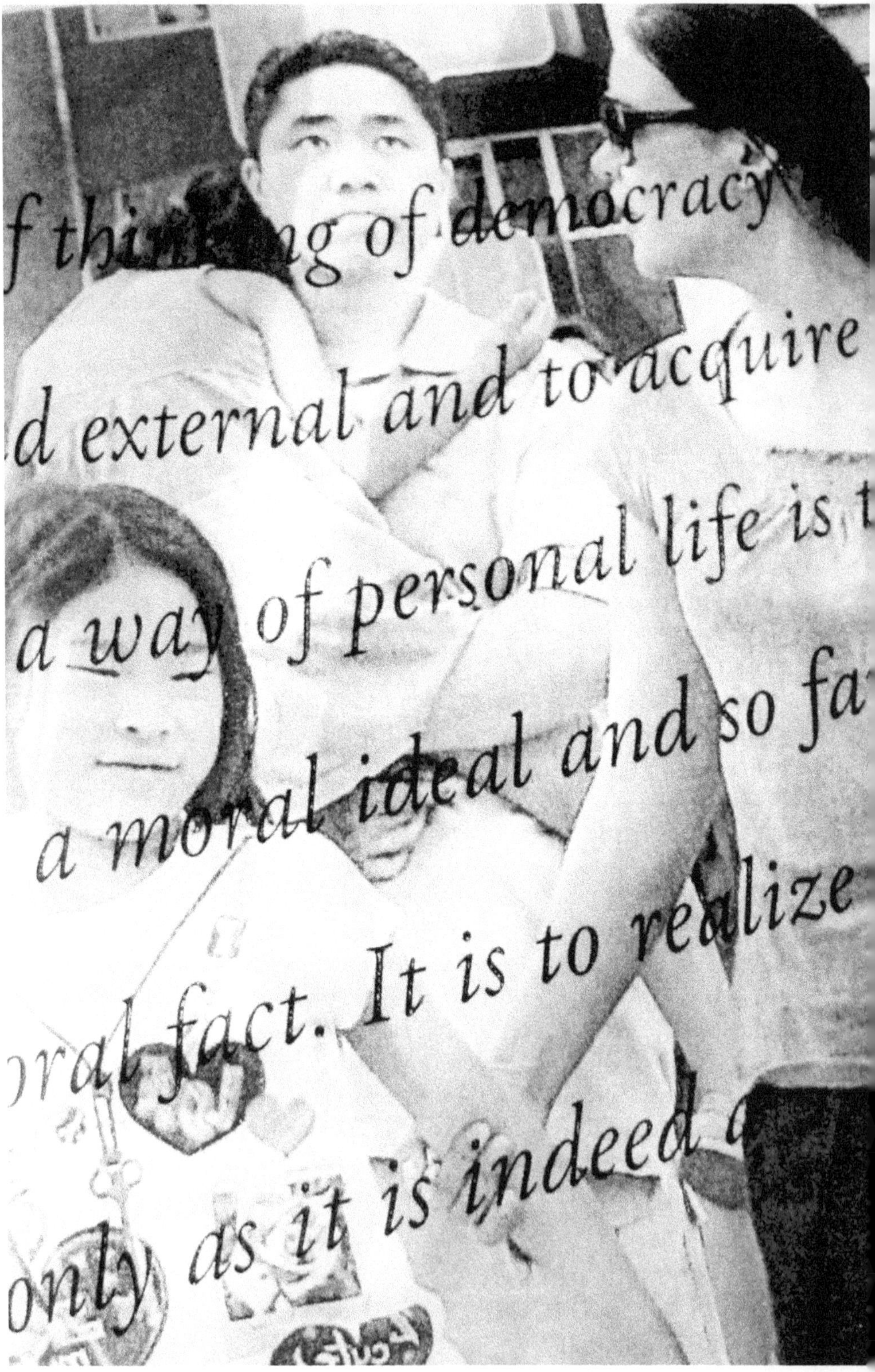

f thinking of democracy

d external and to acquire

a way of personal life is t

a moral ideal and so fa

oral fact. It is to realize

only as it is indeed a

LOSADA FAMILY

Interviewed by Heather Tosteson & Charles Brockett

WE ARE CITIZENS OF THE WORLD

This family interview took place in July 2011 in Palm Beach Gardens, Florida, where the Losada family had recently bought a condo and were vacationing. Zoë, Freddy, and their son Davin live in Caracas, Venezuela. Their daughter, Vanessa Losada Borrego and her husband and infant son Oscar live in Brisbane, Australia. (Elsewhere in this collection, interviews with Freddy Losada's niece Mariana Figuera and nephew William Betancourt explore their different experiences of immigration and citizenship.)

Is national identity something you have given much thought to?

Freddy: We are citizens of the world.

Davin: No, we haven't given it much thought.

Vanessa: I have. I used to think about it more when I was younger. When I was younger, we lived in the United States for a year and a half, and then we lived in Costa Rica, and then we lived in Venezuela. I am Venezuelan. In the U.S. they called me Mexican, in Costa Rica they called me a Venezuelan, but then in Venezuela they called me the *gringa,* the American, then sometimes the Puerto Rican because they forgot that I had come from Costa Rica. I didn't want to be called the *gringa,* I wanted to be called Venezuelan and I think that's why I made a choice not to study in the U.S. because I wanted to have greater roots in Venezuela.

Freddy: Which is why she married a Cuban! And lives in Australia!

Vanessa: That was my reasoning then.

Zoë: I think like many expats I know, I feel as much a foreigner in the U.S. as I do in Venezuela. Or more positively, I feel as at home in Abu Dhabi as I do in Washington, D.C. I don't feel bad because of that. I feel that I've known many different cultures. I also feel it is more real, that nationality no longer matters, that we are all one people.

Freddy: Because you are Baha'i.

Zoë: Yes, I've lived abroad since I was nineteen, but I've been a Baha'i since I was eleven. When I was at the Baha'i World Center last summer, I felt closer to the people there than I do to my neighbors here simply because we all believe that all nations are one. So, that is a religious, idealistic identity that is stronger than my national identity.

How would you identify yourself by nationality if you had to? By culture?

Davin: I would identify myself as a Venezuelan because I was born there. I wouldn't really identify myself as an American, even though I hold both passports, because I haven't lived here long enough and also I don't share the beliefs, so it is kind of tough saying you are a citizen of one nation when your ideals don't match the way it does things.

Zoë: But you can consider yourself a citizen of a country even if you don't approve of everything it does.

Davin: Sure, you can consider yourself a patriot of that country but you don't necessarily agree with that government. You can be a peaceful dissenter and not agree with everything that is being done. I can be a peaceful dissenter in Venezuela as well. I am also in the middle there. I don't like to get into politics too much, but I feel that I can access my feelings if I need. I try to keep as balanced a view as I can, but that isn't possible sometimes, you're always veering to one side or the other.

Freddy: I also don't believe in nationalities. I believe in a utopian world where there wouldn't be any nationalities or borders. However I believe the world is going in the opposite direction. There are more nationalities than ever, at least in the last century. In real life, I feel like I am a Venezuelan for many reasons—language, family, work, culture, geography. I feel I am Venezuelan and I want to die in Venezuela.

Vanessa: I consider myself a Venezuelan, but not a typical Venezuelan because I have an American mom and I have American friends in Venezuela, and I have lived abroad in other places, so I don't fit in exactly as a Venezuelan. In Venezuelan minds, I know they see me as different, but I feel Venezuelan.

Zoë: I definitely feel like an American. I think it is impossible to feel Venezuelan unless you are born there. I've never felt unwelcome because I'm American, but I feel I will never be Venezuelan for Venezuelans—a person they see as similar to them. I have Venezuelan nieces and nephews who I watched grow up and who I'm very fond of. They love and accept me as a member of their family. They call me *Tía Zoë,* which I know is a sign of love and respect, but they will never see me as Venezuelan.

Freddy: I think you would have that feeling in any other country you go to, any one that isn't your own. And Vani, maybe that is what is happening to you too. Having an American mother or living in another country has done the same for you.

Zoë: It's not as if you don't feel loved or accepted—

Freddy: But they won't accept you as the same as them.

Zoë: I can have all Venezuelan friends at the house, but I know I'm different and they do too. Even after forty years. I don't feel that way in the States even though Americans can be very insular. Vani will never be as Venezuelan, for example, as her cousin Mariana [Figuera].

Freddy: But Mariana is changing now that she lives in the U.S.—

Vanessa: She's becoming more American now that she lives here.

Freddy: Or Will [his nephew William Betancourt]. He says that he will never go back to Venezuela. And Mariana will probably end up saying the same thing.

Vanessa: In Australia, you can tell the difference between Australians who have not left the country and Australians who have and who understand that other people exist. So it doesn't have to do with just the U.S.

Freddy: It's a world-wide phenomenon.

Zoë: But I would say that in the rest of the world, most people are more aware that there is a world outside of their borders. Maybe not in Russia because it is so huge. Or Australia. There it makes more sense because it is an island.

Vanessa: Australians find it very difficult to relate to someone from somewhere else. My friends there are the ones who have gone out of Australia.

Do you think that experience of crossing cultures is necessary in order to feel a sense of belonging with someone different from you?

Vanessa: I think it is harder for them to relate to me and for me to relate to them if they haven't had that experience. It is as if we live in different worlds.

Zoë: I feel the Baha'is are my family. When we were in Australia, we made Baha'i friends. Baha'is believe in human beings, so I feel immediately at home with them no matter where.

Would you say as a family you have a cultural or national identity? Are

you a Venezuelan family or an American family?

Freddy: We celebrate Venezuelan traditions.

Vanessa: And Thanksgiving.

Zoë: And Baha'i holidays! We celebrate everything.

Freddy: At Christmas when we make *hallacas*, we're a Venezuelan family.

At what times and in what circumstances would those of you who have it invoke your American citizenship?

Vanessa: When I travel. When I am asking for a scholarship. When I'm asking for an Australian visa. When I am looking for a job in Australia because they look up to America.

Freddy: And when there is a natural emergency and they are evacuating American citizens! Zoë has said that many times.

Zoë: No. I remember during the floods in Venezuela, where 30,000 to 40,000 people died, what did the Americans do? They brought in Black Hawks and evacuated American citizens. I felt it was a great embarrassment.

Davin: I would invoke it whenever it is most convenient. When I am entering the U.S., it is a lot more useful than Venezuelan nationality. But if I'm traveling in South America, for example to Argentina, I present my Venezuelan passport. If not I have to pay! You don't need a visa from Venezuela.

Freddy: And if you go to Cuba, you won't present an American passport.

What does it mean to feel responsible as an American citizen?

Zoë: As an American citizen I feel I bear some responsibility, not huge but definitely some, for some disastrous things that have happened in South America starting with the fall of Allende in Chile, 1954 in Guatemala (even though I wasn't born!). Responsibility in the sense of political responsibility—but as a citizen of the world, not necessarily as an American. I've never voted in an election, but now that we have the condo, I guess I could.

Freddy: She is going to do it soon, so she can vote for Ron Paul!

Davin: I think I could register to vote too. And its more interesting if you have a candidate you want to vote for—like Ron Paul 2012!

Freddy: If this family could vote in 2012, all of us would vote for Ron Paul.

Zoë: Count me out!

Davin: I might do it. I think I will. I wanted to do it in 2008 but I didn't. I have voted in almost every Venezuelan election. It's because it is very easy to do in Venezuela. I have this pacemaker card and they let me in without doing a big line.

Vanessa: I have never voted in the U.S. I have voted in Venezuela. I don't anticipate voting in the U.S. unless I start living here.

Does U.S. citizenship mean anything more than its instrumental advantages to you—like traveling or scholarships?

Vanessa: It means the other half of my family. But I don't feel any loyalty to the U.S. I do feel loyalty to Venezuela. I feel loyalty to Venezuela because I grew up there. I'm identified because of that and because I know how it works, the subtleties. I don't know that about the U.S.

Davin: I don't feel much allegiance to the U.S. mainly because of the politics but I do have family here. If I see a change, then I might feel this is a country I can believe in, that I can look up to. But right now, I don't feel that. It's different in Venezuela. I feel more allegiance, not a hundred percent, but I feel I have participated. Even if my vote hasn't counted much, I feel as if I have a voice.

Do you think Venezuela is a better country than the U.S. and what would that mean? If you were to listen to the different national anthems, which would bring a stronger wave of feeling, for example?

Vanessa: The Venezuelan anthem, "Gloria al Bravo Pueblo," because we call it, *como se llama?*, a lullaby. We put our babies to sleep with that song—and I've been singing it to my baby. I feel more for Venezuela because of the people, the family.

Freddy: Also, part of Venezuelan history and especially the last century, has been affected by U.S. interventions and U.S. policy and it is easier to take sides with the victim and not the oppressor. So there is a psychological effect on that.

Davin: It's hard to pick which country is better. They are both bad. There is a lot to be improved on, but Venezuela is a little better than the U.S. in terms of social inequality.

Zoë: Give me a break, Davin! I don't feel any sadness that their allegiance is more to Venezuela. But in regards to which country is better in terms of one of my major values, which is peace, Venezuela as far as I know has not engaged in any war outside of its borders. So from that point of view, I feel Venezuela is the better country. But does that affect my allegiance? No.

Freddy: What army would you join if there were a war between Venezuela and the U.S.?

Zoë: American.

Freddy: As the Red Cross of course!

Zoë: Of course. But I would join the Red Cross. If the United States were to invade Venezuela as the Venezuelans are always imagining, I don't know.

Vanessa: I would use my U.S. passport—to get out!

Freddy: Like the whores of Bertold Brecht! They used to say, "First to eat. Then tomorrow."

Zoë: In terms of allegiance it's like: I might not like this family, but I'm part of it.

Freddy: As I said, I feel we are citizens of the world. It would not upset me if, after living a long time in Australia, Vani began to feel an allegiance there. Or to Cuba. They can form any bond they want. I don't expect them to be Venezuelans joining the Venezuelan army. I understand what Vanessa says, it isn't only family, history, culture. It is also solidarity. When the landslide happened in Caracas, Vani, Davin, Zoë and I were doing many things to help people. Vani was on the emergency phones, she was doing many things to help people. The same for all of us. Nobody asked us to do this. We wanted to do it and we did. And that bonds you to the country and to the people and the tragedy.

Vanessa: And you know with the Brisbane floods, I didn't feel that way. I was eight-and-a-half months pregnant. But Queenslanders, they all went out and helped people clean their houses and everything. But I didn't feel like I had to. Because in Australia, that bond still is not formed in me.

Freddy: Zoë was acting as a psychologist in the landslide with all the refugees. Every one of us had a role.

Vanessa: But I would feel sad, for example if Oscar—if he grows up in Australia he is going to be an Aussie—he's not going to have that feeling about Venezuela. He's going to have a Cuban and an Aussie side. My father can relate to me because he is Venezuelan. But how can I relate to my child if he is going to be Australian?

Freddy: If he is an Aussie at fifteen, you will have been in Australia for fifteen years.

Zoë: You're saying that he will have more affiliation with the Australian culture than you.

Vanessa: Yes. We have no affiliation with the Australian culture. His father is Cuban. I am Venezuelan.

Zoë: I think I feel more at home in Australia than you do. Do you think it is a function of English? I really like them. I feel very taken care of by Australians.

Vanessa: Because you are American. They *see* you as American. They don't see me as American because they note my accent. You have an American accent.

Zoë: The time I really used my American identity was in Australia when Vani was giving birth. Before that I really liked Australia, but suddenly I found myself in a very foreign system I didn't understand at all, and I found myself thinking, "Is there an American doctor here? Can we transport her to the the U.S.?" I even started talking more like an American. I went to the front desk and said, "I want to talk to the doctor. I want to talk to her now." They said, "She is very busy." I said, "I don't care how busy they are. You have a lot of doctors and I have only one daughter. I want to talk to the doctor now." Eight hours later, the doctor showed up. I think she showed up because I was so pissed off and sounded so American, like a New Yorker.

Venezuela and Cuba currently have conflictual relationships with the U.S. How do you individually reconcile this tension and does that reconciliation shift with context and condition?

Vanessa: Yes. My husband is always going to be a Cuban. I can't speak for him, but we feel when we compare living in Australia or the U.S, that it would be an advantage to live in the U.S. It is not only the proximity to Venezuela and Cuba but also the safety and stable employment of the U.S. that attracts us. Otherwise we would go to Venezuela. Cuba doesn't give us the opportunity for work or economic prosperity—which we like. Venezuela doesn't offer him safety. Or me either, now that I know the difference between living in Australia and in Venezuela and I know how it feels just to be able to walk where I want to walk, not having to hide my rings. It feels very good to be safe. But Australia is also very lonely. And doesn't always feel safe. It is very quiet there, so you always feel someone could come in. In Venezuela it is very loud, there are many people around. That is a kind of safety.

You have recently bought a condo in Florida. Does that affect your sense of citizenship?

Davin: You can have allegiance to the U.S. as a nation, but not as a government. I might begin to feel differently as I have more contact with the U.S.

Freddy: Like Will [his nephew William Betancourt]. You never would have expected him to come here. Davin was the one who convinced him to come here. Will had American nationality but I never expected him to stay and never to return to Venezuela. But he says, "This is my life. This is my country. This is my job."

Davin: He can go back to Venezuela, but not permanently.

Freddy: He says he will go back to visit, but he isn't going to deal with Venezuela. And I understand why also. Everything he did here he couldn't have done in Venezuela. In Venezuela he was a talent that didn't have much future. Here he found opportunity. It wasn't easy for him, but he found the opportunity to develop all the talent he had. It was an amazing transformation. I never doubted that he could do it, or have success either in Venezuela or here, but I understand why he is now preferring to work here, live here, have children here.

Zoë: I think Will began that allegiance when he came to Florida with us when he was twelve.

Vanessa: No! He had a horrible time!

Zoë: I think the material difference—

Freddy: The difference may have given him more confidence. But it was making the decision to come here on his own, to do anything to earn some money and to stay here that was most important. And he found that he could do it, finish several degrees, do very complicated work as an engineer. He's another person. He's always been very *simpatico* and charming, but now he is a complete person.

If you were asked, because you are American citizens who have never lived in the U.S., to make an oath like a naturalized citizen would, would you feel comfortable doing that?

Freddy: Why do you give so much importance to an oath? I don't think any immigrants who take an oath and take all the tests for a nationality, that it makes a difference in how they feel.

Vanessa: If a person doesn't have opportunity in their country and they do feel they have it in the U.S., I am sure that the person would feel emotion, that it would make a difference. They would feel they had been given more chances.

Zoë: Vani, Davin and I have never asked anything of the U.S. They haven't chosen to live in the U.S. I've chosen to live abroad. It's different from Will's choice.

Vanessa: If I made the choice to live here, I think I would do an oath.

Freddy: Perhaps you have interviewed people who have strong emotions about an oath. It's about hope, feeling that you have an opportunity you didn't have before. I think very few people would swear to defend a country no matter what.

Vanessa, your husband is Cuban, has lived in Venezuela, now lives in Australia and may live in the U.S. What are his views about citizenship?

Vanessa: He's very strong about Cuba. He reads up on both sides all the time—the Cuban and the Miami side. He also reads up on Venezuela all the time. He would like to live in Cuba, but he realizes that he will probably never do so, that there aren't the opportunities there. But he will always be *cubano.* He was thirty-three when he first left Cuba.

Zoë: They have a friend in Australia, a Chilean named Marcial, who came to Australia after the fall of Allende. Very leftist guy. His sense of affiliation with Australia is incredible. He idolizes that country.

Vanessa: He doesn't idolize it. He sees it as home.

Zoë: He doesn't even speak that good English.

Vanessa: He speaks very bad English. But he participates in the political process. He has lived in Australia for thirty-nine years. He went back to Chile recently and he said he missed Australia, that he could never go back to Chile to live. But that was because Australia took him in. But it is different for Rodney, even if he lived in Australia thirty-nine years, he would still be Cuban.

Now the next generation—your baby Oscar? How many passports can he potentially travel under?

Vanessa: Spanish, Venezuelan, Australian, and American. He can't travel under a Cuban one because if he gets registered in Cuba, he won't be allowed to leave Cuba. But he will be raised by a Cuban and a Venezuelan. He has the right to claim Cuban citizenship. And if we become Australian residents, then after five years, he can become a citizen. The Spanish passport, Rodney got it because of the access to the European Union.

Freddy: So my grandson is a citizen of the world.

Vanessa: But he will be Australian and we won't understand him!

Oscar Daniel Borrego de Losada received U.S. citizenship in October, 2011, to his mother's delight. She shared her feelings about the process with us in an email from Australia.

The experience of applying for citizenship for my son was sometimes frustrating but in the end it was unexpectedly rewarding. Before Oscar was born, my husband Rod and I started thinking about his citizenship. Rod did most of the work of finding all the paperwork and the requirements for U.S. citizenship for our baby. He asked my mom and me to read all the forms and what we needed to submit but I think my mom thought it was an easy process and not much more thought went into it. She found old papers and letters, even a poem that she won a prize for so that she could prove she had been living in the U.S. for ten years before leaving to go to Venezuela.

When I filled out the form (a few days before our huge trip to the Americas), I was very stressed because I realized the information we were providing wasn't proof enough that she had been living in the U.S. The process requires the person to provide education or work records—not filed tax returns, letters and poems. I made copies of all those papers anyhow, while I was in the U.S. (while my mother drove around in circles with the sleeping baby inside the car to keep him calm).

After I submitted the form with all those papers, I received a very confusing letter that I did not understand. It was very frustrating to not have anyone to ask questions to. In that letter they requested school records or work records, as we had expected, and so Rod and I went about the task of contacting all of my mom's schools from Australia where we are now living. After a month or two, we had all of her school records covering the ten years needed. We elaborated a table with all the contacts at the schools and the years she attended. It was a big task . . . baby sleeping, Rod worried we would not be able to send the response on time. I was so tired!! But I felt compelled to finish it because I needed to give my son the opportunities that I have had, being a dual citizen. I wanted him to be able to, when the time comes, decide if he wants to study in a U.S. university or if he wants to live in the U.S. I just want him to be able to open doors wherever he decides to go. He is now a U.S. citizen and a European Union/Spanish citizen. Perhaps he will also be Aussie and Venezuelan! The more the better.

Working for Oscar's citizenship made me appreciate my own because I kept thinking, what if he doesn't get the U.S. citizenship because of a mistake I make? I thought that his future opportunities could be expanded with the work we were willing to undertake, and so I realized my mom must have gone through some similar ordeal just to give me my own dual citizenship. I value that. Even if he never decides to live or study in the U.S., I have peace of mind because I worked my best to give him that opportunity.

EMILY BEESON

MENNONITE LESSONS FOR COMPLEX TIMES

Mennonites at Home: Lancaster, Pennsylvania

I was born and raised in a fast-paced suburb of New York City, yet I spent my childhood summers on my maternal family's dairy farm in Lancaster County, Pennsylvania. In the heart of Amish country, my brother and I enjoyed the vast green landscape and delighted in the great outdoors. We chased fireflies, collected mint, zigzagged through the cornfields and constantly got in trouble for coming back into the house with dirty feet. One of my sharpest childhood memories is of my great-aunt Anna scrubbing the bottoms of my feet with a soapy washcloth after playing, so that I would be allowed to sit at the supper table. It is well known that Amish and Mennonite households are the epitome of cleanliness and order. My grandmother, Mabel Zook Stoltzfus, was born Amish, then went on to marry a Mennonite: my grandfather, Fred Smoker, also from Lancaster. Hence, she has spent the entirety of her adult life as an Amish-Mennonite: a hybrid not uncommon in Pennsylvania. Grandma Mabel maintains a spotless home, a vibrant garden and spends a considerable part of the day at her quilting wheel. She is eighty-two years old and cooks, cleans, sews and actively writes letters. Thoroughly self-sufficient, she works as a housekeeper and sells handmade cloth Amish dolls to a local market. Grandma Mabel possesses a kind, pious and humble spirit. She values hard work, patience, discipline and calm.

Amish-Mennonites generally have access to television and other modern technologies, including electronic appliances in the home, as opposed to the Amish who are known for their culture of austerity, choosing to live without electricity. My grandma refers to the Amish as being the most plain—she affectionately refers to them as "the plain people"—followed by the Amish-Mennonites. The Mennonites, named after the Dutch priest Menno Simons, founder of the Mennonite sect within the broader Anabaptist movement in Europe during the mid-sixteenth century, are the most liberal in their engagement with modern society. Nonetheless, they are strongly Christian like the Amish, viewing the world through a faith-based lens. Their lifestyle is built accordingly, thus shaping their relationship with politics and society.

The Amish have traditionally upheld a strong degree of separation from government in a desire to control their own decision-making as a faith-based community with a clearly defined set of values: Christian values rooted in the teachings of the Bible. One of the most important needs of the Amish is the freedom to design their own education system for their children, so that religious teachings are woven in with academics. Mennonites, however, are more modern in their use of technology, medicine, and transportation, less insular and more open to interacting with the rest of society. They make an effort to be relatively in tune with what is happening outside of their tight-knit community, at a local, state and national level. Like the Amish, Mennonites uphold somewhat of a separatist attitude toward the U.S. political system, just to a much lesser degree. Nonetheless, this attitude gives a decisively unique view on citizenship compared to the average American.

Mennonite values closely mirror those of the Amish: faith, discipline, hard work, diligence, community and humility. Because their worldview is guided by their spiritual beliefs above all else, both Amish and Mennonites prioritize their allegiances in a hierarchy: God is at the top, earthly things below. They do not believe in a political system or even in their own country more than they believe in Divine Providence to carry them through the stages of their lives and to enable their safety. They pledge their allegiance to God before all earthly things—next, to their fellow Christians. They believe in the Christian church as God's nation, and in God's followers as their family.

I will never forget when my grandmother underwent bypass heart surgery last December, and my great-aunt Sarah and I were outside of the hospital room discussing the intensity of the surgery and all of the medicines involved: I, with fear and she, with complete calm and resolve, stating, "It is not the medicine that will save her. I do not like complicated names of medicines, I do not understand it, and I don't want to think about it! I am telling you dear, it is not the medicine that will carry her through. God is there and will go way beyond in His power and blessing." Spoken like a true believer.

Unlike the Amish who, for the most part, do not vote or have interest in participating in the American political system unless an issue directly affects them, such as zoning, many Mennonites are more connected with politics. Most of the Mennonites who I know in Pennsylvania and Indiana drive cars, so they are dependent on highways and public works. They own property and are taxpayers. Due to their iron-fisted work ethic and frugal lifestyle, they tend to be decisively Republican. After Thanksgiving dinner, it is tradition in my family for the men and women to break off in separate circles and have conversations over coffee and dessert. The women: Grandma Mabel, her two sisters Lydia and Anna, and their sisters-in-law Mary, Susie and Sarah, mostly speak of food, the weather and of recent happenings in the lives of their children. The men, mainly my four uncles Morris, Howard, Omar and Glen, almost always discuss politics, and my brother and I tend to join this group. With an air of lighthearted distance yet also strongly in support of two things, lower taxes and anti-war, they give feedback on the current administration's performance and express their grievances. They speak of America's involvement in war with Iraq and violence in the Middle East in a tone of terror and disgust—yet do pronounce the importance of our country remaining safe and free of harm, just not by violent means or by wasting money on war. Of all things to waste money on, war is one of the vilest. I have delighted in these conversations over the past few years, having taken many political science classes in college.

Dignified in their labors, Mennonites are protective of their land and the money they earn, believing it is rightfully theirs: a byproduct of both their hard work and God's blessing. Most are comfortable financially in that they are extremely resourceful, buying only what is needed and saving the rest, though they always give off an air of being cash-strapped. My relatives fear, and constantly speak of, "hard times" ahead. At my latest family gathering, they jokingly remarked that our country "is going to the pits" due to the lingering recession and high unemployment rates. My grandmother and her seven siblings were young children during the Great Depression and witnessed their parents' struggle for survival. Thus, Grandma Mabel, who as one of the oldest daughters had to support her mother in looking after her younger siblings, has adopted an ingrained fear of future economic depressions. She is always holding on to what she has: from rubber bands, to plastic bags, to pieces of string.

Years of holiday meals, summers spent on the farm, and a very loving relationship with all of my Mennonite and Amish-Mennonite family have placed me in a unique position. My brother and I are modern, but have such deep exposure to family members who are part of a traditional sect of society that as the youngest generation in our family, along with our cousins, we are essentially the last link. My brother and I cannot imagine life any other way: without Grandma Mabel, Anna, Lydia, Sarah, Susie, Morris, Omar, Howard and Glen, and those we have lost along the way: Warren, Wilmer, Mary and Fred. All of them have embedded the values of resourcefulness, frugality, gentleness, hard work and independence within me. They helped raise me to be self-reliant and strong. They perform their long list of daily chores without complaint and are thankful for all of their blessings: each moment, each conversation, and each meal. They are affable and considerate in their dealings with others, cautious of causing no harm. It wasn't until recently that I fully realized how proud I am of my family's Swiss-German Anabaptist roots—we originally hail from Zug, Switzerland—and in the sharply disciplined work ethic that has been passed down for generations.

Mennonites Abroad: The Dominican Republic

My fascination with my Mennonite extended family and their lifestyle, combined with my love of travel and desire to see more of the world, formed the premise for a research project that I designed my senior year of college while applying for the Thomas J. Watson Fellowship, which I was granted that spring. My research project, entitled "The Mennonite Experience with Cultural Identity and Adaptation Abroad," took me around the world in search of American Mennonites who live abroad, either as missionaries or simply as a choice, in search of cheaper land in a less developed country and freedom from the culture of consumerism that pervades the United States. Uprooted from home and exposed to a completely new environment, Mennonites abroad are forced to navigate many cultural challenges as they re-define themselves on foreign soil: culturally, politically, socially and linguistically.

Throughout my year as a Watson Fellow, I traveled across four continents familiarizing myself with the far-reaching web of North American Mennonites abroad, mainly settled in rural areas. I reached many of them through information that I graciously received from members of my grandmother's church in Pennsylvania before starting my journey. Others, I stumbled upon along the way. Many of the Mennonites I encountered, particularly in the Dominican Republic and South America, were born in the United States yet have worked and lived abroad as missionaries for years. They are close enough to the U.S. geographically that they are able to return home to visit.

My travels began on July 31, 2009. I boarded the jam-packed 5:45 a.m. flight to Santo Domingo, Dominican Republic. All announcements were made in Spanish, followed by English, due to the prevalence of Dominicans on board (so many of whom live in New York City's Washington Heights). I spent my first few days in Santo Domingo struggling to figure out the decrepit public transportation system, trying all the fresh fruit juices at roadside *colmados* (small markets) and adjusting to "island time." I reached out to locals, inquiring about Mennonite churches in the city, and ended up attending *Menonita* church at several different spots. It was an experiment in itself, asking around for Mennonites, curious to see whether or not the average Dominican knew of their presence in the country. Many times, they were colloquially referred to as *gente de la leche*, or "people of the milk." Church was an animated and joyous affair; Dominican Mennonites in Santo Domingo love to sing, clap and dance. I was amazed by how deeply it contrasted to the atmosphere of reverence and solemnity I am used to experiencing at Weavertown Amish-Mennonite Church in Lancaster County. It was great fun to sing all of the hymns in Spanish and socialize with fellow churchgoers after the service over a tiny plastic cup of *café*.

So, I set out to find the "people of the milk." Their church service takes place in the countryside, and does not include clapping or dancing. Miles away from Santo Domingo, on the western side of the island not far from the Haitian border, an American Amish-Mennonite missionary family lives and has enacted a church in the rural area surrounding the humble city of San Juan de la Maguana. I found out about them through a Peace Corps volunteer who I met on a *guagua* (mini-bus) ride in Santo Domingo. This missionary family has converted a small yet mighty population of Dominicans to the Mennonite faith, and they are famous in the area for their small *lecheria*, or dairy farm. They produce and sell milk, yogurt, homemade bread and other handmade food items to locals at a small stand on their property. I ended up befriending the family who spearheads this small dairy production and are the lead missionaries of this movement, the Millers, who are originally from Wisconsin but have served as missionaries in the Dominican Republic for over a decade. They were very plainly dressed, equivalent to the Amish. The Mennonites I met in the capital were of the modern sort: driving cars to and from church, joking about happenings in the city, very in tune with politics. They are evangelized, but modern.

Of Amos and Sarah Miller's eight children, three were born in the

U.S. The other five were born in the Dominican Republic and therefore have Spanish names. All of them speak fluent English and Spanish, yet traditional High German is the staple language of the home. They have bibles in all three languages. Their home is a sacred place of tradition and togetherness, and is where their authentic interactions with one another are revealed. To the Dominican population, they show a different face: one that mixes their inherent culture (mannerisms, lifestyle, interactions) with the Dominican cultural traits they have adopted, inclusive of their command of Dominican-style Spanish and perception of time on "island time," meaning you cannot rely on the buses to be on time. Their central role is to serve as deliverers of the Mennonite faith in a predominantly Catholic society, and to continue to keep their traditional lifestyle alive—they were dairy farmers in Wisconsin before they came to the Dominican Republic as missionaries.

The village where the Millers live, Tumbacocos or "falling coconuts" in English, is subtly marked with a small rusty road sign. I got there via two bus rides, a quick motorcycle-taxi ride and a lengthy walk down a muddy road. I arrived in a long navy skirt and a long-sleeved white blouse: the ensemble that became my staple Mennonite research uniform, even in 100-degree weather. Regardless of climate, dressing as modestly and as similarly to them as possible increased my chances of earning their respect and of their being more open to sharing their experiences with me. The Millers expressed, and their actions confirmed, a dedication to their faith-based mission in the Dominican Republic, yet some degree of nostalgia for home. They have had a tumultuous time as missionaries in that several Dominicans who initially converted have since gone back to their families because they were ostracized by Dominican society for leaving Catholicism, and laughed at due to their adopted humble dress and strict behavior (anti-drinking, anti-smoking, anti-loud music). Despite the challenges they have faced as missionaries on foreign soil, in a culture that differs drastically from that of home, the Miller family's allegiance is strictly faith-based and not place-based. Though we never spoke directly of political citizenship, I sensed that they do not really consider themselves American or Dominican—they hold both passports—but rather, as children of God who have lived in both countries. I asked for how much longer they would be placed in the Dominican Republic and Amos answered that really it was indefinite, but they are not placed. Rather, they have chosen to continue their work and will not leave until they feel more spiritually fulfilled and that there is strong leadership amongst the Dominicans, strong enough so that they are able to run their own church and spread the word of God independently, without the Millers' guidance.

Paraguay

My time with the Millers, learning about the challenges and triumphs of church building, provided an amazing foundation for my year. I bid adieu to the Dominican Republic and flew to Lima, Peru and spent about four months traveling across the continent of South America by bus. I explored Peru, traversed through Bolivia and the north of Argentina, and then entered Paraguay via Iguazu Falls. Paraguay, frequently skipped over by tourists, served as the focal point of research in South America. It provided an interesting cultural twist in that the Paraguayan Mennonites predominantly hail from Canada and Germany, not the U.S. There are seventeen Mennonite colonies in Paraguay, and Mennonites are responsible for a large percentage of agricultural production, specializing in dairy and peanut farming in the Chaco region.

I was equipped with contact information for one American family and I set out to find them: three bus rides and a pickup truck ride later. Reminiscent of the Millers in their humble and austere lifestyle, they put me up in the attic of a schoolhouse. Their community is about fifteen families strong: three American missionary families and twelve Paraguayan families that they've converted, all traditionally dressed. I instantly felt out of place, but was welcomed with warm meals and was able to engage them in discussions of Paraguayan culture and to some degree their experience as missionaries. Without fully realizing it, I had entered into the world of a very conservative group of Amish-Mennonites, originally from Indiana, and their life work. Isolated, 40 km from the nearest town, they live a *Life on the Prairie* type of existence. Their colony is made up of simple wooden houses, farmland, livestock and one pick-up truck that everyone shares. In church, men and women sit on opposite sides of the room, like in a traditional Amish service. I left feeling that I had not really gotten to know them, but privileged to have found them and to have experienced life in total peace with the natural landscape, silent nights and country meals. The stifling heat of the attic kept me wide-awake with a string of questions jolting my mind. What would it feel like to wear plain dress and not self-express through fashion? Would I have been capable of killing a live chicken at age ten, then helping my mother prepare it for supper? What does it sound like when a chicken dies?

On my final morning at the homestead, my hosts drove me to the nearest bus station, and I headed back to Asunción to rest before traveling north to the Chaco. I stayed in a low-profile white guesthouse in Asunción called Hogar Menonita: a spotless guesthouse where family-style meals are provided three times a day at an amazingly low price. I talked to a boy at breakfast from Loma Plata, one of the Mennonite colonies in the Chaco, and he told me that he was singlehandedly in charge of ninety cows. His parents were from Canada and his grandparents from Russia. I have heard that is a popular lineage story: Russia—Canada—Paraguay, amongst Mennonites. There was a huge library at the guesthouse and after breakfast, I dove into *Garden in the Wilderness: Mennonite Communities in the Paraguayan Chaco: 1927-1997*. I shared a dorm-style room with just one roommate: a middle-aged German Mennonite woman who lived in the Paraguayan Chaco but was traveling to the capital on a shopping trip. She was married to a Paraguayan, and they spoke German and Spanish in the home—no English. We communicated exclusively in Spanish due to my lack of command of German. We passed the evenings drinking tea after dinner, and I read while she sewed. She shared many stories with me, highlighting the complicated dynamic of being married to a Paraguayan. Unfamiliar with the Latin American tradition of relentless hospitality and sharing, she told me the story of the wooden furniture that her husband worked hard to build for their front porch, and how his extended family came over for dinner then each left with a piece of furniture. If one family member has something that the others don't, it is shared. She felt that he worked hard to make each piece by hand and was devastated to see the furniture go.

After spending a weekend at the Mennonite guesthouse, I made my way to Filadelfia, Paraguay, in the heart of the Chaco, and checked in to the Hotel Florida on Avenida Hindenburg. It was full of tourists who came in search of the classic Pennsylvania Dutch style all-you-can-eat buffet.

The Paraguayan Chaco region is dusty and dry: a notoriously inhospitable climate. It is home to various indigenous tribes and served as battleground of the bloody Chaco War (1932–1935) in which both landlocked Paraguay and Bolivia, two of South America's poorest countries, fought over control of the Chaco region. Paraguay was granted control of most of the Gran Chaco. The Mennonites who emigrated to the Chaco in the mid-1920s, mostly from Russia but also from Canada, were true pioneers, fighting for survival amongst death and disease, yet they prayed and persevered and eventually went on to prosper and pave the way for generations to follow. They made contact with the indigenous community who inhabited the area, though they weren't able to communicate verbally, and the indigenous people shared with them the wisdom of the forest, such as where to find water, while they in turn educated them in the areas of agriculture and health. As foreigners and a minority in Paraguay, their first few decades were marked by struggle, yet many Mennonites in the Chaco have gone on to become successful due to profitable dairy enterprise. They are now faced with the dilemma of becoming rich in a poor country with a staggering economy. Another challenge is to participate responsibly in the Paraguayan political process, which is deeply marred by corruption. Most Mennonites in Paraguay vote, and I believe a few have even served as elected officials.

The Chaco is such a dynamic cultural experiment; everything is marked in both English and German. The landscape is uninspiring—I was exclusively there for research purposes. The Mennonites in the Chaco have car dealerships (Ford pickup trucks) and American-style supersized grocery stores. Local Paraguayans are their employees. I was almost overwhelmed by the degree to which Mennonites have prospered, given their very humble beginnings. They have brought economic opportunity to the area, but have developed the Chaco to the degree that it has taken on a new face, one that, for better or worse, somewhat mirrors the strip mall feel of America. It is almost oppressive to see commercial billboards, massive stores and parking lots amid such a desolate landscape, with traditional churches mixed in.

I encountered many different strains of Mennonites in Paraguay. The missionary experience is clearly distinct from those who have come in search of cheap land and agricultural expansion, or of those who are descendants of the influx of Russian Mennonite refugees in the 1920s. Each encounter provided me with insight into what it means to be a minority religion and culture on foreign soil, and the restructuring of identity this requires. The Mennonite community, both in the U.S. and abroad, is full of intrigue. Because they are more connected to modern society than the Amish, yet retain the same faith-based principles and disciplined work ethic, it is hard to define them in an objective way. Political involvement and view of citizenship is subjective to each family, but God remains the center point, divinely governing their lives.

Lessons Learned

I was overjoyed by the gracious hospitality I received at every

Mennonite household I set foot in while traveling, from the Dominican Republic to Paraguay and beyond. Every home opened up to me, and I truly believe that my connection to the Mennonite church, through my grandmother, made this possible. It made me realize how unique an avenue my brother and I have walked down, with our loving circle of Amish-Mennonite relatives.

I decided to end my trip in Europe, spending considerable time in Switzerland and Holland. I had money to spare because I lived so frugally during my first nine months traveling, and I was ready to live on my own for the final weeks on the road. I absorbed the historical sites of Zurich and explored the Swiss countryside, eating hearty meals that reminded me of Pennsylvania, of my grandma, of home. I returned home after my journey full of experiences, but unsure of where to place them.

I believe that we all sift through life balancing a kaleidoscope of experiences and influences: our parents, our hometowns, our spiritual beliefs, our studies, places we have been, conversations we have had, art and music that have inspired us. The Amish and Mennonite experience illuminates a complex allegiance in many ways—living a simple, traditional way of life on vast acres of graceful farmland right alongside supersized Walmarts in Pennsylvania. Some degree of allure remains; many people find them exotic. They are misfits in society, unfettered in their allegiance to Christian principles above all else, committed to transcending culturally constructed labels and perceptions to carry out a spiritually-driven way of life.

My father's half of the family is not Mennonite, though they hail from a small town called Goshen, Indiana, completely surrounded by Amish and Mennonite farmland. My parents met at Goshen College. My parents were a perfect match for each other because my dad taught my mom how to "walk on the wild side" a little, and my mom, always the straight-A student and perfectionist, reminded him of the value of focus, calm, order and hard work. Upon graduating college, my parents worked hard, saved up, bought their first car, and moved to Philadelphia where my mom attended law school at Temple. Straight out of law school, my mother landed a job at a prestigious New York City law firm, so they headed north and chose to settle in the suburbs, to start a family.

I was born in 1987 and my brother, Morgan, in 1990. We are a product of both environments: the fast-paced life in the suburbs, full of childhood memories of my mom zooming us to school with a full coffee mug in hand, rushing to get to the train in time—and the quiet, calm summers in Pennsylvania. Thinking of my grandma and what she is doing: daily chores, reading, sewing, calmly carrying out her correspondence with friends and going to church, helps center me during times of stress, as I struggle to figure out where I am heading career-wise—trying to define my skills, experience, work ethic and persona on a single sheet of paper, and overwhelmed by the high cost of living in a city. I have, over time, created a safe refuge within myself: I've internalized Mennonite lessons of simplicity during complex times.

My sense of political allegiance is not as complex: I definitely consider myself American and was particularly thrilled when Obama was inaugurated. I am not overly patriotic or a huge fan of American football, but I find modern technology fascinating and stay connected through many social media. I enjoy fashion and individual style. I paint my nails (but had to wait until I was eighteen years old to pierce my ears). Though I appreciate well-made clothes, I am most attracted to the basics: a cream-colored blouse, elegant black boots. I am enchanted by anything homemade. It is actually quite eye opening to step back from my world and realize just how much my Mennonite-ness shines through, even as I remain thoroughly involved in the world: interacting with technology, computer software, pop music, street art, surrounded by entertainment, living in a dynamic, liberal city. I value family, good cooking, and human kindness, above all else.

Globally, I am always dreaming of faraway adventures and the places I'd love to live, volunteer or work abroad. I always try to be up-to-date on international news. I almost believe that my drive to see the world, and familiarize myself with its diverse array of peoples, cultures, languages and landscapes, originates from a desire to escape from the traditional values my grandma preaches: "Stay home, work hard and settle." I know that so many of my Mennonite family members secretly think that I am crazy to not be settled and married—and worst, to not desire to be settled as a young, single woman. This has reason: in their world, it is unheard of for a young woman to actually choose to go off traveling on her own, leaving the comforts of home and the daily routine behind. I have never spoken on the phone with my grandma without her asking me the same two things: Have I found a husband, yet, and, when am I coming home? Yet no matter how busy I am, how far away I am, or how far my dreams in life have led me—whenever I pause and think of my grandma, I come home.

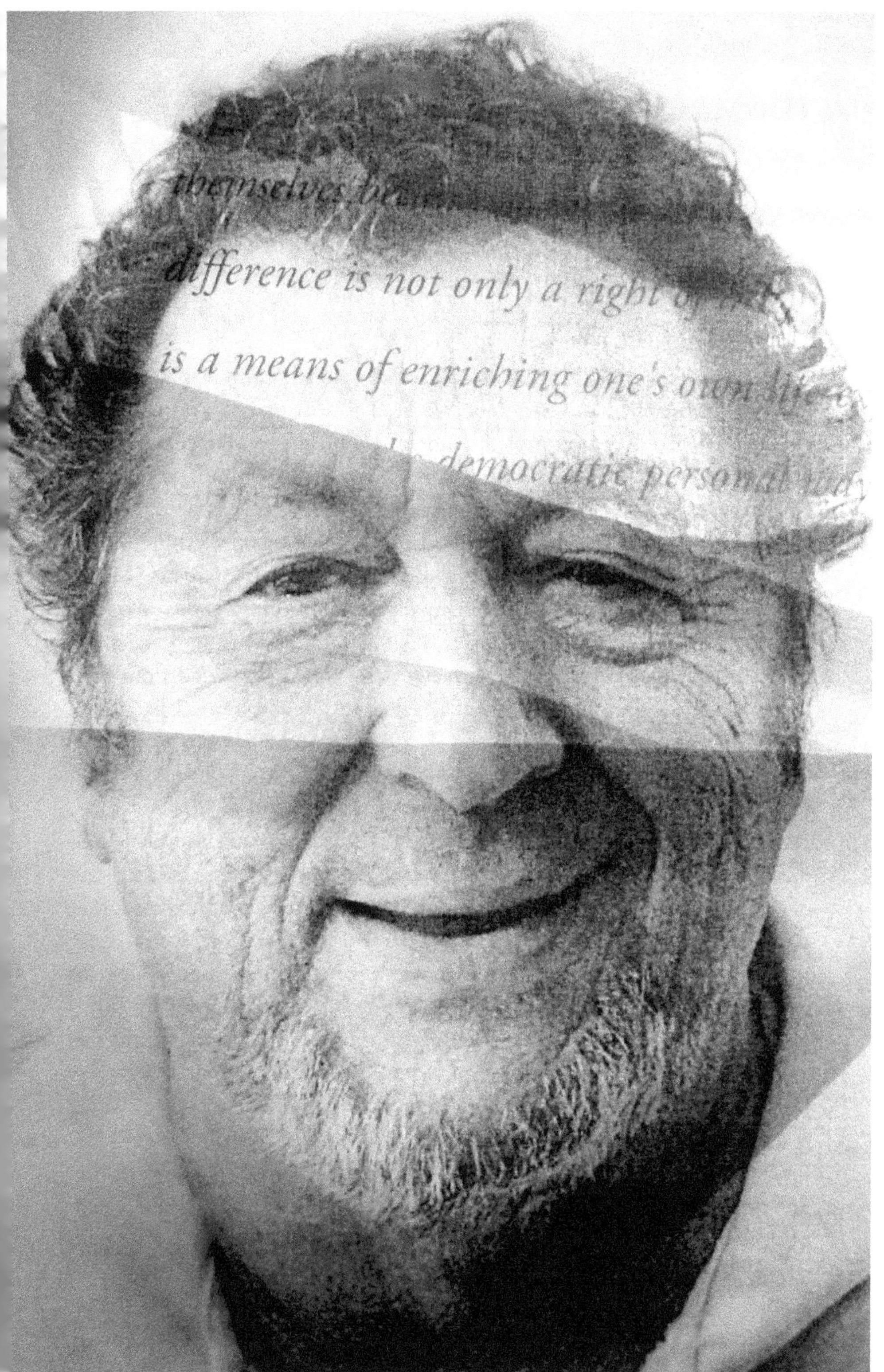
themselves
difference is not only a right
is a means of enriching one's own
democratic personal

THOMAS SPACCARELLI

INTERNATIONALISM

I grew up in Chicago in a working-class neighborhood of apartment buildings, bungalows and two-flats. We lived in a two-flat, a house that has two apartments, one on top of the other. My Italian grandparents lived on the first floor, and we lived on the second—upstairs, downstairs, if you will. Upstairs we were the typical American working-class family. My mother and father both worked. We had an abundance of food, good clothing, and a summer vacation every year that included a wide variety of sights: Miami Beach, Washington, D.C., the Badlands and Mt. Rushmore, etc. We were in many ways the American Dream family. My grandparents downstairs had minimal educations in Europe; both my parents had graduated from high school, and I was on my way to a college education and more. Upstairs we ate "American," watched the *Mickey Mouse Club* and *American Bandstand*, went to Friday-night activity night and sock hop at our high school, and tried every new fad that came along: Velveeta, Diet-rite Cola, and what have you. Downstairs, my grandparents spoke Italian and my grandmother fixed meals that were out of this world. We didn't really have a name for that kind of cooking back then, but when I think of it now, I know exactly what it was: gourmet!

My grandfather had come over to the U.S. when he was twelve years old. He moved around from job to job and state to state, but finally ended up in Chicago where he landed a permanent job distributing bread and pies to grocery stores. At first he used a wagon and a team of mules, and later progressed to a van. As seems appropriate, he was a life-long teamster—the real thing, you might say. My grandmother was born in Chicago, but her family moved back to Italy almost immediately after her birth. When her father died, my great-grandmother took her family to the south of France, so my grandmother grew up in Provence, speaking French in school. Although the family moved back to the U.S. when she was sixteen, grandmother Bambina (born on Christmas Day so appropriately named for the Christ child) thought of herself as French. The basic situation of my childhood years then, was a typical American family upstairs, with my immigrant grandparents downstairs. I grew up hearing daily conversation in Italian and listening to my grandmother sing in French as she fussed and cooked in the kitchen.

It might be hard for some people to believe today, but back in the 1950's, America's public schools were top-notch. I attended the same school my father had attended, and indeed, I had the same first-grade teacher he had. When I got to fifth-grade the school began to offer Spanish classes, and I immediately found the subject I most enjoyed! Perhaps it was because I was always listening to other languages in my home, or perhaps it was the beauty of Miss Lucente, the young fifth-grade teacher I had a crush on. Either way, I took to Spanish immediately, and came to love every lesson, every dialogue, every verb form. Spanish classes continued throughout grammar school and then in high school also, where I dutifully came to have a crush on Miss Stotland, my favorite Spanish teacher ever. I became her assistant and even got to grade the quizzes of the other students. I also began my study of Latin since I thought that every educated person had to have some Latin. My family had no experience of college, so as the time approached to decide on where to go to school, I chose the local branch of the University of Illinois, largely a commuter college. I was chosen to participate in an honors program, and for that we had to choose either French or German. I chose German, and studied it on and off during the whole of my undergraduate years. I had so many courses in German that it was my minor field. Spanish, of course, was my major. Also during those undergraduate years, I was able to squeeze in one year of French, enough to start conversing with my grandmother in the language she most loved.

Back in the 1960's there were not very many American year-abroad programs, so I took a leave of absence from my college and registered for the Program in Hispanic Studies at the University of Granada in the south of Spain. This was the academic year of 1967-68. Franco was alive and well, and Spain was in the midst of the economic boom it had been hoping for since the end of its civil war in the 1930's. The year in Spain changed me forever. I immediately took to Spain's food and its customs, such as taking a break from one to four in the afternoon in order to have the main meal of the day and spend quality time with one's family. Despite the dictatorship, I liked the freedom I perceived in Spaniards, who were willing to talk about any topic, and usually had a very strong opinion about everything. It was in

Spain that for the first time I heard someone actually defend Castro and the Cuban Revolution. I was both astounded and hooked. I wanted to have that freedom, but also I wanted to speak Spanish well enough to talk about every topic and articulate my own strong opinions. Slowly, over the course of the year, that started to become a reality.

Then, as the summer approached and my time in Spain neared its end, I was presented with the most amazing opportunity of my life. My grandparents were going to spend the summer in Italy, visiting relatives and relaxing in my grandfather's hometown on the Adriatic Sea where his father had been a fisherman. I decided that I had to go to Italy to join them and finally learn the language of my ancestors. My grandfather had never forgotten his roots, and all during his career in the U.S., he would send money and gifts to his family in Italy. Several of his nephews were able to attend school or buy books because of my grandfather's generosity, so he was a very welcome and honored guest. I lucked out and was treated with the same love and respect. Before I even got to Italy I had decided that I had to seek formal training in Italian, and my relatives in Italy agreed with me that the place to go was the Università Italiana per Stranieri, the Italian University for Foreigners, in Perugia. My cousins even drove me there and helped me find a suitable apartment for my stay. Classes there were separated according to native language since each group of speakers had different problems with learning Italian. I was able to enter the Spanish group, smaller than the English group and with an easier task since the romance languages share so many features. I was able to make progress very quickly and my cousins were ever so pleased with me on the weekends that I would visit. I was quickly becoming an Italian speaker, and I cannot express the joy I felt as thoughts and emotions began to be articulated without effort.

In short, my year of study in Europe was a life-changing event, and I was determined to get back to Europe as often as possible. I returned to the States and continued my education and was eventually able to take a job at an excellent liberal arts college where I had the opportunity to teach Spanish and some Italian and also obtain leaves of absence in order to direct year-abroad programs in Madrid and Cádiz for other universities. I was also able to create study programs for my home institution that would get me back to Spain as often as possible. In all, I believe I have spent between eight and ten years of my life in Spain. I have worked there, kept house, shopped, and I have made a good number of friends. I find that life in Spain is very pro-life, not in the angry, punitive meaning it has here in the U.S., but rather in the life-affirming habits and customs of the Spaniards. I love the fact that on Saturday morning one can go anywhere in Spain and find people marketing, reading the paper, taking a beer and a tapa, all in public spaces in the middle of the city where one sees no urban decay because Spaniards dwell in their cities and want to be close to work, markets, and places of entertainment and leisure. And these urban dwelling places are not super-expensive, so a person of average salary can afford to live there. I also came to like Spanish politics and aspects of administration such as the fact that the Ministry of Foreign Affairs is also the Ministry of International Cooperation. I like the fact that Spaniards do not have soldiers in countless countries, and that it participates in the international community without the need to dominate. Spaniards live in their public spaces, so that in any town or city, when the afternoon arrives and work is over, countless people can be found in the streets and plazas: children playing; young people holding hands; families taking walks or having a coffee or glass of wine; the elderly visiting with one another or with their families. In a world where so many people suffer from loneliness and solitude in old age, Spain is a place where even widows and widowers can find companionship and company in the local coffee shop.

Most of the European countries have laws that allow the children and grandchildren of emigrants to prove their ancestry and acquire citizenship. My grandfather was a fanatic about documents, and so I was able to find all the pertinent documentation to prove my ancestry. My father was born to my grandparents before they became Americans, so according to Italian law, my father was born Italian even though he was born in the United States. Remarkably, his children were also born Italian even though we did not know it. So when I was able to produce all the paper work (and it took me some two years to put together my case), I was sent my Italian passport. I was asked by some friends if there had been any kind of swearing in ceremony, but I did not become Italian by naturalization. According to Italian law, I was born Italian, and the law under which I obtained my passport is called "Recognition of Citizenship." My Italian citizenship allows me to live and work legally in any of the E.U. countries. Of course, my principal interest is Spain, and so for the last several times I have directed programs in Spain I have done so as a European. Indeed, with Italian citizenship it was very easy to obtain official residency in Spain, which means that I can apply for Spanish citizenship in less than five years from the time of this writing.

I have lived and traveled in a wide variety of countries in Europe, Latin America, Africa, and Asia. My travels have taught me that we are all children of the earth, and I believe that the main reason for seeking dual, and perhaps triple, citizenship is that it provides me with international credentials. At a time when we find many citizens of rich countries complaining about the presence of immigrants in their midst, I find myself in solidarity with the immigrants of today and with my immigrant grandfather whose experiences and tenacity gave me the opportunity to have the excellent education I have, and the ability and right to claim various citizenships. I like to think of myself as a world citizen, and as such I can speak without the chauvinism so common in those who claim to love country above all else. When Americans complain about illegal immigrants, I wonder how they have forgotten about their own ancestry. When Spaniards complain about illegals I remind them that Spaniards went throughout the world and established themselves in many continents without the invitation of anyone. Were THEY illegal? How can one be proud of an imperial past and not take into account basic facts?

One might ask about my allegiance to the various nations in which I am a citizen. And I suppose that many might think that my loyalty can be no better than mixed. I feel loyalty to the United States because it is the country of my birth and the place where three generations of us have been able to achieve the American dream. My loyalty to Italy has to do with cultural and familial roots. Last summer my sister and I visited our family's hometown and we visited the local cemetery with our relatives. In Italy the custom is to attach a photograph of the deceased on each grave. For us it was a joyous reunion with so many members of our family. Our great-grandfather looks exactly like our grandfather and so many of our uncles. We passed through the holy ground with smiles on our faces. How could I not feel loyalty to such a place? And Spain? I have spent most of my life studying its language, history, literature, and culture. I love it dearly and feel totally at home there.

In the end, my citizenship and residency in all these countries is akin to going home to that two-flat in working-class Chicago where I heard various languages and enjoyed many cultures. I have come to realize that the mixture I grew up with is just a small piece of the variety and beauty that exists throughout the planet. I am proud to be an international citizen. In a moment of world history in which there are so many threats to the health of the planet, we need more and more people whose loyalties are not to the small and the particular but rather to the greater and more universal. Gandhi never asked anyone to work for the good of Indians or any other particular people, but rather for the good of human beings in general. The fact that I have different loyalties to my three countries allows me to move closer to that Gandhian ideal.

important do you think each of the
for being truly American?
1) To
been born in America,
lived in America for most of one's life,
3) To be a Christian
able to speak English,
It's Your

AFTERWORD

HEATHER TOSTESON

LISTENING FOR BELONGING II

National identity within American democracy can be a blessing, a curse, or none of the above. Under some conditions, it can enhance participation, trust in government, and one's sense of obligation to the American community. I also find that there is a real yearning among the American people for a sense of unity amid our diversity—rather than a yearning for replacing diversity with uniformity. But national identity within American democracy can be a curse for society as a whole when our attachments are so strong that perceptions of deviation lead to threat and resentment. It can be a curse to members of minority groups who are attached to their American identity, but who also perceive that they suffer from discrimination. It is those people, I find, who are most likely to withdraw from politics and community. Deborah J. Schildkraut

These survey results clearly indicate that the term "community" resonates with ordinary Americans when they are asked about the reasons for their political engagement. They do not tend to explain their activism in terms of self-interest, group interest, or selfless altruism; they are not acting on behalf of only themselves, their families, or other people. Instead, across a wide range of possible political acts, Americans choose to become engaged on behalf of their community. So, even if we do not yet know what the content of "community" is, —i.e., who belongs within the boundaries and how varied are the images of communities in people's imaginations—and how its political effects may vary, we do know community matters. Cara Wong

THE PSYCHOLOGY OF BELONGING

Discussions about immigration are, finally, about belonging. Psychologists and social psychologists have in the last fifteen years begun to discuss the need to belong as a drive as essential to us as drives for attachment and love—one that we are biologically primed for. It is not enough for us as the most profoundly social of species to know that we are safe, loved. We also have a strong need to *feel* we fit in the human condition, that we are, at the most basic level, of the same stuff, the *right* stuff, as others. To feel we belong, we need, in general, deeper bonds not just more social contact. We need to feel that they will continue. Social interactions without these qualities can make us feel more alone.

Intersubjectivity

Daniel Stern, in his book *The Present Moment in Psychotherapy and Everyday Life*, discusses how we are biologically hard-wired for intersubjectivity, this capacity to feel in ourselves what others feel. Like love and attachment, this experience of shared mind is mutually created, it is not something that can take place individually. We are constantly readjusting and negotiating this world-in-common through shared present moments of mutual awareness, not just speaking and listening (non-verbally and also verbally) but also at the same time aware of the other person's participation in this moment, or as Stern would say, feeling that you feel that I feel.

This capacity for intersubectivity, the mystery of my private self resonating with your private self, is the core of our social life. It is essential for our understanding of other's intentions, in fact that may be its most crucial purpose. Our use of it rises with any changes in social position, social ambiguity, our need for personal intimacy, our need to coordinate group action, and when our own identity is in question, for, as Stern says, "We need the eyes of others to form and hold ourselves together." We need it especially, I would suggest, when our social worlds are shifting more rapidly than we can control, as is the case for people facing changes in their communities because of large rapid changes in immigrant population, or when we are moving between various social worlds, which is the case with every immigrant and émigré whose story is included in this anthology.

Reciprocity

One of the intentions we pay most attention to as social beings is reciprocity. Jonathon Haidt writes, "Tit for tat appears to be built into human nature as a set of moral emotions that make us want to return favor for favor, insult for insult, tooth for tooth, and eye for eye." Social trust depends on our choosing the positive side of this response, encouraging and increasing the social reciprocity cycle. One way to do this is to acknowledge that the cycle exists, that we want to do for our neighbors *as we would like them to do for us.* As social beings, we read constantly for intention, and we read constantly for reciprocity because it is so intrinsic to belonging. This isn't a passive stance. We prefer relationships, feel a greater sense of belonging, if we help as well as are helped. Active reciprocity is key to a sense of positive social stability.

Some Evocative Findings about Belonging

In Roy Baumeister and Mark Leary's much cited article "The Need to Belong: Desire for Interpersonal Attachments as a Fundamental Human Motivation," I found their discussion of several cognitive effects that are influenced by our need to belong evocative—especially the findings about how differently we process information and how differently we act if we feel we will interact again with someone. Here are some of the findings most relevant to this anthology:

We have more positive expectations of our own in-group, which means that we tend to forget negative events that happen within our group. However we process information about strangers in black and white terms. In other words, we have the memories of elephants for slights from strangers.

We interpret the importance of an event, its risk or benefit, *most* in terms of how it might affect our relationships rather than the terms more often suggested by risk analysts, such as controllability or globality, which means relationships matter to us, moderate or intensify our sense of vulnerability more than any other factor.

When we interact with people we may interact with again, with the same information we make bolder, but more valid, assessments. We pay extra attention to incongruent information because we're interested in trustworthiness. We think in terms of personal attributes not group characteristics. If we imagine we're going to continue to be in relationship with someone, we present ourselves more modestly. We remember these interactions better. Most importantly to me is that if we believe we will see someone again we will come to their aid when they are in crisis. We won't stand by passively. (Along with Balkanization, the bystander effect is one of the most haunting of social phenomena to me.)

For our discussion here, another observation fascinates me: All of us, when we anticipate interactions with a *group*, even if we are part of a group ourselves, *anticipate conflict.* We do not do this when we imagine interacting with a person, whatever groups they, or we, may belong to. My intuition is that what happens here is that when we think about groups we activate exclusion responses, which are linked with heightened either/or, black/white thinking and heightened flight/fight responses. This observation fascinates me for many reasons. One is that when we talk about democracy, we can talk about it in terms of groups or in terms of individuals, and when we do, we may be priming for very different responses, for intersubjectivity or for threat, for story or for ideology. This is very salient for questions of immigration or structural inequality, which are most often discussed in terms of groups.

National Community and Belonging

In her book *The Limits of Obligation: Geographic, National and Racial Communities*, Cara Wong looks at how different ways we imagine community affect who we see as deserving of reciprocal care and obligation. All community is imagined, Wong says, because it is a concept that exceeds the people we know personally. Community is an animating *idea*. It is our dream of belonging and it means something distinctive to each of us. Even when we use the same word for it—"neighborhood," "community," "nation," "culture"—our image of it is elaborated from our own personal experience with belonging and is distinctively our own. The bounds of that community are where *us* changes into *them* and has very real emotional, social and political consequences.

In general the point where nation becomes part of our imagined community is when we consider immigration. As might be expected, the more narrowly we define the American community, the more ambivalent we are about immigration. Interestingly, in Wong's study those elements of American identity that were most important to everyone had to do with relationship, the possibility of developing and sustaining it: respecting America's political institutions and laws, speaking English as a common language, having American citizenship, and *feeling* American. You may well wonder what feeling American means, but I would think it means wanting to be part of *us*, even more feeling that you already are.

Other expectations—that one be born in the U.S., live here most of your life, or be Christian—were less frequently chosen and can be seen as rigidity and exclusiveness—or as an increasingly precarious sense of national belonging for the people who derive their identity strongly from these experiences and fear that, eventually, they may not fit, may not belong themselves, certainly not exclusively on those criteria alone—and who can't imagine an alternative basis for belonging that will give them more than they will lose.

Deborah Schildkraut, in her book *Americanism in the Twenty-First Century: Public Opinion in the Age of Immigration*, explicitly explores how native-born Americans and immigrants constitute their American identity and imagined community. Her work is especially interesting for several findings: One is that if one looks at the qualities and actions people think are necessary for an American identity they map closely with the ones Wong found—active political and civic participation and assimilation to the extent of a common language. She also helps unpack that interesting expectation that immigrants, to be Americans, should *feel* American. Her findings should make us think. What most affects immigrants' willingness to identify as American is the experience of discrimination. When that happens, they will tend to identify according to their country of origin or according to one of those pan-ethnic identities specific to the U.S. (African-American, Hispanic, Asian), with all their implicit shades of belonging. Their way into the country then is to identify with a group that is fighting for its right to full representation in a contesting and contestable America, and their loyalty will be more to this group than to a more inclusive vision of America *even if their expectations of American citizenship and drive to belong are the same as those of the larger society.*

NEGOTIATING BELONGING THROUGH NARRATIVE

Everybody within a culture must in some measure . . . be able to enter into the exchange of the linguistic community. . . . Another domain that must be widely (though roughly) shared for a culture to operate with requisite effectiveness is the domain of social beliefs and procedures—what we think people are like and how they must get on with each other. . . . These are domains that are, in the main, organized narratively.

Jerome Bruner

Narrative and Belonging: Jerome Bruner suggests in his article "The Narrative Construction of Reality" that story is the mode of thought that humans have developed to "construct and represent the rich and messy domain of human interactions." It is the accrual of stories, each of which is open to interpretation by both the teller and the listener, each of which derives its tension and suspense from how we respond to breaches in our core norms, that is essential to the construction and constant renewal of culture.

Stories depend heavily, as all human interactions do, on the intentions of the characters and what they do with them in the very particular set of circumstances they find themselves. Bruner makes the point that intention alone doesn't determine how an individual will respond to a situation. We may be able to predict how someone might *feel* but not necessarily how they will act. There is always some freedom of choice in a story (or we wouldn't want to know what happened). So we have, through story, an ability to interpret why someone acted as they did—but not necessarily the ability to predict, to establish a clear indisputable relation between a single cause and an effect. Our world becomes more *comprehensible* in relational terms, not necessarily more controllable—but that may be what is most important to us.

Community and the Flow of Story: The debates about immigration, especially illegal immigration, today are often vitriolic, the new state laws in Arizona, Georgia and Alabama punitive and over-reaching, but underlying them, I believe, is that shared drive to belong, to preserve community, to establish limits of obligation and care that are sustainable. But it is interesting to me that community used in this way is a static concept, one that looks to the past rather than to the future. It rarely holds, in a rich, fluent way the richness of our current differences, the reality of our freedom, and the vulnerability of our desire to create and preserve worlds in which we, too, fit.

Our stories of actual experiences of belonging do. The stories in this collection include many experiences of belonging, some voiced, some providing the implicit context for what is said. This awareness of belonging often comes as a surprise, as Julija Suput, looking around the airport in San Francisco on her return from Korea, realizes that home for her now is the diversity she sees around her. Similarly, Ara Sarkissian notes with surprise that, contrary to his assumptions, voting does make a difference in his sense of belonging. "Maybe I should have become a citizen earlier," he muses, for this awareness begins to revise the past as well as the future.

LISTENING TO CREATE BELONGING

. . . if you know if a man is a decided monist or a decided pluralist, you perhaps know more about the rest of his opinions than if you give him any other name ending in ist. . . . What

our intellect really aims at is neither variety nor unity taken singly, but totality. In this, acquaintance with reality's diversities is as important as understanding their connexion. The human passion for curiosity runs on all fours with the systematizing passion.
William James

To be a recipient of a communication is to have an enlarged and changed experience. One shares in what another has thought and felt and, in so far, meagerly or amply, has his own attitude modified. Nor is the one who communicates left unaffected. . . . The experience has to be formulated in order to be communicated. To formulate requires getting outside of it, seeing it as another would see it, considering what points of contact it has with the life of another so that it may be got into such form that he can appreciate its meaning. . . . All communication is like art. John Dewey

The willingness to speak—and the willingness to listen—this continuously negotiated and renegotiated willingness to inhabit each other's worlds, however partial, however briefly, is a moment of shared mind, one of human beings most distinctive gifts, the basis of our ability to work in groups, to understand each other's intentions, to adjust to social ambiguity and change. That we are hard-wired for other minds, for feeling other people's states, means that we are also hard-wired to notice when that resonance is absent. We may listen, but that listening becomes listless if it doesn't lead to intersubjectivity, a shared world—if we become aware that the other person doesn't realize that it is our choice, our effort, our gift to them to listen. But when we listen with a desire to connect and the person we are listening to speaks with a desire to reach us, then something important shifts, a common world emerges, if only for the time of the interchange. These present moments change us, each other, and our imagined futures. For along with reciprocity and intention, we also listen for return, for the possibility of future relationship. That hope too is mutually constructed—through frequent moments like these.

Listening for Core Value

When I suggest that we listen for belonging in immigration stories, I mean it in two ways. First, that we listen in people's accounts of their own allegiances for their own particular constellations of belonging, that we try to imagine, if we had lived their life, being who we are, what our own constellation might be. I suggest we listen for these experiences because we know each other best through our joys—and our experience of belonging is a deep joy.

If we ignore what gives joy, stability, contentment to another, we ignore that which gives their life focus and meaning. We lose a chance to enter into their qualitative universe and it is inside that universe their vision of community comes alive.

Listening for Reciprocity

But that listening of ours isn't detached, abstract—nor should it be. We are listening for relationship. We are listening for our own place in that constellation, whether we are a relative, a friend, a neighbor, a colleague, or a compatriot. *Where do I fit in all this?* is a very valid question. It is also a very hopeful one. "I belong here because I *am* here," Ahmed at the Somali market said to me. By my very presence there, by my engaging him in conversation, I was saying the same thing. In the conversation, in the smile we shared, we were establishing two of the core qualities of community—reciprocity and continuity. I believe that if we act on the assumption that we will interact again, even if the relationship doesn't actually continue, we create a richer dynamic, not just for ourselves but also for the society as a whole. Ahmed will remember me the next time I come in for more than just being one of the few Caucasian women who frequent his store. I will be more willing to come in because he does.

Listening for Choice

When we look at the major concerns the public has about immigration, I invite us to think about them in terms of a sense of belonging and community and to recognize the power each of us has to breathe life into that sense of community or to leave it stillborn. Immigrants certainly don't experience themselves as having the power to exclude, but they do. Which means that they also have the power to welcome. People are concerned that immigrants so limit their attention and resources to their country of origin or to other immigrants of their own ethnicity that the society they are in here and now—the one that includes *us*—is impoverished. In other words, they see the immigrant as having gifts *they can choose* to share. The characteristics they identify as key "to being truly American"—active participation in political and civic process, learning English, becoming a citizen, and feeling American— all speak to what they feel is necessary to keep our society working *as a community*. They want to know that the immigrant has a real commitment to becoming a constructive member of the national *and the local* community. That assurance is something the immigrant has the power to give.

The expectation that an immigrant take some interest in and responsibility for our shared social life from the time they arrive is valid *because the immigrant chooses to come.* Whether they feel they were driven by poverty, driven by wars, driven by ambition, they still had various choices and theirs was to choose to come here. They retain the freedom to leave, not always to stay. This voluntariness is very important to understanding the responses of people here, and immigrants need to take it into account. (Choice is not true for refugees and asylees, or for young people brought as children—and there is an intuitive shift in expectations of acculturation because of this.)

Accommodation to the presence of immigrants is not a choice on the part of the native born. *Constructive* incorporation, however, is. When the native born welcome immigrants, the chances of those immigrants assuming a commitment to the U.S. is much higher. The willingness of an immigrant to self-define as an American is very affected by how much discrimination they feel for being who they are—speakers of foreign languages, lovers of other cultures and countries, holders of different values, the sum of very different experiences. To ignore this is to ignore their deep joys. Stable community needs to draw on all that we know of belonging.

Listening for Mutual Impact

Both immigrants and native-born citizens want reassurance that this relationship matters enough to the other to make the changes in social identity, which are often profound on both sides, worthwhile. Both have the power and the responsibility, individual by individual, to assure each other that this trust is not misplaced or wasted. Immigrants are responsible for recognizing how their presence—especially in the numbers we have now—has changed the socialscape, sometimes drastically, for people whose sense of belonging is already precarious because of other changes in the society. Good first steps are exactly these actions that general opinion lists as key—obeying laws, learning English, applying for citizenship, and, when asked how they identify themselves, saying "American," *for every time they say this, the meaning of that word enlarges.*

The native born has the same responsibility toward every legal immigrant and every citizen—to see them as equal and unique and, as Dewey says, an enrichment to our *own* life-experience. Concerns about the elasticity and tenacity of our society, its capacity to change and the rate at which it can change, might be voiced more powerfully as invitations to help create a more inclusive sense of belonging that is democratic in its demands and its rewards, in other words, depends on each of us for its full realization.

An Open Invitation

The act of listening in itself moves us toward this new more expansive society because it is a moment of shared meaning, an attempt to create even for a moment a world that holds both speaker and listener. In this listening we also begin to collect those stories that create a common culture, a common set of expectations. And we need to do so right here and right now, wherever we live on this globe, whether we are permanent residents, dual citizens, or expats if we hope to create real-time community in a century of mass migration.

I am not suggesting this is easy. Diversity, like democracy, is hard work. It requires more work from us to match minds with someone very different from us. The rewards of that work need to be affective and in the present moment to be sustainable—we need to feel that we are joined in that activity. We need to *feel* that through that listening we are helping to create a world that has a place for us as well as for the person we are listening to, that it deepens our shared sense of belonging.

So, may I suggest to you that you go forth and listen to the neighbor or colleague you feel is most different from you. He or she may be native born or an immigrant, or someone the rest of the world sees as just like you. Listen because you want to enrich your own experience of the world. You may be the wiser for it. You might begin, as I did, with the question, "Where do you experience a sense of belonging?" And after you have listened, I suggest you ask, "Now, would you like to learn about me?" You may be pleasantly surprised. You will certainly be none the less for it.

BIBLIOGRAPHY

Abrams, Dominic, Michael A. Hogg, and Jose M. Marques, Eds. *The Social Psychology of Inclusion and Exclusion.* New York: Psychology Press, 2005.

Baumeister, Roy F. and Leary, Mark R. "The Need to Belong: Desire for Interpersonal Attachments as a Fundamental Human Motivation." *Psychological Bulletin* 1995, Vol. 117, No.3. 497-529.

Bickford, Susan. *The Dissonance of Democracy: Listening, Conflict, and Citizenship.* Ithaca: Cornell University Press, 1996.

Bruner, Jerome. "The Narrative Construction of 'Reality'." *Psychoanalysis and Development: Representations and Narratives.* Eds. Massimo Ammaniti and Daniel N. Stern. New York: New York University Press, 1994. 15-35.

DeToqueville, Alexis. *Democracy in America.* Volumes 1 and 2. New York: Vintage Books, 1945.

Dewey, John. "Creative Democracy—The Task Before Us." *The Essential Dewey, Vol. 1: Pragmatism, Education, Democracy.* Eds. Larry A. Hickman and Thomas M. Alexander. Bloomington: Indiana University Press, 1998. 340-343.

Dewey, John. "Democracy and America." *The Essential Dewey, Vol. 2: Ethics, Logic, Psychology.* Eds. Larry A. Hickman and Thomas M. Alexander. Bloomington: Indiana University Press, 1998. 357-365.

Dewey, John. "Education as a Necessity of Life." <http://listentogenius.com/author.php/38>.

Haidt, Jonathon. *The Happiness Hypothesis: Finding Modern Truth in Ancient Wisdom.* New York: Basic Books, 2006.

Haidt, Jonathon. "The New Synthesis in Moral Psychology." *Science.* 2007, Vol. 316. 998-1001.

Huckfeldt, Robert, Paul E. Johnson, John Sprague, Eds. *Political Disagreement: The Survival of Diverse Opinions within Communication Networks.* New York: Cambridge University Press, 2004.

Iacoboni, Marco. *Mirroring People: The Science of Empathy and How We Connect with Others.* New York: Farrar, Straus and Giroux, 2009.

James, William. "On a Certain Blindness in Human Beings." *William James: Writings 1878-1899.* New York: The Library of America, 1992. 841-860.

James, William. "Percept and Concept—The Import of Concepts." *William James: Writings, 1902-1910.* New York: The Library of America, 1987. 1007-1020.

James, William. "The One and the Many." *William James: Writings, 1902-1910.* New York: The Library of America, 1987. 541-557.

Leach, Jim. "The Tension between Speaking and Listening: Democracy v. Oligarchy." <http://www.neh.gov/whoweare/speeches/02032010.html>.

Putnam, Robert D. "E Pluribus Unum: Diversity and Community in the Twenty-First Century." *Scandinavian Political Studies* 2007, Vol.3, No.2. 137-174.

Sarason, Seymour B. *The Psychological Sense of Community: Prospects for a Community Psychology.* San Francisco: Jossey-Bass, 1974. 157.

Schildkraut, Deborah J. *Americanism in the Twenty-First Century: Public Opinion in the Age of Immigration.* New York: Cambridge University Press, 2011.

Suárez-Orozco, Marcelo M. "Everything You Ever Wanted to Know About Assimilation but Were Afraid to Ask." *Engaging Cultural Differences: The Multicultural Challenge in Liberal Democracies.* Eds. Richard A. Shweder, Martha Minow, and Hazel Rose Markus. New York: Russell Sage Foundation, 2002. 19-42.

Stern, Daniel N. *The Present Moment in Psychotherapy and Everyday Life.* New York: W.W. Norton, 2004.

Wong, Cara J. *Boundaries of Obligation in American Politics: Geographic, National, and Racial Communities.* New York: Cambridge University Press, 2010.

Williams, Kipling D., and Lisa Zadro. "Ostracism: The Indiscriminate Early Detection System." *The Social Outcast: Ostracism, Social Exclusion, Rejection, and Bullying.* Eds. Kipling D. Williams, Joseph P. Forgas and William von Hippel. New York: New York, 2005. 19-34.

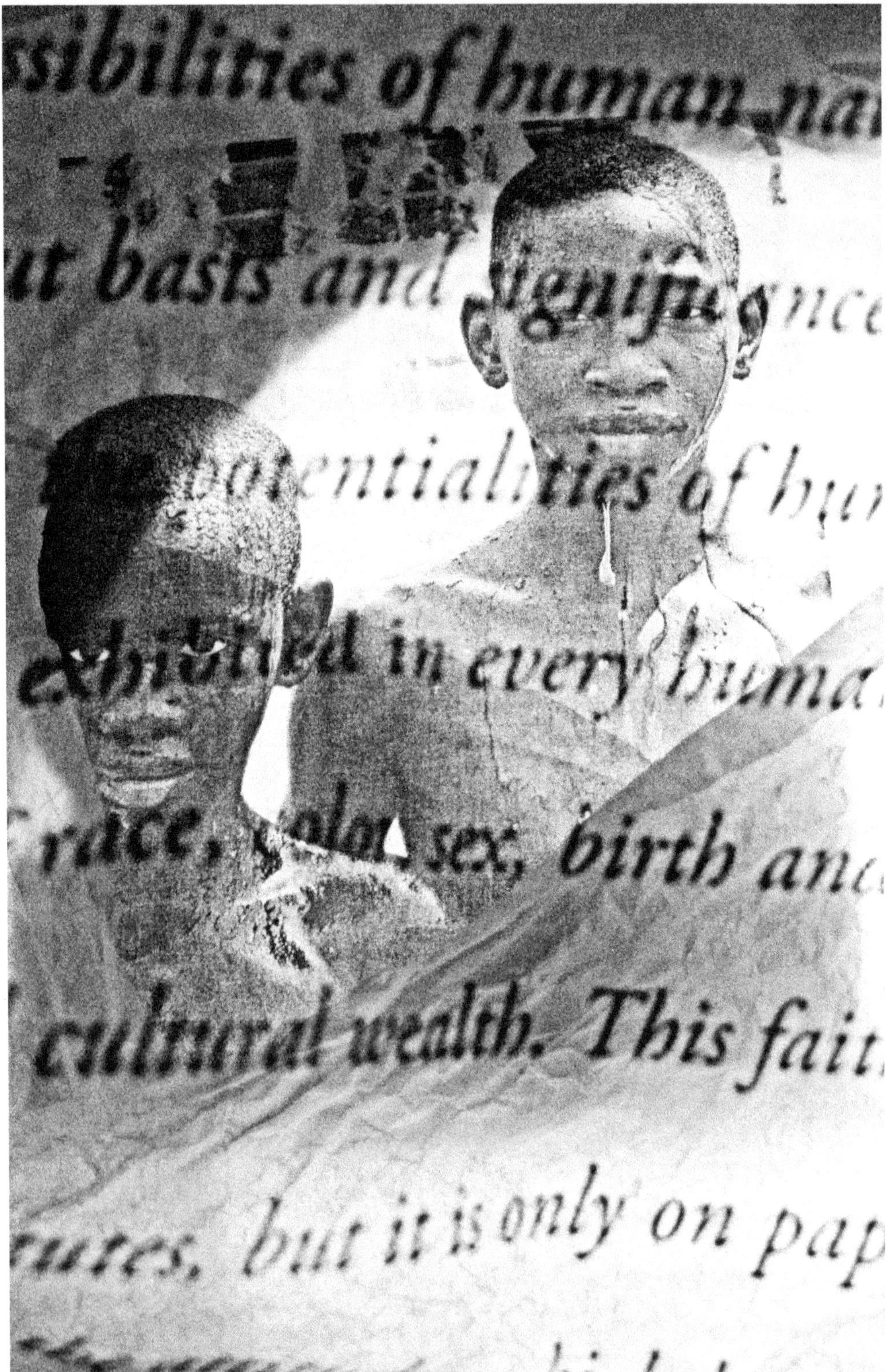

ssibilities of human na

ut basis and significance

potentialities of hu

exhibited in every huma

race, color, sex, birth and

cultural wealth. This fait

utes, but it is only on pap

ACKNOWLEDGEMENTS

Emilio DeGrazia's "Walking on Air in a Field of Greens" was first published in *Walking on Air in a Field of Greens* (Nodin Press, 2009).

Jodi Hottel's "God Bless America" was originally published in *Quill and Parchment.*

Iain Macdonald's "Round Trip" and "Rediscovered Country" first appeared in *Transit Report* (March Street Press, 2011).

Carl Palmer's "Green Card Soldier" was first published in the Seattle weekly *Real Change* (2007).

Photographs by Heather Tosteson, who thanks all those, including contributors, friends, and family, who so generously donated images of themselves to art with no idea what words or ideas they would be brought into association with. The texts used in these images come from John Dewey's "Democracy and Freedom" and "Creative Democracy—the Task Before Us," William James' "Percept and Concept," Congressional hearings on "Dual Citizenship, Birthright Citizenship, and the Meaning of Sovereignty" (Sept. 29, 2005) and "Making Immigration Work for American Minorities"(March 1, 2011), the 1997 Jordan Report: *Becoming an American: Immigration and Immigrant Policy,* and general survey questions found in Cara Wong's *Boundaries of Obligation in American Politics: Geographic, National, and Racial Communities.*

We are very grateful to members of the Wising Up Press Writers Collective, especially Debra Gingerich, Kathleen Housley, Kerry Langan, Anna Steegmann, and Natalia Treviño for so generously and scrupulously reading the manuscript in part or in totality and so ably sharing their skills as writers, editors, and engaged and thoughtful readers.

sk of democracy is forever that of

eer and more humane

in which all share and

DISCUSSION GUIDE

I. Why Does It Matter?

1. What personal experiences have made you interested in immigration? Have these experiences confirmed or challenged your assumptions about immigration? Citizenship? Cultural identity? Belonging?

2. The United States is a very diverse country. What is your mental picture of that diversity? How well does your immediate neighborhood reflect that image? Your city or town? Your region? State? Has this image changed a lot in the last few years particularly in regards to immigration? What have been your responses to that change? Are your responses similar to those who live and work around you?

3. What are your current opinions on immigration and on what it means to be an American? (You might like to consult the survey questions following this guide.) How much are your opinions based on your own direct personal experience? Would other direct personal experiences change them?

4. Do you think that naturalized citizens have as much insight to contribute to immigration discussions as do native-born citizens? Why? Why not?

5. Which people involved in the debate about immigration do you find easiest to understand? Most difficult? Why? Can you image situations where you might have responses similar to those who feel most different from you?

6. Do you think anything you say or do can influence immigration policies? Improve social cohesion in your community? In the country as a whole?

II. Why Do We Come?

1. Which of these stories resonated most with the stories of the immigrants in your own family? Which come closest to your understanding of the "typical" immigrant story?

2. Are there reasons for immigrating to the U.S. that feel more legitimate to you than others? Why? Are there any that cause you discomfort? Why?

3. Do you think that all decent law-abiding people who want to come to the U.S. should be allowed to do so or do you think that the U.S. needs to maintain limits? If limits are needed, at what level, and who should be given preference—people with needed skills, people with close relatives already in the country, people from war-torn countries? Should a desire to eventually become a citizen matter? An ability to speak English or commitment to learning it quickly? Should there be any limits on the number of refugees admitted? Would you be comfortable saying that any of the people whose stories are included in this section should not be able to come?

4. Many immigrants have career accomplishments that might seem out of reach for some native-born citizens. They speak of opportunity as attainable through struggle. Can these stories provide insight or hope to disadvantaged native-born citizens? Why? Why not?

III. Why Do We Stay?

1. Which of the stories in this section moved you the most? Why?

2. Were there some situations people faced in these stories to which you imagine you would have responded differently from the individual in the story? In what way?

3. If you personally had the experiences described in these stories, which ones would make you most willing to stay in the U.S.? Which might cause you to doubt whether you would want to become a citizen or to identify with the U.S.?

IV. Why Do We Go?

1. Do you think that people who have become naturalized citizens should commit to living primarily in the U.S. or should they be free to return to their country of origin or move elsewhere after they have received citizenship? Why?

2. Do you know people well who have lived outside the U.S. for long periods? Do you think of them as less "American" than you? More? Can you still be a good citizen if you are living outside of the country for a long period?

3. Are you comfortable with the reasons U.S. citizens give for living outside of the U.S. for extended period or even permanently? At some point do you think they should become citizens of the country in which they are living? When would that point be? Do their stories affect your understanding of the immigrant experience here?

4. If you are foreign-born, when you return to your country of birth do your cultural allegiances shift at all? Do you feel more "American" there than you do when in the U.S. or is it the other way around?

5. Some of these stories involve people living in the U.S. without legal status. Do you have different responses to the stories of young adults brought here as children and of people who came on their own as adults?

6. Do you support the DREAM Act? If so, would you broaden it? Who would you include? If you don't support it, why not?

7. How much, if at all, does the size of the population of immigrants living in the U.S. illegally affect your feelings about immigration overall and toward legal immigrants? Do you prefer the word undocumented to illegal? Why or why not?

V. Why Do We Commit?

1. Do you expect immigrants to the U.S. to commit to becoming "Americans" earlier than in some of these stories? With less ambivalence than in some of these stories?

2. If you were to become an immigrant to another country, do you think that you might have some of the same complex feelings? Do you think that the people of that country would understand?

3. What level of commitment to the country do you expect from someone becoming a citizen? Some people become citizens more for instrumental reasons

than because they are really committed to the country itself. Does this bother you? What effect do you think this has on community cohesion?

4. Are you comfortable with immigrants choosing to remain permanent resident aliens? Do you think there should be a limit to how long you live in the U.S. without becoming a citizen? How long would that be? What effect do you think not choosing to become a citizen has on community cohesion?

5. Our answers to some of these questions can change when the absolute and the relative number of people involved change. For example, if 80% rather than 25% of the immigrants choosing to become naturalized citizens did so for purely instrumental reasons, would this change your response? If 80% of immigrants living in the U.S. chose to remain permanent resident aliens rather than become citizens, would this change your response? Do these proportions only matter if there are a million immigrants coming into the U.S. each year, rather than 200,000? Do you have such thresholds? Where? Why?

6. If our government's policy is to accept a high number of immigrants, does it have the responsibility to accomodate them to some degree? Where should we limit that accommodation? Why?

7. How might we as a society do a better job of integrating new immigrants into existing communities?

VI. What Does 'American' Have to Do with It?

1. In each of these stories we are getting a complex picture of America and what it means to be American. Which ring the most true for you? The least? Why? When you picture the U.S. and your being American in it, what do you see?

2. Some of these stories portray periods when some Americans were defined as "un-American," and they were either removed from their homes against their will or they left the country to preserve their freedom. How do you incorporate such experiences into your understanding of the American story?

4. Are there public places near your home where you feel that you don't belong because you feel outnumbered, out of place, or unwanted? What did

you want to do in reaction? What did you actually do?

VII. Where Do We Belong?

1. How strong is your own national allegiance compared to other people that you know? Has it changed over your lifetime? Do you have any other national or cultural allegiances that are just as strong or stronger?

2. A number of the authors in this anthology have citizenship in both the United States and another country. Are you comfortable with U.S. citizens having such dual citizenships? If not, why not?

3. If you are comfortable with the idea of dual citizenship, do you think that there might be threshold effects here, that is, if frequent enough it might become an issue for you? Where, if at all, would that threshold be for you?

4. Some dual citizens were U.S. citizens first and then acquired a subsequent citizenship. Most, though, were born elsewhere and kept their original citizenship when naturalizing in the U.S. Does this distinction make any difference to your feelings about the issue?

5. Do you think it important that people have strong national identification and allegiance at this point in history? Do you anticipate much change in the decades ahead?

6. Do you think that most people's identification with a common American identity has been getting stronger in recent years or weaker? Why? If weaker, are you very concerned? What do you think can be done?

Afterword: Learning to Listen

1. Living with diversity can take effort. When, if ever, does it feel like too much work for you? Which aspects of U.S. diversity are the most challenging to you?

2. Have you asked other people to share their immigration story with you? Their native-born story? Have you shared your own? Have you shared it with people very different from you? Did you feel closer or more distant as a result?

3. What was, or what do you imagine would be, most difficult to share about your own experience? What can someone do to make it easier for you to share? What can you do to make it easier for them to share their stories with you?

4. With people who might disagree with you on immigration, do you feel freer to share your *experiences with* or your *opinions about* immigration, cultural allegiance, citizenship and belonging? Why? If you learn about someone's experiences first, does it modify your understanding of their opinions? How?

5. Reading is a form of listening. What have you heard in these stories that has changed you? Is that change in a direction you expected or does it surprise you? Has it made you interested in listening to someone in your life who you haven't listened to before? Who?

OPINION SURVEY QUESTIONS

Some people say the following things are important for being truly American. Others say they are not important. How important do you think each of the following is?

To have been born in America
To have American citizenship
To have lived in America for most of one's life
To be able to speak English
To be a Christian
To respect America's political institutions and laws
To feel American
Blending into the larger society
Seeing people of all backgrounds as American

Do you agree or disagree with the following:

- *It is impossible for people who do not share American customs and traditions to become fully American.*
- *Immigrants increase crime rates.*
- *Immigrants are generally good for America's economy.*
- *Immigrants take jobs away from people who were born in America.*
- *Immigrants make America more open to new ideas and cultures.*
- *Immigrants today strengthen our country because of their hard work and talents.*
- *Immigrants today are a burden on our country because they take our jobs, housing and health care.*
- *Being an American is important to the way I think of myself as a person.*
- *Immigrants today come to think of themselves as Americans just as much as immigrants from earlier eras did.*
- *Blending into the larger society while still maintaining cultural traditions is difficult, but a lot of immigrants today seem to do a good job of it.*
- *If immigrants only tried harder to fit in, then more Americans would accept their cultural differences.*

[Most questions are from the General Social Survey. Also see Deborah Schildkraut, *Americanism in the Twenty-First Century* (2011).]

you as sense of community or a fee

or new friends?

a city/town?

lace of worship?

you work

your e

People

CONTRIBUTORS

Diana Anhalt, formerly a longtime resident of Mexico City, is the author of *A Gathering of Fugitives: Voices of American Political Expatriates in Mexico 1948-1965*. Her articles, essays, book reviews and poetry, published in English and Spanish in Mexico and the United States, have received recognition from *The Writer's Place*, *Common Ground*, Karma Foundation, and Jacobo Rosenberg Foundation, among others.

Emily Beeson received a BA in International and Global Studies from Sewanee: the University of the South in 2009. After graduating, she embarked upon a year of travel as a recipient of the Thomas J. Watson Fellowship, pursuing a self-designed research project. She currently lives in San Francisco.

William Betancourt was born in Washington, D.C. to Venezuelan parents. He was raised in Caracas, Venezuela and came to the U.S. in his early twenties to study. He has a BS and MS in Mechanical Engineering and works for the Navy, designing for ships. He and his wife recently moved to Simi Valley, California.

Jennifer Clark's work has recently appeared or is forthcoming in *Pain and Memory* (Editions Bibliotekos), *All Poetry is Prayer, Raven Chronicles, Dogs Singing: A Tribute Anthology* (Salmon Press), and several others. In 2009 she was nominated for a Pushcart Prize. Her first book of poems, *Necessary Clearings*, will be published by Shabda Press in 2014. She lives and writes in Kalamazoo, Michigan.

Emilio DeGrazia, a longtime resident of Winona, MN, has published two collections of fiction, two novels, and a book of essays. He and his wife Monica co-edited *Twenty-Six Minnesota Writers* (1995) and *Thirty-Three Minnesota Poets* (2000). His short stories, *Seventeen Grams of Soul* (1995), was winner of a Minnesota Book Award, and his recent memoir, *Walking on Air in a Field of Greens*, was one of three finalists for a Midwest Book Award.

D. Elwood Dunn received his PhD from American University in Washington, D.C. He began his career as a professor and diplomat in Liberia. He has taught political science for thirty years at Sewanee: The University of the South and has authored or co-authored ten books. He has been a consultant on Liberian affairs for the State Department and for the current Liberian government of Ellen Johnson Sirleaf.

Aurora Ferrer was born in Havana, Cuba, immigrated to Mexico at age two and then to the United States at three. She is active in fundraising for and bringing awareness to women's rights, green consciousness, and the plight of the immigrant.

Mariana Figuera, a Venezuelan citizen, was raised in Merida, Venezuela. She earned her PhD in Biochemistry from Notre Dame. She is married to **Andy Martin**, a Canadian citizen, and they currently live and work in Florida. She is a cousin of William Betancourt and niece of Zoë Losada.

Debra Gingerich, the author of *Where We Start* (Cascadia), received an MFA from Vermont College. Her poems and essays have appeared in *Mochila Review*, *MARGIE: The American Journal of Poetry*, *The Writer's Chronicle* and others. She received a John Ringling Towers Individual Artist Fellowship in 2007. She works in communications for State College of Florida, Manatee-Sarasota.

Yar Donlah Gonway-Gono, an ordained Methodist minister, received her Doctorate in Women's Studies from Emory University in Atlanta. Her dissertation, *Looking In and Coming Out: A Critical Inquiry into the Life Histories and Moral Dilemmas of Liberian Women in Atlanta* (2001), explored challenges of acculturation for Liberian women in the U.S. A naturalized citizen, she recently returned to Liberia to become the first president of Nimba Community College.

Paige Higbie holds dual citizenships for Australia and the United States. Her family is American but she spent the majority of her childhood overseas in Australia and Germany. She has now returned to the United States and is attending Oberlin College as a junior. This is her first published work.

Jodi Hottel's work has been published or is forthcoming in *Nimrod International, Spillway, Naugatuck Review, Touch, English Journal, Frogpond* and anthologies from the University of Iowa Press, Tebot Bach, and the Healdsburg Arts Council. She recently completed a chapbook of poems about the Japanese American internment. She lives in northern California.

Brian Jungwiwattanaporn lives in Thailand with a shadow theatre artist and a myna bird. He loves stories and prefers listening to talking. Working for a charity, he enjoys his day job.

Murali Kamma is an Atlanta-based writer and the managing editor of *Khabar* magazine. His fiction has appeared in *AIM: America's Intercultural Magazine, South Asian Review, India Abroad*, and *Asian Pacific American Journal*, among other publications.

Marcelle Kasprowicz was born in France and received an MA from the University of Texas at Austin. Marcelle writes in English and French, including translating her French poems to English. Her poems have been published in reviews, anthologies and online and she has been awarded several prizes. Her first book, *Organza Skies: Poems from the Davis Mountains*, was published in 2005.

Janet and Joe Kim are using pseudonyms. Janet grew up in Korea, while her husband Joe, the child of Korean parents, was born, raised, and educated in the U.S. in the New York area. Both are in their mid-thirties and live in Brooklyn where they have two successful clothing stores. Joe also works as a computer consultant.

Nikolina Kulidžan's fiction, nonfiction and poetry have appeared in *The Sun Magazine, Best New Writing 2010, Exquisite Corpse, Reed*, and others. Her short story, "Belgrade Motion Pictures," was nominated for a Pushcart Prize. She is currently at work on her first novel.

Zoë Losada was born in Washington, D.C. but has lived more than thirty years in South and Central America, primarily in Venezuela, where she works as a school counselor in an international school.

Losada Family: Freddy Losada is a retired university professor with a PhD in Marine Biology from Duke University. A Venezuelan citizen, he has been married to Zoë Losada, a U.S. citizen, since 1976. Their two children are both dual Venezuelan/U.S. citizens. Davin, 27, lives in Caracas. Vanessa, 34, has a MS in Environmental Resource Management and lives in Brisbane, Australia with her Cuban husband and their one-year-old son, who is a Spanish (E.U.)/U.S. citizen.

Iain Macdonald, born and raised in Glasgow, Scotland, has earned his bread and beer in a variety of ways, from factory hand to merchant marine officer. He currently lives in Arcata, California, where he works as a high school English teacher. His poetry chapbooks, *Plotting the Course* and *Transit Report,* are available from March Street Press.

Buddhwanti Masih, born in Uttar Pradesh, India, came to the U.S. in the 1970s on scholarship to study religion at the Interdenominational Theological Center in Atlanta. She then earned her MS in Library Science at Atlanta University, working there as an academic librarian until she retired. She has been a permanent resident since 1976, and her son and his children are U.S. citizens.

Alan Masters, along with his wife, directs an international studies abroad program in Monteverde, Costa Rica. He first came to Monteverde in 1983 as a graduate student, and has lived there fairly constantly since 1986. He has a BA in Biological Sciences from Illinois State University and a MS and PhD in Zoology from the University of Florida.

Mary O'Connor is a Sister of Mercy, born in Ireland of Irish and English parents. She has a PhD from UCLA and has taught for the past two decades in South Dakota. She has published essays, short stories, and poetry in Ireland and the U.S. Her essay, "Resilence and Survival: Immigrant and Refugee Women in South Dakota," appears in a collection from SDSU, 2012, and a poetry chapbook, *Windows and Doors*, is forthcoming from Finishing Line Press.

Saad Nabeel grew up in California and Texas. Following his deportation to Bangladesh, he is now a college student in Kuala Lumpur, Malaysia studying electrical engineering.

Carl Palmer, president of the Tacoma Writers Club, nominee for three Pushcart Prizes and the Micro Award, is from Old Mill Road in Ridgeway, VA and now lives in University Place, WA.

Plamen Russev, a graduate of Harvard University and of Georgia State School of Law, has discovered that coaching and breathwork provide much richer opportunities for personal growth and transformation than representing clients in legal matters. He has lived in and enjoyed the peculiarities of Boston and Atlanta during his twenty years in the U.S.

L.S. works as a college professor. In addition to academic publications in her field, she has co-authored a book of poetry with a friend and painter, Oana Lauric, titled *Verses on Canvas.*

Ara Sarkissian came to the U.S. with his family in 1989. A classical pianist and composer, he has pursued studies at Harvard University, New England Conservatory, Longy School of Music, and Boston Conservatory. He is active as a performer and has released two CDs, *The Komitas Project* and *Todd Brunel & Ara Sarkissian.* He lives with his wife and daughter in Boston.

Alexandrina Sergio is the author of a poetry collection, *My Daughter Is Drummer in the Rock 'n Roll Band* (Antrim House). Her work has most recently appeared in *Caduceus, Connecticut River Review* and *Encore* and in several Wising Up Press anthologies. Her poems have received national awards and have been performed by a professional stage company. She frequently performs her poetry, accompanied by her husband, pianist David Sergio.

Lauren Sergio is an associate professor at York University and a research scientist at Southlake Regional Health Centre, both in Toronto, Canada. She has published widely in neuroscience and has made presentations by invitation in Cologne, Rome, Lyon and Marseille, among others. She holds dual U.S.-Canadian citizenship and lives with her spouse, Margaret Gibson, and their two children in Toronto.

Thomas D. Spaccarelli attended the University of Illinois, Chicago; the Universidad de Granada (Spain); and did his doctoral work in Spanish at the University of Wisconsin. He teaches at Sewanee: The University of the South and has directed year-abroad programs in Spain for Sewanee, Vanderbilt University, and the University of Washington. He is a member of the Society of Friends.

Tom Sternberg was born in Romania, moved to Israel after World War II at the age of twelve and then to the U.S. at fifteen. He has a MS from Stanford in Statistics and a long career in business, teaching, and public health.

Julija Suput holds a BA in French and an MA in Teaching Foreign Languages. Her essay, "A Bouquet of Roses," was published in *Shifting Balance Sheets* (Wising Up Press). Her memoir, *In Limbo*, in which she takes the reader into the frightening and indifferent harbors of government bureaucracy, is available as an e-book.

Taye was a librarian in Ethiopia when he won a visa opportunity through the diversity lottery. He lives with his family in the Atlanta area where he continues to work as a librarian.

Natalia O. Treviño has published fiction and poetry in *Mirrors Beneath the Earth* (Curbstone Press), *Bordersenses, Borderlands Texas Poetry Review, Houston Literary Review* and other journals and has received several awards for her work. She is married and has one child. She holds a MA in English and a MFA in Creative Writing. Her first collection of poetry, *Eight Marry Wives*, is forthcoming from Pecan Grove Press.

José Varible was raised in Wisconsin. The only one of six siblings not to have U.S. citizenship, his present location is unknown.

Shantilata Yohan, originally from India, received her MEd from Vanderbilt and her PhD in Counseling and Psychological Services from Georgia State. She taught at Georgia Perimeter College until she retired. She remains very active in ecumenical and interfaith work. She became a naturalized U.S. citizen in the 1970s.

CITIZENSHIP STATUS

Birthright or Inherited U.S. Citizenship

Diana Anhalt
Emily Beeson
William Betancourt
Charles Brockett
Jennifer Clark
Emilio DeGrazia
Debra Gingerich
Aurora Ferrer
Paige Higbie
Jodi Hottel
Brian Jungwiwattanaporn
Joe Kim
Zoë Losada
Davin Losada
Vanessa Losada
Lydia
Alan Masters
Carl Palmer
Alexandrina Sergio
Lauren Sergio
Thomas Spaccarelli
Heather Tosteson

Naturalized U. S. Citizens

Yar Gonway-Gono
Murali Kamma
Marcelle Kasprowicz
Nikolina Kulidžan
Iain Macdonald
Mary O'Connor
Ara Sarkissian
Zvonko Smlatić
Anna Steegmann
Tom Sternberg
Julija Suput
Natalia Treviño
Shan Yohan

Dual Citizens

Paige Higbie
Brian Jungwiwattanaporn
Davin Losada
Vanessa Losada
Mary O'Connor
Lauren Sergio
Zvonko Smlatić
Thomas Spaccarelli
Anna Steegmann
Tom Sternberg
Julija Suput

CITIZENSHIP STATUS

U. S. Permanent Residents

D. Elwood Dunn
Janet Kim
Buddhi Masih
Plamen Russev
Taye
Barbara Toews

U.S. Work Visas

Mariana Figuera
Andy Martin
L.S.

U. S. Undocumented

Mirjana
Saad Nabeel ("unknown")
José Varible

What gives you a sense of community or belonging?

GUEST EDITOR

Anna Steegmann, born in Germany, has lived in New York City since 1980. Her English translations and non-fiction texts have been published by W.W. Norton, *The New York Times, guernicamag.com, sic, 138journal.com, Dimension2, Promethean,* The Wising Up Press, *Epiphany, Ezra, Absinthe, and Trans-Lit.* In German, she has published in several German magazines, written the film script for *New York Memories* and is currently at work on a radio feature. She teaches Writing at the International Summer Academy Venice, Italy and at The City College of New York.

EDITORS/PUBLISHERS

CHARLES BROCKETT, as a scholar of both U.S. and Latin American politics, has taught about immigration issues for over three decades. He has written two well-received books on Central America, *Land, Power, and Poverty* and *Political Movements and Violence*, and numerous social science journal articles. He is a recipient of several Fulbright and National Endowment for the Humanities awards. His PhD is from UNC-Chapel Hill. He lives in Atlanta.

HEATHER TOSTESON is the author of *The Sanctity of the Moment: Poems from Four Decades, Visible Signs, Hearts as Big as Fists* and *God Speaks My Language, Can You?* She has worked as executive editor of two public health journals and in health communications with a focus on communication across professional disciplines, racism, social trust, and how belief systems develop and change. She holds an MFA in Creative Writing (UNC-Greensboro) and PhD in English and Creative Writing (Ohio University). She is founder, with Charles Brockett, of Universal Table and Wising Up Press.

See our booklist and calls for submissions for new anthologies
www.universaltable.org
wisingup@universaltable.org

www.ingramcontent.com/pod-product-compliance
Lightning Source LLC
Chambersburg PA
CBHW020601270326
41927CB00005B/128

9780982726259